EVANGELICAL SPIRITUALITY

Evangelical Spirituality

JAMES M. GORDON

First published in Great Britain 1991
SPCK
Holy Trinity Church
Marylebone Road
London NW1 4DU

British Library Cataloguing in Publication Data

Gordon, James
Evangelical spirituality.
1. Christianity. Spiritual renewal
I. Title
269

ISBN 0-281-04542-9

Typeset by Intype Ltd, London
Printed in Great Britain by
The Longdunn Press Ltd, Bristol

Contents

Preface

The meaning of the term *spirituality* is elusive and successfully evades most attempts to capture it. Used generally, the word describes 'those attitudes, beliefs [and] practices which animate people's lives and help them to reach out towards super-sensible realities'.[1] The same writer defines *Christian* spirituality more specifically as 'derived from and inspired by the revelation of God in Christ'. Christian spirituality is, therefore, 'not simply for the interior life or the inward person, but as much for the body as the soul, and is directed to the implementation of both the commandments of Christ, to love God and our neighbour'. Christianity has a wide variety of spiritual traditions, and each of these its legitimate diversity. Recent works on Christian spirituality have divided the major streams, Anglican, Orthodox, Protestant and Roman Catholic, into smaller tributaries, each with its claim to be recognized as representing an important emphasis which contributes to the overall fertility of the Christian landscape.[2]

The Evangelical tradition is part of this varied landscape, largely unexplored, its riches often unused and perhaps undervalued. My own serious interest was aroused by an invitation to deliver a lecture on Evangelical spirituality as one of a series on Christian spirituality. I chose to study the Olney Hymn Book, including the theology and experience of its joint authors, John Newton and William Cowper. The differences between the two men, in temperament, experience and theological mood, suggested an exploration of Evangelical spiritual life by comparing and contrasting two contemporary examples.

The same method has been adopted in this book. Of the twenty-two Evangelicals who have been studied, some have been so widely influential that they are obvious inclusions, others though less prominent are still remembered while a few are all but forgotten. Selection was controlled by several considerations. The period covered spans from the eighteenth century Revival to the present day. Figures are included from only Britain and

America. Evangelicalism recognizes few denominational barriers and it seemed important to include representatives from a variety of denominations. Nevertheless choices still depend to some extent on the writer's predisposition. I am only too aware of the claims of others to be included in any survey of the Evangelical tradition. Inevitably some inclusions or omissions will surprise or disappoint but I hope the overall impression is one of balance. Perhaps the inclusion of only one Baptist will show how hard this Baptist minister has tried to be fair!

C. H. Spurgeon's printed sermons run to sixty-three volumes, the new edition of John Wesley's works will require over thirty and the volumes of Martyn Lloyd-Jones' expositions of Romans and Ephesians already total sixteen. In trying to understand these personalities and discover the main features of their spirituality it has not been necessary (or remotely possible!) to read everything they wrote. A widely representative sample, carefully chosen and including works which had contemporary influence, has been examined. Secondary works have provided a further check on important sources. For several of the subjects substantial unpublished material is available. These are mentioned in the notes.

The aim throughout has been to provide an appreciative exposition of Evangelical spirituality, with some evaluative comment. In the introductory chapter, rather than attempt a tidy definition of 'spirituality', I have tried to show that, whatever definition is used, it must include the impact of doctrine on experience and moral practice. A too narrow definition produces a distorted picture, lacking in depth and vitality. Evangelical spirituality described as 'early rising, prayer and Bible-study' is one such example of divorcing a spiritual tradition from its context in doctrine and experience and defining it by devotional habit only.[3] I have also tried to define 'Evangelicalism', by showing its historical context and theological emphases. The concluding chapter gathers together many of the themes and characteristics explored throughout the book, finishing with some observations, both critical and appreciative.

The use of so many quotations and sources has resulted in a particular style of notation. Each chapter closes with a bibliography in two sections. The first section, 'Sources Frequently Cited', includes works repeatedly referred to in the chapter. These works are given an abbreviation which is then cited with page reference in the text. The second section includes additional reading much of which will be cited in the Notes.

Keeping company with people who wrote and spoke so much good sense and lived with such spiritual vitality has been a constantly rewarding experience. I have tried to listen with sympathy and understanding, to feel the force of the truths which lie at the heart of the Evangelical experience and to interpret them, not as a detached student, but as one who himself stands within the tradition. The study inevitably reflects the judgements of one particular mind, sifting, filtering and therefore interpreting thought and experience.

In Evangelicalism there is extraordinary diversity in spiritual experience, doctrinal emphasis and personal temperament, to the enrichment of the whole Church. It has its share, too, of weaknesses, blind-spots and inner tensions. But judged by its best representatives, some of them to be found in this book, the Evangelical spiritual tradition is a continuing witness to the power of the gospel and the mission of the Church in the modern world. John Stott, who stands as one example of the vitality of the tradition at its best, has always insisted that Evangelical spirituality is by definition Christ-centred: 'The hallmark of authentic Evangelicalism has always been zeal for the honour and glory of Jesus Christ. With that, I think, we shall be safe.'[4]

While working on this book I have received generous help and have been shown much kindness by many people. My greatest debt is to Dr David Bebbington who has been an enthusiastic supporter and adviser from the beginning. He has read the whole book, chapter by chapter, with meticulous care. His scholarly criticism has always been tempered by encouragement and positive comments. Many of his suggestions have been incorporated and his own published writing has been a rich source of historical detail. I am grateful to him not only for the time he has given to my work, but for friendship and encouragement extending now over a number of years. For the opinions and interpretations offered in the final text, I alone bear responsibility.

I have borrowed books from many friends, not least the Reverend Kenneth Roxburgh whose study is overflowing (literally!) with his fine library of Evangelical history and theology. I am grateful to him and many others for entrusting their books to me. The libraries of Aberdeen University, Cliff College, Calver, New College, Edinburgh, the Scottish Baptist College, Glasgow, and the Dr Williams Library, London, have all been used, and I have greatly appreciated the cheerful responses of their staff to my frequent requests. I also want to acknowledge with gratitude financial support granted by The Baptist Union of Great Britain, the Dr Williams Trust and the Whitley Lectureship.

My family have had to live with this book for over three years. My daughter Aileen and son Andrew have read occasional paragraphs over my shoulder and gone away mystified; but I appreciated their company if not their lack of enthusiasm. Bonnet, our feline friend, has been a curious onlooker ever since she discovered that the top of a computer monitor is warm. My wife Sheila is looking forward to the day when I will no longer be able to use 'the book' as a valid excuse to evade house decoration! I want to thank her for constant encouragement and for carrying the burden of extra work while the book was being written. Of her love I remain both the grateful and surprised recipient. Like Edwin Muir, I consider my marriage the most fortunate event in my life.

The final work on the book has been done during a two-month period of study leave from Crown Terrace Baptist Church, Aberdeen. The seven years I have spent here as minister have brought much personal enrichment through sharing in the life of this church. To the whole congregation, amongst whom I have learned so much about 'the life of grace', I want to express my affection and gratitude. The combination of Evangelical principle, personal devotion and openness to other Christian traditions which characterize this congregation, was exemplified in the life of the late Mrs Winifred McCombie. Her friendship was a source of joy to our family and her encouragement of her minister I will always consider one of God's special gifts. The book is dedicated to her memory, with gratitude to God for a life which to many people was a means of grace.

Notes

1. *A Dictionary of Christian Spirituality*, ed. G. Wakefield (London 1983), 'Spirituality', Wakefield, pp. 361–3.
2. See Wakefield, *Dictionary*; also *The Study of Spirituality*, ed. C. Jones, G. Wainwright and E. Yarnold, London and New York 1986.

3. See M. Hennell, 'Evangelical Spirituality', in Wakefield, *Dictionary*, pp. 138–40; and the same author in Jones etc., *The Study of Spirituality*, pp. 459–63.
4. Timothy Dudley Smith, 'John Stott: An Introduction' in *The Gospel in the Modern World: A Tribute to John Stott*, ed. Martyn Eden and David F. Wells (Leicester 1991), p. 26.

INTRODUCTION

The grace that masters the soul and recreates the will.
P. T. FORSYTH

With passionate intensity the Congregationalist theologian P. T. Forsyth laboured to describe human sin, divine grace, the holy love of God and the finality of the cross. His vision of redemption was often portrayed in words aimed beyond the mind to the reverent imagination most at home in biblical images: 'The end of all is the *grace unspeakable*, the fulness of glory – all the old splendour fixed, with never a one lost good; all the spent toil garnered, all the fragments gathered up, all the lost love found forever, all the lost purity transfigured in holiness, all the promises of the travailing soul now yea and amen, all works immortalised in faith, all sin turned to salvation . . .'[1]

In Forsyth's view Christian life is lived in the power of an inbreaking, disturbing but recreating grace. Much of his writing is an exploration of 'grace unspeakable', the outgoing, demanding love of God as it relates to all the exigencies and experiences of human existence. The life of grace refers to that life which is the free gift of God in Christ, flooding the penitent soul with holy joy and forgiving love, breaking down the barriers of alienation and selfishness, so that the entire life is gladly given back in a living devotion, kindled by gratitude and sustained by the grace that first gave it. New life through grace is the kernel of the Evangelical experience and is consequently a central theme in Evangelical spirituality.

Forsyth had an instinctive feel for words. 'The grace unspeakable' is a phrase which touches a theological nerve centre. Grace *is* unspeakable. By using such a word Forsyth helps to rescue grace from the company of overused superlatives like 'amazing' and 'boundless'. Grace is each of these things, but it is more – unspeakably more. The mystery of God's relationship to man is a 'mystery of grace'; the eternal purpose of God is fulfilled by 'sovereign grace'; the coming of Christ as Redeemer is 'condescending grace'; the death of Christ reveals 'reconciling grace'; the remorseless patience of God is 'pursuing grace'; the forgiving and cleansing power of God is 'saving grace'; the transformation of life by the Holy Spirit is 'sanctifying grace'.[2]

O that my heart were filled with God.

The grace unspeakable suggests depths of mystery, abysmal judgement encountering mercy, ancient enmities dissolved by reconciling love, human sin inflicting suffering on the heart of God and succeeding only in provoking an act of redeeming love which reverberates with eternal consequences. Faced with such thoughts, a theologian like Forsyth unashamedly acknowledged his failure to define the mysterious, demanding and even terrifying impact on the heart of the grace of a crucified God: 'Nothing can justify justifying grace. Sin, grief, death, and grace make a standing rebuke to our lust of lucidity, our rational religion, and our passion to explain. The Lord of death and grace does not explain till we are inexplicably blessed in Him; and then our thought is for ever far in the wake of our faith and our worshipping love.'[3]

Grace, then, is not a comfortable word; if it announces free forgiving love it also intimates the moral demand of an infinite obligation placed on the redeemed heart. 'You are no longer your own . . . you are bought with a price . . . He died that those who live might live no longer for themselves . . . the life I now live in the flesh I live by faith in the Son of God who loved me and gave himself for me. . . .' Grace unspeakable; but also grace flowing in and through human life, the divine gift in Christ, renewing the heart and enabling a new life. Each Christian seeking to live the life of grace derives energy and the will to obedience from the creative fusion in the heart of inexplicable blessing in Christ, profound indebtedness, and grateful adoration. Spirituality includes amongst its deepest motives the glad obedience and disciplined gratitude of worshipping love.

Defining the content and controlling the emphases of Christian spirituality is the revelation of God in Christ. How this revelation is experienced and understood, in Christian communities and in individual lives, decisively shapes each spiritual tradition.[4] In that sense it is true to say that Christian spirituality is lived doctrine, the response of the human heart to divine initiative, the continuing consequences for spiritual life of Christian belief and experience. Martyn Lloyd-Jones, minister of Westminster Chapel for over thirty years, carefully safeguards the trinitarian framework of Christian spiritual experience, and shows how doctrine and spirituality intermingle:

> As I confront this mighty glorious task of denying myself and taking up the cross and following the Lord Jesus Christ I realise that I am to walk through this world as He walked. As I realise that I have been born again and fashioned by God according to the image of His dear Son, and as I begin to ask: 'Who am I ever to live so? How can I ever hope to do that?' – here is the answer, the doctrine of the Holy Spirit, the truth that the Holy Spirit dwells within us.[5]

The life of grace is derived from and inspired by God in Christ, incarnate, crucified and risen. The Spirit of the living Christ is actively and creatively at work, bringing new life to the world, the Church and the individual Christian. Life implies growth and growth implies change, a loss of one kind of stability and security in order to find a deeper rootedness. Christian development is ultimately towards maturity, and involves the struggle to attain to 'the measure of the stature of the fulness of Christ' (Eph. 4. 13). For that reason authentic Christian spirituality is never passive, complacent or morally contented. Charles Wesley believed the Christian's life ought to be lived out of a conscious sense of unremitting indebtedness:

> How shall I thank thee for the grace
> On me and all mankind bestowed?
> O that my every breath were praise!
> O that my heart were filled with God!
> My heart would then with love o'erflow,
> And all my life Thy glory show.[6]

Always the urge is towards Christlikeness and deeper rootedness in his love. R. W. Dale of Birmingham explained the further implications of the spiritual compulsion to grow: 'Christ lives on in those whose life is rooted in Him . . . We place ourselves in His hands, that He may create us afresh, that through the power of His Spirit we may have a new life . . . we do not assume our true position until we surrender all things, virtues as well as vices, strength as well as weakness, that we may make a fresh beginning, and that the will of God may be perfectly accomplished in us.'[7]

The will of God perfectly accomplished in the life of each Christian provides the moral ideal of Christian spirituality. Grace confers both gift and demand. God is love but, because his love is holy, spirituality must exhibit an ethical seriousness consistent with God's love and holiness. Jonathan Edwards argued powerfully for religious experience validated by profound moral change: 'The will is the fountain of the practice, as much as the head of a spring is the fountain of the stream which flows from it. And therefore, if a principle of true grace be seated in this faculty, it must necessarily tend to practice, as much as the flowing of water in the fountain tends to its flowing in the stream.'[8] In Edwards' view, the human personality must be radically renewed before such moral behaviour can flow in a proper purity of motive. The drive of the self must be redirected by an inward work of God, and brought under control by the constraint of divine love: 'The work of redemption which the gospel declares unto us, above all affords motives to love; for that work was the most glorious and wonderful work of love ever seen or thought of. Love is the principal thing which the gospel reveals in God and Christ.'[9]

Lived doctrine centred on Christ, growth towards maturity measured by Christ, and moral renewal after the image of Christ provide the goals of the Christian spiritual life. But the love of God requires active response, a serious pursuit of holiness and obedience. Godliness is neither painless nor inevitable. Christian spirituality therefore presupposes the practice of spiritual discipline. The life of grace is nourished by the means of grace. Disciplined regular devotion is a declaration of love, a daily affirmation of loyalty, an indication of spiritual desire, an admission of need and above all an act of worship which acknowledges the sovereignty of God over the entire life.

According to Hannah More, who pioneered educational work amongst the mining villages of the Mendips, and whose literary works were immensely popular, the success of any given day depended largely on regular devotion: 'The hour of prayer or meditation is a consecration of the hours employed . . . In those hours we may lay in a stock of grace, which if faithfully improved, will shed its odour on every portion of the day'.[10] In that short piece of counsel various traits of Evangelical devotion can be discerned. The regular hour, usually early in the morning, careful watching of the clock to make sure time was carefully used, anxiety to make sure all opportunities were 'improved' and the quite unashamed assumption that one chief purpose of prayer is to replenish the heart with grace. Another side of Evangelical devotion was illustrated by the great evangelist, George Whitefield. Despite his energetic lifestyle he clearly understood the spiritual benefit of meditative silence: 'We often pray best when we speak least. There are times when the heart is too big to speak . . . and perhaps the soul is never in a better frame than when, in a holy stillness and unspeakable serenity, it can put itself as a blank in Jesus' hand, for him to stamp on it just what he pleases.'[11]

Frances Ridley Havergal, hymn-writer and musician, believed meditation to be an act of spiritual concentration, a training of the mind in obedient thought:

> Let every thought
> Be captive brought,
> Lord Jesus Christ, to thine own sweet obedience!
> That I may know,
> In ebbless flow,
> The perfect peace of full and pure allegiance.[12]

Bishop Ryle of Liverpool, Havergal's contemporary, was more blunt and to the point. Referring to Bible reading and prayer he asserted: 'Here are the roots of true Christianity. Wrong HERE, a man is wrong all the way through . . . Private religion must receive our first attention, if we wish our souls to grow.'[13] By such disciplined devotional practice the spiritual life is to be cultivated, corrected and the whole life 'improved'.

In a balanced spiritual life private discipline must be related to the experience of the Christian community, which provides a source of nurture, an informal corrective and a link to the continuing Christian tradition. John Wesley insisted that Christian spirituality must develop in relationship with others and in fellowship with the Church. Holy Communion provides the focal point of corporate Christian worship and a primary means of Christian growth: 'He hath given [the Lord's Supper] for this very end: that through this means we may be assisted to attain those blessings which he hath prepared for us; that we may obtain holiness on earth and everlasting glory in heaven.'[14] The Free Church of Scotland minister Horatius Bonar penetrated deeply into the mystery of grace surrounding the 'ordinance' of the Lord's Supper:

Thy flesh is meat indeed, my God and Lord;
  Thy blood is drink indeed for evermore:
On Thee alone I feed, of Thee I drink,
  That into this sick soul the heavenly health may pour.

Thou WITH us, and Thou IN us – this is life;
  All that the Father is, in Thee we see:
O Christ of God, what art thou not to us,
  And what of wealth is there we may not find in Thee![15]

'Thou with us, and Thou in us – this is life.' Much of what is meant by Christian spirituality is condensed into these four lines: mutual indwelling, the vision of God in Christ, the all-sufficiency of Christ for the believing heart.

From this general exploration of Christian spirituality certain principles have emerged. First, in defining spirituality, the doctrinal content of Christian faith cannot merely be assumed, far less treated as irrelevant or inconvenient. Spirituality is doctrine prayed, experienced and lived in a life of committed obedience to Christ. Second, the conformity of the will to God, the renewal of the mind and the transforming of the moral life by the Spirit of Christ, are the ethical goals of such obedience. Study of a spiritual tradition, then, involves an examination of theological emphases and the relation of these to the experience of sanctification and the growth of the moral personality. Third, this inner dynamic of moral obedience must find external expression in lifestyle and behaviour, and this too is an integral part of spiritual experience. Finally, Christian spiritual life requires stimulus to promote growth and nourishment to sustain it; the means of grace are integral to a balanced spirituality. Bible reading, prayer, meditation, the community of faith, Holy Communion and other spiritual disciplines are God-given means whereby the Christian may grow in the grace and knowledge of Christ. These principles have strongly influenced the studies which follow.

Original, biblical, apostolic Christianity.

The historical starting point of the present study is the 1730s and the subjects span the years from the Evangelical Revival to the present day. These strict historical parameters are not intended to deny the legitimate use of the word 'evangelical' in other disciplines. They are, however, used to differentiate the Evangelicalism which originated in the particular cultural and social context of the eighteenth century from earlier Protestant traditions with which it has much in common.[16] A recent study has identified four defining attributes which have been present in Evangelical religion from the 1730s onwards. They are 'conversionism, activism, biblicism and crucicentrism'.[17] Though the relative emphasis placed on each has changed, together they have remained constant distinctives. The experience of conversion involving repentance towards God and faith in Christ as Saviour; the obligation laid on those who are 'saved by grace through faith' to share the gospel that others may be saved; the submission of mind and heart to the Bible as the authoritative revelation of God; and insistence on the cruciality of the cross in doctrine, experience and piety, are emphases which have given Evangelical spirituality a distinctive place in the Christian tradition.

It is not that any one of these theological characteristics is unique to Evangelicalism, though evangelistic and missionary activism as an imperative imposed on each individual believer was given peculiar impetus by the Revival. Taken together, however, and having regard to the way each of these features is interpreted within the Evangelical tradition, they represent a doctrinal and experiential framework which has produced particular expressions of Christian piety.

Nevertheless the discontinuity must not be overstressed. 'Although evangelicalism is customarily seen as a contemporary phenomenon, the evangelical spirit has manifested itself throughout church history.'[18] John Stott pleads for an even more inclusive approach. In his answer to the question, 'What is the evangelical faith?', he contended: 'The evangelical faith is not a peculiar or esoteric version of the Christian faith – it is the Christian faith. It is not a recent innovation. The evangelical faith is original, biblical, apostolic Christianity.'[19] Stott admitted this might seem an oversimplification, but he has consistently resisted attempts to dismiss Evangelical Christians as 'deviationist', or Evangelical theology as novel. In 1970 he had written: 'The evangelical testimony is to the whole of Scripture . . . Indeed since one important meaning of the word 'catholic' is loyal to the whole truth, one would dare even to say that, properly understood, Christian faith, the catholic faith, the biblical faith and the evangelical faith are one and the same thing'.[20]

Certainly many Evangelicals would argue for inclusions from earlier periods. A powerful case might be made for Luther, Calvin and other continental Reformers; but also for the English Protestant Reformers such as Hugh Latimer and Nicholas Ridley, Puritan divines such as William Perkins, John Owen, Richard Baxter and the Scottish Covenanter, Samuel Rutherford, as well as Independents like Isaac Watts and Matthew Henry. These and many others share the same spiritual and theological heritage as Evangelicalism.

But by the 1730s a whole new cultural mood prevailed, nurtured on Enlightenment attitudes and in the process of changing the ways in which truth was apprehended. Experience became a primary criterion for establishing the veracity of any proposition, affecting the way biblical statements were understood, for example those concerning personal salvation. The pattern of cause and effect, such a fruitful assumption in the realm of science, began to be applied to spiritual experience. The eighteenth-century idea of human progress and the optimistic mood from which it developed found its theological counterpart in the Arminian 'optimism of grace', expressed in a universal gospel invitation and an emphasis on the freedom of humanity to respond to the divine initiative. Calvinism was moderated as greater stress was laid on the moral responsibilities accompanying salvation. On these and other aspects of the Reformed tradition, cultural factors impinged on Christian thought, deeply affecting spiritual experience. Evangelicalism was therefore decisively shaped by its cultural matrix. Without in any way undervaluing the contribution of earlier Protestant traditions, it is the spirituality of the Evangelical revival and its heirs which provides the subject matter for this book.[21]

Many Evangelicals themselves have drawn deeply and satisfyingly from the wells of these earlier traditions. Wesley's Christian

Library is a monument of 'devout eclecticism'. From almost the entire range of Christian literature he sought to 'extract the gold out of the baser mixtures', creating a Reader's Digest of spiritual writings.[22] Bishop Ryle weighted his argument against Keswick teaching and its emphasis on holiness by faith as a second experience of grace, with solid ballast obtained from the 'English Divines' stretching from Latimer to Baxter. John Calvin and the Puritan Richard Sibbes were two favourites of Charles Haddon Spurgeon, whose love for all things Puritan included enjoyment of a game of bowls, the Puritans' favourite pastime. The Methodist Samuel Chadwick, 'that stout apostle of Protestantism . . . heartily loved Catholic devotional manuals'.[23] Alexander Whyte, Minister of Free St George's, Edinburgh, was thoroughly catholic in his taste and encouraged his students 'to get into a relation of indebtedness with some great authors of past days'.[24] His own relation of indebtedness included the Puritan Thomas Goodwin, the Carmelite Teresa of Avila and Cardinal Newman. Such examples demonstrate the willingness of Evangelicals to find nourishment far beyond their own fences.

The whole Christian tradition is the common inheritance of the people of God. Evangelicalism has many debts to earlier and different traditions and the spirituality of Evangelical Christians continues to be enriched, challenged and broadened when mind and heart are open to others. The Puritan Thomas Goodwin combined profound Christian sentiment with rare and humble catholicity:

> As for my part, this I say, and I say it with much integrity, I never yet took up party religion in the lump. For I have found by a long trial of such matters that there is some truth on all sides. I have found Gospel holiness where you would little think it to be, and so likewise truth. And I have learned this principle, which I hope I shall never lay down till I am swallowed up of immortality, and that is, to acknowledge every truth and every goodness wherever I find it.[25]

Goodwin's phrase, 'Gospel holiness . . . and so likewise truth', provides a succinct description of spiritual priorities which lie close to the heart of Evangelical spirituality. If Evangelicals are debtors to the wider tradition they are also spiritual creditors. In the study that follows, the Evangelical contribution to Christian spirituality will be examined through the experience and the writing of a varied selection of Evangelical Christians who had this in common, that they were seeking to live 'the life of grace' in pursuit of 'Gospel holiness . . . and so likewise truth'.

Notes

1. P. T. Forsyth, *The Holy Father* (London 1957), p. 79.
2. See John Wesley, *Works*, Oxford edn, vol. 7 (Oxford 1983), p. 840.
3. Forsyth, *Holy Father*, p. 75.
4. See *A Dictionary of Christian Spirituality*, ed. G. Wakefield (London 1983), where there are general articles on, for example, Calvinist, Carmelite, Lutheran, Puritan, and Quaker spirituality. Regional articles include African, Indian, and Russian spirituality.
5. Martyn Lloyd-Jones, *Spiritual Depression* (London 1965), pp. 169–70.
6. Wesley, *Works*, vol. 7, p. 536.
7. R. W. Dale, *Lectures on the Ephesians* (London 1895), p. 200.
8. Jonathan Edwards, *Ethical Writings* (New Haven 1989), p. 298.
9. ibid., p. 143.
10. J. and M. Collingwood, *Hannah More* (Oxford 1990), p. 133.
11. George Whitefield, *Sermons* (London 1825), p. 179.
12. F. R. Havergal, *Poetical Works* (London n.d.), p. 735.
13. J. C. Ryle, *Holiness* (London 1952), p. 92.
14. A. C. Outler, *John Wesley* (New York 1980 edn), p. 338.
15. J. N. Bonar, *Hymns by Horatius Bonar* (London 1904), p. 219.
16. The problem of definition is tackled in D. W. Bebbington, *Evangelicalism in Modern Britain: A History from the 1730s to the 1980s*, (London 1989), ch. 1.
17. Bebbington, *Evangelicalism*, pp. 2–17.
18. See R. V. Pierard, 'Evangelicalism', in W. Elwell, *Evangelical Dictionary of Theology*, pp. 379–82.
19. R. Manwaring, *From Controversy to Co-existence* (Cambridge 1985), p. 192.
20. ibid.
21. Bebbington, op. cit. pp. 50–74.
22. W. Leary, *Man of One Book*, Wesley Historical Society Lecture, No. 53, 1987, p. 31.
23. G. Wakefield, *Methodist Devotion* (London 1966), pp. 104–5.
24. A. Whyte, *Thirteen Appreciations* (Edinburgh 1913), p. 157.
25. ibid., p. 169.

1

JOHN and CHARLES WESLEY

So free, so infinite His grace.
CHARLES WESLEY

'I am persuaded that Wesley never rose above the region of logic and strong volition. The moment an idea presents itself to him, his understanding intervenes to eclipse it, and he substitutes a conception by some process of deduction. Nothing is immediate to him.'[1] This estimate of John Wesley suggests that he was cool, detached, incapable of simply enjoying experience, but rather subjecting all of life to the calm scrutiny of objective reason. As a way of describing Wesley's way of thinking it may be true enough; it comes nowhere near describing the man, or doing justice to the richness of his experience. Wesley's diary, journal and letters give abundant evidence of his total involvement in life around him. What emerges from these personal documents is a man who is a complex and elusive mixture. Sensitive and tactless, compliant and overbearing, endlessly active and yet, he claimed, 'Though I am always in haste, I am never in a hurry; because I never undertake any more work than I can go through in perfect calmness of spirit.'[2] For more than fifty years Wesley recorded in his journal the work he undertook. It is the diary of an activist par excellence. The narrative throbs with energy and leaves the reader struggling to keep up with the comings and goings, the doings and writings, the preaching, teaching, praying, organizing and reorganizing of the human dynamo at the centre of revival. It is a day by day account of God at work in conversion, answered prayer and triumph over persecution. Hundreds of people are met in the passing, but his itineraries are narrated with brevity, matter of factness and a minimum of description.

The impersonal tone of the journal was mainly due to its nature and purpose. It was first and foremost an exercise in public relations, answering the critics of the Revival and informing the faithful of the progress of the gospel. Yet what began as an apologia developed into a travelogue as Wesley himself became an increasingly sought-after presence in towns and homes. As a gospel activist Wesley crammed his time with evangelistic effort, leaving little space for the developing of relationships with converts. For the reader of the journal, the result is a multitude of names which are given brief mention and then are left behind as horse, and later post-chaise, went careering off elsewhere. While the journal offers little documentation on Wesley's spirituality, it provides the context within which his spiritual life developed.[3]

He had taken away my sins, even mine.

In all of John's writing there is a relentlessly logical tone clothed in economic prose as he presents Christian truth in carefully constructed discourses, pastoral letters, polemical pamphlets and sermons often heavy with theological argumentation. John's formidable intellect was the prism through which his spiritual experience was passed, emerging as a fully reasoned spectrum of experiential theology. In his writing and theologizing, emotion was held under the discipline of reason while mystical or speculative insight was subjugated to a biblically controlled logic.

After the Aldersgate experience Wesley was convinced that only a gospel which kindled emotion, moved the will and persuaded the mind could penetrate to the centre of human personality and lay claim to the soul's allegiance. John had little use and even less patience for mere doctrinal rectitude. 'Orthodoxy or right opinions is at best but a slender part of religion, if it can be allowed to be any part of it at all,' (W p. 8). The gospel is to be believed in such a way that the primary truths of man's fallen state, God's grace and provision of reconciliation and atonement through the death of Christ, the inner renewal wrought by the Holy Spirit in conversion and the perfection of love, become vitally and transformingly real. Christ is not simply to be believed in; he is to be encountered and trusted. His death for sin is not only to be acknowledged as historic fact, but experienced as personal present reality. Holiness is not an elusive ideal but a gift of grace to be lived out in the perfection of love. Wesley came to such convictions by a lengthy and varied process, including the religious formation of his childhood, the decisive impact of spiritual experience and the assimilation of many insights from the Christian tradition.

Born into a serious and devout home, the child of two singularly strong minded parents, John and the other Wesley children learned early the value of obedience and the shaping power of a firm discipline. At Oxford John's intellect was honed and his mind trained while at the same time he began to explore the Christian spiritual tradition. From Jeremy Taylor he learned the importance of purity of intention; Thomas à Kempis taught him that real religion is of the heart, and from William Law he heard the uncompromising call to a wholehearted Christian commitment.[4] He and Charles were founder members of the Holy Club, a group with the twofold aim of personal religious discipline involving daily Bible study and frequent Holy Communion, and good works as a means to spiritual growth. At this point, and for some years after Aldersgate, Wesley was influenced by the classic mystical writings, particularly from Germany and France. He seems to have ignored the fourteenth-century English mystics. Wesley's relationship with the mystics was an on-and-off affair for some years, but eventually he all but broke the relationship completely when he complained, 'All other enemies of Christianity are triflers; the mystics are the most dangerous of all its enemies. They stab it in the vitals' (CH p. 492). In 1735 the Wesley brothers embarked on the ill-fated mission to Georgia where the experience of failure and hostility combined with their admiration for the beliefs and conduct of the Moravians led them to a process of profound self-examination and intensified spiritual search.

Thirty-two years of life had resulted in a man decisively shaped by his upbringing, richly gifted in temperament and ability with a highly developed sense of spiritual discipline and religious fervour, and carrying a substantial burden of self-knowledge acquired through, amongst other humiliations, the catastrophic failure of the Georgia mission. Despite all John had received from the rich tradition of the Christian faith, spanning seventeen centuries, there was as yet no organizing principle around which such disparate insights and confusingly varied experiences could be arranged. Something was needed to unite spiritual truth and personal experience in a creative fusion. He needed some new inner dynamic, a creative spark that would set his heart alight with renewed purpose and replenished spiritual resources. However the Aldersgate experience is interpreted, the result for John Wesley was a life of energetic efficiency and single-minded discipleship which made him leader of the Revival and a preacher of experiential Christianity.

'I felt my heart strangely warmed. I felt I did trust in Christ, Christ alone, for my salvation; and an assurance was given me that he had taken away *my* sins, even mine, and saved me from the law of sin and death.' In these now celebrated words of testimony, key words of Wesleyan spirituality are already apparent. 'I felt', in the sense of inner conviction confirmed by experience; 'I did trust', in the sense of total dependence on the grace of God; 'Christ alone', to the exclusion of personal moral effort, religious compliance or mystical experience as the basis of justification; 'salvation', a word Wesley would spend his life describing, proclaiming and celebrating; 'assurance', the joyful confidence in a full, free and present salvation; and of course the first person singular, and especially the possessive case, used in relation to the sins that are 'mine' and the Saviour who is 'mine'. It was from the standpoint of one whose life had been redeemed that Wesley informed the world, 'It was of mere grace, of free love, of undeserved mercy that God hath vouchsafed to sinful man any way of reconciliation with Himself'.[5]

Where shall my wondering soul begin?

In contrast to the earnest, energetic but cool temperament of John, Charles was exuberant, easy-going and popular. His warmth and winsomeness were complimented by a fellow student. 'Charles Wesley was a man made for friendship; who by his cheerfulness and vivacity would refresh his friends' heart . . .'[6] He was a sensitive soul, easily hurt and feeling deeply the opposition or dislike of others. As John's younger brother he observed that 'my brother always had the ascendant over me' (BL p. 20). That is not strictly true, for Charles had a resilient steel core to his nature which made him stubborn even by John's standards, and he had a volatile temper when, in John's words, 'He was all off the hooks again' (T p. 17). At such times Charles could be harsh to the point of causing deep offence. He speaks of a meeting where he 'sharply rebuked three or four inflexible Pharisees'; during the Calvinist controversy he threatened to 'renounce (*sic*)

George Whitefield from the house-top'.[7] Later in his pastoral work he showed similar severity with one who needed to be taught humility. His account of this shows how drastic and yet how psychologically subtle Charles could be. 'My weapons were mighty through God to the pulling down of his strongholds, yet would I not tell him that I now think him humble . . . For *my* heart showeth me the wickedness of his, that was I to observe it to him, he would be proud of his humility' (BL p. 120).

Like John, Charles was shaped by his home, inheriting the strength of will and mind of his parents. He developed an intense religiosity at Oxford, accompanied John to Georgia and returned in real danger of physical and spiritual disintegration, seriously ill and spiritually confused. Two years later, influenced by Zinzendorf and Peter Bohler, and after a prolonged period of seeking, he wrote, 'I found myself convinced. I now found myself at peace with God, and now rejoiced in hope of loving Christ.'[8] The hymn often associated with the conversion of the Wesleys begins with a question of perplexed gratitude, 'Where shall my wondering soul begin?' The journal, letters and hymns throb with emotion and an intense concentration on the love of the crucified Christ. On announcing his text, 'It is finished', the newly converted preacher burst into tears, 'the love of Christ so constrained me'. It was his love for Christ and his vivid sense of Christ's love for him and for all mankind, that drove Charles, almost against his nature, to preach and work, often facing ferocious opposition, especially in the early days. Given a temperament naturally intense, an experience that ignited everything in him that would burn, and the personal cost of his own obedience to the divine imperative to preach the gospel, it is not entirely surprising that Charles displayed strong feelings ranging from sheer tactlessness to sublime devotion. The tensions in Charles' character are well summarized by F. C. Gill: 'What are we to make of his paradoxical nature – patient yet impulsive; retiring yet resolute; frail yet a fighter; controversial and hot tempered yet gentle and forbearing; otherworldly yet intensely human; introspective yet exhilarating; a rigid conformist yet a bold pioneer . . . ?'[9]

It was from such experiences of personal conversion that the powerful stream of Wesleyan spirituality began to flow outward in mission. The two brothers were linked in a spiritual partnership of work, purpose, spiritual experience and natural loyalty. There would be occasions when their relationship was tested by controversy; in details and emphasis their doctrines, especially concerning Christian perfection, would begin to show significant differences. In essentials they were agreed, their spirituality presupposing the cardinal doctrines of a free gospel, defined in Charles' crisp sentence, as 'the two great truths of the everlasting gospel, a universal redemption and Christian perfection'.[10]

Poetry . . . the handmaid of piety.

In 1780 John Wesley published a hymn book 'not so large as to be either cumbersome or expensive', but containing 'such a variety of hymns as will not soon be worn threadbare' (CH p. 73). Acknowledging, as humbly as a brother was able, the poetic skill, the literary taste, the theological and practical comprehensiveness and the pervading spirit of piety in his brother's work, John predicted, 'When poetry thus keeps its place, as the handmaid of piety, it shall attain, not a poor perishable wreath, but a crown that fadeth not away' (CH p. 75). His estimate of the book as 'a little body of experimental and practical divinity', 'a full account of religion speculative and practical' and a 'declaration of the heights and depths of scriptural Christianity' gives it decisive importance in a study of the spirituality of the Wesleys.

Calculated in simple statistics the poetic achievement of Charles Wesley was remarkable. One estimate suggests 9,000 poems, containing 27,000 stanzas and 180,000 lines (BV p. 7). Even in the 1780 collection John probably overstates his case when he claims that there are no 'doggerel . . . botches . . . or feeble expletives'. Two examples from the larger corpus, show that even Charles Wesley could write poor poetry:

Some put their trust in chariots,
And horses some rely on,
But Christ alone,
His people own,
The health and strength of Zion.[11]

In his address to the city of London the reader is as astonished as the Londoners at the ingenuity which produces a couplet like:

And with astonish'd Europe sees
Your truly wonderful police.[12]

These were exceptions, offset by a vast output of devotional lyricism unique in Christian history. The hymns were the confessions of a redeemed sinner, the evangelistic tools of a gospel preacher and an account of the varied experience of one whose religion was 'holiness and happiness, the image of God impressed on a created spirit; a fountain of peace and love springing up into eternal life' (W p. 129). These words of John help to pinpoint why it is that the hymns retain their hold on the minds and hearts of subsequent generations of Christians. By the construction, the tone and the content of his poems, Charles was intending not only to express but to induce the experience he described. The singer is invited to take the centre stage in the drama. In this sense some of these hymns are 'unparalleled examples of communicable theology' (T pp. 20, 50). Communicable, not only because the writer knows and feels the truth he describes, but because he has, by a combination of consummate skill and intuitive gift, made plain language an effective vehicle for communicating vital religious truth. As a sophisticated young Oxford graduate John had early discovered the off-putting effects of an overdeveloped vocabulary. 'When I talked to plain people . . . I observed they gaped and stared.' Accessible language was an essential component of the Wesleyan strategy, both in evangelism and in Christian nurture.[13]

The hymns reveal an Oxford-trained classicist and skilled linguist who has a feel for words, and particularly for the resonance of meaning and allusion that can be created by a word with the right associations. Many of his sentences are loaded with 'the restrained energy of a coiled spring' (BV p. 36). His care with words can be examined by simply glancing at surviving manuscripts which are disfigured with corrections and suggested alternatives in word and structure. Sometimes polysyllabic latinisms are placed in a verse otherwise made up of short, staccato phrases in Anglo-Saxon, and often to great effect, as for example in the couplet: 'There let it for thy glory burn, with inextinguishable blaze.'

His use of personal pronouns, the abundance of superlatives, his forceful use of the question mark, the effectiveness of the hard-worked exclamation mark, the varieties of metre and the flowing logical progression of argument are all features of Charles' style which have been admired and studied. It is important to bear in mind that the stylistic features of the poems provide the technical sub-structure of 'communicable theology'. And if the finer points of composition technique were lost on the plain people, many of whom either could not read or could not afford books, that did not detract from the spiritual effectiveness of the hymns in stimulating and shaping religious experience.[14]

Many of the hymns are little more than 'Biblical mosaics cemented together by a master craftsman'.[15] The commentary of Matthew Henry, which was trundled around in the specially installed bookcase of Charles' coach, provided many a seed thought. The goodness of God is beautifully pictured as a vast unfathomable sea whose:

> Streams the whole creation reach,
> So plenteous is the store,
> Enough for all, enough for each,
> Enough for evermore.

The characteristically warm comment of Matthew Henry on Exod. 34.5–9 is virtually a prose equivalent: 'The springs of mercy are always full, the streams of mercy always flowing. There is mercy enough in God, enough for all, enough for each, enough for ever' (CH p. 383). In an age when only a minority could read and when many converts were too new to the faith to be familiar with the Bible, Charles provided hymns which made biblical truth memorable. To the modern Christian, with the edge of the imagination blunted by the rigours of critical scholarship, some of Charles' expositions and applications seem fanciful. The well-loved story of David and Goliath is given an unlikely twist. 'Who is this gigantic foe that proudly stalks along?' He is none other than 'my own wickedness, my own besetting sin'. Since God has helped in past weakness, and since he has delivered in Jesus' name from the bear and the lion, he can be trusted to give victory now:

> Faith in Jesus' conquering name
> Slings the sin-destroying stone,
> Points the Word's unerring aim
> And brings the monster down.
> (CH p. 415)

To complain about the exegesis is to miss the point. It is precisely this identification of the singer's experience with the Bible story that creates an openness to the possibility that the same spiritual truths can be operative here and now.

In what has to be one of the most spectacularly obscure punch lines he ever wrote Charles gives a good illustration of the liberties he was prepared to take with the text of the Authorised Version. The closing rhetorical flourish is one of the celebrated features of Wesleyan hymnody. Usually the hymn rises to heights of devotional aspiration, praising the everlasting love of God, or anticipating the bliss of heaven when the redeemed will be lost in wonder, love and praise. Compared with such lyricism the last line of 'Father of omnipresent grace' leaves a sense of almost total anti-climax . . . almost:

> Then, then acknowledge and set free
> The people bought, O Lord, by thee,
> The sheep for whom their shepherd bled,
> For whom we in thy Spirit plead;
> Let all in thee redemption find,
> And not an hoof be left behind.
>
> (CH p. 179)

The near comic picture of the last line is a direct quotation from Exodus 10.26 in the Authorised Version. Pharaoh is reluctant to allow a total exodus of people, property and cattle, and tries to keep back the cattle. Moses dug in his heels, insisted on the total all-inclusive exodus in which all God's people with all their possessions would be set free 'and not an hoof be left behind'. It does not matter that Charles changes the species from cattle to sheep. He is content to have found a telling phrase to show the completeness of redemption and the all-inclusive claims of the divine grace.

A plain account and a collection of prayers.

In 1765 John published his *Plain Account of Christian Perfection*. The treatise 'gathers up into itself all that he ever said on the subject that is of real importance' (W p. xv). Like so much of John's writing, it was done in haste and in response to a crisis. It is a rather rambling assemblage of autobiography, extracts from minutes, previously published prefaces, private letters and reported conversations. He was writing with hindsight, under some pressure and it is not too surprising that some have detected discrepancies between the *Plain Account* and other published sources.[16]

In the treatise Wesley was contending for what he regarded as the peculiar spiritual gift entrusted to the Methodist people, the doctrine of Christian perfection. Perhaps the pot-pourri format was not the most persuasive he could have chosen, but he has still produced a powerful argument for what he variously called scriptural holiness, perfect love, Christian perfection, but never sinless perfection. Near the end he passionately insists on a fair hearing, suggesting that any reasonable person must conclude that this doctrine is: 'Mr Wesley's doctrine, [only] insofar as Mr Wesley teaches the doctrines of Christ . . . It is the doctrine of Jesus Christ . . . it is His doctrine, emphatically and particularly His' (W p. 375). Wesley became impatient with the wrangling over semantics. Christian perfection is not either this or that New Testament concept. It is not a matter of neatly adjusted definition or mutually approved vocabulary. It is the 'dedication of all our life to Him', but if people prefer other terms Wesley generously supplies a string of options:

> In one view it is purity of intention, dedicating all the life to God. It is the giving God all our heart; it is desire and design ruling all our tempers. It is the devoting, not a part, but all our soul, body, and substance to God. In another view it is all the mind which was in Christ, enabling us to walk as Christ walked. It is the circumcision of the heart from all filthiness, all inward as well as outward pollution. It is a renewal of the heart in the whole image of God, the full likeness of Him who created it. In yet another it is the loving God with all our heart, and our neighbour as ourselves. Now take it in which of these views you please (for there is no material difference) and this is the whole and sole perfection, as a train of writings prove to a demonstration . . .
>
> (W p. 376)

John Wesley was more than capable of holding his own in the rough and tumble of theological in-fighting.

John's first publication was *A collection of Forms of Prayer for Every Day in the Week*, issued in 1733. Two later collections show that Wesley retained his methodical approach and his liking for order and forethought in approaching God. He never outgrew these prayers. Many of them are long and discursive, and demand a high level of application and attention to get through them without, at least mentally, beginning to fidget. Indeed some of the prayers include requests for mental composition; they reveal a striving for concentration which suggests Wesley himself knew the recurring problem of distractions. He prayed 'that my wandering thoughts may all be fixed on Thee, my tumultuous affections composed, and my flat, cold desires quickened into fervent longings and thirstings after Thee' (G p. 24). The controlled mind is integral to spirituality, so he prays that 'Thy love may fill my heart, and be the motive of all the use I make of my understanding' (G p. 25). A fixed regularity in time, a definiteness of purpose, clarity of language and deliberately created habit helped to avoid piecemeal devotion. 'Cure us of this intermittent piety and fix it into an even and constant holiness' (G p. 90). Inner constancy of devotion must be matched by an outwardly 'zealous obedience'. Against lukewarmness and dejection he urged God to 'give me a lively, zealous, active and cheerful spirit, that I may vigorously perform whatever Thou commandest' (G p. 26). There are frequent prayers that he might be helped so to order his affairs, and so to strive after holy efficiency, that he will be enabled to live the useful life of the well-organized saint.

A concern about inner religion is evident from the level of watchfulness he displays, examining motives, identifying weaknesses and questioning the integrity of his own character. Appetites, passions and understanding are to be carefully guarded, 'that I may resolutely deny them every gratification which has no tendency to Thy glory' (G p. 34). He asks that he might live 'as one who knows this life to be the seed-time of an eternal harvest', and that 'in this dangerous labyrinth of the world . . . Thy heavenly dictates be our map and Thy holy life our guide' (G pp. 65, 75, 78). In a lovely sentence John prays 'Let me as a pure crystal transmit all the light Thou pourest upon me' (G p. 33).

All of this reflects the serious moralism of his Oxford days. The inclusion of these prayers in his later collected works suggests that he never found such moral seriousness out of place, so long as it was a disciplined yet free response to the love of God.

A mere lump of ungodliness.

John Wesley carefully defined sin as 'an actual voluntary transgression of the law . . . of any commandment of God, acknowledged to be such at the time it is transgressed' (T p. 52). Sin is the inevitable outcome of a distorted will. It is a moral rebellion for which each person is held accountable by God. Such defiance incurs the wrath of God, experienced as guilt now and impending judgement in the future. The remedy for a distorted will does not lie within human grasp. Only a radical renewal of the heart, by a work of God, will deliver from both the guilt and the power of sin. There is a deep pessimism in the Wesleys' view of unregenerate human nature. John argued that we need to be convinced 'that confusion, and ignorance, and error reign over our understanding; that unreasonable, earthly, sensual, devilish passions usurp authority over our will; in a word there is no whole part in our soul, that all the foundations of our nature are out of course'.[17]

Though sin is often described in terms of its effects, as for example when it is called defilement, disease, bondage, death, and weariness, the Wesleys could be quite explicit about particular sins. The gospel they preached not only saved from sin in general but from the daily sins that ravaged the lives of the people. In one hymn, 'Lovers of pleasure', 'misers', drunkards and 'swearers' are urged to believe and be saved. A particularly interesting example of Charles' straightforward language is found in a hymn written for the Kingswood colliers. There are allusions to the everyday life of miners; several phrases had particular relevance to the hard life of the collier. They knew from hard experience the misery of being 'sons of the night'; they understood the meaning of the 'bared arm', and the futility of digging away at 'senseless stones'; and for miners who sometimes worked lying down in seams measured in inches there would be grim reality in the metaphor 'the people that in darkness lay'. Kingswood was a rough mining community, described in uncomplimentary terms as 'so ignorant of sacred things that they seemed but one remove from the beasts that perish. They were utterly without desire of instruction, as well as without the means of it. The place resounded with cursing and blasphemy. It was filled with clamour and bitterness, wrath and envyings, idle diversions, drunkenness and uncleanness; a hell upon earth.'[18] When due allowance is made for the colourful exaggerations of the Victorian biographer, Kingswood was clearly no picnic for evangelists. Many of these rough colliers were converted and found themselves singing such rugged testimonies as these:

> Suffice that for the season past
>   Hell's horrid language filled our tongues,

We all Thy words behind us cast,
And lewdly sang the drunkard's songs.

But oh the power of grace divine,
In hymns we now our voices raise,
Loudly in strange hosannas join,
And blasphemies are turned to praise.
(CH p. 326)

In one sense these verses show the attractiveness and realism of revival spirituality, as the power of the gospel works to change the habits of ingrained sin. The power of grace divine was demonstrated not by impressive triumphs of spiritual discipline but by the much more earthy victory over obscene language and habitual drunkenness. Less wholesome, and revealing the moral rigour that often accompanies intense religious experience, was the case of James Rodgers, a fiddle-playing miner who smashed his fiddle to witness to his conversion.[19] It is difficult not to feel regret that the evangelists failed to approve and appreciate the simple harmless pleasures of ordinary folk. However, for those who were converted, the experience was so radically disruptive and the effects so profound that it did seem to require some symbolic rejection of the sinful past.

Both John and Charles liked to describe the gospel as God's method of healing a diseased soul. 'Hereby the great Physician of souls applies medicine to heal this sickness; to restore human nature, totally corrupted in all its faculties.'[20] In the hymns Christ is variously described as a balm, a cordial, a mantle in which the bruised soul is wrapped, a medicine for every wound. In one of his daring, biblical metaphors Christ is urged to take the healing knife:

Wound, and pour in, my wounds to heal,
The balm of pardoning love.
(CH p. 208)

Before sinners turn to Christ they must be made to feel the need of a Saviour. Conviction of sin is closely related to self-knowledge; not in the sense of unaided knowledge, but as the work of the Spirit of God: 'Ah give me Lord myself to feel,/my total misery reveal.' This request comes after a long process of self-accusation in which the sinner describes himself as 'naked, poor and void of Thee', 'wayward impotent and blind' and 'averse to good and prone to ill' (CH p. 208). But hammering away at a stony heart to break it with a vision of its own hardness will bring neither forgiveness nor relief. The realistic appraisal of the self is only a preparation for the believing look to the crucified Christ, the one who bore the penalty of sin, and whose suffering and death speak with heartbreaking force to the world, of the all-embracing love of God:

Bleeding love – I long to feel it!
 Let the smart Break my heart;
Break my heart and heal it.

(T p. 131)

To 'feel' one's own personally acknowledged sins are a direct cause of Christ's death is to touch the nerve centre of Evangelical penitence. Jesus' death is portrayed in some of the hymns as the ultimate consequence of a morally sick world, so unendurable that even the inanimate creation shuddered with revulsion. The earth is contorted in horror, rocks explode in protest as Jesus dies:

The earth could to her centre quake,
 Convulsed, while her Creator died . . .

The rocks could feel Thy powerful death,
 And tremble and asunder part.

(CH pp. 110–11)

Jesus groans 'and nature shakes and earth's strong pillars bend' (CH p. 107). The putting to death of Jesus was so morally malignant, and expressed such defiant hatred, that the cosmos trembled on the brink of collapse. In this divine tragedy every soul is implicated. Each individual soul bears the weight of its own responsibility for the crucifixion of Jesus:

Extended on a cursed tree,
 Besmeared with dust, and sweat, and blood,
See there, the King of Glory see!
 Sinks and expires, the Son of God.

Who, Who, my Saviour this has done?
 Who could thy sacred body wound? . . .

I, I, alone have done the deed!
 'Tis I thy sacred flesh have torn.

(CH p. 107)

Faced with the vision of the crucified Lord each sinner personally confronts the dreadful consequence of sin, the moral horror of crucifying God. The great gospel paradox is that the same event is the means whereby God expresses his redeeming love and fulfils his saving purpose.

Amazing love! How can it be?

The love of God is so incomprehensibly gracious that in trying to expound it Charles often resorted to paradox. Love by its very nature is uncoerced gift; it is essentially self-giving to others. That God in Christ should give himself, freely and fully on the cross, not just for sinners, but for him, and not just for him but for all, was a truth that staggered the mind and strained even the language of worship. In what is perhaps the finest piece of devotional theology he ever wrote Charles exulted in the incomprehensibility of grace:

> 'Tis myst'ry all; th'Immortal dies!
>   Who can explore his strange design?
> In vain the first-born seraph tries
>   To sound the depths of Love divine.
> 'Tis mercy all! Let earth adore!
> Let angel minds enquire no more.
>
> (CH p. 322)

The paradoxical nature of divine love creates a tension between divine will and human freedom. There is a gentle restraint in God that will not short-circuit the moral freedom, the consenting will and the self-donation that give love its value and meaning. But in another sense the love of God is persuasive, persistent and self-expending. Such love will not merely wait. It will seek to awaken an answering love. Charles was a skilled expositor of this graciously persistent aspect of the divine love:

> His love is mighty to compel;
> His conquering love consent to feel.
> Yield to His love's resistless power
> And fight against your God no more.
>
> (CH p. 82)

The compulsion of love, the persistence of grace, the 'vehement love' of Christ, are phrases which convey the inner experience of being drawn, reluctantly but freely, with trepidation and yet with expectancy. Jesus stands as the 'lure of love', the definitive advertisement of a God whose nature and whose name is love. The love of God is not a truth arrived at by deduction. It is neither an implicate drawn from the observed data of an ordered creation, nor is it an assumed but vaguely defined benevolence in God, which would be more akin to sentiment than faith. The love of God is crucicentric. The cross reveals the nature, extent and purpose of divine love as it encounters human sin. On the cross Christ bore the weight and burden of sin; but the person who comes to the cross must experience something of that weight too. The line, 'Lay thy weighty cross on me', read alongside another verse, conveys something of the oppressiveness of divine love:

Infinite thy mercies are,
Beneath the weight I cannot move,
Oh! 'tis more than I can bear;
The sense of pardoning love.
(CH pp. 300, 306)

In a typical rhetorical flourish one hymn ends with the theologically startling prayer, 'Force me to be saved by grace'. Similarly, 'Bend by thy grace, Oh bend or break, the iron sinew in my neck', becomes the rather drastic prayer of the returning backslider (CH pp. 304, 272). All this language of bending and breaking, of melting, drawing, compelling and yielding, is within the context of the divine love tirelessly, even remorselessly, inviting response.

The conviction that God loves all people, and that consequently Christ died for all, is the theological and spiritual basis of Wesleyan evangelism. The idea of a limited atonement was not only theologically suspect to the Wesleys, it seemed an unwarranted restriction on the sovereignty of grace. In a famous piece of devotional polemic (a phrase which is not a contradiction when used of some of his hymns) Charles insisted, 'For all my Lord was crucified, For all, for all, my Saviour died' (CH p. 123). The experience of grace compels every Christian to ask with Charles Wesley, 'O how shall I the goodness tell, Father, which Thou to me hast showed?' It is part of conversion experience, and integral to Evangelical spirituality, to become a witness to the goodness and love of God. The connection between the universal love of God for all men, made particular to each person, and the obligation to publicize the gospel to all mankind, is neatly shown in these quotations:

Great God of universal love
 If all the world through Thee may live,
In us a quickening spirit be
And witness Thou hast died for me.

O let Thy love my heart constrain,
 Thy love for every sinner free,
That every fallen soul of man
 May taste the grace that found out me;
That all mankind with me may prove,
Thy sovereign, everlasting love.

(CH pp. 120–1)

And that sovereign everlasting love patiently, persistently and even forcefully seeks the sinner. It is a love that is self-giving, forgiving, atoning and it is finally and utterly revealed in the crucified Son of God. It would be easy to miss the disturbing theological implications of Charles' poetical absolutes:

All the names that love could find,
 All the forms that love could take;
Jesus in himself has joined,
 Thee, my soul, his own to make.

(CH p. 315)

All that love is capable of being, all that the divine love can achieve in redemption of sinners, all the creative self-expenditure of God, finds fulfilment in Christ. And it is *that* love which becomes operative in the life of the redeemed sinner, bestowing the power, the urge and the possibility of a life perfected in love.

The heaven of heavens is love.

It were well you should be thoroughly sensible of this; the heaven of heavens is love. There is nothing higher in religion; there is in effect nothing else . . . And when you are asking others, 'Have you received this or that blessing?', if you mean anything but more love, you mean wrong; you are leading them out of the way and putting them upon a false scent. Settle it then in your heart, that from the moment God has saved you from all sin, you are to aim at nothing more, but more love . . . you can go no higher than this till you are carried into Abraham's bosom.

(W p. 362)

The highest achievement of grace in the renewed heart and the conclusive test of the worth of any spiritual experience is how far it contributes to growth in love. Wesley used many phrases in an attempt to silence those who charged him with teaching a sinless perfection which had no further need of grace, or which seemed to deny the reality of sin in the life of the Christian. His rueful impatience with constant criticism is barely hidden when he accuses a critic of confusing the issue by introducing 'the scarecrow of Sinless Perfection' (TL ii p. 229). From another opponent he asked for tolerance, but if that was not forthcoming he indicated what his future attitude would be. 'I think and let think . . . I am sick of disputing; let them beat the air and triumph without an opponent' (TL iv pp. 216–17).

In trying to do justice to Wesley's view of perfection it is important to remember that the doctrine was shaped and reshaped in response to criticism and in the context of controversy. It is a doctrine which he passionately believed was biblical, and which he claimed he had taught from the beginning. While he frequently speaks in the letters of concessions, retractions, and corrections, these affect the details. The central truth remained.

When asked to explain his view of perfection Wesley consistently rooted it in love, the gracious redeeming love of God poured into the heart by the Holy Spirit, who, through regeneration and sanctification, restores the image of God in the heart. The perfect Christian is one whose 'soul is all love'; whose heart is so 'all flaming with the love of God as continually to offer up every thought, word, and work as a spiritual sacrifice. . . .' It is 'another term for the image of God in man'; or it is 'loving God with all the heart, rejoicing evermore, praying without ceasing, in everything giving thanks'. The clue to these phrases lies in the absolute terms Wesley uses. Works like 'all', 'every', 'always' and 'evermore' are enough to make any Christian who knows the reality of sin's persistence a little nervous. But with what he called his 'dogmaticalness', Wesley let loose a volley of well-aimed replies:

> By Christian Perfection I mean (1) loving God with all our heart. Do you object to this? I mean (2) an heart and life all devoted to God. Do you desire less? I mean (3) regaining the whole image of God. What objection to this? I mean (4) having all the mind that was in Christ. Is this going too far? I mean

(5) walking uniformly as Christ walked. And this surely no Christian will object to.[21]

Pressed about the nature of the experience, Wesley could claim, 'I know hundreds of persons . . . who experienced such a love of God and so fervent a goodwill to all mankind (attended with power over all sin)' (TL ii p. 62). Charles describes this overwhelming experience of love as the kingdom from above, established in the heart:

> The kingdom of established peace
> Which can no more remove;
> The perfect power of godliness,
> The omnipotence of love.
>
> (CH p. 384).

John expended a lot of energy and ink in trying to overcome the difficulty of using the word 'perfection'; but it is a biblical word and no other says precisely the same thing. In any case, for Wesley it was more important to understand and experience it than to replace it. Given its biblical origins, Wesley argued for his position on scriptural grounds. 'If the scripture supports my doctrine it will stand; if not, the sooner it falls the better.' He claimed that he 'taught nothing beyond or contrary to the word of God'.[22] Once the scriptural principle was established he looked for the confirmation of scriptural truth in Christian experience. For that reason his references to Christian Perfection, especially in the letters, begin to read like a compilation of case studies gathered by a religious sociologist.

The real sticking point, and the reason why the 'whole religious world' had 'set themselves in array' against Wesley's teaching were simple enough. The Calvinist tradition taught a gradual sanctification, wrought out in the experience of conflict and struggle with indwelling sin. Wesley came to believe in perfection as a 'simple act of faith wrought in the soul . . . in an instant'. His argument became hard for Calvinists to pin down when he introduced a qualification which seemed very like the theological equivalent of having his cake and eating it. Having made his statement about simple faith and the work of an instant, he added, 'But I believe a gradual work both preceding and following that instant' (TL iv p. 187). But what is the nature of that gradual work? Is it to improve upon the grace already given in an 'instant'? Does the simple act of faith remove the desire, or the ability to sin? If not, what does it achieve, and whatever it is, why use the word perfection to describe it?

Wesley believed in the sovereign efficacy of grace and that a life given over utterly to God would be enabled to give all that God requires, namely 'our full consent, our whole desires, our undivided hearts'. Wesley never equated uninterrupted obedience with static saintliness. The psychological astuteness with which he and Charles detected the hidden motives, the subtle nudges and the dangerous attractiveness of sin, makes nonsense of the charge that they believed in an experience which renders the Christian soul unimprovable. John readily admitted that the blessing could be lost, but it need not be: 'The only conclusion I deny is that all Christians do and must commit sin so long as they live,' (TL iii p. 170). He dismissed the convenient distinction between committing occasional sin and continuing in sin. The notion that there is a decisive difference between intermittent lapses and habitual sin is a 'loop-hole subversive of all holiness' (TL iii p. 169). John refused ever to set limits to what the grace of God could achieve in the restoration of the divine image in fallen man. The second work of grace in the heart was, he believed, biblical, and confirmed by what he believed were indisputable cases of people who testified to an inner assurance of having been made perfect in love. This assurance was given by 'a direct, positive testimony of the Spirit' (TL iii p. 213). This simple act of faith is an opening of the heart to the fullness of the divine love so that God is felt and known to be powerfully present. In Wesley's beautiful sentence, 'Faith is the voice of God in the heart proclaiming Himself' (TL iv p. 265).

Perhaps the most rewarding way to explore Wesley's meaning is to concentrate on the 'heaven of heavens', love. John built a moral theology on the ethical principle that one cannot will two mutually exclusive ends at one and the same time. When the soul is filled with God's love there is simply no living space for sin. Love excludes all that is inconsistent with itself. That is the perfect law of love:

> Love excludes the selfish passion,
>   Love destroys the carnal mind;
> Love be here my full salvation,
>   Love for Thee and all mankind.
>
> (T p. 162)

In one hymn Charles even makes love synonymous with God himself. Notice the personification and the capitals at the end of the verse:

Love our real holiness,
 Love our spotless character,
Love is liberty and peace,
 Pardon and perfection here;
Less than this cannot suffice;
 Love be Thou our all in all;
Then we in Thine image rise,
 Then we into nothing fall.
 (T p. 163)

To claim such an experience of holiness seems tantamount to spiritual pride. Yet Wesley encouraged those who felt they had experienced the perfection of love to speak about it. That this did not to lead to self-advertisment was due in large part to Wesley's approach to spiritual things. Though there were occasions when his doctrine was discredited by exaggerated claims and inconsistent lives, it was Wesley's practice to test and evaluate experience. Spiritual experience has its own authority but it is subordinate to the Bible, which teaches that fruit is the evidence of species. Those who claim to have been perfected in love must show a character and lifestyle consistent with love. The fruits of the Spirit provided John with a formidable check-list, so that even the most intense spiritual experience was subjected to rigorous ethical examination. When Wesley made such an evaluation he conveyed the result with blunt honesty, as when he told one correspondent; 'I dislike your littleness of love . . . your impatience of contradiction . . . your censoriousness . . . your overvaluing of yourselves and undervaluing of others' (TL iv p. 193).

Charles was equally firm in maintaining the connection between perfect love and an observably Christlike character. The mind of Christ, indwelling and acting through the believer, was one of his favourite themes. One particularly fine meditation on the mind of Jesus contrasts the unreliable wavering of the heart with the 'settled peace', the mind of Christ 'fix'd within' and the soul 'stablished with abiding grace'. The whole poem is a prayer for the mind of Christ to be reproduced in the Christian's daily experience:

Plant, and root, and fix in me
All the mind that was in Thee;
Settled peace I then shall find –
Jesu's is a quiet mind.

Lowly, loving, meek, and pure,
I shall to the end endure;
Be no more to sin inclined –
Jesu's is a constant mind.

I shall fully be restored
To the image of my Lord,
Witnessing to all mankind –
Jesu's is a perfect mind.

(CH p. 508f)

Consistent with his view of perfection as instant but followed by a gradual work, John urged the need to improve upon the grace received. He told a preacher in Derbyshire: 'Continually exhort them to go on unto perfection, steadily to use all the grace they have received and every moment to expect full salvation.' He warned a female correspondent not to 'stop on the threshold of perfection' but to 'press on to the mark . . . till you experimentally know all that love of God which passes all (speculative) knowledge' (TL v p. 290; vi p. 153).

A poem on 'The True Use of Musick' uses the musical metaphor to reflect on Christian progress. Jesus is asked to 'compose' his people into thankfulness, and to 'tune their hearts'. Sins of 'secret pride and subtle sin' are not to be allowed to 'desecrate our hallowed strain':

That hurrying strife far off remove,
That noisy burst of selfish love
  Which swells the formal song;
The joy from out our heart arise,
And speak, and sparkle in our eyes,
  And vibrate on our tongue.

When the whole life has been composed and arranged by Jesus, and the performance is under way, the whole piece of 'Musick' moves towards it climax:

Jesus Thyself in us reveal,
And all our faculties shall feel
  Thy harmonising name.

With calmly reverential joy
O let us all our lives employ
In setting forth Thy love.
(CH pp. 326f)

Only a musician who has heard his music murdered by discordant voices, out-of-tune singers and musical show-offs, will fully appreciate the aptness of Charles' metaphor. As a description of the discipline and purpose of Christian progress it is superb.

Prayer . . . Scripture . . . and receiving the Lord's Supper.

In spiritual matters John warned against what he called 'expecting the end without the means . . . the expecting knowledge . . . without searching the scriptures, and consulting the children of God; the expecting spiritual strength . . . without constant prayer . . .' (W p. 361). The perfection of love is the end of Christian living; God in his goodness has provided various means to the attaining of that end. The 'chief of these means are prayer . . . searching the scriptures (which implies reading, hearing, and meditating thereon), and receiving the Lord's Supper.'[23]

Charles recognized that a complex range of feelings come into play when a Christian personally and privately seeks God in prayer. Inevitably there will be feelings of unworthiness, a chronic sense of self-abasement which creates a longing for increased holiness and a deliverance from even small sins. For the soul seeking holiness, 'a very little dust will disorder a clock, and the least sand will obscure our sight, so the least grain of sin which is upon the heart will hinder its right motion towards God' (W p. 370). The motion of the heart towards God is a vital element in prayer; it is the sign of hunger and thirst after righteousness; it is the soul's Yes to the offer of grace.

For the Wesleys, prayer was christocentric. In prayer the eye of faith is drawn irresistibly to the crucified Christ; beneath the cross sin is owned, confessed and forgiven. The Christian will never cease to be an adoring penitent. Yet consciousness of sin must not be overdone. The focus of devotion is not sin but Christ. Grace operates negatively to purge the heart but it also works positively to bring it into conformity with Christ. Remorse for sin, the answering love of the forgiven heart, adoring gratitude and the desire to be made Christlike, are inseparable strands of Evangelical devotion. When a Christian prays it is with a profound sense of unworthiness which begins as penitence, and then evokes a mystified but joyful wonder at the gracious love of God, which struggles for articulation but is finally expressed in a prayer of almost unattainable aspiration . . . to share the holiness of Christ:

A heart in every thought renewed
  And full of love divine;
Perfect, and right, and pure, and good,
  A copy Lord of Thine.

(CH p. 491)

Such holiness is the outcome of costly discipline. To know God in the fulness of his love demands time spent in his presence. Charles wrote a hymn, 'In an Hurry of Business', in which he asks: 'From all entanglements beneath, call off my peaceful heart'. So vital to the soul's health is such time with God that Charles uses language more suited to the criminal court: 'Arrest the prisoner of Thy love,/and shut me up in God' (CH p. 439). In a letter to a young army surgeon he urged 'Watch and pray. Watching implies early rising . . . prayer never hinders business' (BL p. 125). In the same vein, and with particular reference to prayerful reading, John gently crushed a lay preacher, telling him he was 'lively but not deep; there is little variety; there is no compass of thought. Reading only can supply this, with daily prayer' (TL iv p. 103). Both John and Charles were unwavering in their conviction that Christian progress was gradual, disciplined and dependent on the faithful use of the means of grace. In an undisguised broadside aimed at the quietist tendencies of the Moravians Charles urged believers to 'Pray . . . every moment pray, and never, never faint' (CH p. 439).

Concern for personal holiness was balanced by an outward-looking concern for the world around. In John's published prayers the Ministers of state, the Houses of Lords and Commons, the universities, the monarch and the magistrates are all mentioned. He found space to include 'the afflicted in mind and body', those 'condemned to death', Gentiles, Jews, heretics, prisoners, the poor and the dying. In fact in these prayers Wesley seems to be deliberately careful to include all mankind. 'Show mercy to the whole world . . . magnify thy goodness to all thy children . . . Shine into all the dark corners of the world.' There is theological breadth in the address to 'God the eternal source and necessity of being, on whose free overflowing that of the whole creation every moment depends'. His concern for the whole creation is unmistakeable and is seen at its most optimistic when he looks forward to the time when God 'has wrought his glorious design to finish the world in a beauteous close' (G pp. 78, 76). Such prayers grew naturally out of a universal gospel. The creative love of God is all-pervasive and yearns to be all-inclusive, and that love prays through each Christian heart.

A whole section of the hymn book is devoted to intercession and some of the hymns show that same world-embracing faith. Several times God is called the 'universal Friend', prayers are offered for the heathen, the Jews, the fallen and several for England. Charles encourages Christians to 'Extend the arms of mighty prayer, Ingrasping all mankind,' (CH p. 402). 'Ingrasping' suggests outstretched arms of welcome, the beckoning gesture, the all-inclusive invitation or an embrace that cherishes the whole world. It is a brilliantly evocative word which gives the distilled essence of a universal gospel.

As noted earlier, the Bible was a formative influence in the lives of the Wesleys. At one stage John had 'conversed much' with the mystics but 'found at length the absolute necessity of giving up either them or the Bible'. He 'fixed his choice' and from then onwards the Bible became his basis of argument, the repository of divine truth, the guidebook for souls in pilgrimage and the primary source of Evangelical religion (L iv p. 234). The significance of the Bible for spiritual growth is well explained in Wesley's *Notes on the New Testament.* 'The Spirit of God not only once inspired those who wrote it, but continually inspires, supernaturally assists, those who read it with earnest prayer' (CH p. 178). The same thought is present in the well known verse:

> Come Holy Ghost (for moved by Thee
>   The prophets wrote and spoke);
> Unlock the truth, Thyself the key,
>   Unseal the sacred book.

'God through Himself we then shall know . . .' (CH p. 185). Since God speaks directly through the Bible, personal diligent reading was reckoned to be indispensable for spiritual health. At least two hours of daily Bible reading was the optimistic advice given to Miss Lewen, 'a remarkable monument to divine mercy'; John congratulated another correspondent on her resolve to be a

Bible Christian; yet another female correspondent was informed that 'all the knowledge you want is comprised of one book – the Bible' (TL iv p. 247; v p. 221). He explained his own practice in a passage written with verve and enthusiasm: 'At any price give me the book of God! I have it! Here is knowledge enough for me. Let me be "a man of one book". Here then I am, far from the busy ways of men. I sit down alone; only God is here. In his presence I open, I read his book; for this end, to find the way to heaven . . . I meditate thereon with all the attention and earnestness of which my mind is capable.'[24]

The Lord's Supper held a central place in the spirituality of the Wesleys, for in the celebration of Holy Communion the Church reaffirmed the historic reality of the cross. The excesses of enthusiasm, and the careless dispensing with means by the Quietists, were checked and corrected by the biblical injunction, 'This do in remembrance of me'. In obedience to Christ, and as an act of oblation, Christians deliberately recall the manner and purpose of Christ's death. 'It may still be questioned whether any lenses have yet been constructed as perfect for visualizing Jesus, as penitent tears.'[25] Tears may dim the sight but they clarify spiritual vision. Only those who have experienced the cross by mourning the death of Jesus for them, can fully understand and clearly perceive God's redemptive purpose.

The Lord's Supper is an occasion, ordained by Christ for the intimate fellowship of believers with their Lord:

> Our hearts we open wide,
> To meet the Saviour
> And lo! the Lamb, the Crucified,
> The sinner's Friend, is come!
> His presence makes the feast;
> And now our bosoms feel,
> The glory not to be exprest,
> The joy unspeakable.[26]

The joy unspeakable flows directly from the experience in the heart of the eternal, sufficient and finished work of Christ. In celebrating the Lord's Supper Christians catch a glimpse of the incalculable costliness of grace, the ineffable mystery of Calvary and the eternal consequences of the atonement:

> Thou standest in the holiest place,
> As now for guilty sinners slain;

Thy blood of sprinkling speaks, and prays
  All-prevalent for helpless man . . .
(W p. 265)

With eyes firmly fixed on heaven Charles anticipates the fulness of salvation when the heavenly life will suffuse the Christian soul:

The light of life eternal darts
  Into our souls a dazzling ray,
A drop of heaven o'erflows our hearts,
  And deluges the house of clay.

Sure pledge of ecstasies unknown,
  Shall this divine communion be;
The ray shall rise into a sun,
  The drop shall swell into a sea.
(W pp. 264–5)

The dominant mood of the Eucharist is joy, because the Lord's Supper is not only commemoration and communion; it is an act of celebration and a festival of praise. Charles's exuberance leaves no room for emotional restraint and he asks the congregation to sing:

Louder than gathered waters,
Or bursting peals of thunder,
  We lift our voice
  And speak our joys,
And shout our loving wonder.[27]

Strident celebration is an appropriate but of itself inadequate response. Commemoration, communion and celebration fuse into spiritual worship only in a climactic gesture of self-consecration:

Take my soul and body's powers;
  Take my memory, mind and will;
All my goods, and all my hours,
  All I know and all I feel,
All I think, or speak, or do;
Take my heart but make it new.
(CH p. 593)

'Take my heart but make it new.' The spirituality of the Wesley brothers was unmistakeably experiential. It was a religion of the renewed heart. Central to their preaching, praying and piety was a profound gratitude to God for his grace shown to sinful mankind through the atoning death of Jesus. Divine judgement placed an eternal burden of guilt and death on sin; but through the death of Christ divine love bore that burden away as an act of sheer self-giving grace. By faith in the redeeming love of God every sinner can know forgiveness, can feel peace and can experience a personal renewal amounting to a total inner renovation. Such love and grace will not be thwarted by the limitations of human nature, because it is the eternal, 'exhaustless' love of God that pours into the new heart. The love divine excels all other loves.

The literature pulses and vibrates with wondering love. One of the hymns movingly celebrates the incoherence of the grateful heart:

Remember, Lord, my sins no more,
  That then I may no more forget,
But sunk in guiltless shame adore,
  With speechless wonder at Thy feet.

O'erwhelmed with Thy stupendous grace,
  I shall not in Thy presence move
But breathe unutterable praise,
  And rapturous awe, and silent love.

(CH p. 527)

The gospel of a loving redeeming God, reaching down to sinful, lost humanity with the offer of grace, new birth and inner renewal, made possible a life free from the guilt and power of sin, a life given over completely to the service of God. That service is to be expressed in a life of perfect love, and will come full circle as the new born Christian feels the drive of the divine imperative to witness before the world to the loving, dying Saviour. The last verse of Charles' most used hymn seems to sum up the great hope and goal of Wesleyan spirituality, and lifts the eyes beyond the daily struggle for holiness, looking to the final consummation of God's creative love:

Finish, then, Thy new creation,
  Pure and spotless let us be;
Let us see thy great salvation,
  Perfectly restored in Thee;
Changed from Glory into Glory,
  Till in heaven we take our place,
Till we cast our crowns before thee
  Lost in wonder, love, and praise.

(CH p. 547)

Sources frequently cited

Baker, F., *Charles Wesley as Revealed in His Letters*. London 1948. (BL)

—— *Charles Wesley's Verse*. London 1989. (BV)

Gill, F. C., *John Wesley's Prayers*. London 1951. (G)

Telford, J., *Letters of John Wesley*, Standard edn, ed. Telford. 8 vols., London 1931. (TL)

Tyson, J. R., *Charles Wesley on Sanctification*. Grand Rapids 1986. (T)

Wesley, J., *A Collection of Hymns for the Use of the People Called Methodists*. Works of John Wesley, Oxford edn, vol. 7. Oxford 1983. (CH)

Whaling, F., *John and Charles Wesley: Selected Writings and Hymns*. London 1981. (W)

Additional reading

Davies, R., and Rupp, G., *A History of the Methodist Church in Great Britain*, vol. 1 (London, 1965), vol. 4 (London 1989), contains a comprehensive bibliography on all aspects of the Wesleys' theology and spirituality.

Gill, F. C., *Charles Wesley, The First Methodist*. London 1964.

Marshall, M., and Todd, J., *English Congregational Hymns in the Eighteenth Century*. University of Kentucky Press 1982.

Rack, H., *Reasonable Enthusiast*. London 1989.

Rupp, G., *Religion in England: 1688–1791*. Oxford 1986.

Turner, J. M., *Conflict and Reconciliation: Studies in Methodism and Ecumenism in England, 1740–1982* (London 1985), chaps. 1–4.

Tyerman, L., *Life and Times of John Wesley, A.M.* 3 vols, London 1871.

Tyson, J. R., *Charles Wesley. A Reader*. New York 1989.

Notes

1. Note by S. T. Coleridge in his copy of Robert Southey's *Life of Wesley*, quoted in *Light on C. S. Lewis*, ed. Jocelyn Gibb (New York 1965), p. xvii.
2. *Works of John Wesley*, Oxford edn. vol. 25 (Oxford 1980), p. 9.
3. E. Jay, ed., *The Journal of John Wesley* (Oxford 1988), gives a brief introduction.
4. W. Leary, *Man of One Book*, Wesley Historical Society, Lecture no. 53, 1987.
5. H. Lindstrom, *Wesley and Sanctification* (London 1950), ch. 2, esp. p. 66.

6. A. Dallimore, *A Heart Set Free, Life of Charles Wesley* (Welwyn 1988), p. 31.
7. ibid. pp. 98, 107.
8. T. Jackson, *Journal of Charles Wesley*, 2 vols. (Kansas City 1980), vol. 1, p. 92.
9. Gill, *The First Methodist*, pp. 231–2. Tyson, *A Reader*, gives a clear profile of Charles's personality, pp. 3–10; see also Rack, *Reasonable Enthusiast*, pp. 251–7.
10. T. Jackson, *Journal*, vol. 1, p. 286. See also Tyson, *A Reader*, pp. 35–48, for a summary of Charles's theology. See A. M. Allchin, *Participation in God* (London 1988), for an important article, 'Man as God and God as Man', pp. 24–35.
11. T. Dudley-Smith, *A Flame of Love* (London 1988), p. xiii.
12. G. Rupp, *Religion in England 1688 to 1791* (Oxford 1986), p. 410.
13. *Works of John Wesley*, Oxford edn, vol. 25 (Oxford 1980) p. 132.
14. Tyson, *Sanctification*, pp. 20, 50f.; J. E. Rattenbury, *The Evangelical Doctrines of Charles Wesley's Hymns* (London 1941), remains a classic study, see ch. 3; Marshall and Todd, *English Hymns*, pp. 73–83, and Tyson, *A Reader*, pp. 20–35, highlight the connection between the hymns and the Wesleys' preaching.
15. Tyson, *Sanctification*, p. 24; O. Beckerlegge, 'A Man of One Book: Charles Wesley and the Scriptures', *Epworth Review*, vol. 15, no. 2, pp. 44–50.
16. *Works of John Wesley*, Oxford edn, vol. 2 (Nashville 1985), p. 97.
17. Lindstrom, *Wesley*, p. 20.
18. L. Tyerman, *The Life and Times of John Wesley, A.M.*, 3 vols. (London 1871), vol. 1, p. 269.
19. ibid., vol. 1, p. 333.
20. *Works of John Wesley*, Oxford edn, vol. 2 (Nashville 1985), p. 184.
21. Telford, *Letters*, vol. ii, p. 281; vol. iii, p. 167; vol. iv, p. 10; vol. v, p. 141.
22. Telford, *Letters*, vol. ii, p. 281; vol. iii, p. 157.
23. *Works of John Wesley*, Oxford edn, vol. 1 (Nashville 1985), p. 381.
24. ibid., pp. 105f.
25. Rattenbury, *Evangelical Doctrines*, p. 158, cf. G. Wakefield, *Methodist Devotion* (London 1966), ch. 1.
26. Rattenbury, *Evangelical Doctrines*, p. 220; J. E. Rattenbury, *The Eucharistic Hymns of John and Charles Wesley* (London 1948), provides a thorough study of Wesleyan eucharistic theology as reflected in the hymns.
27. ibid., p. 228.

2

JONATHAN EDWARDS and GEORGE WHITEFIELD

Grace! Grace! What hath God wrought?
WHITEFIELD

On Sunday, 19 October 1740, while on a preaching tour of New England, George Whitefield enjoyed the hospitality of Jonathan Edwards and his wife. Mr Edwards, he remarked, 'is a solid, excellent Christian', while Mrs Edwards was described as a woman 'adorned with a meek, quiet spirit', who 'talked solidly of the things of God' (JGW p. 476). Aged 25, Whitefield had recently embarked on an evangelistic itinerary which would gather momentum and become part of a widespread Evangelical Awakening with far-reaching effects on both sides of the Atlantic. Together the two preachers embodied an evangelistic Calvinism in which the theological principle of sovereign grace and the Evangelical imperative of gospel proclamation merged in a creative fusion.

Edwards was born in 'an obscure colony [East Windsor], in the midst of a wilderness, and educated at a seminary just commencing its existence [Yale], passing the better part of his life as the pastor of a frontier village [Northampton], and the residue as an Indian missionary [Stockbridge] . . .' (WJE 1 p. xi). He was the fifth child, the only boy in a family of eleven. His father was a frontier minister in a community numbering just over three hundred. His mother was the daughter of the venerable Solomon Stoddard, minister of Northampton, Massachusetts, from 1672 to 1729, a man known for his facility in both conversation and controversy, Edwards described him as 'an eminently holy man [though] of a dogmatical temper'.[1] Edwards became his grandfather's assistant in 1726 and his successor in 1729.

Throughout the 1730s sporadic spiritual awakenings occurred

in the colonies, the most significant being a number of 'surprising conversions' in Edwards' own area, of which he gave an account in his *Faithful Narrative*. An extraordinary surge of religious excitement swept through the colonies in 1740, partially stimulated by earlier movements but given decisive impetus by the preaching of Edwards and particularly the young George Whitefield. The two men poured out their lives in the promotion and explication of the Revival. Whitefield, the itinerant evangelist, preached a message of spiritual crisis with unequalled dramatic fervour. Edwards, the settled pastor, already experienced in directing the spiritual energies of a revival, established the criteria for authenticating 'a genuine work of God'. Whitefield exulted in his work: 'I am in my element as an evangelist'. Edwards fulfilled the more cerebral ministry of controlling the revival by theological explanation and profound spiritual analysis.

A sense of the glory of the divine Being.

Edwards' early religious training 'rendered him, when a child, familiarly conversant with God and with Christ, with his own character and duty, and with the nature of that eternal life which, begun on earth, is perfected in heaven' (WJE 1 p. xii). As a boy he spent much time in 'religious conversation', and at one stage was praying five times daily, even going so far as to build a prayer booth in a secluded swamp for the purpose of corporate prayer with two friends! Such intense religiosity and overdeveloped seriousness began to subside during college days at Yale. Then a near fatal illness when he felt 'God shook him over the pit of Hell,' provoked 'violent inward struggles' which compelled a fresh search for salvation, but without that 'affection and delight' which had given warmth to his earlier experience. Edwards later doubted that such terrified seeking represented authentic spiritual search, arguing, with characteristic subtlety, that self-preservation is untrustworthy as the primary motivation of the spiritual life.

In his late teens Edwards had an experience of God which he later called his 'first conversion' (WJE 1 p. xlviii). Reflecting on 1 Timothy 1.17, he felt his soul suffused with a sense of the glory of the Divine Being. 'I thought with myself how excellent a Being that was, and how happy I should be if I might enjoy that God, and be rapt up to Him in heaven; and be as it were swallowed up in him forever' (WJE 1 p. xiii).

From his reading of Puritan and Dissenting divines Edwards expected conversion to be an experience with 'particular steps'. His own conversion did not follow the normal pattern and he confessed with perplexity: 'I do not remember that I experienced regeneration, exactly in those steps, in which divines say it is generally wrought . . .' (WJE 1 p. xxiv). For several years he followed a programme of diligent self-examination in pursuit of assurance. During this period he compiled seventy 'Resolutions' as a personal check-list. These amount to a highly developed strategy to sustain and protect his relationship with God. Resolution twenty-five reads: 'To examine carefully and constantly, what that one thing in me is, which causes me in the least to doubt the love of God; and so direct all my forces against it'. He resolved to 'trace' each sin back 'to the original cause', and more specifically 'to maintain the strictest temperance in eating and drinking'. Several record occasions of self-dedication: 'Resolved, never, henceforward, till I die, to act as if I were any way my own, but entirely and altogether God's. . . .' This resolution is a reaffirmation of an earlier act of dedication, cast significantly in trinitarian terms. He had 'given himself clear away to God' . . . 'did believe in Jesus Christ, and did receive Him as a Prince and Saviour', . . . and 'did receive the blessed Spirit as my Teacher [and] Sanctifier . . . and cherish all his motions to enlighten, purify, confirm, comfort and assist me' (WJE 1 p. xxv). The deliberate encouragement of self-doubt was related to the theology of election which lay at the heart of Puritan spirituality. No Christian can guarantee that they are of the elect; the evidence must be found in the spiritual life, in a sense of sin, a yearning for holiness, a lively faith in Christ and a submission to the sovereign will of God.

Ten years later, in 1733, by which time he was well established as pastor of the Northampton church, he concluded that he ought to live on the assumption that he was indeed converted, though with adequate safeguards against presumption: 'It seems to me, that whether I am now converted or not, I am so settled in the state I am in that I shall go on in it all my life. But however settled I may be, yet I will continue to pray to God, not to suffer me to be deceived about it . . . and ever and anon, will call all into question and try myself, using for helps some of our old divines . . .' (WJE 1 p. xxxvi). He intended to look to God for his 'whole portion and felicity' and aim at being 'a complete Christian, in all respects of a right stamp'. Exploring the spiralling realms of metaphysical theology and the subterranean depths of religious psychology Edwards would indeed 'call all into question' and try himself by seeking the authenticating stamp of God's 'sovereign and excellent grace' in his spiritual experience.

The doctrine of the Trinity and the concepts of beauty and harmony helped Edwards to develop a richly experimental theology. He felt, to a remarkable degree, the inward compulsion to worship the Lord in the *beauty* of holiness. The human soul finds utter fulfilment only as it stands in proper relation to a holy God:

> Holiness is . . . the highest beauty and amiableness . . . It makes the soul a little sweet and delightful image of the blessed Jehovah . . . What sweet calmness, what calm ecstasies, doth it bring to the soul. How doth it make the soul love itself . . . how doth God love it and delight in it; how do even the sun, the fields and trees love a humble holiness . . . It makes the soul like a garden planted by God . . . where the sun is Jesus Christ, and the blessed beams and calm breeze, the Holy Spirit.
> (J p. 16)

The ultimate perfection of beauty and harmony are found only in the inner life of the Trinity, expressed in an entire mutual consent. The consent of the Father to give the Son, the consent of the Son to fulfill the divine purpose in obedience to the Father, and the Spirit as the loving consent by which the divine creative and redemptive purposes are accomplished, suggested to Edwards a soaring vision of the glory of God. He sensed in the Godhead a harmony which could only be adequately portrayed by using the analogy of music. The origin and destiny of each soul is an essential part of the divine magnum opus in which the movements express the harmonious beauty and moral excellences of God. The finale of the work of God, in which all things come to their consummation, is likened to a 'very complex tune, where respect is to be had to the proportion of a great many notes together' (J p. 20). Each individual life is an indispensable note, essential to an authentic performance and a faithful reproduction in history of the work of the divine composer.

The same image of musical harmony illumines Edwards' view of sanctification. 'Holiness of heart doth of its own nature . . . keep men from errors in judgement about religion . . . The reason is, that as the sanctified mind is let into the spiritual world . . . it easily perceives what ideas are *harmonious* and what are not . . . the soul distinguishes *as a musical ear*' (J p. 87). Edwards had described his early experiences of God as a receiving of 'new dispositions . . . and a new sense of things', but his later analysis of conversion shows that he had come to believe conversion involved nothing less that the radical renewal of personality by the operation of the sovereign, electing grace of God. 'New dispositions' included a new sense of the beauty of God expressed in the purposeful harmony and moral perfection of the divine Trinity, a new sense of sin as inordinate self-love springing from inborn moral corruption and a new sense of the divine love reproducing in Christian character and Christian community, a life in moral harmony with God.

The native depravity of the heart of man.

'The principles on which the power of godliness depends, are in great measure exploded', lamented Edwards; and those who held to such principles are 'commonly looked upon to be crack-brained and beside their right mind' (Y3 p. 2). In other words, to enlightened men, such principles were contrary to reason. Edwards shared the 'Enlightenment passion for critique'. Isaac Newton had forced radical changes in the experimental procedures of physics by an investigative method based on distrust of initial observations. Applied to the physical world such questioning, unimpeded by preconceptions, shed light on many puzzles. By sheer weight of results, inductive reasoning established itself as the primary basis for the pursuit of scientific knowledge. What Newton achieved in physics, Locke and Hume attempted in the human sciences of politics, epistemology and psychology with shattering implications for theology. This hunger for knowledge and enlightenment dominated the intellectual climate of Edwards' generation. As a precocious teenager he prepared papers on natural philosophy covering such diverse subjects as 'Of Insects', 'Of the Rainbow', 'Of Light Rays', and 'Of Atoms'. The search for order and harmony by probing and examining evidence, stimulated by the underlying confidence that the world can be understood according to established laws, provided the intellectual framework within which Edwards did his most creative thinking. If others used the new sciences to discredit the Christian revelation, Edwards found them admirably suited to the exploration of the excellency of the Divine Being as expressed in the harmony, beauty, and purposefulness of the creation.

The autonomous reason had unlocked and illumined the mysteries of the natural world, conferring new knowledge and exposing superstition. When reason was given the same clarifying and progressive function in theology, many believed similar benefits accrued. The idea of supernatural revelation was discredited in favour of the sufficiency of reason; original sin, a condition of total ruin imputed from Adam to the whole race, and carrying with it moral culpability, seemed to contradict reason and justice; human depravity, the belief that through the fall humanity's intellectual and moral capacity had not only been damaged, but had been corrupted into enmity against God expressed in pride and self-will, was exactly contrary to the spirit of the Enlightenment; the wrath of God, as punitive response to sin, the atonement as an act of representative penal substitution, and salvation as the sovereign act of God offered in free grace to the elect only, all alike offended the new perceptions of what was reasonable and morally acceptable.[2]

Edwards' most significant writing provided a massively reasoned defence of orthodox doctrine, motivated by concern that vital religion would shrivel and die if the doctrines of grace were reasoned out of existence. 'Things are going downhill so fast, and truth and religion, both of heart and practice, are departing by such swift steps that I think it must needs be, that a crisis is not very far off' (Y3 p. 20). The crisis he feared was further provoked by a volume entitled *The Scripture–Doctrine of Original Sin, Proposed to Free and Candid Examination*, written by an English Congregationalist, John Taylor. The title betrays the determination to subject the doctrine to examination in the court of unfettered reason. Another title, published in New England in 1757, highlights the main issue: *A Winter's Evening's Conversation upon the Doctrine of Original Sin . . . Wherein the Notion of Our Having Sinned in Adam and Being on That Account Only Liable to Eternal Damnation is Proved to be Unscriptural, Emotional and of Dangerous Tendency*. The same year Edwards published his own treatise, *The Great Christian Doctrine of Original Sin*. It reveals the philosopher–pastor using the tools of his opponents to establish a doctrine which by its pessimistic estimate of the corrupt human intellect threatened the integrity of the whole enlightenment enterprise.

The extent of human depravity, the destiny of infants, the righteousness of God glorified in the damnation of sinners, the nature of Christ's death and the necessity of new birth present theological dilemmas the resolution of which depends on establishing the precise nature of sin. Edwards had no doubts. History and human experience confirm the biblical evidence. Humanity is universally, unfailingly and irremediably sinful. A steady effect requires a steady cause. What other reason can there be for universal moral failure than that each person is inherently flawed, the rebellious possessor of a nature sympathetic to sin and antagonistic to God? Sin itself is a heinous disregard of a God who is infinitely worthy and rightfully demands of his creatures an infinite obligation. Sin is not only a misuse of free will, a wrong moral choice; it is both an act of self-determination and an act predetermined by a sinful nature which renders the sinner 'odious to God' (Y3 p. 129).

Edwards was impatient with any gradation of sin. Sin is not an isolated act to be judged by its intention or consequences. It is the expression of a nature so subverted by wickedness that it lacks native integrity. To say that man is not totally corrupt because he is capable of good as well as evil is as unreasonable as to argue the seaworthiness of a ship to cross 'the Atlantick Ocean', against all positive evidence to the contrary, 'under a notion that it may probably go [a] great part of the way before it sinks, or that it will proceed and sail above water more hours than it will be sinking . . .' (J p. 145). The divine abhorrence of all sins, however small, and however infrequent, arises from the personal offence against the majesty and infinite worthiness of God which every sin implies. A sinner's supposed good deeds count for nothing against the insult and injury done to God. To insist otherwise is to argue that 'the domestic of a prince was not a bad servant because . . . he did not spit in his master's face so often as he performed acts of service' (J p. 146).

True religion . . . consists in holy affections.

Such personal insult is symptomatic of pride and 'the predominancy of self-love' in the unregenerate. Sin is deliberate blindness to all that makes God lovable, and rebellion against all that God demands, in preference to an inward-turning love of self and a corresponding hatred of all that challenges the right to self-determination. Egocentricity is an all-pervasive corruption of the basic constituents of personality, poisoning the moral life at its source. The drive of the self is so powerful that it distorts even religion, by using devotional practice in an attempt to oblige God to bless. Response to the gospel of the grace of God then becomes a calculated manoeuvre engineered by the survival instinct of the self. It is not surprising therefore that Edwards prized, above all other spiritual signs, disinterested love expressed in holy affections.

In 1746 Edwards published his classic account, *Religious Affections*'. Along with other works, it was written both to defend the Awakening as a work of God and to define carefully the nature of true conversion. Edwards, confronted with the undeniable excesses of revival spirituality and troubled by the accusations of opponents that emotional fervour was spiritually spurious, insisted that the observable evidence of conversion is holiness of life under the governing impulse of love to God. Holiness is an affair of the heart (or will) and is expressed in holy affections. The enlightenment of reason by doctrinal truth and the correction of behaviour by ethical insight are necessary aspects of the conversion experience, but it is the supernatural inner change wrought by the Spirit in the soul which gives a new disposition and taste for the things of God so that the heart begins to recognize, relish, love and consent to spiritual things. Such relish and delight consists of love to God pure and simple, with no self-reference. 'By this you may examine your love to God, and to Jesus Christ, and to the Word of God, and your joy in them, and also your love to the people of God, and your desires after heaven; whether they be from a supreme delight in this sort of beauty, without being primarily moved from your own imagined interest in them, or expectations from them' (Y2 p. 240). By such tests the mercenary spirit of much revivalist experience was exposed. With considered scorn he castigated the self-indulgence of those who boasted of elevated experiences: 'What they are principally taken and elevated with, is not the glory of God, or beauty of Christ, but the beauty of their experiences. They keep thinking of themselves, what a good experience is this! . . . and so they put their experiences in place of Christ, and his beauty and fulness; and instead of rejoicing in Christ Jesus, they rejoice in their admirable experiences' (Y2 p. 251).

A sinner's consent to God ought not to be conditional on blessing, but should be an unconditional Yes to the inherent beauty of God's moral excellence. Conversion is then identified with the communication of divine truth to human consciousness by the Spirit, in such a way that it is grasped by intellectual apprehension, admired in appreciative contemplation and obeyed by a new moral inclination. The result is 'a sense of the heart of the supreme beauty and sweetness of the holiness and moral perfection of divine things, together with all the discerning and knowledge of things religious, that depends upon and flows from such a sense' (Y2 p. 272). Such renewal of the moral personality must then be manifested in a life consistently Christian. 'For Edwards grace is an abiding principle of holy action in the heart'.[3]

Charity and its fruits.

In 1741 a young female convert wrote to Edwards asking for advice as to 'the best manner of maintaining a religious life'. In the course of a seventeen-paragraph reply Edwards exhorted, 'Pray that your eyes may be opened . . . that you may know yourself and be brought to God's footstool; and that you may see the Glory of God and Christ . . . and have the love of Christ shed abroad in your heart' (WJE 1 p. liii). Spiritual sight, self-knowledge, the sense of the glory of God and the love of Christ in the heart depend amongst other things on the use of the Bible. 'Most persons are to blame for their inattentive, unobserving way of reading the scriptures', he complained. Yet even the most apparently arid parts of Scripture are 'mines and treasures of gospel knowledge'. Edwards remonstrated with those who neglected the Bible, which he believed was 'the proper means to bring the world to the knowledge of God'. He loved and studied the Bible more than all other books and for over thirty-five years expended enormous labour compiling notes, writing his *Miscellanies* and harvesting his fruits into notebooks, a blank-leaved Bible and over 1100 surviving sermon manuscripts. In his devotional reading he valued the commentators Matthew Henry and Philip Doddridge and read the Scriptures believing that the Spirit who inspired them was the essential interpreter and communicator of the truth contained in them. Prolonged absorption of the biblical text provided a firm objective base from which to test the reality of spiritual experiences.

Much of Edwards' best teaching is in his sermons where he deals with charity, purity of heart, the attractiveness of Christ, self-examination and the various forms of self-deceit, a subject on which Edwards was both theologically and psychologically expert. One series of sermons, not included in earlier editions of his works, *Charity and its Fruits*, is a superb exposition of 1 Corinthians chapter thirteen, a part of the New Testament which, in its balancing cautions and positive assertions about the priorities of Christian spirituality, was a required corrective to revivalist enthusiasm.

'The Spirit of God is a Spirit of love', and 'that is the most precious gift which is most of an evidence of God's love' (Y8 p. 160). Love is the 'acting, working, spirit in faith' so that in Christian obedience the will to perform, the inclination to obey and the imagination to discern are all energized by an enlivening love. Indeed 'all [that] is saving and distinguishing in Christianity does radically consist and is summarily comprehended in love' (Y8 p. 141). Love expressed in holy action validates experience, and of all spiritual gifts love provides decisive evidential value of grace.

Obedience to the love command is not a legal requirement with which the Christian must comply; it is the natural and unsurprising attitude of one in vital relationship with God whose love has been poured into the renewed heart. Love is the unmistakeable feature which betrays family likeness to God. Not only so, 'it is the nature of love . . . to incline and dispose to imitation', and consequently Edwards preached a demanding love in which each of love's attributes answered to a corresponding aspect of the character of God (Y8 p. 194). The incomparable love of God is the standard by which Christian spirituality is tested. Considering the long-suffering of love, Edwards urged his congregation to imitate the long-suffering of God: 'He that possesses his mind after such a manner that when others reproach him and injure him, and show a spiteful spirit towards him, can notwithstanding maintain in calmness a hearty good will to his injurer, and look down on him with real pity for him without any tumult or bitterness; he herein as it were manifests a godlike greatness of soul' (Y8 pp. 200–1).

Edwards was well aware that he was comparing human behaviour with that which is incomparable; human love, however sublime in its vision, however ungrudging in sacrifice and however consistent in practice, falls short of the glory and love of God. Nevertheless, though blurred and faded, the pattern of divine love will be discernible in Christian character, and will answer, however faintly, to the love of God. So when he considers the kindness of love, Edwards applies the same principle: 'Love of benevolence is that disposition which a man has who desires or delights in the good of another. And this is the main thing in Christian love, the most essential thing, and that whereby our love is most of an imitation of the eternal love and grace of God, and the dying love of Christ, which consists in benevolence or good will' (Y8 p. 213).

While Christian love is compared with divine love, Edwards never lessens the distance between humanity and God. He is relentless in his accusations concerning envy, pride and self-love. Real love to God is necessarily accompanied by a constant and frank humility: 'If we are ignorant of our meanness as compared with Him, the most essential thing and that which is original in true humility is wanting' (Y8 pp. 234–5). Man's 'natural meanness is his littleness; his moral meanness is his filthiness'. Such moral and spiritual inadequacy accounts for the infinite distance between man and God. So the mood of the Christian heart as humble, grateful, receptive and uncalculating, arises from awareness of this vast moral distance between God in his loveliness and man in his ugliness. That such love should reach out in redemptive self-expending love was for Edwards a miracle capable of breaking the chronic egocentricity of the human heart.

In a magnificent sermon, powerful in rhetoric, soaring in vision and vibrating with theological passion, Edwards described 'Heaven as a World of Love'. There, in the community of the redeemed, the divine love will be appreciated and apprehended by minds and hearts finally in harmony with God, filled with heavenly love to the exclusion of all that is unlovely, and made fully sensitive to the beauty of holiness: 'There [in heaven] this glorious God is manifested and shines forth in full glory, in beams of love and delight, enough for all to drink at, and to swim in, yea, so as to overflow the world as it were with a deluge of love' (Y8 p. 370). The love of God, which so enriches the life of the Christian, is that same love which guarantees the eternal unity of the Godhead: 'The infinite essential love of God is, as it were, an infinite and eternal mutual holy energy between the Father and the Son, a pure, holy act whereby the Deity becomes nothing but an infinite and unchangeable act of love, which proceeds from both the Father and the Son' (Y8 p. 373). The essential unselfishness of God is supremely demonstrated in Christ's atoning death. Edwards urges his hearers to anticipate now the future joy of liberated faculties in an unrestrained acknowledgement of the dying love of Christ: 'The saints will love God with an inconceivable ardor of heart . . . with the same ardor will the saints love the Lord Jesus Christ . . . They shall then be more sensible than they are now what great love is manifested in Christ, that he should lay his life down for them. Then Christ will open to their view the great fountain of love in his heart far beyond what they ever before saw . . .' (Y8 p. 377).

The spirituality of Jonathan Edwards is entirely centred in the glory of God. He tolerated nothing which diminished that glory or subtracted from the absolute sovereignty of the divine will. The awakening of the heart, the regeneration of the soul and growth in holiness were all alike at the disposal of the Lord God omnipotent. His intellect took hold of the mixed phenomena of revival experience, and by a process of dissection and analysis he exposed the spurious and established the genuine. Like a scientist pursuing a new discipline, he proposed a series of 'distinguishing signs of truly gracious and holy affections'. Chief among these, as the measure of maturity and the test of reality, is disinterested love, expressed in a life of ethical obedience which draws its power from the Holy Spirit, at work in the renewed heart, conforming the life to the image of Christ, crucified and glorified.

Strict application of such logic in pastoral discipline provoked serious conflict leading eventually to Edwards' dismissal from the Northampton church in July 1750. He had insisted that only such as profess personal faith in Christ as Saviour from sin, and whose profession is substantiated by a corresponding life of credible piety, should be admitted to Holy Communion, a position radically different from his grandfather's view that Holy Communion is itself a converting ordinance. To Edwards' mind such practice at best merely encouraged a false sense of security and at worst subverted the gospel by blurring the edges of the truth that all are sinners at enmity with God until reconciled in Christ. Until such reconciliation was effected by 'closing with Christ' it was intolerable to Edwards that God's enemies should come to the table pretending to be friends. Underlying the controversy were festering grievances, family in-fighting, local jealousies and, on Edwards' part, a powerful intellect able to argue theological principle combined with a sense of pastoral responsibility incapable of pragmatic compromise.[4]

Many factors contributed to the tragedy of Edwards' life. After vacating the Northampton pulpit he remained a focus of dispute. Discredited in the eyes of many, he eventually accepted the call to the frontier post of Stockbridge. Without access to libraries and removed from the intellectual stimulus of demanding pastoral charge he still produced works on which his reputation as 'America's Theologian' would rest. His rare gifts were recognized in 1757 when he was offered the Presidency of the College of New Jersey. The pain of rejection seemed to be giving way to deserved recognition. Edwards died after an inoculation for smallpox before he could begin his Presidency. Behind the sad circumstances of Edwards' later life was a man whose personality and integrity prevented him from successfully combining rarefied theological exploration with pastoral expediency. The expositor of the glory of God, a glory now inspiring terror of judgement and now radiating redemptive love, was simply incapable of transposing spiritual vision into the lower key of pastoral reality.

When the weight of sin went off.

Powerful currents of spiritual activity are bound to give rise to controversy, and this was as true for the itinerant Whitefield as it was for the resident pastor of Northampton. Whitefield was repeatedly accused of wild 'enthusiasm', his field preaching was seen as subversive of church order and as a provocation to riot and mob violence. Many of his strictures on the church were anti-clerical in tone and drew from his critics the charge that he 'preached a new gospel as unknown to the generality of ministers and people.' A late Member of the University of Oxford fulminated: 'Your sermons are off-hand harangues – mere enthusiastic rant – a wild rhapsody of nonsense – the foam of an overheated imagination, the spuings of the heart upon the people in unconcerted sentences.'[5]

Whitefield's early life was spent in Gloucester where his parents were the proprietors of the prosperous Bell Inn. He was the last of seven children and it seems to have been taken for granted, both by his mother and himself, that he would become a clergyman. In an autobiographical fragment Whitefield outlined his education, mentioning his skill at drama and elocution, his enjoyment in reading plays and an imaginative intensity by which he became engrossed in the parts he played. All of these native gifts would combine with spiritual fervour to produce the most electrifying public orator of the age.

He remembered 'some early convictions of sin', and pleaded guilty to 'an impudent temper' and a 'sensual appetite', in the satisfying of which he stole money from his mother to buy 'fruits, tarts' and other treats. He gave up school at fifteen and served in the inn as a 'professed and common drawer'.[6] The eighteenth-century inn was a social kaleidoscope providing a liberal education in the subtleties and crudities of human nature. He matriculated at Pembroke College, Oxford, in 1732, paying his way by working as a servitor. By now he was eighteen and had been seriously engaged in a life of religious discipline for over a year. He came to 'a lively and experimental knowledge of Christ' only after a protracted programme of ascetic discipline which left him broken in health. He cut his diet by 'leaving off fruits' and choosing 'the worst sorts of food', his 'apparel was mean', and he spent an anguished five or six weeks of 'fights with [my] corruptions'. Whitefield descended into a vortex of spiritual anxiety which was expressed in increasingly bizarre behaviour and led to his breakdown during Lent 1735.[7]

Earlier he had read *The Life of God in the Soul of Man*, a mystical work by Henry Scougal of Aberdeen, and had been impressed by its teaching that vital religion must arise from the life of God within and not from external religious duties, however strenuously performed. Confined to bed as a result of his illness, he read the Greek New Testament and Bishop Hall's *Contemplations*. Sometime during his convalescence he was filled with the joy of assurance and forgiveness. 'God was pleased to remove the heavy load . . . O with what joy . . . joy that was full of and big with glory, was my soul filled, when the weight of sin went off, and an abiding sense of the pardoning love of God, and a full assurance of faith, broke in on my disconsolate soul' (JGW p. 58).

Oh the blessedness of these evangelical truths!

In time, the abiding sense of pardoning love and full assurance of faith were to be condensed into a spirituality derived from 'the doctrines of Grace'. A later sermon includes the confession, 'I know the place! . . . where Jesus Christ first revealed himself to me and gave me the new birth.' The initiative of God, the necessity of new birth, and salvation understood as free gift were theological principles which shaped Whitefield's later thought. His experience of futile discipline, meticulous legality and self-destructive asceticism had culminated in spiritual failure and utter exhaustion. Deliverance from such bondage released new energy and gave him a profound sense of liberation, of being an object of God's love. Election was neither theological conundrum nor moral scandal; it was an act of 'distinguishing love,' of 'electing, soul transforming love'. By 1739 he wrote of his comfort in Jesus Christ: 'He saw me from all eternity; He gave me being; He called me in time; He has freely justified me through faith in His blood; He has in part sanctified me by His Spirit; He will preserve me underneath His everlasting arms till time shall be no more . . .' (WGW 1 p. 98).

His preaching in London, Bath and Bristol in 1737 'literally startled the nation. He was a new phenomenon in the Church of England' (JGW p. 22). Later itineraries included Dublin, Glasgow, Newcastle and Edinburgh. Soon after, he made the first of seven visits to America, preaching in such places as Boston, New York and Charleston, and centring much of his work in New England and Georgia. Evangelistic zeal sharpened his criticism of weak or erroneous doctrine. As a controversialist he took on John Wesley and the Bishop of London, he sharply criticized the works of the revered Anglican Archbishop Tillotson, and argued at various times against Moravians, Quakers, Deists, Arminians and any others he identified as opponents of a gospel of free grace.[8] In a characteristic passage he asserts: 'I bless God His Spirit has convinced me of our eternal election by the Father through the Son, of our free justification through faith in His blood, of our sanctification as the consequence of that, and of our final perseverance and glorification as the result of all. These

I am persuaded God has joined together; these, neither men nor devils shall ever be able to put asunder.'[9]

Despite such definite doctrinal commitment there was in Whitefield a persistent strain of catholicity and a real desire for unity with other Christians. 'I would willingly be of so catholic a spirit as to love the image of my divine master, wherever I see it: I am far from thinking God's grace is confined to any set of men whatsoever.'[10] The same breadth of sympathy led to Whitefield's involvement in all kinds of social concern. At different times he was involved in orphan care, improved treatment of slaves, education of children, and to his credit made a blistering attack on anti-Semitism at Lisbon (WGW 3 p. 84). Equally, he never hesitated to interfere with what he perceived to be the sins of his age. He preached against horse racing. His preaching persuaded the manager of the Glasgow Playhouse to 'take the roof down'. The letters abound with glimpses of Whitefield the 'troubler of Israel'; 'several clods were thrown . . . some rude people kicked a football . . .'; 'we were serenaded by a copper furnace' being beaten.

By 1739 the Wesleys were equally busy, preaching 'free salvation' and provoking riotous opposition. In Whitefield they encountered opposition from an ally.[11] Whitefield carefully qualified 'free salvation' in a letter to Wesley in which he began with the quaint disclaimer, 'Jonah could not go with more reluctance against Nineveh than I now take pen in hand to write against you'. The Wesleys proclaimed a universal atonement, salvation free for all who believe; Whitefield insisted God's grace is 'free, because not free to all; but free, because God may withold or give it to whom and when He pleases'.[12] Both agreed that grace was the source of salvation; but they profoundly disagreed as to its method of operation. In a passage reminiscent of Edwards in its trinitarian emphases, Whitefield firmly stated, 'It was grace, free grace, that moved the Father so to love the world, as to give his only begotten Son . . . It was grace, free grace, that moved the Son to come down and die. It was grace, free grace, that moved the Holy Ghost to undertake to sanctify the elect people of God' (SGW p. 421). Earlier letters contain lengthy apologetic defences of his Calvinism, but gradually he is content with shorthand exclamations, 'O Grace, Grace', and it is noticeable that the exultant note persists through the whole correspondence. A letter written when he was fifty-five is almost childish in enthusiasm and yet reveals cautious distrust of his own heart; innocence and self-knowledge fuse in the paradox of a grace that gives value to the worthless and which transforms guilt into the gratitude of the forgiven. As a 'very worthless worm' he felt he had no rights before God: 'and yet, (O amazing love!) Jesus, a never-failing, ever-loving, altogether-lovely Jesus, careth for and comforts him on every side . . . Grace! Grace! What hath God wrought? With all thy mercies glorious Emmanuel, deny not the mercy of a thankful heart' (WGW 3 p. 393).

Grace and sovereign purpose, intent on man's salvation, issued finally in the cross. In numerous letters Whitefield exulted in the cross. 'Forget not a bleeding God', he urged; he trusted one of his converts would 'know what it is to feast on a crucified Jesus'; he pointed out 'how mean and contemptible does every creature appear, when the soul gets a near view of the crucified Redeemer', and he encouraged meditation on 'the agony and bloody sweat of an incarnate God' (WGW 1 pp. 154, 161; 2 p. 95).

Personal experience and biblical precedent convinced Whitefield that regeneration is entirely the work of the Spirit of God. By faith the soul enters into a mystic union and receives a transfusion of the divine life. Explaining the text, 2 Cor. 5.17, 'If any man be in Christ he is a new creature', Whitefield boldly asserted what to be in Christ means '. . . to be in Him so as to partake of the benefits of God's sufferings. To be in him not only by an outward profession, but by an inward change and purity of heart, and cohabitation of his holy Spirit. To be in him so as to be mystically united to him by a true and lively faith, and thereby to receive spiritual virtue from him . . .' (SGW p. 544).

The new creature in Christ is continuous with the old, though there is now a radical discontinuity of legal status before God and of inner moral condition:

> As it may be said of a piece of gold, that was once in the ore, after it has been cleansed, purified and polished, that it is a new piece of gold; as it may be said of a bright glass that has been covered over with filth, when it is wiped, and so become transparent and clear, that it is a new glass; . . . so our souls, though still the same as to essence, yet are so purged, purified and cleansed from their natural dross . . . by the blessed influence of the holy Spirit, that they may be properly said to be made anew. (SGW p. 545)

By an imputed righteousness the barriers of legal condemnation and moral impurity are removed enabling the soul to be restored to fellowship with God. Probably his Oxford experiences underlie his warning that the constant and conscientious use of all the means of grace is proof, not of being a Christian, but only of seriousness in seeking new birth. Those who sincerely long for salvation will not 'lazily seek but laboriously strive to enter the narrow way'. But in the end, the new birth and peace with God are the 'least of those mercies God has prepared for those that are in Christ . . . this is but the beginning of an eternal succession of pleasures . . .' (SGW p. 552).

What is a Christian without a holy warmth?

Throughout his life Whitefield felt himself a 'meer [*sic*] novice' in Christ's school. He never felt he had killed the root of pride, he upbraided himself for his lack of love, and repeatedly lamented his lack of zeal. Though expenditure of energy is no guarantee of spirituality, there is no doubt Whitefield had little time for comfortable complacency. The gospel concerns ultimate questions which permit no trifling. 'Strive as strivers for eternity', he urged, his own frenetic pace of life serving as a daunting example and making nonsense of his self-estimate as an unprofitable servant. 'O that my head was water, and mine eyes fountains of tears, that I might bewail my barrenness and unfruitfulness in the chuch of God . . . I blush and am confounded when I think for what little purpose I have lived' (WGW 2 p. 304). Whitefield was constantly taking his spiritual temperature and measuring his love for Christ by his zeal in his work. He prayed to be saved from the 'fatal langour': 'For what', he asked, 'is a Christian without a holy warmth?'

Fire was a favourite metaphor. The image of heat, the self-expenditure of fuel, the giving of light and the diffusion of energy all answered to the activist strain in Whitefield's temperament. 'What a mystery of love is the mystery of godliness! Whilst I am writing the fire kindles . . . I would fain die blazing, not with human glory but with the love of Jesus' (WGW 2 p. 4). Such ardour was neither contrived nor exaggerated but was the genuine by-product of an experience which ignited an intense and imaginative personality. Whitefield's sense of failure was relative; compared with the love God had shown him, and the cost of redemption through the sufferings of God, he thought his efforts were so insignificant as to be unmeasurable. Yet they who have been forgiven much, love much, and those who love much must find ways of expressing their devotion. Whitefield's Calvinism never for a moment tolerated the antinomian heresy. Again and again he called Christians to a life of unsparing discipleship, ethical obedience and determined perseverance. 'Grace omnipotent, grace alone, can enable us to see our compleatness in Christ, and yet excite us, from principles of gratitude and love, to faithfulness and zeal, as though we were to be entirely saved by them. Glorious mystery!' (WGW 3 p. 43). This is his own explanation for his punishing lifestyle and it rescues some of his more effusive exclamations from the charge of artificiality. 'Had I a thousand hands I could employ them all . . . had I a thousand lives my dear Lord Jesus would have them all.' A more wistful note creeps into the later letters, including the delightful prayer: 'Keep me travelling, keep me working, or at least beginning to begin to work for thee till I die!' (WGW 3 p. 26).

Sermons, letters, social concerns, personal counselling and encouraging of local societies were all part of a non-stop evangelistic campaign. Whitefield preached on thousands of occasions, though only seventy-five sermons were ever published. Bishop Ryle, staunch admirer of Whitefield, commented acidly on the inefficiency of Whitefield's stenographers: 'These worthy men appear to have done their work very indifferently, and were evidently ignorant alike of stopping and paragraphing, of grammar and of gospel.'[13] The sermons are bare bones stripped of flesh and lacking the vitality, power and immediacy of a living personality. Whitefield's gift of improvisation and dramatic sense, his uncanny discernment of mood and the overwhelming sense of earnestness he conveyed to his audience are all muted by the flattening effect of sermons hastily recorded secondhand, thereby losing the overall emotional impact of a preacher in living touch with the minds of his hearers. Wesley's printed sermons can be equally flat, but they convince by their internal logic and doctrinal engagement. Edwards' sermons throb with intellectual and theological power, marshalled into tightly structured argument and informed by pastoral and biblical reflection. Edwards was a philosopher theologian who for pastoral reasons argued massively against Arminianism; Wesley was an eclectic theologian and an organizational genius in whom various streams of the Christian tradition coalesced and found expression in Arminian Methodism; while George Whitefield was an evangelist pure and simple, in whom Calvinist theology and Methodist enthusiasm fused and released extraordinary resources of evangelistic effort.

What the sermons obscure of the real Whitefield is largely recovered in the letters. For the years between 1734 and 1770 the collected edition contains 1,465 letters recording notes, replies, rebukes, spiritual directions, reflections on his own spiritual life, business matters and family concerns. Correspondents included 'a child at the Orphanage House, Georgia', a soldier stationed at Gibraltar, the Bishop of Bangor, Gabriel Harris his bookseller, the Erskines of Scotland, the Earl of Leven and Melville and countless known and unknown individuals seeking counsel or being given unsolicited spiritual advice.

Many of his own spiritual struggles can be chronicled, as for example his lifelong inner battle against the sin of pride. The egocentric tone and lack of tact in the early journal is well known, and was regretted by the mature Whitefield. 'I am a proud, imperious, sinful worm', he confessed, 'It is difficult to go through the fiery trial of popularity and applause untainted', he admitted ruefully (WGW 1 pp. 32, 60, 69). Self-understanding was hard won, wrung from the pain of rejection, conflict and an almost habitual sense of remorse. 'O for further leadings into the chambers of that selfish, sensual and devilish imagery that yet lie latent in my partly renewed heart' (WGW 2 p. 150). Whitefield had a profound sense of personal incompleteness, of being a sinner in process of being saved daily from sin, of sanctification as gradual growth and often painful cultivation. He almost ran out of acceptable epithets in lamenting the persistence of self-love and self-will. 'This remaining body of sin, what an antichrist! what a scarlet whore! what a hell! what a red dragon! . . . how hard, how slow he dies! . . . O for a heart gladly to embrace every cross, every trying dispensation, that may have a tendency to poison, or starve, or nip the buddings of the old, and cherish, promote, or cause to bloom and blossom the graces and tempers of the new man in my soul!' (WGW 2 p. 150). The horticultural image recurs at an earthier level when he rejoices that God is still pleased to 'dig and dung, round me, and not cut me down as a cumberer of the ground' (WGW 1, p. 65).

Spiritual growth is possible only as the heart is opened by God, to receive divine grace. New life is organic, growth is progressive, and as imperceptible as the changes by which a mountain spring becomes, over many miles, an impressive river. 'Young Christians are like little rivulets; ye know rivulets are shallow, yet make great noise; but an old Christian, he makes not much noise, he goes on sweetly, like a deep river sliding into the ocean' (SGW p. 274).

As the loadstone attracts the needle.

The dangers of complete passivity and his refusal to do anything towards his own progress in the spiritual life, due to a misguided and exaggerated reliance on faith alone, had led to spiritual paralysis at Oxford. Whitefield never made that mistake again. There is mature balance and insight in his counsel to a young convert: 'We have nothing to do; but to lay hold on him by faith, and to depend on him for wisdom, righteousness, sanctification and redemption. Not but we must be workers together with him; for a true faith in JESUS CHRIST will not suffer us to be idle. No it is an active, lively, restless principle; it fills the heart, so that it cannot be easy, till it is doing something for JESUS CHRIST' (WGW 1 p. 47).

The Bible held first claim on Whitefield's attention as a means of grace. 'The scriptures contain the deep things of God, and therefore can never be sufficiently searched into by a careless, superficial, cursory way of reading them, but by an industrious, close and humble application' (SGW p. 429). The sense and purpose of Scripture is spiritual and can be discerned only with the help of the Holy Spirit as interpreter. 'The divine image and superscription is written upon every line', making the Scriptures an inexhaustible source of truth and means of grace. Reading is to be 'devout and daily', interspersed with ejaculatory prayer, and should conclude with a prayer that 'the words which you have read, may be inwardly engrafted in your hearts, and bring forth in you the fruits of good life . . . Do this and you will with a holy violence, draw down God's Holy Spirit into your hearts; you will experience his gracious influence, and feel him enlightening, quickening and inflaming your souls' (SGW p. 429). The English Bible, the Greek Testament and Matthew Henry's exposition became the regular tools of Whitefield's devotions. He spoke of 'praying over every line and word' of both the English and Greek texts, a practice which gradually formed a mind soaked in biblical terminology. Many of his more quaint phrases are echoes of the Authorised Version. Referring to times of spiritual satisfaction, he enjoys 'eating spiritual morsels, full clusters of grapes from the heavenly Canaan', 'the Ram's Horns sound in Jericho' is his way of announcing success in Wales, while the spiritual torpor of the land is like an 'Egyptian darkness'. More importantly, such regular absorption of the scriptural text nourished and sustained a personality which was prodigal in self-expenditure for over forty years.

From the beginning Whitefield read 'useful' books, that is books which promoted the spiritual life by expounding sound doctrine. On his first transatlantic voyage, in an act of drastic censorship, he threw some 'bad books' overboard and replaced them with 'good ones'. He noted in his journal that 'bad books are become fashionable among the tutors and students' in the Harvard college for ministers at Cambridge, New England. In defence of solid reading he argued, 'What, if the Holy Spirit is to lead us into all truth, does not the Holy Spirit make use of, and lead us by the means? Has he not indited the Scriptures? Has he not helped holy men to explain those scriptures? And why may I not, in a due subordination to the Holy Spirit, make use of those men's writings?' (WGW 1 p. 253). This was a plea for sensible balance, and a recognition of the dangers of uncontrolled exegesis and spirituality isolated from the corrective of the community of faith. Whitefield enjoyed Matthew Henry, Philip Doddridge, and learned from Thomas Goodwin, John Flavel, Thomas Boston and William Law, all of whom he frequently quotes or commends.

The relation between such reading and prayer was sometimes so close as to be indistinguishable. He used his voyages as times of prolonged spiritual exercises, attributed the results of his ministry to the prayers of others and urged correspondents to assist him with their prayers, to pray with 'strong crying and tears at the throne of grace'. He complained to a young friend from Leeds about the tardiness of a letter sent by hand to avoid the cost of a stamp: 'Write to me; I do not like your sending such round-about ways; friends' letters always pay postage. O let us send often by post to heaven; I mean on the wings of faith and love . . .', this gentle rebuke being followed by the disarming signature. 'In haste, but much greater love . . . G. W.' (WGW 3 pp. 12–13).

The power of prayer to create and sustain fellowship was greatly valued by Whitefield. The neglect of intercession and the absence of imaginative empathy was, he believed, a primary cause of lovelessness and division. 'In the heart of every true believer there is a heavenly tendency, a divine attraction, which as sensibly draws him to converse with God, as the loadstone attracts the needle' (SGW p. 586). Intercession, then, is natural and is not a sign of an 'uncommon degree of charity' or 'an high pitch of perfection'. It is every Christian's duty, it is to be universal in scope and as a regular discipline is a stimulus to love. Intercession effects 'a blessed attention in the heart' so that envy becomes thanksgiving for another's blessing, condemnation becomes prayer for forgiveness and criticism is silenced by a humbling sense of equal unworthiness. Yet the underlying thrust of Whitefield's prayers was quite simply his belief that prayer works. He said to one whose 'stature reminds me of little Zaccheus': 'I would advise you to plead the promises for temporal blessings. In the name of Jesus, many a sweet morsel and opportune supply, have I fetched in from God by this means. That is the way I live . . .' (WGW 1 p. 116).

The differences between Edwards and Whitefield are many and obvious. Whitefield was emotionally volatile, a dramatic and colourful orator, a man well able to relate to people of all classes. Edwards was much more controlled, even restrained in the living out of his faith. As Ryle warned, readers will not encounter in Whitefield's sermons 'a commanding intellect or grasp of mind', but that is exactly what the reader of Edwards does encounter. There are two kinds of sermons; the written and the spoken. In delivery and forceful application of the gospel Whitefield was unrivalled in his day, perhaps in any day. But the content lived only in the presence and personality of the preacher. The sense of immediacy, of vital contact with a man in living touch with God, was what made the dry bones of Whitefield's sermons, as we now have them, once live and speak with power. Edwards too could move congregations to profound depths of fear and penitence, but his strength was in the firm grasp with which he took hold of the gospel he preached, and hammered out a reasoned, biblical psychology of Christian experience.

Whitefield was a restless, energetic activist, happy only when burning the candle at both ends. There was little time in his life for reflection, and always the threat that the dissipation of his energies would bring him to an early grave. Edwards lived most of his life in a comparatively small area, perhaps in his later years a prophet without honour in his own country. The two men came to faith in Christ after prolonged spiritual struggle; in their respective circles they resisted the inroads of Arminian theology and consequently their spirituality reveals the hallmarks of the Calvinism they promoted. In Whitefield there is little that is new or subtle. The awfulness of sin and the necessity of new birth, the substitutionary death of Christ and the electing grace of God, the Christian life as perseverance in conflict sustained by the Holy Spirit; these are the doctrines of the evangelist and their simple exposition satisfied Whitefield. By contrast Edwards conveyed a towering sense of the majesty of God. A mind subtle, analytic, and powerfully intelligent, not only defended the doctrines of grace, but by an imaginative and daring application of logic to biblical truth and spiritual experience, recaptured something of the glory, beauty and coherence of the truth, without doing violence to the sovereign mystery at the heart of the divine–human encounter.

Sources frequently cited

Dallimore, A., *George Whitefield*. Edinburgh, vol. 1 1970, vol. 2 1980. (D)

Edwards, J., *Religious Affections*. ed. J. E. Smith. New Haven 1959. (Y3)

——, *Ethical Writings*, ed. Paul Ramsey. New Haven 1989. (Y8)

——, *Original Sin*, ed. C. A. Holbrook. New Haven 1970. (Y2)

——, *Works*, ed. Hickman. Edinburgh reprint, 1974, 2 vols. (WJE)

Jenson, R. W., *America's Theologian*. New York 1988. (J)

Whitefield, G., *Works*, 6 vols. London and Edinburgh 1771. (WGW)

——, *Journal*. London 1960. (JGW)

——, *Sermons on Important Subjects*. London nd. (SGW)

Additional reading

Clifford, A. C., *Atonement and Justification*. Oxford 1990.

Davies, R., George, A. R., and Rupp, G., *A History of the Methodist Church in Great Britain*, vol. 4 (London 1989), pp. 701–2 (Bibliography).

Hatch, N. O., and Stout, H. S., *Jonathan Edwards and the American Experience*. New York 1988.
Miller, P., *Jonathan Edwards*. New York 1963.
Morgan, D. L., *The Great Awakening in Wales*. London 1988.
Murray, I. H., *Jonathan Edwards*. Edinburgh 1987.
Noll, M., 'Jonathan Edwards', in *Evangelical Dictionary of Theology*. Basingstoke 1984.
Philip, R., *The Life and Times of the Rev. George Whitefield*. London 1837.
Reist, I. W., 'John Wesley and George Whitefield', *Evangelical Quarterly* (1975), vol. 47: 1, pp. 26–40.
Russell, S. H., 'Jonathan Edwards and the Evangelical Discernment of Spirits', *Epworth Review*, vol. 16:2 (May 1990), pp. 74–85.
Ryle, J. C., *Christian Leaders of the 18th Century*. Edinburgh 1978.
Sherriff, C. B., The Theology of George Whitefield, PhD Thesis, Edinburgh 1950.
Tyerman, L., *The Life of George Whitefield*, 2 vols. London 1876.

Notes

1. Murray, *Edwards*, p. 90.
2. See Bebbington, *Evangelicalism in Modern Britain* (London 1988), pp. 50–69; see also G. R. Evans, A. E. McGrath and A. D. Galloway, *The Science of Theology* (Basingstoke 1986), pp. 107–229.
3. Hatch and Stout, *American Experience*, p. 183.
4. See Miller, *Edwards*, pp. 201–33; Murray, *Edwards*, pp. 311–49 for two conflicting interpretations of the rights and wrongs of the controversy.
5. Rack, *Reasonable Enthusiast*, p. 193.
6. Dallimore, *Whitefield*, vol. 1, pp. 46–7; Philip, *Whitefield*, ch. 1; *Journal*, pp. 33–72.
7. During this time he had met and was being directed by the Wesley brothers. Whatever later judgements are made on their influence on Whitefield, he spoke with appreciation of Charles as 'my never to be forgotten friend', and thanked John for his 'excellent advice and management of me under God'. *Journal*, pp. 47, 75; Philip, *Whitefield*, pp. 14–24, esp. p. 22, is highly critical of the Wesleys' role.
8. Whitefield's attack on Tillotson caused grievous offence to admiring Anglicans. See Dallimore, *Whitefield*, vol. 1, pp. 482f. Clifford, *Atonement*, clarifies many of the theological issues surrounding Whitefield and Wesley; he also gives sympathetic consideration to Tillotson, ch. 3.
9. Dallimore, *Whitefield*, vol. 1, p. 408.
10. WGW 1 p. 33. See also pp. 58, 66, 81, 115, 126, 132, 142; 2, p. 114 etc.
11. The Whitefield–Wesley controversy can be followed in their correspondence and the biographies. See also F. Baker, 'Whitefield's

break with the Wesleys', *Church Quarterly*, vol. 3 (1970–1), pp. 103–13. The conciliatory but firm tone of Whitefield, and the memorial sermon of Wesley preached at Whitefield's funeral stand to the credit of both men. For a quite different controversial approach see O. Beckerlegge, 'Toplady and Wesley', *Epworth Review*, vol. 17, pp. 48–53.

12. Reist, p. 28.
13. Ryle, *Christian Leaders*, pp. 50–1.
14. The influence of Matthew Henry's *Exposition* on Charles Wesley has already been noted. For Whitefield's use of Henry see the index in Dallimore. The aids used by Edwards noted in Hatch and Stout, p. 123, include Henry and Doddridge. For a full survey of Edwards' theological reading see Y3 *Religious Affections*, pp. 52–73.
15. Edwards' contemporary relevance is well argued by Jenson. For the relation between his Calvinism and later developments in Princeton, see D. Meyer, 'The Dissolution of Calvinism', in *Paths of American Thought*, ed. A. M. Schlesinger and M. White (London 1964), pp. 71–85; and also M. Noll, 'Jonathan Edwards and Nineteenth Century Thought', in Hatch and Stout, *American Experience*, pp. 260–87.

3

JOHN NEWTON and WILLIAM COWPER

Boundless stores of grace.
NEWTON

John Newton was the son of a shipmaster. Early in life he made five voyages to the Mediterranean. He joined the navy and was flogged for desertion; later he joined the merchant marine and was so profane in language he outraged even a hardened naval crew. Following shipwreck off the coast of Africa he was for a time a slave of a planter's black mistress and suffered great humiliation and brutality. Eventually he became involved in the slave trade and was master of a slave ship. His experience of providential deliverance, his reading of *The Imitation of Christ* and his study of Scripture led to his conversion. After surviving a storm at sea he recorded, 'I found I was no longer an infidel . . . I began to know that there is a God who hears and answers prayer . . . Though I cannot doubt that this change, so far as it prevailed was wrought by the Spirit and power of God, my views of the true character of the Christian life were still very defective' (B 25–7). Newton understood his conversion as the beginning of a lifelong process of grace, a gradual growth in understanding and maturity.

A stroke forced him to retire from the sea aged 29, and he became tide surveyor at Liverpool. His application to be ordained to the ministry in the Church of England was repeatedly refused, due apparently, to his lack of a university education. Eventually after intervention by a sympathetic supporter he was appointed to the parish of Olney in 1764, at the age of 39.[1]

All the fulness and completeness of my justification.

Cowper was born into a genteel and comfortable family. From the beginning he seemed to lack initiative and direction in life. His tutor was 'indolent', and used his 'genius as a cloak for everything that could disgust you in his person'. Cowper made an abortive attempt to study law at the Inner Temple in London, then he suffered a serious nervous breakdown when faced with the formality of a civil service examination. It was during such a period of mental and emotional turmoil that Cowper was converted. He later wrote describing his experience as 'not merely an acquiescence in the gospel as a truth, but an actual laying hold upon and embracing it as a salvation wrought out for and offered to me, personally and particularly . . . immediately I received strength to believe it. I saw the sufficiency of the atonement He had made, my pardon sealed in His blood, and all the fullness and completeness of my justification.'[2] This intense personalizing of the atonement and the dramatic, dateable conversion, are recurring themes in the earlier thought of Cowper. In later years the glow and the joyous assurance would be replaced by bleak despair, and the smiling face of God would be hidden behind a frowning providence. Unable to stay alone, he lodged with a clergyman and his wife, called Unwin, until the death of Mr Unwin following a riding accident. Soon afterwards he and Mrs Unwin came under the pastoral care of John Newton.

When Cowper moved to Olney in 1767 he began a lifelong friendship with Newton. The mutual and enduring affection of these two quite different people provides a rich study of friendship. Newton was a classic example of 'a brand pluck'd from the burning', a worldly-wise ex-seaman, plain and uncomplicated in his enjoyment of life, utterly certain of the grace of God and freely partaking of the solid joys and lasting treasures which none but Zion's children know. Cowper was the refined gentleman, whose nature was inherently fragile, converted during a mental breakdown and lapsing into periodic depressions, oscillating between faith in God's mercy and terror of God's wrath. Cowper was one whose darkest poetry was written with 'the pen of misery dipped in the ink of despair', and yet whose darkness of soul was occasionally lit up by flashing glimpses of insight into the merciful heart of God.

Cowper's mental torment and sense of personal lostness is

sometimes blamed on Evangelical theology in general and Newton in particular. However, for a decade Cowper's faith seemed to act as a bulwark against depression. A recent champion of Newton offers a caricature which has some serious exponents amongst Cowper's biographers:

> The name conjures up a grotesque image, both comic and horrifying, of a Pecksniffian hypocrite who walked the planks of his slaveship in the Atlantic, reflecting aloud, for the sake of the human cattle chained to their gratings below, 'Glorious things of Thee are spoken'; a monster of complacency who after a well publicised conversion, harried into insanity his parishioner, Wm. Cowper, by hell-fire sermons expounding Calvinist doctrine at its most rigid and ferocious.[3]

Perhaps the most telling evidence against the view of Newton the religious tyrant is the impression we gain of him from incidentals. When Cowper was finding friendship and support in the home of the widowed Mrs Unwin, Newton outfaced scandalized parishioners. During a long period of incapacity Cowper stayed with the Newtons and Newton noted the first smile to cross his friend's face for sixteen months.[4] Newton refused to hunt game, especially partridge and hares, for fear of hurting 'those of a sensitive nature' (WN 1 p. 513), and there are clear indications in his letters of both sympathy and tolerance concerning Cowper's illness. 'He always judiciously regarded his friend's depression and despondency as a physical defect, for the removal of which he prayed, but never reasoned or argued with him concerning it' (B pp. 185; 191). The whole tenor of Newton's pastoral ministry gives an impression of warmth, large–heartedness and an absence of that rigid impersonal dogmatism of which religious bullies are made.

Perspicuity, simplicity and ease.

Widely regarded as one of the finest exponents of the art of letter writing, Cowper succeeded in communicating on paper much that was difficult to articulate more immediately. Affection, criticism, anger and spiritual bewilderment can all appear in one letter. Cowper had an instinct for significant trivia and a penchant for interesting gossip. In his letters the details of human life were observed and recorded by one whose curiosity was devoid of malice. Such daily ordinariness served as a stimulus to playfulness and provided reassuring testimony to the worthwhileness of life. New neighbours, accidental meetings, the state of his greenhouse, descriptions of the antics of his beloved hares, his impatience at the delayed arrival of a new desk and a stream of other domestic details provided subject matter on which he mused with refined humour and moral sense. In the letters, more than anywhere else, Cowper can be heard laughing without bitterness.

Newton's correspondence grew into a substantial and effective ministry of spiritual direction. 'Anatomy is my favourite branch; I mean the study of the human heart with its workings and counterworkings, as it is differently affected in a state of nature or of grace, in the different seasons of prosperity, adversity, conviction, temptation, sickness and the approach to death.' The same pastoral theology informs the letters. One correspondent paid him a dubious compliment when he remarked, 'Your letter shows you are deep read in the wiles of Satan, and able to give good counsel to the afflicted' (B p. 175). Leading Evangelicals like William Wilberforce, Charles Simeon and Hannah More were to benefit from Newton's commonsense approach to spiritual life.

The two friends collaborated in the production of the Olney hymn book, a project intended to help Cowper by giving him definite and useful direction for his talent. The long delay in publication is explained by Newton in the preface, in 1779:

> The book would have appeared much sooner . . . if the wise, though mysterious, providence of God, had not seen fit to cross my wishes. We had not proceeded far upon our proposed plan, before my dear friend was prevented, by a long and affecting disposition, from affording me any further assistance. My grief and disappointment were great; I hung my harp upon the willows, and for some time thought myself determined to proceed no further without him.
>
> (WN 3 pp. 301–5)

Cowper's 67 hymns were written in 1771–2; the remaining 348 were by Newton.[5] These are the only genuine hymns Cowper wrote before the onset of a depression which seldom lifted entirely and often sucked him into a vortex of despair.

Newton wrote throughout his curacy, sometimes churning out hymns at the rate of one per week, these hymns often being used to illustrate the text of the sermon. Inspiration was often sparked by the ordinary events of village life: changing seasons, a hard frost, a local fire, an unexpected surgical operation, provided homely illustrations of gospel truth.

The visit of a lion gave him the opportunity to reflect on the fickleness of his devotion to God: 'Last week we had a lion in town. He was wonderfully tame . . . as docile as a spaniel; yet the man told me he had his surly fits . . . no looking glass could express my face more justly than this lion did my heart . . . as wild and fierce by nature . . . but grace has in some measure tamed me . . . I know and love my Keeper . . . but I have my surly fits too . . . I got a hymn out of this lion' (B p. 229). The Olney congregation found themselves singing:

Yet we are but renewed in part,
The lion still remains,
  Lord, drive him wholly from my heart,
Or keep him fast in chains.

(WN 3 p. 559)

Some of Newton's hymns would find an honourable place in an anthology of 'Verse and Worse'; others fulfil his modest aim of bringing the mysteries of the faith vividly into the life experience of ordinary people. For Newton the language of hymnody must be plain and clear. In his own words 'perspicuity, simplicity and ease should be chiefly attended to'; he hoped that his hymn writing might qualify him for 'usefulness to the weak and poor without quite disgusting persons of superior discernment' (WN 3 pp. 301–5). Perhaps Newton was oversensitive to the likely criticisms of those who, unlike him, had enjoyed a university education. If so it was unnecessary, for what his letters and sermons lacked in formal culture was compensated for by wide and conscientious study. A good number of his hymns are classic examples of the good hymn; profound experience, expressed in familiar imagery and accessible to the mixed abilities of a congregation engaged in corporate worship.

Cowper shared his friend's avowed aim of communicating truth in a plain style. He let his publisher know his opinion in no uncertain terms: 'Give me a manly rough line, with a deal of meaning in it, rather than a whole poem full of musical periods that have nothing but their oily smoothness to recommend them.'[6] In the pursuit of a compact plainness of style the two hymnwriters were reflecting the literary fashion of their age.[7] Nevertheless, 'To make verse speak the language of prose without being prosaic', is an aim both pastorally and educationally sound.

The guilty but returning soul.

'My first principle in religion is what the scripture teaches me of the utter depravity of human nature . . . I believe we are by nature sinners and by practice universally transgressors . . . and that the bent of our natural spirit is enmity against the holiness, government and grace of God' (WN 1 p. 534). The colourful events in Newton's past suggest that his pessimistic view of human nature owed as much to his own experience as to the Scriptures. Speaking of his utter inability to save himself, he explained his experience in terms of a moderate Calvinism. Newton often traced his view of election to his past experiences of deliverance and divine interference: 'By nature I was too blind to know him, too proud to trust him, too obstinate to serve him, too base minded to love him . . . the love I bear him is but a faint and feeble spark . . . but he kindled it and he keeps it alive' (WN 1 p. 608). There is genuine self-knowledge in the words:

In evil long I took delight,
Unawed by shame or fear;
Till a new object struck my sight,
And stopp'd my wild career.

This is one of many hymns exploring conviction of sin. Guilt is here experienced as remorse; the guilty heart is smitten with shame in the presence of crucified love:

My conscience felt and owned the guilt
And plunged me in despair;
I saw my sins his blood had spilt
And help'd to nail him there.

By an intense personalizing of the atonement Newton emphasizes the mystery of the gospel, that God should of his sovereign grace absorb the penalty of sin. He expresses his wonder in the language of paradox:

Thus while his death my sin displays
  In all its blackest hue;
Such is the mystery of grace,
  It seals my pardon too.

With pleasing grief, and mournful joy,
  My spirit now is fill'd;
That I should such a life destroy
  Yet live by him I killed.

(WN 3 p. 522)

It is an odd ending for a congregational hymn. The intermingling of grief and joy give the impression of perplexed wonder while the last two lines have the force of a question directed inwards, the reflecting heart seeking to penetrate the gospel paradox of life through death. The sense of personal involvement in, and responsibility for, the death of Christ invested Newton's spiritual life with moral urgency and spiritual warmth.

For his part, Cowper presented a grimly forensic description of the atonement in which he painted the peril of the soul and the efficacy of Christ's death in the starkest possible colours:

To reconcile offending man
  Make justice drop her angry rod;
What creature could have form'd the plan,
  Or who fulfil it but a God.

No drop remains of all the curse
  For wretches who deserved the whole;
No arrows dipt in wrath to pierce
  The guilty but returning soul.

(P p. 144)

'Praise for the Fountain Opened' is a hymn both loved and hated. Cowper fused two biblical references, bringing together the image of a fountain for sin and uncleanliness, and the sacrificial image of washing in blood (Zech. 13.8; Rev. 7.14):

There is a fountain fill'd with blood,
  Drawn from EMMANUEL'S veins;
And sinners, plunged beneath that flood,
  Lose all their guilty stains.

(P p. 154)

Newey concedes, 'It is a fine hymn in an idiom alien to us.'[8] To many minds today it seems tasteless, even morbid, the product of an anguished conscience and a diseased mind. Few can have known more intimately than Cowper the inner wilderness created by guilt and self-hatred; the chilling sense of desolation, the clinging pollution of sin, persistent despair which threatened to suffocate all moral aspiration, and, overclouding the moral consciousness, the terrifying vision of an unappeased God.

Sometimes the person who lives on the extremities of human experience gains the sharpest perceptions of the ambiguities of moral existence. Cowper was a man acquainted with guilt, and perhaps his hymn would be considered more sympathetically if it were seen as an attempt to minister to his own condition of soul. Judged even by that standard the hymn remains a shock to the system. A man with a lacerated conscience, his mind tortured by a self-rejection which he saw as the mirror image of God's displeasure, was trying to find comfort in the gospel. By emphasizing the physical horror of God's act in Christ, was he in some sense seeking reassurance? Is there a desperate logic being worked out? The more revolting the cross, the more convincing is the love of Emmanuel who died there; the fountain is filled, guaranteeing an unfailing and sufficient supply even for one 'as vile' as Cowper believed himself. Alongside the tragic cost of divine judgement and reconciling mercy, his own exaggerated sense of sin is made more manageable and less mortally dangerous. The very horror of the cross is the sinner's hope, the worst that can happen has happened.

In the first verse Cowper is courageously confronting his recurring nightmare of damnation, by a forced contemplation of the strongest biblical images he can conceive, namely, bloody sacrifice and substitutionary atonement. That done, he placed his own sense of vile sinfulness alongside the great atoning act and began to move with more confidence into the language of absolutes. Sinners who are plunged beneath that flood, lose *all* their guilty stains; the fountain will *never* lose its power; in that fountain *all* sins are washed away, and those washed are saved to sin *no more*. In the fourth verse, the last in which he uses the fountain of blood image, Cowper recalls his own first discovery of the cross, in words which suggest a level of stability and wellbeing which was to desert him, a few brief periods excepted, for the rest of his life:

E'er since by faith I saw the stream,
  Thy flowing wounds supply,
Redeeming love has been my theme,
  And shall be till I die.

The last two verses are often omitted from Evangelical hymn books, giving the hymn in its truncated versions an unintended severity.[9] The hymn did not originally end with the word 'grave', but with an image which, in its childlike naiveté, rescued Cowper's sense of worth and usefulness to God. Anticipating the time when 'all the ransom'd church of God' will 'be sav'd to sin no more', and recognizing the limitations of 'this poor lisping stamm'ring tongue' as an instrument to 'sing thy power to save', Cowper affirmed his faith and his hope in 'Redeeming love' in unqualified terms:

Lord, I believe thou hast prepar'd
  (Unworthy though I be)
For me a blood-bought free reward,
  A golden harp for me!

'Tis strung, and tun'd, for endless years,
  And form'd by pow'r divine;
To sound, in God the Father's ears,
  No other name but thine.

(P p. 154–5)

For once, Cowper's sense of exclusion recedes and the image of musical harmony is used to express his tentative faith in the creative purposes of God. 'The harp, like the player, is made good by God; from a beginning in blood, we move to an end in music. All the human being can do is to wash his sins at the fountain and sing in paradise; the rest (in T. S. Eliot's phrase) is not our business.'[10]

Both Newton and Cowper understood conversion to be the human response to divine love and an essential and initiating stage of Christian experience. The note of unequivocal loyalty to Christ gave much of Newton's writing an exultant mood: 'We are His by every tie and right; He made us, He redeemed us, He reclaimed us and we are His by our own voluntary surrender of ourselves . . . He knocked at the door of our hearts but we barred and fastened it against Him, . . . but when He revealed His love we could stand out no longer' (WN 1 p. 463). The love which forces the glad capitulation of the heart is the generous eternal love of a crucified Saviour. In a lesser known hymn Cowper reflected, with something of Newton's optimism, on God's eternal love affair with mankind:

Thus wisdom's words discover
   Thy glory and Thy grace,
Thou everlasting lover
   Of our unworthy race!
Thy gracious eye survey'd us
   Ere stars were seen above;
In wisdom Thou hast made us
   And died for us in love.

And could Thou be delighted
   With creatures such as we,
Who when we saw Thee, slighted
   And nail'd Thee to the tree?
Unfathomable wonder
   And mystery divine,
The voice that speaks in thunder
   Says sinner, I am thine.

(P p. 145)

How sweet the name of Jesus sounds.

The essential connection between conversion and spirituality was succinctly put by Newton in a letter to Thomas Scott, an Anglican curate who owed his adoption of Evangelical principles to his correspondence with Newton: 'Hence a twofold necessity of a Saviour . . . His blood for the pardon of our sins, and His life, Spirit and grace to quicken our souls and form us anew for Himself that we may feel His love and show forth His praise' (WN 1 p. 544). The primary response of the human heart is praise for all that God in Christ has given to sinful humanity. 'To love Christ is the greatest dignity of man',[11] Cowper declared, and such love expressed in praise is true worship:

My song shall bless the Lord of all,
   My praise shall climb to his abode;
Thee, Saviour, by that name I call
   The great Supreme, the mighty God.

Of all the crowns JEHOVAH bears
   Salvation is his dearest claim;

That gracious sound well pleased he hears,
And owns EMMANUEL for His name.
(P p. 165)

This sprightly hymn with the doctrinally loaded title, 'Jehovah Jesus', gives Christian praise theological balance. The whole plan of salvation demonstrates the nature of God as gracious. The loving purpose of God and the atonement made by Jesus reveal no conflict in the Godhead. The cross is a demonstration of the unity of purpose, the harmony of will and the eternal love which underlie the divine sovereignty. The praise of a saviour God is common in the Olney hymn book but the note of unqualified praise is rare in Cowper's contribution. Frequently his mood is interrogative, hopeful but hesitant. This is poignantly evident in a hymn to Jesus Emmanuel, God with us;

Heal us EMMANUEL, here we are,
Waiting to feel thy touch,
Deep wounded souls to Thee repair,
And Saviour we are such.

Amongst the deep wounded souls who came was a woman who furtively touched Jesus' clothing and found her hesitant uncertainty rewarded:

Conceal'd amid the gathering throng
She would have shunned Thy view;
And if her faith was firm and strong
Had strong misgivings too.
(P p. 141)

That is a compact definition of the ambiguity of Cowper's faith: strong, with strong misgivings. For Cowper faith was always qualified, assurance never absolute and devotion always tinged with the fear that his own unworthiness would lead to an ultimate and eternal exclusion from the presence and succour of God.

By contrast Newton could be exuberant to the point of extravagance in his descriptive praise of Jesus. Two quotations illustrate his cumulative style. 'The whole deportment of a Christian should show that a knowledge of Jesus, which he has received from the gospel, affords him all he could expect of it; a balm for every grief, an amend for every evil, a pattern for every thing which he is called to do or suffer, and a principle sufficient to constitute the actions of everyday acts of religion . . . He will guide me by His counsel, support me by His power, comfort me with His presence; and afterward, when flesh and heart fail, He will receive me to His glory' (WN 1 pp. 456, 632).

The converted blasphemer now revels in the beauty and glory of Jesus' name. His hymn on the names of Jesus shows the christocentric element of his spirituality at its best. The hymn is a classic example of Evangelical hymnology; richly experimental, intensely personal, full of scriptural allusion, showing a humble awareness of dependence on grace and with a forward look to heaven as the goal and glory of Christian hope while still remaining practical enough to take present responsibility seriously. The hymn needs no further comment:

How sweet the name of Jesus sounds,
In a believer's ear;
It soothes his sorrows, heals his wounds
And drives away his fear.

It makes the wounded spirit whole
And calms the troubled breast;
'Tis manna to the hungry soul,
And to the weary rest.

Dear name, the Rock on which I build,
My shield and hiding place;
My never failing treasury filled
With boundless stores of grace.

Jesus! My Shepherd, Husband, Friend,
My Prophet, Priest and King;
My Lord, my Life, my Way, my End,
Accept the praise I bring.

(WN 3 p. 370)

Our life is a warfare.

If Evangelical spirituality is warmed by fervent devotion to Christ, it is also marked by a keen awareness of the frustrating power of sin. To grow in grace means to die to sin, and that process is a lifelong struggle. For Newton the spiritual battle was vivid, costly and deadly serious; victory over sin will be hard won, but by God's grace and through the merits of Christ, it is ultimately certain. Nevertheless Newton recognized the value of conflict. It strengthens the muscles and sinews of Christian character. He was by temperament robust and realistic, and his balanced understanding of sin was informed by personal experience of moral defeat and keeping grace. Without in any way reducing the offensiveness of sin he accepted the fact that Christians still live within human limitations.

For Cowper the struggle was fiercer and the stakes ultimate. The sensitive soul of Cowper became increasingly enmeshed in a web of guilt, fear and personal worthlessness, creating an unbearable spiritual suspense, and placing a crushing question mark over his eternal fate. The objective promises of God which are given in Scripture, vie with Cowper's own feelings of guilt and lostness, setting up an inner tug-of-war which he never resolved. His spiritual anguish hangs heavily in a hymn which, ironically, connects God and happiness in its first line.

The Lord will happiness divine
  On contrite hearts bestow;
Then tell me gracious God is mine
  A contrite heart or no?

I hear but seem to hear in vain,
  Insensible as steel;
If aught is felt, 'tis only pain
  To find I cannot feel.

Experience of the warm fellowship of the prayer meeting lies behind the sad perplexity of verse 5:

Thy saints are comforted I know,
  And love Thy house of prayer;
I therefore go where others go
  But find no comfort there.

He ends with a desperate plea for an adequate contrition:

O make this heart rejoice or ache;
  Decide this doubt for me;
And if it be not broken, break,
  And heal it, if it be.

(P p. 199)

The tensions remain unresolved. Decision and doubt, brokenness and healing, the total lack of any self-confidence before God leave him stripped and vulnerable in the hands of God whose violence might break him in order to heal him. To ask broken-hearted contrition as a gift from God reveals longing of such intensity and passion that it is incapable of facile or undemanding fulfilment. This feature of Cowper's spirituality helps explain the constant use of qualifying words like 'if' or 'but'. In his search for spiritual wholeness Cowper almost invariably found reasons which might disqualify him from blessing. For example comfort, that inner sense of spiritual wellbeing which Cowper found so elusive, seems to be within his grasp in the hymn 'Sometimes a light surprises'. It is a fine hymn of assurance and trust in the God who heals, sets free, bears and provides for his child. But the first word, 'Sometimes', casts a shadow of qualification over all that follows.[12]

No hymn expresses Cowper's spiritual longing more poignantly than the famous 'O for a closer walk with God'. A 'calm and heavenly frame', and 'a light upon the road', are simple images expressing the experience of assurance. But they are overshadowed by two regret-filled questions:

Where is the blessedness I knew
  When first I saw the Lord?
Where is the soul-refreshing dew
  Of Jesus and his word?

'Peaceful hours' and 'sweet memories' are now swallowed up by the 'aching void' which is as inexplicable as it is unbearable. Did sin drive the Holy Spirit out? Is it a cherished idol which displaced him? Cowper uses a violent verb to convince God of his sincerity. He will 'tear' the usurping idol from his heart. The whole hymn is an almost unbearably moving account of a vulnerable soul, smitten and desolated by the absence of God; wistfulness, regret, self-searching, spiritual dejection and renewed resolve, merge and mingle into a beautiful prayer of penitence and longed-for restoration.[13]

In contrast to Newton's healthy realism, Cowper conceived of sin as more than the frustration of grace. Acute feelings of personal guilt created a harrowing sense of foreboding which sometimes distilled into resigned terror. One of his favourite images for his inner conflict was the storm. In hymns and poems he explored the psychic turmoil of doubt, the towering waves of impending judgement and the threatening darkness which engulfs the soul that senses hostility in God. In a poem written to honour his mother's memory he compared her safe anchorage with his storm-tossed existence:

Always from port withheld, always distressed;
Me, howling winds drive devious, tempest toss'd.
Sails ript, seams op'ning wide, and compass lost,
And day by day some current's thwarting force
Sets me more distant from a prosp'rous course.[14]

The accusations against God are thinly veiled. While the theme of a wise loving providence pervades the Olney hymn book, in the experience of Cowper there is an ambivalence in God which confused him. He wrote to the Olney schoolmaster, Samuel Teedon: 'There is no text in Scripture less calculated to comfort me, than that which promises comfort to the broken heart . . . I believe myself the only instance of a man to whom God will promise every thing and perform nothing.'[15] He tried to find some constructive reasons for his suffering: 'Every scene of life has two sides, a dark and a bright one, and the mind that has an equal mixture of melancholy and vivacity, is best of all qualified for the contemplation of either. It can be lively without levity, pensive without dejection'.[16] Cowper seldom achieved the balance which insured against dejection. Still, when he felt more confident in God's goodness, he could write in a mood as near to optimism as he ever came:

Happy the man who sees a God employed
In all the good and ill that chequer life!
Resolving all events, with their effects
And manifold results, into the will
And arbitration wise of the supreme.[17]

Cowper's faith in the ultimate benevolence of providence is unforgettably portrayed in 'Light Shining out of Darkness'. The first line, 'God moves in a mysterious way', is an immediate admission of God's right to a sovereign secrecy, but there is nothing sinister in the hiddenness of the divine purpose. Verse two depicts God, not as an evil genius bent on wrecking lives, but as a skilled artificer:

Deep in unfathomable Mines,
Of neverfailing Skill,
He treasures up His bright designs,
And works His Sovereign Will.

Cowper's own experience of fear and depression lend weight to what would otherwise be mere exhortation:

> Ye fearfull Saints fresh courage take,
> The clouds ye so much dread,
> Are big with Mercy, and shall break
> In blessings on your head.

'Dread' is placed in a position of emphasis and the ominous warning of imminent storm seems confirmed by 'big'. Then Cowper springs his two surprises: the clouds are big, but with mercy; and they shall break, but with blessings. In the fifth verse a gentler image provides another surprise:

> His purposes will ripen fast,
> Unfolding every hour,
> The Bud may have a bitter taste,
> But WAIT, to SMELL THE FLOWER.[18]

In this hymn, Cowper has almost created a Christian theodicy which could make sense of his own suffering. Not because he has found a theory which explains everything, but because he is content to trust the 'never failing Skill', 'the Sovereign Will', and the 'Smiling face' of the God whose purposes will 'ripen fast', whose 'bright designs' are treasures in his keeping and whose grace guarantees ultimate mercy and blessing. Anticipation of such blessing underlies Cowper's playful line, 'Wait, to smell the flower'; believing patience rather than mute resignation enables him to confess, 'God is his own Interpreter, And he will make it plain.'

The surprising twists in the hymn equally suggest the apparently random happenings of providence. Life too has its unexpected twists. Not all clouds are big with mercy and when they break there can be a crushing sense of loss. However reassured Cowper seems, he remained perplexed by the mysterious movements of God. A strong doctrine of providence may encourage assurance. If however, God is understood to be capricious, and omnipotence is detached from personal care, then assurance is impossible, for then faith has no foundation in the nature of God. Even mercies are felt to be mere postponement of judgement, and like the shipwrecked mariner, 'He but escapes the troubled sea, to perish on the shore'. In a lesser-known hymn, entitled

'Peace after a Storm', Cowper apologizes to God for harbouring hard thoughts about him:

When darkness long has veiled my mind,
   And smiling day once more appears,
Then, my redeemer, then I find,
   The folly of my doubts and fears.

O let me then at length be taught
   What I am still so slow to learn,
That God is love and changes not,
   Nor knows the shadow of a turn.

(P p. 180)

'God is love and changes not'. There in simple language was the theological answer to Cowper's dilemma. God is not inscrutable unpredictable power. Ironically and tragically, Cowper points the way to a peace which, after his breakdown in 1783, he never fully found again. Years after Newton left Olney, Cowper wrote to his friend, 'We think of you often and one of us prays for you; the other will, when he can pray for himself.' Encouraged to start writing hymns again by William Bull, Cowper replied, 'Ask possibilities and they shall be performed; not hymns from a man suffering despair as I do. I could not sing the Lord's song were it to save my life, banished as I am, not to a strange land, but to a remoteness from His presence, in comparison with which the distance from east to west is no distance.'[19]

Newton's view of human life, and particularly human sin in relation to God, was both more realistic and more optimistic. Realistic in that he recognized the radically destructive power of sin; optimistic because he, unlike his friend, was firmly convinced of the ultimate triumph of grace in his life. In 'The Sick Soul' he described sin as dangerously pernicious:

No words of mine can fully paint
   That worst distemper, sin.

It lies not in a single part
   But through my frame is spread;
A burning fever in my heart,
   A palsy in my head.

It makes me deaf and dumb and blind
   And impotent and lame;

It overclouds and fills my mind
With folly, fear and shame.

He ends with a question, but it is a rhetorical one:

Say cans't thou let a sinner die
Who longs to live for Thee?
(WN 3 p. 397)

'Of course not', says Newton. 'Though sin wars it shall not reign; and though it breaks our peace it cannot separate from His love.' Another of his hymns was written as a comment on Gal. 5.17, and reveals the psychological honesty that made Newton such a fine pastor of souls. The verse from Galatians reads, 'For the desires of the flesh are against the Spirit and the desires of the spirit are against the flesh; for these are opposed to each other, to prevent you from doing what you would.' From this verse Newton offers a self analysis which is transparently honest:

Strange and mysterious is my life
What opposites I feel within!
A stable peace, a constant strife,
The rule of grace, the power of sin . . .

Thus different powers within me strive
And grace and sin by turns prevail,
I grieve, rejoice, decline, revive
And victory hangs in doubtful scale,
But Jesus has his promise pass'd
That grace shall overcome at last.
(WN 3 pp. 450–1).

Newton has cleverly portrayed the paradox of salvation. The Christian is saved from sin yet still a sinner; desiring to serve God yet obstinately wilful; at peace with God yet embroiled in conflict. Nevertheless Newton exults in the power of grace, using a metaphor which is the last word in incongruity: 'What is weaker than a worm? Yet the Lord's worms shall, in His strength, thresh the mountains and make the hills as chaff' (WN 1 p. 457).

Love, the inner spring of obedience.

'A Christian is not of hasty growth like a mushroom, but rather like the oak, the progress of which is hardly perceptible but in time becomes a great deep-rooted tree' (WN 1 p. 606). Newton used several metaphors to make the point that Christians will always be in process in this life. 'The work of grace in its first stages I sometimes compare to the lighting of a fire where for a while there is abundance of smoke, but it burns clearer and clearer' (WN 2 p. 8). The work of grace is like building: 'In a building, if it be large there is much to be done in preparing and laying the foundation before the walls appear above ground; much is doing within when the work does not seem perhaps to advance without . . . when encumbered with scaffolds and rubbish a bystander sees it at a great disadvantage and can form but an imperfect judgment of it' (WN 1 p. 602).

Here again the pastoral realism of Newton is evident. Imperceptible growth, the slow burning fire and the cluttered building site suggest the need to be patient, tolerant of failure and prepared for disappointment. On the other hand the solid oak, the glowing fire and the well-proportioned building point to the promise of future completion. While he supposed perfection in this life to be unattainable, Newton nevertheless considered it a goal worth striving for. With wise tolerance he said he would rather pray for it than dispute against it, though he expected to be saved as a sinner and not as a saint.

Growth in grace is understood as a daily, vital and progressive experience involving forgiveness, obedience to God and service to others. Newton rejected any view of conversion which allowed a Christian to live off the spiritual capital of past experience. Recalling the wilderness experience of Israel being provided with daily manna, he insisted that Christian experience must be in the present tense:

The truths by which the soul is fed
  Must thus be had afresh;
For notions resting in the head
  Will only feed the flesh.

Nor can the best experience past
  The life of faith maintain;
The brightest hope will faint at last
  Unless supplied again.

(WN 3 p. 324)

The emphasis on daily experience gave rise to the ever present danger of over-reliance on feelings. Newton was no wild enthusiast, but neither was he afraid of emotion in religion. He recognized the perils of overdone introspection and insisted on a proper balance between excited affections and objective gospel truth:

> A moonlight head knowledge however true is a poor thing; nor am I an admirer of those rapturous sallies, which are more owing to a warm imagination than to a just perception of gospel truth. The gospel addresses both head and heart; and where it is received as the word of God and is clothed with the energy and authority of the Holy Spirit, the understanding is enlightened, the affections awakened and engaged, the will brought into subjection, and the whole soul delivered to its impress as wax to the seal.
>
> (WN 2 p. 18)

The experience of grace must be fresh and it must reflect a proper balance between head and heart, but it must not remain an internal, private affair. Conversion, love for the Saviour and an incessant spiritual struggle for holiness gave rise to a moral seriousness which affected the whole of life. Music, amusements like cards and dancing were alike condemned. Cowper begins to sound like a spoilsport when he warns against the joy that vain amusements give, comparing them to 'the honey of a crowded hive, defended by a thousand stings' (WN 3 p. 368).

It is in the daily pursuit of grace and ethical direction that we find the characteristic expressions of Evangelical devotion such as 'early rising, Bible reading and prayer'. Several scholars have remarked on the eccentricity of the section in the hymn book entitled 'Seasons'. There are no hymns for such major church festivals as Advent, Epiphany, Lent, Eastertide or Whitsuntide. On the other hand much is made of Evening, Saturday Evening and the End of the Year. The heavy sense of accountability to God for the use of time made the close of the day, the end of the week and the last day of the year significant times of spiritual stocktaking.

Time is God's gift; the soul has been redeemed at infinite cost, and Christians are therefore obliged to live wisely and usefully. 'A life divided between God and the world is desirable: when one part of it is spent in retirement, seeking after and conversing with Him whom our souls love; and the other part of it is employed in active service for the good of our family, friends, the church and society, for His sake' (WN 1 p. 516). Prayer and activity 'for His sake' are the two poles around which much of the spiritual life revolves.

Newton's principles and practice of prayer are childlike in their simplicity. He encouraged the Olney congregation, 'Thou art coming to a king, large petitions with thee bring.' This hymn becomes a series of uncomplicated petitions for a conscience freed from guilt, a heart at rest, a character reflecting Christ, the inner assurance of God's love, and finishes with two requests: 'Show me what I have to do, every hour my strength renew'. This sense of moment-by-moment dependence on God meant that, for Newton, prayer was never inappropriate and the throne of grace was always accessible. Frequent prayer and a constancy of devotion reinforce the sense of the immediacy of God in daily life. Cowper affirmed the omnipresence of God in the hymn specially written for the commencement of the Olney prayer meeting:

> For Thou within no walls confined
> Inhabitest the humble mind;
> Such ever bring Thee where they come,
> And going, take Thee to their home.
>
> (P p. 166)

In the process of sanctification, openness to God and inner alertness to his voice as mediated through the Scriptures, promote the development of Christian taste and nourish and inform the Christian mind. Newton was wary of any form of legalism and saw little value and perhaps danger in a life regulated by the endless rules and ethical maxims which make up the received tradition of Evangelical piety. 'By frequent prayer and close acquaintance with the scripture, and an habitual application of the same to our hearts, there is a certain delicacy of spiritual taste and discernment to be acquired.' Newton assumes development of character, growth of moral awareness, the gradual evolution of a Christian mind, able to apply the principles of Scripture to the endlessly varied circumstances and the countless moral choices confronting the Christian involved in the life of the world.

To negotiate the many challenges and decisions of each day the Christian requires heavenly wisdom, which, according to Newton, 'does not consist in forming a bundle of rules and maxims, but in a spiritual taste and discernment, derived from an experiential knowledge of the truth and of the heart of man as described in the word of God; and its exercise consists much in a simple dependence upon the Lord . . . We seldom act wrong when we truly depend on Him' (WN 1 p. 637). In another letter he develops this theme even further, calling this spiritual discernment 'something analogous to the word taste when applied to music or good breeding by which discords and improprieties are observed and avoided as it were by instinct, and what is right is felt and followed not so much by force of rules, as by a habit insensibly acquired and in which the substance of all necessary rules are digested' (WN 1 p. 511).

Newton is really arguing for an instinctive but acquired obedience which draws energy and moral decisiveness from devotion to Christ. On more than one occasion he taught, 'love is the clearest and most persuasive casuist'. But this was not an eighteenth-century progenitor of situation ethics. He qualified and limited his meaning elsewhere: 'The love of God is the best casuist . . . the principle of acting simply for God will, in general make the path of duty plain, and solve a thousand otherwise dubious questions.' While many other Evangelicals agonized over such 'dubious questions' of Christian behaviour, Newton relied on the guidance of the Spirit through the medium of prayer and Bible teaching. The overarching principle however, was a desire to act in accordance with the love of God: 'The love of Christ is the joy of his heart, and the spring of his obedience.'[20]

Such a spirit of freedom and direct dependence on God for moral guidance is far removed from the censoriousness sometimes associated with later Evangelicalism, and from that of Cowper at his most sharply disapproving. Not for Newton the scrupulous soul meticulously avoiding sin by rules and prohibitions. He preferred the freedom and risks of those who trusted God to show them what was right in the immediacy of each situation. What controlled this freedom was a life of prayer, the continuous exposure of the heart to Scripture, and the keen desire in the believer's heart to imitate Jesus. Christians are predestined to be conformed to the image of God's Son; to repeat Newton's own phrase, it is the work of the Spirit to give each Christian an 'experimental knowledge' of that truth.

In a passage attractive for its warm and gentle theology, Newton expounds the heart of his spirituality:

> The love of God, as manifested in Jesus Christ, is what I would wish to be the abiding object of my contemplation; not merely

> to speculate upon it as a doctrine, but so to feel it, and my own interest in it, as to have my heart filled with its effects, and transformed into its resemblance; that with this glorious exemplar in my view, I may be animated to a spirit of benevolence, love and compassion to all around me; that my love may be primarily fixed upon Him who has loved me, and then, for His sake, diffused to all His children and all his creatures . . . then I should be active and diligent in improving all my talents and powers in His service and for His glory; and live not to myself, but to Him who loved me and gave Himself for me.
> (WN 2 p. 18)

Newton and Cowper shared the same basic theology. The Calvinism of Cowper was perhaps more inflexible than that of Newton, but in essentials they agreed. The inner corruption of the human heart, sin as enmity against God, the death of Christ as the sinner's substitute and as a propitiation for sin, faith in Christ alone as the basis of salvation and a progressive view of Christian sanctification provide the doctrinal content of the Olney hymns. However, it was at the point when objective doctrine had to be translated into personal religious experience that the differences were marked.

The crucial difference was in their experience of assurance. The nature and basis of assurance is integral to Calvinistic theology and spirituality. Newton claimed he was as sure of the way of salvation as he was of the way to London. His confidence in the sovereignty of grace and in the security of the elect was vigorously and enthusiastically trumpeted forth in his hymn 'Glorious Things of Thee are Spoken'. God is 'He whose word cannot be broken', grace 'never fails from age to age' and Christians exclusively enjoy the 'Solid joys and lasting treasure' of the City of God. The eternal security of the believer carries with it an unconditional guarantee:

> On the Rock of Ages founded
> What can shake Thy sure repose?
> With salvations walls surrounded
> Thou may'st smile at all thy foes.

Cowper could never sing these words with the whole heart. Not because he did not believe them, but because they referred to a spiritual condition which was impossible for one whose life experience had often been a bleak negation of all he desperately tried to believe. Chronic feelings of guilt triggered recurring bouts of self-despair, and underlying his whole existence a subterranean dread which repeatedly surfaced in his consciousness in the form of a God who was unalterably indifferent to him and his fate. In such a bleak atmosphere assurance was impossible and breakdown all but inevitable. No argument of logic, theology or philosophy can verify the doctrines of grace; assurance is something given, not achieved. It is a gift to the believing heart, confirmed by the evidence of new birth in the life, arising out of a faith whose foundation pillars are plunged deep into the sovereign, electing and keeping love of God. Cowper found such faith permanently elusive. His spirituality is most genuinely expressed in hymns which convey yearning and hesitation. Question and affirmation are followed by question again, revealing an inner frustration, prolonged indefinitely because of his refusal to take Yes for an answer. The result is a mood of resigned sadness which occasionally gives way to hope but never permanently, and never to the extent that he was able to experience 'a calm and heavenly frame'.

In a poetic fragment attributed to Newton, the poet imagined the first conversation between Newton and Cowper when they meet in heaven. All Cowper's worst fears evaporate in the warm welcoming atmosphere of God's presence and there is humour as well as warm sympathy in Newton's words as he gently reminds Cowper, 'I told you so':

> O let thy memory wake! I told thee so;
> I told thee thus would end thy heaviest woe;
> I told thee that thy God would bring thee here,
> And God's own hand would wipe away thy tear,
> While I should claim a mansion by thy side;
> I told thee so – for our Emmanuel died.[21]

Sources frequently cited

Baird, J. D., and Ryskamp, C., *The Poems of William Cowper*. vol. 1. Oxford 1980. (P)

Bull, J., *John Newton*. Religious Tract Society, London 1868. (B)

Newton, J., *Works*, 6 vols. Reprinted Banner of Truth, Edinburgh 1984. (WN)

Additional reading

Bennett, I., *The Poetry of the Passion*. Oxford 1982.

Davie, D., *English Hymnology in the 18th Century*. California 1980.

Edwards, B. H., *Through Many Dangers*. Aylesbury 1975.

Ella, G. M., *Paradise and Poetry: an In-Depth Study of William Cowper's Poetic Mind*. Olney 1989, available from Cowper and Newton Museum, Olney.

Hartley, L., 'The Worm and the Thorn: A Study of Cowper's Olney Hymns', *Journal of Religion*, xxix (1949), pp. 220–9.

King, J., *William Cowper*. Duke University Press 1986.

King, J. and Ryskamp, C., *The Letters and Prose Writings of William Cowper*, 5 vols. Oxford 1979–85.

Leaver, J., 'Olney Hymns 1779', *Churchman*, vol. 93 (1979), pp. 327–42, and vol. 94 (1980), pp. 58–66.

Marshall, M., and Todd, J., *English Congregational Hymns in the Eighteenth Century*. University of Kentucky Press 1982.

Newey, V., *Cowper's Poetry: A Critical Study and Reassessment*. Liverpool University Press 1982.

Pollock, J., *John Newton*. London 1981.

Thomas, G., *William Cowper and the Eighteenth Century*, London 1935.

Watson, J. R., 'Cowper's Olney Hymns', *Essays and Studies*, New Series, vol. 38 (1985), pp. 45–65.

Notes

1. For a description of Olney, see King, *Cowper*, pp. 72–6; G. R. Nuttall, 'Baptists and Independents in Olney to the Time of John Newton', *Baptist Quarterly*, vol. xxx (1983), pp. 26–37, reveals Newton's ecumenical spirit. T. Wright, *The Town of Cowper* (London 1886), is a fascinating collection of local and natural history.
2. King, *Cowper*, p. 54.
3. Davie, *English Hymnology*, p. 14; Marshall and Todd, *English Hymns*, pp. 89–98.
4. J. Whittle, *Solid Joys and Lasting Treasure* (London 1985), p. 68.
5. In the 1779 edition of the *Olney Hymn Book*, Newton revised some of Cowper's work. For Newton's hymns I have used the collected edition of his works. For Cowper's hymns, I have used the Oxford edition. The critical notes and commentary shed much light on the hymn texts.

   In addition to specific works cited above further material on the Olney Hymns can be found in Bill Hutchings, *The Poetry of William Cowper* (London 1983), ch. 2; King, *Cowper*, pp. 82–6; P. M. Spacks, *The Poetry of Vision* (Cambridge 1967), ch. 8; R. D. Stock, *The Holy and the Daemonic from Sir Thomas Browne to William Blake* (Princeton 1982), pp. 330–46; Marshall and Todd, *English Hymns*, pp. 132–40, on Cowper's 'fearful hymns'; and an older work, W.

J. Courthope, *A History of English Poetry*, 'Religious lyrical poetry in the Eighteenth Century', vol. 5, pp. 327–59.

6. Newey, *Cowper's Poetry*, p. 330.
7. Bebbington, *Evangelicalism in Modern Britain* (London 1989), pp. 67–8, briefly discusses the features of Augustan England. See also D. Davie, *Purity of Diction in English Verse* (London 1952).
8. Newey, p. 296; Marshall and Todd, *English Hymns*, pp. 125–6.
9. Neither Spurgeon's nor Sankey's collections use the whole hymn.
10. Watson, 'Olney Hymns', p. 61. This is a particularly helpful article in which the author highlights the theological implications of Cowper's poetic devices.
11. To William Unwin, 28–9 July 1785, *Letters*, vol. II, p. 366.
12. See Donald Davie, *New Oxford Book of Christian Verse* (Oxford 1981), pp. xvii-xxix.
13. See *Oxford Poems*, p. 480, for the life-setting of this hymn and the suggestion that Mrs Unwin's illness prompted it.
14. *Poetical Works of William Cowper*, ed. H. Milford (Oxford 1905), p. 396.
15. To Samuel Teedon, 16 May 1793, *Letters*, vol. IV, p. 338.
16. Ella, *Paradise and Poetry*, p. 267.
17. *The Task*, Bk 2, lines 161–6, Milford, p. 149.
18. *Oxford Poems*, p. 175. Watson brings out well the importance of the word 'wait'. Hope and even playfulness underlie the serious point that the unfolding of God's purpose is worth waiting for. Newton's revision, 'Sweet will be the flower', weakens the force and ruins the poetry.
19. To William Bull, 25 May 1788, *Letters*, vol. IV, p. 165.
20. WN, pp. 511, 436, 503.
21. Quoted with no authenticating source by F. W. Boreham in *A Bunch of Everlastings* (London, Epworth Press, 1955), p. 208. I am indebted to Kate Durie for this reference.

4

CHARLES SIMEON and HANNAH MORE

Grace . . . displayed toward us in ten thousand ways.

SIMEON

By the beginning of the nineteenth century, Evangelicalism had begun to gain important footholds within the established Church, extending its influence into many areas of social life. Clergymen like John Newton, Thomas Scott and Henry Venn became exemplars of Evangelical churchmanship, combining vigorous biblical preaching, Evangelical conviction and loyalty to the Church of England. By the turn of the century Evangelical clergy were estimated to be 300–500 strong. Influenced by Newton, Wesley and especially William Wilberforce, the movement for the abolition of slavery gathered momentum. The 'Clapham Sect', a group of influential laymen, began to organize and use their resources in pursuit of social reform and other Evangelical goals. The Church Missionary Society, the British and Foreign Bible Society and the Religious Tract Society came into existence as powerful organs of missionary activity and Evangelical propaganda. The strategic value of being able to place 'godly and devout' men in parishes, with or without the parishoners' consent, began to be recognized and exploited by Evangelical leaders. During this period of consolidation and initiative Charles Simeon and Hannah More emerged as influential leaders of the resurgent movement.[1]

Remember the day . . . all the days of thy life.

Simeon came from a moderately wealthy middle-class family in which religion was mostly a matter of social conformity. From

Eton he entered King's College, Cambridge, in 1779, a fashion-conscious poseur who spent £50 a year on personal clothing, loved horses, frequented Newmarket races, and enjoyed cards, dancing, wine, and a lifestyle which gave the impression he never had a serious thought in his life. However in 1776, when he was seventeen, he observed the national Fast Day, and later recorded: 'I thought that if there was one who had more displeased God than others, it was I' (C p. 5).

In the university lectures were infrequent, attendance occasional and academic standards reduced to the level of farce by the absence of adequate examinations. Yet Cambridge life influenced Simeon in at least two decisive ways. Firstly, as he remarked in conversation, 'One of the great blessings of a Cambridge education is that we lose our rigidity; as stones on the sea shore lose their angles by rough friction, so do we. Love, and collision with others soon rub off our asperity of doctrine' (P p. 40). Secondly, when his first series of sermon outlines was published, one grateful recipient discerned 'the correct, orderly, logical brain of a Cambridge graduate' (C p. 133).

However lax academic discipline, religious protocol was still observed. In February 1779, Simeon received from the College Provost the customary summons to Holy Communion three weeks later. Feeling his integrity threatened he began to prepare himself to receive communion and was overwhelmed by feelings of unworthiness. 'Satan himself was as fit to attend as I.' Frantic bouts of reading brought little reassurance. The Communion service came and went and Simeon makes no mention of how he coped with it. By Holy Week, still poring over *Instruction for the Lord's Supper*, by Bishop Wilson, a classic text from earlier in the century, he was arrested by a comment about the Jews transferring their sin to the head of their offering: 'The thought rushed into my mind, What! may I transfer all my guilt to another? Has God provided an offering for me, that I may lay my sins on his head? then God willing, I will not bear them on my soul one moment longer. Accordingly I sought to lay my sins upon the sacred head of Jesus. . . .' The week climaxed on Easter Sunday morning. 'I awoke early with those words upon my heart and lips, "Jesus Christ is risen today! Hallelujah! Hallelujah!" From that hour peace flowed in rich abundance into my soul . . .' (C p. 9).

Fifty-six years later, Simeon confided, 'When the light of God's countenance . . . first visited me . . . I was enabled by His grace to set my face towards Zion.' Alongside the text, Deut. 26.3, 'That thou mayest remember the day when thou camest forth out of the land of Egypt, all the days of thy life . . .', Simeon had written in his huge copy of Brown's *Self-Interpreting Bible*: 'So must I, and God helping me so will I, the Easter week and especially the Easter Sunday, when my deliverance was complete, in 1779' (H p. 29). The unexpected nature of his conversion, the absence of human agency and the sense of liberation from guilt convinced Simeon of the sovereign freedom of the Redeemer to call sinners to himself.

Each year during Passion Week Simeon felt himself personally addressed, and summoned to penitent wonder by the Christ who died and is alive for evermore. So he sought to 'improve that solemn week to the uttermost'. Later he was conscious of being 'heavy and stupid' in 'calling to mind my former sins and the mercy I obtained twenty-eight years ago', a candid recognition of his inability to supply appropriate feelings on demand (C pp. 218, 222). Nevertheless, the fusion of his personal experience with the Easter gospel generated an enormous output of spiritual energy spanning half a century.

Simeon's literary legacy consists of fifty-three years of preaching condensed into 2,536 sermons, divided almost equally between Old and New Testaments, the whole constituting a homiletical commentary on the Bible. *Horae Homileticae* was issued in twenty-one thick volumes, in sixteen months, a feat which makes it churlish to cavil at the unabashed self-praise of his introductory letter: 'an expedition never known or heard of in the writings of a private man' (C p. 721). It is a preacher's legacy, much of his life's work reduced to words, albeit several millions of them. More importantly, his sermons reveal the biblical spirituality of one gripped by 'stupendous mystery' made personal in 'God's unbounded mercy to me'.[2]

At the end of a Scottish 'holiday' he calculated he had delivered seventy-five addresses to 87,310 people in three months! (H p. 140). Simeon was a meticulous correspondent and once remarked that he had 7,000 copies of his own letters, kept to forestall misrepresentation of his opinions. Most of these letters gave spiritual and pastoral advice. Missionaries were encouraged, curates advised, hotheaded Evangelical clergymen rebuked, critical bishops answered, worried parents comforted and a miscellany of enquiries treated with courteous consideration.

Students were invited to his sermon classes to be taught the value of addresses which were structured, biblical and competently delivered. By 1812 he held informal conversation parties for the discussion of religious matters. These weekly commitments built up a substantial pastoral workload which Simeon accepted unasked. Remarkably he found time to guide the initiatives which culminated in the formation of the Church Missionary Society in 1799; he gave lifelong support to the Bible Society, raised funds for evangelism amongst the Jews and, within his own Church, laid the foundations for Evangelical control of numerous clerical appointments by purchasing rights of appointment. Cambridge during Simeon's tenure had become a centre for the implementation of Evangelical strategy.[3] But again, the generating source of all his gospel activism was the redeeming love that found him on Easter Sunday 1779.

The cross laid upon me that I might bear it after Jesus.

An Easter conversion repeatedly recalled, and annually celebrated within a Church which had produced a rich liturgy, woven around the great redemptive events of the Christian year, encouraged Simeon's spirituality to focus on Christ crucified, risen and experienced. His gospel flowed from the rich fountainhead of the cross and so survived vigorous opposition, unending repetition in countless sermons, and released influences which slowly transformed early nineteenth-century Anglicanism. 'The cross', he stated, 'is so extensive a field for meditation, that, though we traverse it ever so often, we need never resume the same track: and it is such a marvellous fountain of blessedness to the soul, that if we have ever drunk of its refreshing streams, we shall find none other so pleasant to our taste' (HH 8 p. 323).

Simeon preached the cross with little concern for theological sophistication. 'The True Cause of Our Lord's Suffering' he found in Christ, 'expiating our guilt, effecting our peace and renovating our nature' (HH 8 pp. 356f.). The cross cast its shadow over the whole of human existence as a demonstration of law and love, a divine imperative summoning sinners to repentance. His own faith he described as 'the religion of a sinner at the foot of the cross' (C p. 731). One of his most important sermons, 'Christ Crucified, Or Evangelical Religion Described', argued that the atonement is the only adequate basis for Christian spirituality. In the cross Christ was 'set forth as the only foundation of a sinner's hope'; by appeal to the cross, 'holiness in all its branches must be enforced and a sense of Christ's love in dying for us . . . inculcated, as the main spring and motive of all our obedience' (HH 16 p. 40). When such 'a sense of redeeming love occupies the soul', obedience becomes 'ingenuous, hearty, affectionate, unreserved [because] there is no other principle in the universe so powerful as the love of Christ' (HH 16 p. 40).

The sermon describing Evangelical religion was the personal apologia of a minister whose life-work had been the explanation and defence of gospel principles in an environment hostile to the least suggestion of religious enthusiasm. In the message of the suffering Christ, Simeon found a paradigm for his own crossbearing. It is impossible to separate his passionate loyalty to Christ crucified from the opposition, ridicule and hostility he encountered for prolonged periods at Cambridge. They were connected in his mind by an incident to which he attached great significance. Depressed because of 'much contempt and derision in the university', he prayerfully opened his Greek Testament for a text to sustain him: ' "They found a man of Cyrene, Simon by name: him they compelled to bear his Cross." You know Simon is the same as Simeon . . . what a blessed hint of encouragement! To have the Cross laid upon me, that I might bear it after Jesus – what a privilege! it was enough. Now I could leap and sing for joy as one whom Jesus was honouring with a participation in his sufferings . . . I henceforth bound persecution as a wreath of glory round my brow' (C p. 676).

On his appointment to Holy Trinity he had immediately encountered opposition. Locked pews, conspiring churchwardens who locked the church doors and threw out benches Simeon had installed, student disturbances and a general atmosphere of hostility are all part of a remarkable story of pastoral perseverance. His motto, 'The servant of the Lord must not strive', described his ideal though it cut against the grain of an impulsive nature with a streak of quick temper. Yet there is an attractive whimsicality in his logic as he tried to make the best of a bad situation: 'It was painful indeed to see the church, with the exception of the aisles, almost forsaken; but I thought that if God would only give a double blessing to the congregation that did attend, there would on the whole be as much good done, as if the congregation were doubled, and the blessing limited to half the amount' (C p. 44).

Painful experience of ill-will and sneering indifference gave Simeon some of his sharpest insights. 'They who are most earnest in prayer for grace, are often most afflicted because the graces which they pray for, e.g. faith, hope, patience, humility, are only to be wrought in us by means of those trials which call forth the several graces into acts and exercises' (C p. 71). Nor did he always blame the other person: 'I have often found upon reflection, that self has been gratified under the cloak of zeal, and my own will consulted, rather than the will of God' (C p. 387). He recognized belligerent zeal as the besetting sin of some Evangelicals and pleaded, 'Win souls by kindness, rather than convert them by harshness, and what I once called fidelity' (C p. 450). To heresy hunters and crusaders for truth he warned, 'Let a man once engage in controversy, and it is surprising how the love of it will grow upon him; and he will find a hare in every bush, and follow it with something of a huntsman's feelings' (C p. 634). One of his parables illustrates perfectly his pastoral wisdom: 'Two ships were aground at London Bridge. The proprietors of the one sent for a hundred horses and pulled it to pieces. Proprietors of the other waited for the tide: and with sails and rudder directed it as they pleased.'[4] Many times Simeon resisted the temptation to 'send for a hundred horses', preferring to 'wait for the tide'. Patient wisdom was the valuable by-product of his lonely 'participation in the sufferings of Jesus' in the unspectacular arena of Cambridge academia.

Adoration and humiliation.

Simeon's battles with himself and decades of opposition provided 'rough friction', grinding down a character in which colourful eccentricity and Christian sanity coexisted. But not without cost. From the beginning of his ministry, Simeon recognized a strain of arrogance and vanity in his personality. His friends noticed too. Henry Thornton had written pointedly, 'The three lessons a minister has to learn are 1. Humility. 2. Humility. 3. Humility' (C p. 74). Criticism of one of his earliest sermons forced a conclusion which became a primary conviction in all his later Christian experience. 'Our great apostasy seems to consist primarily in making a God of self' (C p. 55).

Simeon recognized that redeemed personality is not perfect, and sanctification is a painful and lifelong struggle. In a characteristic display of pastoral realism he argued that each Christian must carry the burden of individual temperament: 'Religion does not so alter the character as to leave nothing remaining . . . An ardent and enthusiastic man, when he becomes religious, will still be of the same temperament . . . the person who shuddered at a toad before conversion, will do the same afterwards. Religion gives, indeed, a new direction and tone to the mind. We are vessels, and religion, when poured into us, will taste . . . of the tan or the wood of our natural dispositions' (H p. 171).

In the struggle against his 'natural disposition' Simeon was merciless in self-criticism. 'What a blot is my whole life! God knoweth that I loathe myself, and THAT because I cannot loathe myself more' (C p. 103). When asked what he considered the principal mark of regeneration, he gave the disconcerting reply, 'The first and indispensable sign is self-loathing and abhorrence' (C p. 651). He attributed his own conversion to his frank recognition of complete personal unworthiness. The same principle, he believed, was operative throughout Christian life: 'I was once brought very low before God, when mine eyes were first opened to see my real state . . . Without this habitual experience of our sinfulness and natural depravity, even an active religion is a vain thing' (C p. 654).

On religious questions Simeon believed truth did not lie in one extreme, or the other, or even in the middle, but in both extremes held together. This principle related primarily to the Calvinist-Arminian debate in which Simeon held that divine predestination and human responsibility are held together in creative tension.[5] However the same conviction sheds light on his drastic view of human nature. A spirituality which demands only self-loathing must ultimately degenerate into destructive self-hatred. In Simeon's thought self-loathing stood at one extreme. In thought and experience it coexisted with an attitude of adoring awe, compelling worship in the presence of the Almighty. Simeon did not loathe himself in relation to others, but in relation to the pristine holiness of God. In the prayer of adoration 'God is in His place and the sinner is in his'.[6]

It was significant to Simeon that the cherubim in Isaiah chapter six used only one pair of wings to fly; with two they hid their faces and with two they covered their feet. The infinite distance between the moral majesty of God and the utter dependence of even unfallen creatures compels a severe reticence. How much greater the distance between the Lord, high and lifted up, and the sinner who dares to invade his presence? The adoring Christian lives under the burden of privilege. Awesome attraction and terrifying joy are somehow mixed with profound unworthiness, as the searing light of God flashes from the throne, exposing all sin, while by the same light irradiating the cross and cleansing 'the man of unclean lips'. Only in penitent adoration can the Christian fully experience the truth of two extremes: God and self, holiness and sin, grace and weakness, joy and contrition, salvation and judgement. The inner contradiction is inevitable because the Christian is and will always be a redeemed sinner.

'This is the religion I love. I would have conscious unworthiness to pervade every habit, and act of my soul; and whether the warp be more or less brilliant I would have humility to be the woof.'[7] Adoration and humiliation, such a formative tension in Simeon's development, were given moving expression near the end of his life:

> I am, I know, the chief of sinners; and I hope for nothing but the mercy of God in Christ Jesus to life eternal. And I shall be, if not the greatest monument of God's mercy in heaven, yet the very next to it . . . and I lie adoring the SOVEREIGNTY of God in choosing such a one – and the MERCY of God in pardoning such a one – and the PATIENCE of God in bearing with such a one – and the FAITHFULNESS of God in perfecting His work and performing all his promises to such a one.
>
> (C pp. 810–11)

From the refining process of opposition Simeon emerged chastened and changed, with 'an elasticity of heart' that 'rebounded to the pressure of love'. A fascinating glimpse of the impact of devotional practice on relationships is preserved in his diary: 'When reading 1 Cor. xiii this morning, I asked myself how I should act towards Mr and Mrs Edwards . . . and regretted that the same spirit did not animate me towards every other person. I began to pray for our Provost . . . I apprehend that the best mode of understanding the nature and extent of Christian love, is to consider what dispositions we shew towards the dearest objects of our affections, and to put every human being in their place' (C p. 219). The way to love others is to pray for them. After this incident Simeon began to pray for his enemies, 'particularly the most violent and inveterate'. One of his quaint witticisms hints at friction in the university committee rooms: 'Whatever be the number or quality of your counsellors, always put love in the chair, and give him a casting vote'. No such reserve checked his unhappiness at the 'envy and jealousy' which surfaced at a CMS meeting. The rivalry and in-fighting of missionary zealots hurt him: 'Love to God and man should be the only feeling of the soul' (C pp. 727; 572).

Simeon was a forceful, emotionally intense man, sometimes quick-tempered and occasionally reacting out of all proportion to the perceived offence. A well-meaning servant who poked the fire wrongly was strongly disabused by Simeon, the bachelor with a love of creature comforts. But in such outbursts there was no malice and no enduring damage if Simeon could help it. A letter of abject apology was sent in response to a well-meaning rebuke. An indication of how important uncompromised relationships were to Simeon is given in a memorandum in which he carefully anticipated how to deal with the character assassination rife in a university town. He finished by noting, 'I consider love as wealth; and as I would resist a man who should come to rob my house, so would I a man who would weaken my regard for any human being' (C p. 451). In the matter of Christian love there should be no ungenerous restraint. 'That we may show our love improperly I readily grant; but that we can love one another too much, I utterly deny, provided only it be in subserviency to the love of God' (C pp. 770–2).

Scripture read in the spirit of prayer.

As an Evangelical churchman Simeon's devotional discipline revolved around the Bible and the Prayer Book. 'The Bible first, the Prayer Book next, and all other books and doings in subordination to both' (P p. 29). He was persuaded that the liturgy of the Church of England was 'in perfect conformity to the Holy Scriptures', so that the doctrines of the Prayer Book were not so much subordinate to the Bible, as derived from it. They should therefore be accorded due authority, exerting theological control over practical devotion.[8]

Throughout his life Simeon's spirituality was held in orbit by the pull of Scripture. The devotional priority of the Bible was absolute: 'Religion is the regulation of our lives by God's holy word' (P p. 41). A guest at his rooms in King's College recorded: 'Mr Simeon invariably rose every morning, though it was the winter session, at four o'clock; and, after lighting his fire, he devoted the first four hours of the day to private prayer, and the devotional study of the Scriptures' (C p. 67). The lighted fire was no mere incidental. He made acceptance of a preaching engagement conditional on having 'a tolerably warm room'. 'A tinder box, a little wood to kindle a fire speedily, a few roundish coals . . . are but small matters in themselves; but to one who rises early, and longs to serve his God without distraction, they are of some importance.' Having ensured that, he then hinted, 'a warm room, and all my wants (with the exception of a little bread and cheese) are supplied' (C p. 233). Simeon was strict but reasonable with himself. Discomfort had no intrinsic value as a way of holiness.

Believing the Bible conveyed 'the mind of God' he approached it with reverence. 'This is the word of Him who came down from heaven to instruct me; of Him who died upon the cross to save me; of Him who now sits enthroned in glory' (HH 18 p. 252). The one indispensable faculty is a teachable mind, sensitive to the direction of the Holy Spirit, and humbly receptive to divine truth: 'If we look at a sundial, we may understand the use and import of the figures; yet can we not attain a knowledge of the time unless the sun shine upon it. So it is with respect to the Word of God . . . scripture read in the spirit of prayer teaches practical wisdom; but read in another spirit only enlightens the understanding, and not always that' (P p. 36). It was no part of the Christian's duty to question the wisdom of the Bible or try to reconcile its difficulties. For himself, he 'was content to sit as a learner at the feet of the holy Apostles' with 'no ambition to teach them how they ought to have spoken'.[9] So the Bible was an objective touchstone, a ladder to heaven, a map to find our way home; in a sermon on the Bible as a lantern, an illustration drawn from Newmarket races must have raised a few Evangelical eyebrows: 'In all important points the path we are to follow is made as clear to us as the racer's course'.[10]

A set of practical principles exerted sensible control over his exegesis. He sought to bring out 'what is there', not to 'thrust in' what he thought should be there. The text must be treated in a 'natural manner', allowing every verse 'its just meaning, its natural bearing and its legitimate use'. Given such responsible receptiveness, the Christian should 'make a practice of selecting daily some portion of Scripture for . . . meditation through the day'. Ethical direction and Christian maturity are the fruit of biblical obedience: 'With the Scripture as his guide, and the Holy Spirit as his instructor [the Christian] needs no casuist but an upright heart; no director but a mind bent on doing the will of God' (HH 15 p. 53). God's Word 'humbles the proudest spirit, and subdues the most obdurate heart to the obedience of faith. Nor is it to the adoption of new principles only that it brings the soul, but to the acquisition of new habits; so that it becomes set on Christ and heavenly things as once it was set on self and earthly things' (HH 5 p. 109).

The spiritual impact of biblical truth is reinforced by being shared in the liturgy and fellowship of the worshipping church. Simeon scorned 'extemporaneous effusions' as the liturgical norm. The 'precomposed forms' of the Prayer Book contained breadth of sympathy, depth of experience, beauty of language and precision of theology, conveying a sense of corporate identity to the people of God. He knew of one who had been awakened by the petition 'From everlasting damnation, good Lord, deliver us'; and he found personal comfort in the confession, 'there is no health in us'. Indeed the comprehensiveness of the Prayer Book made it an unparalleled vehicle for expressing human experience in the presence of God. 'There is no possible situation in which we can be placed but the prayers are precisely suited to us; nor can we be in any frame of mind, wherein they will not express our feelings . . . strongly and forcibly' (HH 2 p. 266).

After one of his trips to Scotland, as he crossed the border he raised his hands in praise that he was back within his liturgical home territory. His experience of Scotland provided more than one deprivation. He attended a full Presbyterian Communion where there were 1,000 communicants, recording in his diary: 'They who could stay there from beginning to end, with any profit to their souls, must be made of different materials from me' (C p. 120). For Simeon the Lord's Supper was an opportunity for private enrichment. Three weeks later, after a similar service, he wrote: 'I had a delightful season, and Christ was peculiarly precious to my soul. I did not attend to the exhortation, but to my own meditations' (C p. 125). Simeon preferred familiar order, well-loved prayers and the freedom of mind and heart to assimilate truth and commune with God without the intrusion of hortatory voices.

The same sensitivity to spiritual occasion marked his readings from the Prayer Book. 'Never do I find myself nearer to God than I often am in the reading desk' (H p. 147). In defence of the 'Excellency of the Liturgy' he asked, 'If it be lawful to worship God in forms of verse, is it not equally so in forms of prose?' In answer, Simeon went on to defend the advantages of the liturgy. More than once he argued against those who found the liturgy dull, or confining: 'Let him only examine his frame of mind . . . and he will find that his formality is not confined to the service of the Church, but is the sad fruit and consequence of his own weakness and corruption.'[11] His own high view of the liturgy invested such 'formal' acts as pronouncing the benediction with spiritual vitality. 'In pronouncing it, I do not do it as a mere finale, but I feel that I am actually dispensing peace from God, and at God's command. I know not the individuals to whom my benediction is a blessing; but I know that I am the appointed instrument by whom God is conveying the blessing to those who are able to receive it'.[12]

By his loyalty to the Church of England Simeon encouraged other Evangelicals to stay within their spiritual home. Evangelical spirituality, far from being incompatible with firm churchmanship had been shown to flourish in the deep soil of the Anglican tradition. Nor had church allegiance frustrated Evangelical co-operation. Across the denominations work on reform, education, evangelism and other philanthropic interests was consolidated. Simeon was an outstanding contributor to the overall process by which Evangelicalism became a socially acceptable expression of Christian faith in the early nineteenth century.

I have a stronger sense of sin than of pardon.

On 6 April 1807, the Eclectic Society, a group of Evangelical clergymen meeting in London, addressed the question, 'How may pious women best subserve the interests of religion?' Simeon notes, 'The generality seemed to think they did best by keeping at home and minding their own business. My ideas did not perfectly coincide with theirs' (C p. 224). One woman who neither kept at home nor minded her own business was Hannah More, born in 1745 and the second youngest of five sisters. Her father, master of a charity school near Bristol, married a woman of 'plain education, the daughter of a creditable farmer, but endowed, like himself, with a vigorous intellect' (R 1 p. 7). As a child with an academic turn of mind, she quickly became competent in Latin and gained a good command of French, Italian and Spanish. She became so proficient in mathematics that her father stopped her classes in deference to popular notions concerning the delicacy of the female brain![13] Economic circumstances compelled the five sisters to earn their own living and they set up a private school in Bristol where 'French, Writing, Arithmetic and Needlework would be carefully taught'. More began as a pupil, soon became a teacher and began to write dramas for the school. Later, having suffered the humiliation of being jilted three times, she was compensated with an annuity for £200 and used her financial independence to make lengthy visits to London.

She moved into exalted literary circles, forming friendships with Dr Johnson and Horace Walpole, David Garrick the Shakespearean actor, Sir Joshua Reynolds the portrait painter, Edmund Burke the statesman, and an increasing number of wealthy and aristocratic figures in high society. She was a member of the Blue Stockings, a select group of literary women who met regularly to engage in profitable conversation. Her plays, directed and produced by Garrick in the Drury Lane Theatre, made her a much sought-after London celebrity. More thrived on witty conversation and the intellectual give and take of late eighteenth-century London, but after some years disenchantment began to surface in her letters. Society was 'frivolous', suffering from 'fatal levity' and overindulged appetites. She was shocked that 'the strawberries at Lady Stormont's breakfast cost one hundred and fifty pounds' (R 1 p. 285). Conversation was poisoned by flattery, lethal gossip, and mindless trivialities. 'They talk of the high price of sugar and pepper, as if THESE were the only source of the evils we suffer.' She complained about the 'follies, distresses and vices of this town' which 'throw a gloom over and sadden the spirit of pleasure in society' (R 1 p. 244).

There is no classic account of conversion in Hannah More's story. Her change of heart was a gradual process of withdrawal from the values and goals of a society in which she felt less and less at home.[14] Her visits to London became less frequent, as she preferred the retreat of her cottage at Cowslip Green, 'ten miles from Bristol on the Exeter road'. The faith which gradually emerged was rooted in historic Anglicanism but open to other creative influences. Pious habits learned from her parents were reinforced by wide and disciplined reading, especially in the fields of devotional and apologetic literature. Johnson playfully rebuked her for reading the 'papist Pascal'; she worked through such tomes as Bishop Kennicott's *Critical Text of the Old Testament*, and was an admirer of the works of Richard Hooker, Richard Baxter and Philip Doddridge.

Her reading of John Newton's *Cardiphonia* was a significant turning point in her experience. She went to London to hear him preach and came back with 'two pocketfuls of his sermons and tracts'. So began a friendship lasting seventeen years in which Newton became her spiritual adviser, guiding her through a painful process of doubt when she questioned if she 'loved God cordially, effectually, entirely'. Already involved in philanthropic activity, she came into contact with William Wilberforce, who combined high spirits with spiritual seriousness, further evidence that Evangelical religion could be both attractive and aggressively active in reform. Additional impetus towards Evangelical principles was given by contact with the Clapham community which, under the sober leadership of Henry Thornton, represented 'a hardy, serviceable, fruit-bearing patrimonial religion'.[15]

Gradually such influences convinced More that her religion lacked the vitalizing encounter between the soul and God which was the heart of Evangelical spiritual life. She had no personal experience of penitent, trusting faith in the atoning death of Christ, by which conscience is cleansed and the soul renewed through the Holy Spirit. Newton had pointed this out from the start. 'As sinners, the first things we need are pardon, reconciliation and a principle of life and conduct entirely new' (R 2 p. 92). By 'looking to Jesus and feeling [her] need of a Saviour', she could 'know him to be . . . the sun of the world and of the soul; the source of all spiritual light'. Newton was a good listener and gifted at reading between the spiritual lines. His letter continued by reassuring her that the work of grace begins 'faint and indistinct, like the peep of the dawn. The beginnings of the Christian life are likewise small in the true Christian, who likewise passes through a succession of various dispensations, but advances, though silently and slowly, yet surely, and will stand forever' (R 2 p. 93).

Four years later, More continued to bemoan 'a weak faith' and 'little progress in the divine life'; three more years and she was still dissecting her soul: 'I trust my faith is sound, but it is not lively . . . there must be something amiss in my heart which I do not know of . . . because I have little sensible joy . . . I have a stronger sense of sin than of pardon and acceptance; though I have the firmest belief of both on the gospel terms; but it is not an operative principle' (R 2 p. 277).

Holiness of life . . . the only true evidence of a saving faith.

More's diary for 1798, when she was fifty-three, reveals the intensity with which she felt her spiritual failure. 'I will confess my sins – repent of them – plead the atonement – resolve to love God and Christ – implore the aid of the Spirit for light, strength and direction – examine if these things be done – be humbled for my failures – Watch and pray' (R 2 p. 55). Her spiritual agitation had its origin in a profoundly moral view of Christianity. 'Holiness of life is the only true evidence of a saving faith . . . the gospel is strict . . . the standard of religion should always be kept high' (R 2 pp. 120; 338–9). More was ruthlessly honest and far too self-aware to make excuses for herself. She was caught in the crossfire of a hyper-sensitive conscience and a mind skilled in decoding the moral ambiguities of her inner life.

In an age of exaggerated flattery and quickly changing fashion, popularity and acclaim were weak currency. More's attitude to praise became ambivalent.[16] Enjoyment of achievement fuelled the temptation to vanity and made her success a spiritual testing ground. 'Alas', she reflected, 'when I receive these undue compliments, I am ready to answer with my old friend Johnson, "Sir, I am a miserable sinner" ' (R 2 p. 437). She offended many in the upper classes by insisting that human nature is essentially corrupt and that all without distinction share the shame and guilt of fallen humanity.[17] Indeed she argued that human corruption was the starting point of experimental theology: 'Genuine Christianity can never be grafted on any other stock than the apostasy of man. The design to reinstate beings who have not fallen, to propose a restoration without a previous loss, a cure where there was no radical disease is altogether an incongruity' (W 8 p. 6).

Consistent with Evangelical principles, More believed the human heart requires to be changed so that man's 'dark understanding is illuminated, his rebellious will is subdued, his irregular desires are rectified; his judgment is informed, his imagination is chastised, his inclinations are sanctified' (W 8 p. 3). By a new birth, which, whether sudden or gradual, must be definite, a complete reorientation of the personality takes place. Christianity then becomes a 'religion of the heart': 'THERE [religion] subsists as the fountain of spiritual life; THENCE it sends forth, as from the central seat of its existence, supplies of life and warmth through the whole frame; THERE is the soul of virtue, THERE is the vital principle which animates the whole being of a Christian' (W 8 p. 8). Even then, sin is only dealt with at the level of a reconciled relationship with God. The renewed heart is set on a collision course with the world outside while being threatened by 'imperfectly subdued corruptions' within.

The world applauded much of More's literary work; Christian friends repeatedly praised her for the great good done by her writings, often falling into the same sin of uncritical flattery which she found so objectionable in the world; she played hostess to a constant stream of bishops, literary figures, Christian workers, friends and strangers, on one occasion noting ruefully that she had nineteen visitors, six of whom she had never met before. More was too honest not to recognize the dangers of such admiration; and too scrupulous to enjoy it innocently. Throughout her life, bouts of self-examination uncovered yet another subterfuge of her recalcitrant ego. 'Self love is a Proteus of all shapes, shades and complexions, it has the power of dilation and contraction as best serves the occasion. There is no crevice so small through which its subtle essence cannot work its way, no space so ample that it cannot stretch itself to fill' (W 8 p. 216). It is 'a malignant distemper which has possession of the moral constitution', a 'tempest which agitates the sleeping ocean'. Its ingenuity is inexhaustible, so that 'it is no low attainment to detect this lurking injustice in our hearts, to strive against it, to pray against it, and especially to conquer it' (W 8 p. 226). Like much of her didactic writing, these words are patently autobiographical.

Eventually she worked out a comprehensive strategy for self-examination. Motives were specially suspect. 'These we should follow up to their remotest springs, scrutinise to their deepest recesses, trace through their most perplexing windings' (W 8 p. 194). To the charge that such intense self-preoccupation was spiritually unhealthy she would insist: 'This inward eye, this power of introversion is given us for a continual watch upon the soul.' As she went deeper and deeper into the labyrinth of motive and intention she exposed further moral distortions, but only at the cost of casting suspicion over the whole moral life, and subjecting every encouraging compliment to such fine filtering that all affirmation was extracted, leaving a sense of perpetual unworthiness. She made the valid point that Christians are more inclined to examine their hearts when they think they are in the right, and was well aware that such inspection often 'gratifies self-love'. But rather than suggesting the need for honesty in confronting the total self, bad and good, she argued against the credibility of her own goodness. 'Let us establish it into a habit to ruminate on our faults. With the recollection of our virtues we need not feed our vanity. They will if that vanity does not obliterate them be recorded elsewhere' (W 8 p. 199).

Sin, once discovered, must be forsaken. She found no peace in general confession: 'It will not do to repent in the lump. The sorrow must be as circumstantial as the sin. Indefinite repentance is no repentance . . . it is one grand use of self-enquiry, to remind us that all unforsaken sins are unrepented sins' (W 8 p. 204). So self-examination is likened to an author revising, correcting, rewriting then proof-reading the copy of his literary efforts. 'He finds much to amend, and even to expunge, in what he had before admired.' Even then the soul has its own list of errata. 'When by rigorous castigation the most acknowledged faults are corrected, his critical acumen, improved by exercise, and a more habitual acquaintance with his subject, still detects and will forever detect new imperfections' (W 8 pp. 205–6).

Surprisingly, vigilant editing of her inner life did not lead to despair of making progress. After she had spelt out the extent of self-abasement she conceded: 'If we consider ourselves in our natural state, our estimation cannot be too low; if we reflect at what price we have been bought, we can hardly overrate ourselves in the view of immortality' (W 8 p. 7). A Christian cannot hate what God loves, including the imperfect but redeemed self. In a fallen world the goal of Christian growth cannot be perfection, but, at best, progress towards perfection. Christian maturity must be pursued with a humbling knowledge of inner corruption and unrelenting mortification of the propensity to self-love.

A welcome note of realism brings the high standards of her 'strict gospel' within reach of ordinary flesh aspiring to sanctity. A long passage illustrates her ability to weaken her case for the prosecution by offering significant clues to the defence. Growth need not be measured by the amount of corruption still discovered, but by the 'perceptible change in [our] desires, tastes, pleasures . . . and progress however small in holiness of heart and life'. The happiness of the Christian consists in

> a settled, calm conviction that God and eternal things have the predominance in his heart; in a clear perception that they have, though with much alloy of infirmity, the supreme, if not undisturbed, possession of his mind; in an experimental persuasion that his chief remaining sorrow is, that he does not surrender himself with so complete an acquiescence as he ought to his convictions. These abatements, though sufficient to keep us humble, are not powerful enough to make us unhappy.
>
> (W 8 p. 17)

Despite this modest disclaimer, in the later More the spontaneous sparkle of vitality was dulled by a film of accumulated seriousness.

Retirement for the improvement of ourselves.

Conflict with 'the world' created a further spiritual dilemma; how to serve God in the world without being contaminated by its values. Does obedience to God involve separation from, or involvement in, the world? Attracted to a life of retreat, quiet study and spiritual cultivation, she was impelled by an equally powerful need to work towards her optimum level of usefulness for God. Inevitably she was torn between the conflicting, and often contradictory, demands of being and doing.

On the subject of meditation and the cultivation of the inner life More set herself exacting standards. With characteristic caution she warned: 'A retirement which does not involve benefit to others, as well as improvement to ourselves' fails 'the great purpose for which we came into the world [and] for which we withdraw from it' (W 9 p. 226). Self-improvement and benefit to others became the overriding spiritual ambitions of the later Hannah More. In fulfilling them she was required to be a woman of leisure and exertion, privacy and publicity, contemplation and action, qualities so apparently irreconcilable that each ambition could only be attained at the expense of the other. Eventually each was achieved with limited success and More, unreasonably, would blame herself.

When she withdrew from London society she planned a place of quiet retreat with leisure to 'store her mind with . . . maxims of wisdom' and be 'safe from temptations'. But as she confessed to Newton: 'I am certainly happier here than in the agitation of the world but I do not find I am one bit better; with full leisure to rectify my heart and affections the dispositions do not come' (R 2 p. 88). Severe self-criticism marred the joy of communion with God. She took herself to task for distracted thoughts, cold affections and selfish motives. 'Escaped from hurry, vexation, gaiety and temptation to peace, leisure and retirement. Where I had planned much progress . . . I find a languor, a drowsiness . . . sloth and self-love getting strong dominion, and much time wasted which I had devoted to self-improvement' (R 2 p. 416). Unreasonably, she rebuked herself for not meditating during a migraine, and struggled guiltily with her inability to make sufficient use of bouts of insomnia![18]

As a strict Sabbatarian she devoted Sundays to prayer and serious reading. When bad weather prevented her going the rounds of her Sunday Schools, she tried to use the time with a spiritual thrift which forgave no wasted moment. 'I have seldom a Sabbath to spend on myself. Let me not trifle away this precious opportunity but pass it in extraordinary prayer, reading and meditation. Enable me to make conversation one of my pious exercises' (R 2 p. 421). The last petition, ominous in its implications for friendship, was never fulfilled to her satisfaction. In 'worldly company' she worried about her 'mind being secularised', and noted on one occasion 'I was tempted to be warm in politics' (R 3 pp. 55–7). In 'godly company' similar dangers lurked. 'I fear I do not profit enough when I get with pious people – joy evaporates in self-satisfied feelings, and serious talk, without reaching the heart' (R 3 p. 59).

The Romanticism of the new generation as personified in Coleridge, Byron, Scott and Wordsworth had little appeal to Hannah More. She thoroughly enjoyed Scott's poetry but loathed Byron's 'sin and infamy' (J p. 225). Yet some of her letters reveal a love of nature in keeping with the Romantic vision of the world. Of course the beautiful world is attributed to the wise Creator, and it must not usurp first place in the affections, but with these provisos More viewed the beauty of the natural world with positive pleasure.[19] What she could not enjoy at first hand, she enjoyed vicariously in the poems of her favourite poet, William Cowper, who lovingly observed and described the domestic world of gardens, greenhouses, hedgerows and riversides. Descriptions of her own horticultural efforts are light-hearted and enthusiastic: 'I spend almost my whole time in my little garden which mocks my scant manuring. From morn to noon, from noon to morn, I am employed in raising dejected pinks, and reforming disorderly honeysuckles' (R 2 p. 73). She was criticized by some over-zealous converts for not writing a tract condemning the sin of wearing flowers; no such sin existed in her extensive catalogue! As an octogenarian she confessed without a hint of remorse, 'The only one of my youthful fond attachments which exists still in its full force, is a passion for scenery, raising flowers, and landscape gardening' (R 4 p. 303). Slipped into a paragraph on the moral benefits of tedious reading, is the remarkable confession: 'I cannot afford to buy [books] because I have spent all my money on trees' (R 3 p. 172). Few duties were as uncomplicated to More as her garden; few taken more seriously than her reading.

Despite the whirlwind of social engagements in the early London days she found time to read through all the Epistles three times, then a fourth, using John Locke's *Paraphrase*. She once 'read through a shelf of books as they came to hand without any choice or selection' and was amazed at the 'mass of crudities swallowed' (R 2 p. 198). Later she was reading Matthew Henry and David Hume, an incongruous combination of devotion and metaphysics. As she became confirmed in her Evangelical stance her taste became much more selective. 'Taste is of all ages, and truth is eternal; and there is a truth in taste almost as demonstrable as any mathematical proposition' (R 2 p. 147). So Gibbon's *Decline and Fall* was read and subjected to severe and perceptive criticism.[20] Cowper retained his favoured place but was reproved for wasting his genius on mere translations of Homer. More gave thanks to God that she had stopped reading the classics and 'now willingly read little of which religion is not the subject'. Robert Leighton's *First Peter* she judged 'a mine of intellectual and spiritual wealth . . . He always catches hold of the heart' (R 3 p. 357). The Bampton Lectures on *Mahomet and Christ*, West on *The Resurrection*, Bishop Lowth's critical *Commentary on Isaiah* began to replace less 'improving' works. Scott's *Waverley Novels* she judged non-moral and not worth the investment of God-given time. Novel reading offended against the principles of usefulness and self-improvement.[21]

The number of biblical commentaries she studied and prayed over emphasized the place she gave to the Bible. She subjected literary and doctrinal works to acute criticism but for the Bible she claimed privileged exemption. 'Though Holy Scripture was given to be searched [it] was not given to be criticized . . . Christianity is no appropriate field for the perplexities of metaphysics . . . It is not to be endured . . . to hear questions on which hang all our hopes and fears, speculated upon as if they were a question of physics or history' (J p. 232). She plainly did not undervalue the intellect, and explained her own position clearly: 'I put religion on my right hand and learning on my left. Learning should not be despised even as an auxiliary.'[22]

Bible reading and prayer went together in her devotions. Read prayerfully the Bible could be 'nutriment to the heart', 'an unerring line to ascertain our own rectitude' or 'oil to the lamp of prayer'. A primary benefit of her own extensive study was a mental treasury of theological and biblical knowledge from which she drew material for meditation. In that sense all her reading was 'spiritual reading'. Prayers of confession should be marked by humiliation not complaint. A sense of sin humbles, but the promised grace makes despair vanish. More's writing on prayer is less preoccupied with personal failure. Undoubtedly she experienced release from herself when she turned her thoughts towards God. She still moulded the objective promises of Scripture to the shape of her own needs, but in doing so she found those needs met. 'Prayer is the application of want to Him who alone can relieve it, the voice of sin to Him who alone can pardon it . . . Our love to God arises out of want, God's love to us out of fulness' (W 8 pp. 74, 109). 'The beauty of Scripture consists of pronouns'; for her the personal, possessive pronouns invested prayer with delight. 'The consummation of the joy arises from the peculiarity, the intimacy, the endearment of the relation' (W 8 p. 82).

In prayer More experienced the love of God through Christ as a healing and recreating influence. 'When the adoring soul is gratefully expatiating on the inexhaustible instances of the love of God to us, let it never forget to rise to its most exalted pitch, to rest on its loftiest object, His inestimable love in the redemption of the world by our Lord Jesus Christ' (W 8 p. 110). Her vivid sense of a providence which was detailed in purpose and faithful in love, enabled her to enjoy all 'earthly blessings'. Such pleasures must include 'a thankful reflection on the goodness of the Giver, a deep sense of the unworthiness of the receiver, and a sober recollection of the precarious tenure by which we hold it' (W 8 p. 118).

In prayer the Christian mind and heart confront the mystery and majesty of God with acknowledged incapacity. Amongst the most enduring and enriching gifts of God to redeemed humanity is the vision of the fulness of his grace, ever available to empty hearts. Such generous love bestows the promise of all the grace the human heart can contain, and that promise creates an aching and inarticulate longing for God, which is the prayer of supplication, not for God's gifts, but for God himself.

> It is the glory of religion to supply an object worthy of the entire consecration of every power, faculty and affection of an immaterial, immortal being . . . Christianity demands the energies of the entire man; its worship, the choicest portion of his time; its doctrines, the strenuous exertion of his intellectual powers; its duties, the stretch and compass of his widest endeavours; its truths, the highest exercise of his faith.
>
> (W 8 p. 126)

I would rather work for God than meditate on him.

With financial independence More had leisure to read widely, think deeply and pursue a life of personal holiness. In her garden she found relaxation and a creative outlet and in the quiet seclusion of her home she assiduously cultivated her soul. But until 'every faculty [was] stretched in the service of the Lord' her other ambition, 'the good of others', would remain unfulfilled.

William Wilberforce had a galvanizing effect on Hannah More. Through him she became deeply committed to the abolition of the slave trade. On principle she boycotted West Indian sugar and carried a plan of a slave ship with which she ruined many an evening planned by unsuspecting hostesses for agreeably harmless conversation. Between 1788 and 1805 she published several works in which she criticized the morals and manners of 'the Great'. The *Estimate of the Religion of the Fashionable World* and *Strictures on the Modern System of Female Education* caused offence to some, but became very popular with the upper classes. Westminster schoolboys burnt an effigy of the woman who had dared write about 'the dissipation of youth'.[23]

Her motivation in writing such books has been the subject of much critical research.[24] Her own avowed purpose, again influenced by Wilberforce, was related to her perception of what was wrong with society. When they met in 1787, Wilberforce and his friends had put moral reform on the political agenda by obtaining the promise of a royal proclamation against vice and immorality defined as neglect of Sunday observance, excessive drinking, blasphemy, profane swearing, gambling and 'loose, licentious, indecent and blasphemous publications' (J p. 104). More's strategy was simple: 'To expect to reform the poor while the opulent are corrupt, is to throw odours into the stream while the springs are poisoned' (J p. 152).

She was suspicious of 'corrupt poets and philosophers'. In the ferment of the war with revolutionary France and under pressure from the Bishop of London, she wrote *Village Politics*, an antidote to *The Rights of Man* by Thomas Paine. It was written for the poorer classes and the barely literate and is an unquestioning defence of an established order which confined the underprivileged to poverty and social powerlessness. Hannah had become a spokesperson for radical conservatism. The tract became an immediate bestseller and extravagant claims were made that she had prevented revolution in England. Many more Cheap Repository Tracts followed, initiating a publishing phenomenon.[25]

During the 1790s More and her sisters, at the instigation of Wilberforce, had begun a programme of basic education amongst the mining families and villagers of Cheddar. The scheme spread to cover many villages all over the Mendip Hills, so that by 1796 over 1600 were enrolled in ten parishes.[26] As the work began she wrote to her friend Mrs Carter:

> A friend of mine and myself having with great concern discovered a large village, at many miles distance from me, containing incredible multitudes of poor, plunged in an excess of

> vice, poverty, and ignorance beyond what one would suppose possible in a civilized and Christian country, have undertaken the task of seeing if we cannot become humble instruments of usefulness to these poor creatures in the way of schools and a little sort of manufactory.
>
> (R p. 178)

It was for such people that More wrote, and by the time she did she had become familiar with their lives, vocabulary and values.

Hannah More has been called 'one of the most successfully innovative writers of popular political literature'.[27] She advocated quiet obedience to the decrees of providence and encouraged attitudes of law-abiding decency in which each person knew their place, and learned to be content with it. Having carefully studied the chapbooks sold by local hawkers, she wrote tracts in which virtue was rewarded and the vicious got what they deserved. Characters such as Sinful Sally, Mr Fantom and Mr Bragwell came alive in the telling of the stories. She shows detailed knowledge of apprenticeship, poaching, working in a coal mine, getting drunk, the techniques of weaving and many other aspects of the daily life of the poor.

The flood of writings which flowed from her 'consecrated pen' was inevitably of mixed quality. Much of it was written in unscholarly haste; many were so historically specific that they must remain period pieces; her popular tracts, and especially her views on the place of women in society continue to provoke interest; her educational approach was blatantly paternalistic and her political stance reactionary. But in terms of her spirituality the work of writing and teaching was the obverse side of her piety, the active expression of an inner compulsion to do good. She would not have understood the criticism of modern political and social theorists, living as she did through political revolution and dying just after the 1832 Reform Act, which she opposed. A casual comment to her spiritual director, John Newton, provides an accurate self-estimate, tinted as always with a sense of failure: 'God is sometimes pleased to work by the most unpromising and unworthy instruments; I suppose to take away every shadow of doubt that it is his own doing. It always gives me the idea of a great author writing with a very bad pen' (R p. 464).

Both Charles Simeon and Hannah More lived long lives, spanning momentous changes in Church and state. By the influence of personal ministry, evangelical propaganda, gifts of energetic organization and strategic thinking, they contributed significantly to the consolidation of the Evangelical party in the established Church. Neither of them married, and their singleness made possible life-styles in which singleminded activity and punishing timetables did not conflict with family responsibility. Simeon set the tone of Evangelical ministry by an example whose influence is incalculable. By personal training of hundreds of ordinands and by securing for Evangelicals a share of rights of appointment he strengthened the hold of Evangelicals within the Church. More laid the foundations of a moral reformation which at best attempted to change the behaviour of the privileged classes, and at worst conspired to perpetuate an unjust social system. The lasting effects of her moral teaching were discernible in the norms and habits of Victorian Evangelicalism, as for example the emphasis on stewardship of time, the dangers of fiction, strict Sabbath observance and the middle-class preoccupation with doing good among the poor.

A persistent sense of unworthiness imbued their spirituality with a spirit of discontent which always pointed inwards to find its cause. When More confessed that she often had a stronger sense of her sin than of God's pardon she echoed Simeon's experience. He had learned to live with his unworthiness by seeing himself from the viewpoint of a holy God. In adoration he worshipped and trusted a God whose love and judgement coincided in the cross and placed him, despite his sin, in a different and merciful light. Hannah, too, found comfort in truths bigger than her failures, and often returned to the Pauline argument that she was bought with a price, a fact which placed her value to God beyond ultimate dispute.

Simeon allowed his mind to soak in the Bible and seldom referred to his wider reading. More's mind was cultured and well stored, an example of 'the Puritan work ethic of the mind'.[28] Though her taste in religious books was remarkably catholic, like Simeon she claimed that her religion was rooted in the Bible. In 1803 she anticipated the sentiments of Simeon's spirited but eirenic 'Preface' and in doing so placed herself alongside her contemporary as an avowed Evangelical, entirely at home in the Church of England. 'How I hate the little narrowing names of Arminian and Calvinist. Christianity is a broad basis. Bible

Christianity is what I love . . . a Christianity practical and pure, which teaches holiness, humility, repentence and faith in Christ; and which after summing up all the evangelical graces, declares that the greatest of these is charity' (R 3 p. 196).

Sources frequently cited

Carus, W., *Memoirs of the Life of Rev. Charles Simeon*. London 1847. (C)

Hopkins, H., *Charles Simeon of Cambridge*. London 1977. (H)

Jones, M. G., *Hannah More*. Cambridge 1952. (J)

More, H., *Works*, 11 vols. London 1830. (W)

Pollard, A., and Hennell, M., ed., *Charles Simeon, 1759–1836*. London 1964. (P)

Roberts, W., *Memoirs of the life and Correspondence of Mrs Hannah More*, 4 vols. 2nd edn London 1834. (R)

Simeon, C., *Horae Homileticae*, 21 vols. Grand Rapids 1988. (HH)

Additional reading

Brown, A. W., *Recollections of the Conversation parties of the Rev. Chas. Simeon*. London 1863.

Centenary Addresses, *Charles Simeon: An Interpretation*. London 1936.

Collingwood, J. and M., *Hannah More*. Oxford 1990.

Hopkins, M. A., *Hannah More and Her Circle*. New York 1947.

Moule, H. C. G., *Charles Simeon*. London 1965.

Rosman, D. M., *Evangelicals and Culture*. London 1984.

Smyth, C., *Simeon and Church Order*. Cambridge 1940.

Notes

1. See Pollard and Hennell, *Simeon*, ch. 1; Hopkins, *Simeon*, pp. 15–23.
2. Carus, *Memoir*, p. 232. See Hopkins, *Simeon*, pp. 59–62, for details of 'Horae Homileticae'.
3. See Max Warren, 'Charles Simeon: His methods in the local church, the Church of England and the nation', *Churchman*, vol. 92 (1978), pp. 112–23; Moule, *Simeon*, ch. 12; Pollard and Hennell, *Simeon*, pp. 140–7. The vexed question of patronage is dealt with by Warren; Pollard and Hennell, pp. 170ff; see R. W. Heinze, 'Charles Simeon – through the eyes of an American Lutheran', *Churchman*, vol. 93 (1978), pp. 240–52, for a sympathetic view by an outsider.
4. Heinze, p. 241.

5. Smyth, *Church Order*, p. 185.
6. For Simeon on the Calvinist–Arminian Controversy see HH 1 pp. xiv-xxii.
7. Quoted in A. Bennett, 'Charles Simeon: Prince of Evangelicals', *Churchman*, vol. 102 (1988), p. 134.
8. Carus, *Memoir*, p. 298; See the footnote in HH 1 p. xiv. Simeon's preface remains an important document in the history of exegesis. Few Evangelicals treated the literary integrity of the different books of the Bible with so much sensible respect.
9. Quoted in Donald Coggan, 'Charles Simeon', in Great Preachers series, *Theology* (1951), pp. 136–40. Coggan returned to Simeon in *These Were His Gifts*, (Exeter 1978). The influence of Simeon on Lord Coggan has been documented in Margaret Pawley's biography of the former Archbishop. The contribution of C. M. Chavasse in Centenary Addresses, 'Simeon and his Love for the Bible', has many quotations from Simeon himself. See the important section dealing with Simeon's theology of the Scriptures in H. D. McDonald, *Ideas of Revelation. An Historical Study, A.D. 1700 to A.D. 1860*, especially pp. 213–44.
10. *Centenary Addresses*, p. 65.
11. See Douglas Webster, 'Charles Simeon and the Liturgy', *Theology* (1951), p. 299. The same author's essay in Pollard and Hennell, *Simeon*, is particularly helpful in clarifying Simeon's attitude to the liturgy. But Simeon's sermons, especially the second, should be read to appreciate the measured argument of an Evangelical churchman defending his liturgical heritage, cf. HH 2, Sermon Nos. 191–4.
12. Coggan, 'Charles Simeon', p. 139.
13. C p. 224; See J. Pratt, *The Thought of the Evangelical Leaders* (Edinburgh), for the 'minutes' of these discussions.
14. M. Hopkins, *Hannah More*, p. 14.
15. Sir James Stephen, quoted in Jones, *More*, p. 93.
16. During her London days Hannah was equally guilty of 'bespattering' her friends with flattery. See *Quarterly Review*, vol. 52 (1834), p. 427. Incidentally, this review article on Roberts' *Memoir* is a highly entertaining though unsparing criticism of the work and its author. It highlights serious weaknesses in Roberts' treatment of the sources.
17. See especially her *Strictures on the Modern System of Female Education*, ch. 20, and Jones' comments, pp. 114–21.
18. See Rosman, *Evangelicals and Culture*, for a comprehensive treatment of Evangelical attitudes.
19. On Romanticism and Evangelicalism generally see D. W. Bebbington, 'Evangelical Christianity and Romanticism', *Crux*, vol. xxvi 1 (1990), pp. 9–15.
20. Hannah's 'Strictures' on Gibbon can be found in Roberts, vol. 2, pp. 132, 137, 175, 415, 435.
21. Hannah's 'Estimate' of Scott can be found in Roberts, vol. 3, pp. 372, 390; 4, pp. 182, 205. S. Pickering, *The Moral Tradition in English Fiction* (New Hampshire 1976), pp. 89–105, compares Hannah's novel 'Coelebs in Search of a Wife' with Scott's 'Waverley'.

22. Her contribution to educational development has received considerable scholarly attention. Paul Sangster, *Pity My Simplicity* (London 1963), examines the motives, methods and content of Evangelical educational enterprises. S. O'Donnell, 'Mr Locke and the Ladies', *Studies in Eighteenth Century Culture*, vol. 8, pp. 156ff., is critical of Hannah's views on female education.
23. 'The Cool World of S. T. Coleridge: More for the Millions', P. M. Zall, *Wordsworth Circle* (1973), vol. 4, pp. 152f.
24. In addition to Zall, see O. Smith, *The Politics of Language* (Oxford 1983), ch. 3. M. Myers, 'Reform or Ruin: A Revolution in Female Manners', *Studies in Eighteenth Century Culture*, vol. 11 (1982), pp. 199–216. B. Hilton, *The Age of Atonement: the Influence of Evangelicals on Social and Economic Thought, 1785–1865* (Oxford 1989), p. 204, describes Hannah's approach as 'moral majoritarianism'.
25. By 1796 two million had been sold. Some, with extracts from Practical Piety were translated into Swedish, Dutch, Icelandic, Tamil and Sinhalese. A Russian translation of 'The Shepherd of Salisbury Plain' was prepared by a Russian Crown Princess whose delightful letter is in Roberts, vol. 4, p. 42.
26. Sangster and Jones each give different perspectives on the Mendip experiment.
27. Smith, *Politics of Language*, p. 80.
28. See Myers, 'Female Manners', pp. 209–12.

5

HORATIUS BONAR and ROBERT MURRAY McCHEYNE

Absolutely sovereign, yet infinitely gracious.
BONAR

John Bonar was ordained minister at Torphichen, near Edinburgh, in 1693. When Horatius his great-great-grandson died in 1889 the Bonar family had served as ministers of the Church of Scotland and the Free Church of Scotland for an aggregate of 364 years. Horatius Bonar's ministry stretched over half a century, from his induction at Kelso in 1837 to his death in 1889 as minister of Chalmer's Memorial Free Church in Edinburgh.

Robert Murray McCheyne was born on May 21, 1813, the youngest of a family of five. His father was a prominent Edinburgh lawyer and a hard-line Tory who once wrote to ask one of his sons in India: 'Have you any vermin called Whigs and Radicals in Hindustan?' (Y p. 5). By the time Bonar and McCheyne met at Edinburgh University, Bonar was already training for the ministry and committed to Evangelical principles. McCheyne was studying classics and moral philosophy with spare-time pursuits including geography, elocution, music, gymnastics and sketching. When McCheyne entered the Divinity Hall in September 1831, he began a friendship with the Bonar brothers, David, James, Andrew and Horatius, which lasted until his death in 1843, aged 29.

Through the teaching of Thomas Chalmers, the most original and one of the most able thinkers in the Church of Scotland, McCheyne and Bonar received a theological education which permanently enriched their ministry. Chalmers was an avowed

Evangelical whose own parish ministry had been revitalized by his conversion. In 1805, he had published a pamphlet with the remarkable admission: 'The author . . . can assert, from what is to him the highest of all authority, the authority of his own experience, that after the satisfactory discharge of all his parish duties, a minister may enjoy five days in the week of uninterrupted leisure, for the prosecution of any science in which his taste may dispose him to engage.'[1] Following his conversion he pursued an energetic parish ministry characterized by powerful preaching, intellectual vitality and far-sighted economic and social experiments, especially in Glasgow. His appointment as Professor of Divinity at Edinburgh exposed substantial numbers of students like Bonar and McCheyne to the passionate thinking of a powerful mind and the rich experience of an innovative and socially aware parish minister.

The Evangelical zeal of Bonar, McCheyne and many other young ministers of their generation was poured into parish ministry. Bonar spent fifty-three years in pastoral charge at Kelso then Edinburgh. McCheyne spent one year at Larbert and a mere seven years at St Peter's, Dundee. During his Kelso ministry Bonar was a tireless evangelist. He wrote many books of practical divinity of which *God's Way of Peace* and *God's Way of Holiness* were the most significant, the former selling 285,000 copies during his lifetime. He was editor of several journals including *The Quarterly Journal of Prophecy*. He wrote over six hundred hymns, his collection, *Hymns of Faith and Hope*, reaching a circulation of 140,000. McCheyne's life was so short there was little time for maturing of ideas, growth of character and influence or any significant literary output. Yet from a short ministry of seven years emerged a model of pastoral care, legendary both for conscientious visiting and searching preaching. When allowance is made for hagiography, what remains is one of the most impressive pastorates in the life of the Scottish Church. Visitation notebooks, Bible study notebooks, sermon manuscripts, letters and other extant sources bear witness to a profoundly effective ministry.

This wilderness of chimney pots.

Following the death of his brother David in 1831, McCheyne began to have a stronger sense of his personal unworthiness. His diary records: 'Deep penitence, not unmixed with tears. I never before saw myself so vile, so useless, so poor, and, above all, so ungrateful. May these tears be the pledges of my self-dedication' (B p. 14). He read *The Sum of Saving Knowledge*', an appendix to the *Confession of Faith*, and was conscious of a spiritual change. This led to a gradual refining of moral tastes as he sought to live out his faith in Christ. Cards, theatre and dancing were all proscribed; sabbath observance was more carefully planned; Bible reading, prayer and Holy Communion became meaningful acts of devotion.

At university McCheyne read the lives of Henry Martyn, Alexander Duff of India, David Brainerd and Jonathan Edwards. Evangelistic fervour and keen missionary interest became permanent elements in his pastoral theology and spiritual development. In Edinburgh, while participating in parish mission work, he was shocked at the 'miserable habitations' in which the poor lived. 'What imbedded masses of human beings are huddled together, unvisited by friend or minister' (B p. 24). He conducted a survey in the Lawnmarket and the Canongate and found that fewer than one in seven of the inhabitants had any meaningful church connection.[2] A student ministry in Larbert provided further evidence of the spiritual needs of industrialized towns. By 1835 Larbert was a busy industrial town of 6,000, with mines, mills and railways all serving the Carron Ironworks. 'The people are savages for ignorance – but very amenable to kindness as all savages are', he wrote to his father.[3] When he moved in 1836, Dundee was all but established as a key centre for linen, rope and jute manufacture. Here too he encountered the juxtaposition of poverty and prosperity. In one parish there were eleven bread shops and one hundred and eight public houses. St Peter's was a new extension congregation made up of weavers, warpers, spinners, bankers and merchants, reflecting a wide social spectrum and offering endless evangelistic opportunity. The thought of a small undemanding rural parish never seriously tempted him. God, he said, 'has set me down among the noisy mechanics and political weavers of this godless town . . . Perhaps the Lord will make this wilderness of chimney-tops to be green and beautiful as the garden of the Lord' (B p. 67).

Assiduous pastoral visiting was a matter of spiritual discipline to McCheyne. Visitation notebooks record names of house occupants, family details, illnesses, special needs. In red ink he noted the text he had expounded and any conversation on spiritual matters. He was known to visit those who were ill several times a day and made the dying a special concern. His notebooks contain neat diagrams of the streets of the parish with names, details of families, and even his own prayers for their spiritual welfare. McCheyne worked his parish with devotion and zeal, sustained by a profound sense of responsibility to Christ, the head of the Church.[4]

Like autumn winds over Scottish hills.

Horatius Bonar's most enduring literary contribution is to be found in his better hymns. It was the 1870s before hymns were generally tolerated within the Free Church of Scotland. Significantly one of his best hymns, 'Here O my Lord, I see Thee face to face', was written to be *read* at the end of a Communion service in his brother's church at Greenock. Bonar was a careful scholar, familiar with Chaucer, Spenser, Milton, Shakespeare, Scott and Coleridge.[5] Opinions differ about the quality of his productions. They have been called melancholy, solemn, plaintive, 'like autumn winds over Scottish hills', though the deaths of five of the nine children born to the Bonars reinforced the sombre notes in a temperament naturally quiet, even withdrawn. More critical is the judgement that his hymns are 'diffuse, loosely constructed, feeble stanzas, halting rhythm, defective rhyme, meaningless iteration'.[6] But they were hymns 'for a preacher's purpose', one defender suggests. Certainly many of them seek to explain various religious moods and to explore theological truth. Consequently some of them are little more than versified dogma. In others, good ideas are weakened by being overspun so that many have to be substantially reduced to give them a tighter structure. Some editors even feel compelled to rearrange verses so that the climax is not wasted by a further two or three verses. Many compositions were written on scraps of paper, numerous notebooks, even old envelopes, and rarely changed afterwards. Others were written in railway carriages or while hill-walking.

The demand created by Moody and Sankey for gospel songs stimulated such productions as 'Rejoice and be glad' and 'Yet there is room', but because he was careless of dates, or circumstances, many hymns are difficult to place in his own experience. Yet there are some intriguing clues. Sometimes an aphorism from

Augustine, Jerome, Virgil or Paul provides the seed thought. One particularly atmospheric poem was inspired by the eerie dangerous sea-fog around St Abb's Head on the south-east coast of Scotland. Another was written almost as a poetic equivalent of Mendelssohn's Hebridean Overture. On holiday in Oban in Argyllshire, he wrote 'Fingal's Cave', which begins with the poetically unpromising line, 'Booming in, booming in!', but becomes a well observed word picture of the waves crashing in on Staffa.

One other feature, important because it balances the world-denying tone of many of Bonar's hymns and poems, is the occasional happily contented note. One humorous effect was inspired by the sight of his brother Andrew, at the time Moderator of the General Assembly of the Free Church of Scotland (an office to be carried with proper dignity), trying to rescue a duck floundering in a mud pond without falling in himself. One verse gives the flavour:

His valour in a moment cooled
  At touch of that dark ooze;
He would have risked his life to save
  But could not risk his shoes!

(H p. xxxvii)

Other joyful celebrations of life can be found in such hymns as 'Summer Gladness', 'Praise goeth up to Thee' and 'The Fountainhead of Beauty'. This last hymn explores the changed attitude of the born again believer to the created world, and it is unhesitatingly positive. Before conversion:

The tide's great ebb and flow, to me
Was speech, and psalm and ministrelsy;
O musical and mighty sea . . .

Now, with the simplicity and innocence of childhood restored, he can look on the world in the light of the cross and still see it 'Bright with the undefiled':

And shall I cease to love you now,
Ye hills above, ye rocks below,
Because I see your beauty flow
  From God the only wise?

(H pp. 164–5)

The love I need is righteous love.

Bonar and McCheyne were committed to pastoral evangelism based on the twin premises of man's lost condition and God's free offer of grace. Bonar asked bluntly, 'Is man a totally and thoroughly depraved being by nature? Is he ruined, helpless, blind, dead in trespasses and sin?' Using a favourite metaphor, he answered his own question, 'Man is bankrupt; totally so; his credit in the market has gone' (GWP p. 14). Sin constitutes more than moral aberration; it arises, not from social disadvantage, nor from ignorance, nor is it a temporary handicap in the slow but sure advancement of man on his ethical pilgrimage. Sin is an infinite debt, an ineradicable blot on the soul. 'One single transgression of a soul is ineffaceable. Once done it stands; and with it stands its penalty. To efface the ineffaceable! To eradicate the ineradicable! How vain and hopeless!'[7] Yet the essence of sin lies deeper than moral pollution. Sin is an act which violates the relationship between creature and Creator. The legitimate authority of a holy, sovereign and loving God is flouted by a personality inherently, and without radical renewal, incurably rebellious:

Infinite, infinite
  Sin upon sin,
Sin of not loving Thee,
Sin of not trusting Thee,
  Infinite sin.

(H p. 139)

Though Bonar understood the atoning death of Christ in the apparently impersonal terms of transaction, he was profoundly aware of God's dealings with humanity as personal. Sin is not merely to make a wrong moral choice; it is by its very nature an act of loveless and faithless rejection of God and the gospel offer of a completed atonement. It involves a deliberate stepping outside of grace into the sphere and penalty of lawlessness. For Bonar the love and holiness of God are held in harmonic tension. God is 'holy yet loving; the love not interfering with the holiness, nor the holiness with the love; absolutely sovereign, yet infinitely gracious; the sovereignty not straitening the grace nor the grace relaxing the sovereignty . . .' (GWP pp. 33, 51). Where the nature of God and the demand of his law is concerned there is no room for negotiation. God must be consistent with his own holy character; the law's demands must be met, otherwise the essential expression of the will of God could be violated with impunity. The gospel not only reveals the heart of God it manifests the righteousness of God. 'It is not by incarnation, but by blood-shedding that we are saved' (GWP 65). The exacting demand of divine law is established beyond argument in a long sombre hymn:

No, not the love without the blood;
  That were to me no love at all;
It could not reach my sinful soul,
  Nor hush the fears which me appal.

The love I need is righteous love,
  Inscribed on the sin-bearing tree,
Love that exacts the sinner's debt,
  Yet, in exacting, sets him free.

Love boundless as Jehovah's self,
  Love holy as His righteous law,
Love unsolicited, unbought,
  The love proclaimed at Golgotha.
(HFH III p. 101)

The love of God proclaimed on Golgotha must not be weakened into mere demonstration; the cross reveals the wrath of God against sin, borne by Christ in the sinner's place. Consciousness of such holy love and penal suffering should awaken sinners both to their danger and to the only source of safety in the righteous love of God.

The wrath of God, the reality of hell and the imminent return of Christ were given graphic and explicit treatment in the sermons of McCheyne and Bonar. If a soul was to be awakened to 'its perilous condition', then an honest statement of the spiritual facts was in order. McCheyne, reviewing his first four years in Dundee, suggested that since he came, some souls had been converted, some had climbed a rung or two of Jacob's ladder, others were four years nearer heaven, but others were four years nearer hell! The blinding and deceiving power of sin obscures the eternal consequences of evil and exaggerates the immediate pleasure of gratification. 'Alas', McCheyne complained, 'you think sin freedom, though it is forging chains for your soul . . . sweet though it is the very wormwood of hell . . . light though it is the source of the blackness of darkness' (Y p. 212). To those who ignored the gospel warnings he dared, 'Go on, love the world; grasp every pleasure; gather heaps of money; feed and fatten your lusts; take your fill. What will it profit you when you lose your soul?'[8]

These negative warning notes were balanced by a constant appeal to the sovereign love of God most fully exercised in the work of atonement. The forensic basis of reconciliation, the origins of salvation in the electing love of God and the believer's response in taking God at his word and believing the gospel, provided Bonar and McCheyne with a solid doctrinal foundation on which to build a life of personal devotion and uncalculating service. Their spirituality, though warmly affective and revealing a sense of vital and personal communion with God, was nevertheless anchored in a theological system which unashamedly used the contractual language of the legal transaction. 'On our part there is the believing; on God's part, the imputing or reckoning. We believe, He imputes; and the whole transaction is done, the blood washes off our guilt; the righteousness presents us before God as legally entitled to the position of righteousness which our Surety holds, as being Himself not merely the righteous One, but Jehovah OUR Righteousness.'[9]

O you that are in Christ, prize Him!

McCheyne greatly admired the letters of the Scottish seventeenth-century divine, Samuel Rutherford, and the influence is obvious in the sermons and letters. He used images familiar to any reader of Rutherford; honey to describe 'sweet' emotions, sunlight to describe warmth of feeling and well-being of soul, embracing and reclining as expressions of spiritual intimacy, and overall a tone of confidential joy in the presence of the 'Altogether Lovely One'. A source critic would be hard put to distinguish Rutherford from McCheyne in a sentence like this: 'Live much in the smile of God. Bask in his beams . . . Let your soul be filled with a heart-ravishing sense of the sweetness and excellency of Christ' (B p. 293).

McCheyne's style has been called 'winsome', exhibiting an 'almost feminine quality', indicating a spirituality in which feelings of love and longing were creatively integrated with intellect and activity. McCheyne seemed to have a heightened awareness of the reality and near presence of Christ, and sensed in him a fragrance and loveliness that was breathtaking in power and attraction. The suffering of the crucified Jesus kindled an ardour and devotion he could sometimes barely contain. He declared, 'If there were ten thousand other ways of pardon, I would pass them all by and flee to Him.' He could never erase the knowledge that 'Christ held down his head for shame on account of my sin so that I may hold up my heart in peace on account of His righteousness', so he urged his church members, 'You that are in Christ prize Him! You that are in doubt solve it by running to Him! You that are out of Him, choose Him now!' (Y pp. 97, 208).

In his search for an adequate vocabulary he resorted to the Song of Solomon. In eight years of ministry it is significant that this was the Old Testament book he preached on most after Psalms and Isaiah. Amongst Evangelical preachers it was a favourite hunting ground for texts which celebrated the joy, rapture and lightheartedness of love. In keeping with orthodox exegesis the book was understood as an allegory of the love between Christ and the redeemed soul, or, depending on the text, between Christ and the Church. 'There is no book that more thoroughly tests the depth of a man's Christianity . . . it is filled with the tenderest breathings of believer and Saviour.'[10] In various sermons the soul of the believer is likened to a garden which is sown, tended and watered by Christ. Song of Sol. 8.13–14: 'I sleep but my heart waketh', becomes an exhortation to early rising, prayer and a 'keeping of trysting times'; the finest example, 'Christ and the Believer', is an exploration of personal religion in which the rhetorical, figurative and pleading elements of McCheyne's preaching are seen at their best.[11]

The Gospels were a more obvious source for the raw material of devotion. In a prolonged meditation on the love of Jesus he let his imagination interpret the gospel story. 'Travelling to Bethlehem I see love incarnate . . . Tracking his steps as he went about doing good, I see love labouring . . . Visiting the home of Bethany I see love sympathising. Standing by the grave of Lazarus I see love weeping . . . passing on to Calvary I see love suffering, bleeding, expiring. The whole scene of His life is but an unfolding of the deep, awful, and precious mystery of redeeming love' (Y p. 233). McCheyne interrupted the meditation with a characteristic appeal. 'No more sit unmelted under that wondrous love which burns with so vehement a flame', and avoiding the implication that Christ is love and God is a wrathful sovereign requiring to be placated, he places the whole enterprise of salvation within the loving heart of God. 'Christ is not the originator but the gift of this love; he is not the cause but the exponent of it' (Y pp. 233–4). In a crisp sentence he demonstrated neat theological balance. 'Love is the fulfilling of the law; God is love; Christ is God.'[12]

O love of God how strong and true.

Bonar's hymns offer a more objective statement of the possibilities and purposes of the divine love. There is still a persistent individualism but it is usually accompanied by substantial theological statement. Like many of his hymns, 'O Love of God how strong and true' has benefitted from editorial pruning though compilers differ in their inclusions. The best verses are those which use unexpected words and ideas, which may not work too successfully as poetry but attract attention and insist on being sung thoughtfully:

O Love of God, how strong and true!
Eternal and yet ever new,
Uncomprehended and unbought,
Beyond all knowledge and all thought.

O love of God, how deep and great!
Far deeper than man's deepest hate;
Self-fed, self-kindled like the light,
Changeless, eternal, infinite.

(H p. 76)

Most of the ten verses of the original explain where this love is most clearly 'read'. But none of them have the arresting power of that disturbing phrase . . . 'deeper than man's deepest hate'. Where hatred is at its most destructive, where the depths of evil threaten to extinguish all light, there the self-fed, self-kindled love of God shines, and for Horatius Bonar as for Murray McCheyne its source was the cross.

The substitutionary view of the death of Jesus caused no embarrassment to preachers who generally avoided the cruder pictures of a loving Christ accepting punishment for the world's sins to placate a wrathful God.[13]

Thy cross not mine, O Christ,
Has borne the awful load
Of sins, that none in heaven
Or earth could bear, but God.

(H p. 46)

'But God.' In that telling qualification Bonar held the cross and the love of God together in the suffering of Jesus. While McCheyne never understated the cross as the centre of all Christian experience, more than Bonar he was caught up in the wonder and loveliness of Jesus and shared in sermons and letters a faith glowing with gratitude. McCheyne dwelt upon the subjective experience of an objective atonement, Bonar explored the mystery itself, admittedly with frequent use of the first person pronoun, but with a tone less intense. A hymn popular in Bonar's own day explores well the relationship between subjective feeling and objective truth:

My love is ofttimes low,
My joy still ebbs and flows;
But peace with Him remains the same,
No change Jehovah knows

That which can shake the cross
May shake the peace it gave,
Which tells me Christ has never died,
Or never left the grave

Till then my peace is sure,
It will not, cannot yield;
Jesus, I know, has died and lives;
On this sure rock I build.

I change, He changes not,
The Christ can never die;
His love, not mine, the resting place,
His truth, not mine, the tie.

The cross is still unchanged . . .

(H p. 100)

The point is established early; inner feelings fluctuate but God is constant. The unthinkable is suggested, that the cross, so pivotal in the divine purpose of salvation should be shaken, and the crucifixion and resurrection be reversed. But that is impossible, for what holds the Christian securely within the love of God is not feeling but the established facts of the gospel; love is the resting place, but it is truth that is the tie. For Bonar the love of God expressed in Christ crucified is irreversible truth, making the cross the believer's guarantee of eternal life. Two short simple verses summarize what for him were the essential facts of salvation:

Bearer of sin, He came to earth,
Though rich, for us becoming poor,
God manifest in flesh for us,
Our lot of darkness to endure.

'Tis finished: He has done it all;
Peace He has made 'twixt earth and heaven
That cross proclaims the Father's love,
The cancelled debt, the sin forgiven.[14]

Love not the world that hated Him!

Antipathy towards the world of human affairs pervades Bonar's poetry. There is an almost pathological fear in the first verse of a hymn innocuously entitled 'Passing Through':

I walk as one who knows that he is treading
  A stranger soil,
As one round whom a serpent-world is spreading
  Its subtle coil.

(H p. 63)

The moral catastrophe of a blighted Eden haunts the writer, who goes on to speak of 'breathing ungenial air', walking on 'plains of danger' and passing along in 'haste and fear'. An attitude of suspicion generates countless phrases, equally negative: 'this mass of human sin', 'the world's bewitching melodies', 'hell's sophistries' and 'earth's hot haunts of riot'. Various images are used to reinforce his sense of alienation; 'grim cities', 'dark crags', 'rugged hills', 'bleak muirs', 'deep mist settling darkly down' and 'Chill moorland where the flowers are few', have a theological rather than a topographical significance. Many of Bonar's hymns display homesickness, a chronic suspicion of life, a wistfulness that seems world-denying and jaundiced. After admitting he is 'least at home upon this earth' he by-passes life in the world to enlarge on the glory of heaven:

Most at home amid the glory
  Of the everlasting throne;
Most at home amid the splendour
  Of the one unsetting sun.

Most at home amid the praises
  Of the never silent throng;
Who through ages of the ages
  Sing their never-jarring song.

Most at home in heaven . . . [15]

The world crucified Jesus, it is the sphere of spiritual conflict for Christians and by unbelief seeks to undermine the truth of the gospel. Bonar's negative view of the world was reinforced by all of these perceptions, but it was his belief in the pre-millennial return of Christ which provided the theological rationale for his world-rejecting stance.

Firstly, Bonar held the unbelieving world responsible for the death of Jesus, not simply in historical but in theological terms; the world remains at enmity with God. The hatred that crucified Jesus still governs the behaviour of an unbelieving world, making an alliance with the Christian's heart impossible. As Bonar reminded the Christian disciple:

Him whom ye love it smote,
The Christ that died for you:
Love not the world that hated Him;
The world Thy Lord that slew.

(HFH III p. 93)

A second reason for Bonar's antipathy arose from the theological perspective he shared with McCheyne. Christian life is a battle against sin. Conflict is inevitable, unrelenting and spiritually perilous, involving a 'life-long battle with all evil things'. In the 'War Song of the Church', Christians are urged to 'Rise! Arm! Fight!', for 'Life with death and death with life,/Closes now in deadly strife'. As encouragement to the 'warriors of the crown and cross' he issued a call to militant heroism:

Spare not toil, nor blood nor pain,
  Not a stroke descends in vain:
Wounded, still no foot we yield
  On this ancient battle-field.

(H p. 129)

The same embattled spirituality is encountered in McCheyne's letters and sermons. In a pastoral circular to his church he observed, 'The most of God's people are contented to be saved from the hell that is without. They are not so anxious to be saved from the hell that is within' (B p. 236). Sanctification consists in the mortification of sin, slaying sin by killing it at its source. But that is never entirely achievable so long as the Christian lives in a sinful world and inhabits 'a body of sin'. The Christian is vulnerable to spiritual attack and moral subversion from the world because: 'Every natural heart is a wilderness – a dead place without a drop of water; and then all natural hearts put together make up a wilderness world' (B p. 302). 'Do not think then', warned McCheyne, 'any sin trivial; remember it will have everlasting consequences' (B p. 289). McCheyne distinguished between the natural unconverted heart, the awakened heart (aware of sin and judgement) and the believing heart (which closes with and cleaves to Christ). Like Bonar, he saw the world as the life of natural man organized in opposition to God, and bringing pressure to bear on the sworn allegiance of the child of God.

I ask a perfect creed.

In his Moderator's Address to the Free Church of Scotland in 1883, Bonar was in pugnacious mood. 'Every revealed truth has a distinct personal claim to be believed, however offensive to the taste or spirit of the age. Truth never demands a vote' (P p. 230). In a closing broadside he refused to countenance any accommodation of the gospel to the intellectual preferences of the prevailing culture:

> Our advanced thinkers and men of expansion demand a Christ for the nineteenth century, but . . . it must be either the first-century cross, the first century Gospel, the first-century Christ, or no cross, no Gospel, no Christ at all. A cultured world now calls aloud for a cultured Christ, and refuses its allegiance to any other; but there shall no other Christ be given but the son of the carpenter . . . who was wounded for our transgressions, and bruised for our iniquities . . .
>
> (P p. 231)

He distrusted deeply 'the ever-shifting changes and contradictions of public opinion', 'the effacement of ancient landmarks and the slackening of the most trusted keystones'. He sensed an enemy of the gospel in the progressive thinking of his age, an enemy 'fertile in stratagem' with an extended front, shifting positions and 'his ambuscades multiplying on all sides'. He commented sadly, 'Faith in our day is sometimes shallow; unbelief has gone down deep.' The threat an unbelieving world posed to the truth of the gospel then suggests another reason for Bonar's world-rejecting stance.

When Bonar delivered the above addresses he was seventy-five. But he was not simply voicing the sour sentiments of an aged and nostalgic divine. The tone and content were entirely consistent with Bonar's thought from the beginning of his ministry. In his poem on the Great Exhibition of 1851, studied sarcasm combines with a fervent impatience for the glory of heaven to produce a poem which documents powerfully the profound antipathy with which some Evangelicals viewed the advances of science. He contrasts the transient glitter of the earthly city with the enduring splendour of the City of God. The first line, describing the great glass exhibition hall, is unmistakably ironic: 'Ha! yon burst of crystal splendour'; it is like 'Arabia's matchless palace', and it is built to house 'all creation's jewelry', 'earth's uncovered waste of riches', 'forms of beauty, shapes of wonder, Trophies of triumphant toil'. Yet the writer detects a mood of hubris pervading this man-centred celebration:

From the crowd, in wonder gazing,
   Science claims the prostrate knee:
This her temple, diamond blazing,
   Shrine of her idolatry . . .

Listen to her tale of wonder,
   Of her plastic, potent spell,
'Tis a big and braggart story,
   Yet she tells it fair and well.

(H p. 16)

Eight years later, Darwin published *The Origin of Species*. By the late nineteenth century people like Bonar sensed the baleful implications for a theology of divine sovereignty and human fallenness. According to Bonar, the human intellect is fallen; its processes, its values and its conclusions are all provisional and subject to truth as revealed in the Bible. Yet Bonar clearly knew the unsettling effects of doubt and spoke movingly of the loss of the believing heart, 'a heavy sense of loss – of a treasure lost – lost in the crowd, lost in business and bustle, lost in strife, lost in pleasure and politics – too thoroughly lost to be recovered, and far too priceless to be replaced by anything else'. And in a world that was becoming more impressed by visible, empirical 'scientific' knowledge, he warned that in such an atmosphere of radical questioning: 'Invisible personalities lose all reality, and Him who is infinitely personal, the King eternal, immortal, and invisible, we often find the most difficult to realise' (P p. 227). It is from a heart honestly afraid of losing its bearings that the prayer CREDO, NON OPINOR is offered:

I ask a perfect creed!
  Oh that to me were given
The teaching that leads none astray,
  The scholarship of heaven;

Sure wisdom and pure light,
  With lowly, loving fear;
The steadfast ever-looking eye,
  The ever-listening ear;

The one whole truth I seek
  In this sad age of strife,
The truth of Him who is the Truth,
  And in whose truth is life.

(H p. 104)

Bonar believed truth was a moral issue. 'Error injures, truth heals; error is the root of sin, truth of purity and perfection' (GWH p. 8). Whether the error was in the scientific conclusions of unbelievers, or in false teaching within the Church, the only remedy was to be led into truth by the Spirit of truth. Belief and ethics, doctrine and spirituality, must be interwoven in the same fabric. Sound theology is to be acted out in life. 'It should give to the Christian character and bearing a divine erectness and simplicity; true dignity of demeanour, without pride or stiffness or coldness; true strength of will without obstinacy, or caprice, or waywardness. The higher the doctrine is, the more ought it to bring us into contact with the MIND of God, which is "the truth" and with the WILL of God which is "the law" ' (GWH p. 195). Such truth is not arrived at by mere reflection, prayer and Bible study, important as they are. Truth is the gift of the

Spirit of truth, that 'workman within, quickening, fashioning, moulding, all things to His will – bringing every part of the soul into contact with the truth that is without, by means of the pressure of His own hand from within' (O p. 110). It is a Christian duty to defend such truth against a world which has 'a secret preference for doubt', 'rejects finality and completeness' and regards faith as 'a restraint upon thought, not an instrument for its development' (P p. 228). 'We would be advanced thinkers too but our thinking should be in deepening sympathy with the mind of God, and fuller understanding of His never obsolete Word. We would be progressing theologians but not at the expense of truth and soundness' (P p. 229).

Behold I come quickly!

Bonar was one of a growing number of Evangelicals influenced by a resurgent pre-millennial interpretation of the second coming of Christ. The world-denying attitude so prevalent in Bonar originated in his eschatology. Pre-millennial theology held that the physical, visible return of Christ would precede the establishing of the millennial Kingdom in which Christ and his saints would reign for a thousand years before the consummation of all things. The years between the first and second advent were understood as the 'last days', as days of grace when the elect would be saved but also evil days when the world would descend into ever-increasing wickedness until, by the catastrophic intervention of God, Christ would return, evil be overthrown, and the reign of Christ established. The signs of such all-pervasive evil were numerous and obvious to alert and discerning saints, and predictive prophecy based on observed events became a new pastime of the pious.

Post-millennial theology, widely regarded as the orthodox view at the beginning of the nineteenth century, held by contrast that the preaching of the gospel by Spirit-empowered preachers would lead to the inauguration of the Kingdom of God which would last a thousand years and then would follow the bodily return of Jesus. The differences went deeper though. Post-millennialists tended to look with optimism on the world of affairs. Missionary activity gave the human contribution to the spread of the gospel a significant role in the purpose of God so that revivals and missionary advances were viewed as signs of progress towards the conversion of the world. Such a theology fitted well with the spirit of the later nineteenth century. As post-millennial thinking moved closer to secular ideas of progress many Evangelicals moved to a pre-millennial position, finding that reading of the world more accordant with biblical fact and historical events.

The revival of pre-millennialism is closely associated with the meteoric but tragic life of Edward Irving. Deeply influenced by Romanticism, especially as exemplified by Coleridge (one of Bonar's favourites), Irving became critical of what he saw as the stultifying influence of Enlightenment thinking on religious life, and reacted in favour of a religion in which emotion, spontaneity and immediacy were regarded as equally valid in articulating experience. The new prophetic interpretation of world history in pre-millennial terms which emerged from Irving and his circle gradually won widespread acceptance amongst Evangelicals. McCheyne attended a meeting in Edinburgh in 1829 and took careful notes of Irving's address. He later noted ruefully in his diary 'The horror of some good people in Glasgow at the millenarian views is very great, while at the same time their objections seem very weak' (B p. 124). Bonar, too, was an out-and-out pre-millennialist. His first sermon in Kelso and his last sermon in Edinburgh fifty-two years later contained the text 'Behold I come quickly!'[16]

The pessimistic world-view of pre-millennialism coloured Bonar's whole attitude to Christian living and the world of human affairs. Darkness, gathering clouds, the anguished cry of a travailing creation and countless other metaphors cover his writing with an apocalyptic shadow. The period between Christ's birth and the second coming are, in the purpose of God, years of antichristianity:

> During it, God's object seems to be, to allow human and Satanic wickedness to evolve and overflow to the uttermost. In former dispensations he tried many a check, but all failed; and now he has let loose creature lawlessness and evil, in order that, when it has reached its height, he may effectually interpose to arrest it, by sending his own Son into the world, to destroy Antichrist and to bind Satan. Then, under the righteous rule of Jesus and His Bride, shall holiness be established, iniquity swept away, and peace shed its vernal gladness over the long desolations of earth.
>
> (O p. 122)

That is a succinct summary of the pre-millennial hope. Expanding it further, Bonar exulted, 'What deliverance and joy! Christ upon the throne, Antichrist in the abyss, and Satan bound in chains! The saints exalted and glorified, the wicked trodden down and put to shame! The curse removed, Paradise restored, Israel gathered, the Gentiles converted, creation blessed, and Jehovah in the person of Immanuel taking up his everlasting abode with the children of men' (O p. 123).

Such an explicit hope, embodied in powerful biblical imagery, inevitably gave Bonar's mind a forward-looking cast. Added to his hostility to the world and suspicion of progressive thought was a yearning that remained unappeased, and an impatience to move beyond this world to the nearer presence of Christ. That his attitude was world-denying is beyond argument, but it was a denial born of an imaginative vision of a different world, a world restored to the glory God originally intended. So he comforted himself, 'It is but a little while . . . One more outburst of the warring winds, and then the earth's storms are hushed, and the long dissonances of time melt into the one harmony of creation's boundless song' (O p. 124).

The breathings of God's heart.

Near the end of his life, McCheyne published *Daily Bread*, a calendar for reading the Bible through in one year. It was intended to encourage a disciplined, consistent reading of the whole Bible, and reflected something of his own practice. In fact one of his notebooks contains similar plans for reading the whole Bible through in one and two months! 'We must be driven more to our Bible and the mercy seat', he urged. He warned against formality, self-righteousness and the danger of 'living without any divine work in the soul – unpardoned, unsanctified and ready to persist – yet spending appointed times in secret and family devotion'. 'This', he said with little concession to tact, 'is going to hell with a lie in the right hand.' He further warned against careless reading, but told those who found the plan too exacting to 'throw aside the fetter, and feed at liberty in the garden of God' (B pp. 618–28).

'I love the word of God and find it sweetest nourishment to my soul', he wrote to Bonar. His handwritten sermon and Bible study notes show how he took texts, phrases or just one word and ruminated, examined cross references, and gradually shaped and moulded the passage till it spoke to him of Christ. 'All, all tell of Jesus . . . Jesus pervades the Bible . . . it is the standing witness to Jesus' (Y p. 198). He encouraged the practice of praying the Bible by going through the daily portion saying such prayers as, 'O Lord, give me the blessedness of . . .' (B p. 50). This he believed was the 'best way of knowing the meaning of the Bible, of learning to pray', and of knowing God, for 'the words of the Bible are just the breathings of God's heart', and to study them is to become intimate with God (Y p. 196).

McCheyne measured his spiritual vitality by the enjoyment and help he gained from regular reading of Scripture. He confessed in his diary, 'Humble purpose-like reading omitted. What plant can be unwatered and not wither?' Christian growth requires spiritual nourishment, indeed food for thought, for it is the assimilation of the truth of God that enables the believer to begin 'to comprehend with all the saints what is the height and depth and length and breadth, and to know the love of God that passes knowledge.' At university McCheyne and the Bonars had been part of an exegetical society in which they freely used their facility in the original biblical languages. But all such critical study was firmly put in its subordinate place. His diary records 'Biblical criticism. This must not supersede heart work' (B p. 21).

Both men encouraged a comprehensive reading of the Bible, including the barren genealogies and 'all the bloody battles which are chronicled'. Bonar warned against a 'vitiated spiritual taste' arising from selective Bible reading and urged that 'the whole soul be fed by the study of the whole Bible . . . that there be no irregularity nor inequality in the growth of its parts and powers' (GWH p. 193). Every part of the Bible is given for blessing. McCheyne, again using imagery reminiscent of Rutherford, wrote to comfort a bereaved friend: 'The Bible is like the leaves of the lemon tree – the more you bruise and wring them the sweeter the fragrance they may throw around' (B p. 322).

During the period between McCheyne's death and Bonar's later years critical study of the Bible advanced swiftly.[17] Much of Bonar's writing was defensive, and intended to reassure Christians of the trustworthiness and unassailable authority of the Bible.[18] 'Each word in the Bible is to be dealt with as a sacred thing, a vessel of the sanctuary, not to be lightly handled or profanely mutilated, but to be received just as it stands. There may be passages difficult to reconcile, doctrines which apparently conflict with each other . . . but God has spoken them . . . they cannot really be at variance with each other. The day is coming when we shall fully understand their harmony.'[19] So Bonar accepted that difficulties existed, but they were to be put up with until critical scholarship was rendered redundant, its conclusions superseded by an eschatological unveiling of the mind and purpose of God. As Moderator he defied the critics: 'We add nothing to, and we subtract nothing from, the perfection of that profoundest of profound volumes, but we make daily discoveries of its depths. We do not pretend to prop it up as if it were on any side giving way; we confide in it as a fortress impregnable against all assault.'[20]

Here grasp with firmer hand the eternal grace.

When McCheyne linked Bible reading and prayer he was reflecting a background in which family devotions and personal piety still had a formative influence in the home. At St Peter's he encouraged 'prayer concerts', deliberately arranged occasions when the congregation met together for brief Bible exposition and corporate prayer. At their peak, attendances reached eight hundred. Prayer was more an attitude than a regular duty, and though McCheyne was meticulous about the regularity of his own devotions, his ideal was to develop 'the habit of looking upward all the day, and drawing down gleams from the reconciled countenance' (B p. 55). Nevertheless the early hours were of primary importance as a time to set the day's priorities. Bonar also commended the practice of early rising:

Begin the day with God!
He is thy sun and day;
He is the radiance of thy dawn,
To Him address thy lay.

Take thy first meal with God!
He is thy heavenly food;
Feed with and on Him; He with thee
Will feast in brotherhood.

(H p. 98)

McCheyne used maps and 'missionary intelligence' to widen the scope of his and his people's prayers, convinced that prevailing prayer and mission are profoundly connected in the divine purpose. Put simply, he believed prayer worked: 'If the veil of the world's machinery were lifted off, how much we would find done in answer to the prayers of God's children' (B p. 93). The same large-hearted impulse is evident in Bonar. His hymn 'Intercession' is reminiscent of the careful inclusiveness of some of Bishop Andrewes' intercessions:

> Pray for thy friends: let the full heart go out
> For all thou lovest here; forget not one:
> Count o'er the precious names; nor let a doubt
> Obtrude that God upon thy cry can frown.

There is nothing selfish in praying for those he loves. In any case God is a willing listener who recognizes some of the hesitations ordinary people feel. Prayer should be offered:

> For the dear Church of God thy prayers prolong,
> The one wide family of God below . . .
> For all the many members of that throng,
> And for each fellow-pilgrim lone and faint;
> Known or unknown, the feeble or the strong,
> For each hard-pressed and sorrow-stricken saint.

Perhaps a man of Bonar's reserve, who had lost five children, was more sensitive than most to the need for the prayers of unknown fellow-pilgrims, and he goes on to urge prayers asking the God of health to make a wounded world whole.

> Plead for the advent of the promised king,
> The reign of heavenly glory here on earth,
> The budding of the world's eternal spring,
> The coming of creation's second birth.
> (H pp. 165–66)

Here intercession is placed firmly within the advent hope, thereby raising the gaze of faith beyond earth to the altogether further horizon of God's ultimate purpose in the consummation of all things. In that sense all of life was felt to be provisional; until he come!

Holy Communion, with its special season, has long held a special place in Scottish spiritual life. Both Bonar and McCheyne made full use of the Communion service as a time of spiritual reflection. One of the first major changes McCheyne made when he went to Dundee was to increase the number of Communion services from two to four each year. While observing the ordinance of the Lord's Supper as a corporate act, McCheyne valued the opportunity for personal communion between Christ and the soul. He noted in his diary: 'At the communion. Felt less use for the minister than ever. Let the Master of the feast alone speak to my heart' (B p. 25).

Communion Sunday was the climax of several days of spiritual preparation, followed in St Peter's by a Monday night thanksgiving service. The notes of solemnity, celebration and anticipation merged to generate powerful spiritual responses amongst the communicants.[21] In a beautiful communion meditation on Col. 1.21–3 he wondered out loud: 'Ah brethren, herein was infinite love. Infidels scoff at it – fools despise it; but it is the wonder of all heaven. The Lamb that was slain will be the wonder of all eternity. Today Christ is evidently set forth crucified among you. Angels, I doubt not, will look down in amazing wonder at that table. Will you look on with cold, unmoved hearts?'[22] 'That table' was meant to move cold hearts, and Evangelicals like McCheyne and the Bonars placed it at the centre of a penitent and wondering devotion. It was described as a 'lovely keepsake of Immanuel' and a 'sweet silent sermon' intended to break the heart, convert the sinner, reassure the believer and give nourishment to all who see the broken poured out Christ in the bread and wine.

The Scottish experience of the Communion season inspired some of Bonar's best poetry. The hymn, 'One Christ we feed upon, one living Christ', weaves a richly theological pattern around themes of life, health, feeding and satisfaction.

Thou with us, and Thou in us – this is life
  All that the Father is, in Thee we see:
O Christ of God, what art Thou not to us,
  And what of wealth is there we may not find in Thee!

On Thee alone I feed, of Thee I drink,
That into this sick soul the heavenly health may pour.

My life, my everlasting life art Thou,
  My health, my joy, my strength, I owe to Thee.

(H p. 218)

The connection between the cross, the communion and the health of the soul recurs in Bonar. The cross is 'Life's tree, its glorious wealth, laden with everlasting health', flowing out in healing and restoration. The image of the tree of life is quite deliberate and speaks of a restored Eden, reconciled communion and renewed creation, ideas which find adventurous expression in his description of the cross as the 'womb of nature's second birth'.

The personal communion of the believing soul with Christ is memorably unfolded in 'Here O my Lord, I see Thee face to face'. The mood conveys a sense of relaxed joy which is preserved from complacency by awareness of need, a sense of wondering love and wistful longing for the time when such fellowship will be complete and uninterrupted. For the present, bread and wine nourish the soul by bringing the Christian face to face with the mystery of saving love.

Here O my Lord, I see Thee face to face;
  Here would I touch and handle things unseen,
Here grasp with firmer hands the eternal grace,
  And all my weariness upon Thee lean.

Here would I feed upon the bread of God,
  Here drink with Thee the royal wine of heaven.
Here would I lay aside each earthly load,
  Here taste afresh the calm of sin forgiven.

Too soon we rise: the symbols disappear;
  The feast, though not the love, is past and gone;
The bread and wine remove, but thou art here,
  Nearer than ever, still my Shield and Sun.

(H p. 235)

Bonar lived fifty years longer than McCheyne, yet there is a remarkable degree of correspondence which belies the age difference. Their basic doctrinal position was largely dictated by the Westminster Confession, but kindled by an Evangelical fervour which grasped such highly charged theology and preached it for a verdict. Through evangelistic commitment and pastoral activism they gave full expression not only to their native gifts, but to a pastoral spirituality both devout and energetic. McCheyne died before the Disruption, but his intention to secede was clear, being, like Bonar, a staunch defender of the Church's freedom from external interference. The gospel they preached implied uncompromising rejection of 'the world', and envisaged a life of conflict and yet of consolation, a life of watchfulness against temptation balanced by the advent hope.

Bonar's negative response to the progress of contemporary thought, his firm rejection of a critical enterprise which claimed the right to do historical criticism free of dogmatic presuppositions and his lifelong pre-occupation with pre-millennial thinking, created a spirituality which was powerfully reactionary. Yet the same man was capable of gentleness, sensitivity and a spiritual warmth that remains immensely attractive when encountered in his best hymns.

To speculate on what McCheyne might have become is pointless, and needless. The impact of his short ministry set off vibrations still felt generations later. The assessment by a Free Church of Scotland professor is hardly impartial, but it eloquently conveys the view, at least amongst his friends, that the young minister of St Peter's summed up all that was best in Scottish Evangelicalism before the Disruption: 'McCheyne brought into the pulpit all the reverence for Scripture of the Reformation period; all the honour for the headship of Christ of the Covenanter struggle; all the freeness of the gospel offer of the Marrow theology; all the bright imagery of Samuel Rutherford; all the delight of the Erskines in the fulness of Christ.'[23]

Sources frequently cited

Bonar, A., *Memoirs and Remains of R. M. McCheyne*. Edinburgh 1966. (B)
Bonar, H., *Hymns by Horatius Bonar*. London 1904. (H)
——, *Hymns of Faith and Hope*, 3 vols. London 1871. (HFH)
——, *God's Way of Peace*. London 1861. (GWP)
——, *God's Way of Holiness*. London 1874. (GWH)
Oliphint, B. R., *Horatius Bonar*, Edinburgh PhD. Thesis 1951. (O)
Proceedings of the Assembly of the Free Church of Scotland, 1883. (P)
Yeaworth, *R. M. McCheyne*, Edinburgh PhD. Thesis 1955. (Y)

Additional reading

Blakey, R. S., *The Man in the Manse*. Edinburgh 1978.
Brown, S. J., *Thomas Chalmers and the Godly Commonwealth*. London 1982.
Cheyne, A. C., *The Transforming of the Kirk*. Edinburgh 1983.
——, 'The Bible and Change in the Nineteenth Century', ch. 12 in *The Bible in Scottish Life and Literature*, ed. D. Wright. Edinburgh 1988.

Drummond, A. L., and Bulloch, J., *The Scottish Church, 1688–1843*. Edinburgh 1973.

——, *The Church in Victorian Scotland, 1843–1874*. Edinburgh 1975.

——, *The Church in Late Victorian Scotland, 1874–1900*. Edinburgh 1978.

Hewat, K., *R. M. McCheyne: A View from the Pew*. Belfast 1987.

McCheyne, R. M., *Additional Remains*. Edinburgh 1857.

——, *A Basket of Fragments*. Aberdeen n.d.

MacInnes, J., *The Evangelical Movement in the Highlands of Scotland, 1688 to 1800* (Aberdeen 1951), pp. 79–196.

Memories of Dr Horatius Bonar, by Relatives and Public Men. Edinburgh 1909. New College Library, Edinburgh, holds many of McCheyne's manuscripts, including a large body of correspondence, both from and to McCheyne, various sermon notebooks, visitation pocketbooks and other important sources. Yeaworth lists approximately 300 unpublished sermons. His own biblical index of known sermons, and full listing of the correspondence are very useful.

Riesen, R. A., ' "Higher Criticism" in the Free Church Fathers', *Records of the Scottish Church History Society*, vol. xx, pp. 119–42.

Smellie, A., *Robert Murray McCheyne*. London 1913.

Tait, J., *Two Centuries of Scottish Church Border Life* (Kelso 1889), pp. 335–43.

Tulloch, J., *Movements of Religious Thought in Britain during the Nineteenth Century* (London 1885), Lecture iv.

Voges, F., 'Moderate and Evangelical Thinking in the Later Eighteenth Century: Differences and Shared Attitudes', *Records of the Scottish Church History Society*, vol. xxii, pp. 141–58.

Add Bibliography from RSCHS 1990.

Notes

1. Brown, *Thomas Chalmers*, p. 26.
2. Blakey, *The Man in the Manse*, p. 31.
3. Letter, 16 Nov. 1835.
4. The various McCheyne notebooks are primary examples of how one man practised his theology. The visitation notebooks are full of social and pastoral detail; the Bible study notes a fascinating view of a preacher's devotional discipline.
5. See Bonar, *Hymns*, Introduction, for further details of Bonar's methods and sources.
6. Julian, *Dictionary of Hymnology* (London 1892), p. 161.
7. H. Bonar, *Man, His Religion and His World* (London, n.d.). p. 52.
8. Sermon, Galatians 6.14, Oct. 1840.
9. H. Bonar, *The Everlasting Righteousness* (London 1873), p. 72.
10. MS Sermon, Song of Songs, Notebook iii, New College.
11. See also *Additional Remains*, pp. 210, 230; Bonar, *Memoir*, pp. 350, 378, 383, 454, 480.

12. Notebook xii, New College.
13. This has to be qualified by the use McCheyne made of the doctrine of hell in preaching. The doctrine of eternal punishment as God's righteous wrath on sin, and even his descriptive sermon on the mental agonies of hell, stay within orthodox theology. But his sermon on 'The Eternal Torment of the Wicked, Matter of Eternal Song to the Redeemed' is a doctrinal overstatement which is not only speculative, but attributes an attitude to the redeemed which the Bible nowhere attributes to God. See *A Basket of Fragments*, 6th edn (Aberdeen n.d.), pp. 298–347.
14. H. Bonar, *Until the Day Break*. (London 1890), p. 29.
15. ibid., pp. 114–15.
16. For further details on Irving and a clear presentation of the theological intricacies, see Bebbington, *Evangelicalism*, pp. 78–86; also 'The advent hope in British Evangelicalism since 1800', *Scottish Journal of Religious Studies*, vol. ix, No. 2 (Autumn 1988). For Simeon's view of Irving see Carus, p. 690. The pre-millennial position was viewed with great suspicion within Bonar's own communion which has tended to favour the amillennial position. There is a helpful general article by R. G. Clouse in the *Evangelical Dictionary of Theology*, ed. Elwell, 'Millennium'. In addition to Journal contributions Bonar developed a close connection with the Mildmay conferences, where pre-millennial thought was sympathetically expounded.
17. See the essays by Cheyne in *Bible in Scottish Life*, and by Riesen, 'Higher Criticism' *Records*.
18. See also Bebbington, *Evangelicalism*, pp. 86–91.
19. H. Bonar, *Truth and Error* (Edinburgh 1846), pp. 5f.
20. *Proceedings of Assembly*, p. 229.
21. See K. Hewat, *McCheyne from the Pew*, pp. 67–88, for a contemporary account of McCheyne's conduct of a 'Communion season'.
22. MS Sermon, Colossians 1.21–3, August 1841, New College.
23. W. G. Blaikie, *Preachers of Scotland* (Edinburgh 1888), p. 294.

6
ROBERT W. DALE and CHARLES H. SPURGEON

Grace transcends love.
DALE

1873 saw the publication of volume three of *The Treasury of David*, the magnum opus of Charles Haddon Spurgeon. Robert William Dale, then editor of *The Congregationalist*, was warmly appreciative. 'All that he writes is full of juice . . . We have never felt so strongly before how like he is to an old Puritan . . . He is very strong on those passages which express the experience of the human heart . . . where the exposition requires historical imagination he is less successful.[1] Two years later Spurgeon returned the compliment, together with the gentle criticism, in his *Commenting and Commentaries*. Dale's volume on Hebrews fell just short of an alpha rating: 'Daring and bold in thought, and yet for the most part warmly on the side of orthodoxy, his works command the appreciation of cultured minds'.[2] Spurgeon would gladly own the description of 'old Puritan', and Dale would not deny the qualification implied by the phrase 'for the most part'.

These two commanding figures share many incidental similarities. Their conversions followed a similar pattern of devout upbringing, anxious self-scrutiny and resolved crisis. Though neither had a typical theological education they became celebrated youthful preachers and after brief probationary periods, each gave a lifetime's ministry to a large city church. On separate occasions they caused offence to Church of England Evangelicals by charging them with inconsistency in holding Evangelical opinions and yet remaining in a church which, they claimed, taught baptismal regeneration.[3] Dale was involved in a defensive campaign on the side of orthodoxy against an over-enthusiastic liberalism given explicit voice at a Congregational conference at Leicester in 1877.[4] Spurgeon played a central part in a denominational crisis in 1887 following allegations concerning the 'downgrade' of Evangelical doctrine amongst ministers of the Baptist Union.[5] Politically both ministers were convinced supporters of the Liberal party, and entered into correspondence with its leader W. E. Gladstone.

In matters theological, Spurgeon was immutably orthodox and never felt the need to modify the Calvinist framework within which his spiritual life had developed. His spirituality stood on a bedrock of Calvinistic Puritanism, as defiant of modernity as any historical monument intended to bear witness to older, better values. Spurgeon did not mind the epithet Puritan. He was content to use the vocabulary and conceptuality of a bygone age because it answered to his own experience.

By contrast Dale's Evangelical orthodoxy became more and more suspect as he modified, redefined and finally rejected his Calvinist heritage. His first expository series of sermons on Romans created uproar. The doctrine of original sin and universal guilt by the imputation of Adam's sin upon the whole race, he declared 'unintelligible'. Against the harsher conclusions of a system which allowed for infant damnation he protested: 'I know not how to repress my indignation; there are no words strong enough to express my abhorrence, loathing and disgust' (D p. 113). In preaching, as in debate, Dale drove in nails so hard that he split the wood. By the time he reached the fifth chapter 'the congregation was like one great Bible Class: there was a Bible open in every hand . . . excitement deepened into alarm, and alarm rose to the height of panic'.[6]

He rejected the traditional interpretation of original sin and predestination because to him their moral implications were intolerable and their intellectual credibility no longer tenable. The challenge posed by biblical criticism, scientific advance and social change forced a man of Dale's intellectual bent to attempt a defensive restatement of Evangelical doctrine. With profound faith in the invulnerability of Christ the Truth, and in response to the prevailing winds of contemporary thought, Dale 'worked out his own salvation with fear and trembling'.[7] In direct contrast, Spurgeon was uncompromisingly hostile to 'the spirit of the age', suspicious of the intellectual and social changes which were becoming more and more unsympathetic to the old theology. Spurgeon's was a spirituality of conservation, of reverence for the past and of protest against the eroding forces of the present; Dale's was a spirituality of reconstruction, equally concerned to preserve, but prepared to use modern materials if they proved more durable.

The grandest moment in the moral history of God.

For ten years Dale was an only child, four other children dying soon after birth. An overanxious mother passionately intent on her son becoming a minister, and home relationships in which 'affection though tongue-tied and inarticulate was deep and strong', did nothing to help Dale overcome a shy temperament, an unathletic awkwardness and an overserious bookishness. At the age of fourteen he was reading Butler's *Analogy* and Paley's *Evidences* in a frantic search for religious certainty. The recollection of the influence exerted on his inner life at this time by James' *Anxious Enquirer* carries an unmistakeable note of remembered desperation. 'I read it on my knees and in keen distress about my personal salvation. Night after night I waited with eager impatience for the house to become still, that in undisturbed solitude I might agonize over the book which had taught so many to trust in God.'[8] Eventually after many 'metaphysical adventures' he found peace: 'At last – how I cannot tell – all became clear; I ceased thinking of myself and of my faith, and thought only of Christ; and then I wondered that I should have been perplexed for a single hour' (D p. 17).

Despite his growing popularity as a preacher, his first application for the ministry met with a discouraging lack of enthusiasm from his minister. For a time he worked as a schoolmaster, an experience which helped to dismantle some of his walls of reserve. Later he was accepted for training and became co-pastor with John Angell James at the influential Carr's Lane Church in Birmingham, becoming sole pastor on James' death in 1859.

During his co-pastorate he preached the sermons on Romans which marked the start of his controversial work of theological redefinition. In rejecting the Calvinist interpretation of original sin Dale had no intention of understating human guilt:

> The sins once committed remain a part of our moral history for ever. What is done cannot be undone . . . You may commit

> a sin tomorrow; it will be your sin, if you are still alive, thirty, forty, fifty years hence – yours when you are seventy though you committed it when you were five and twenty. You cannot escape from it. The malignant lie, the deliberate dishonesty, will cling to you, year after year, and you will not by any moral effort be able to throw it off.
>
> (E pp. 62–3)

Sin is not alien to human nature, nor is it confined in commission or consequences to the individual. There is, he argued, complicity in evil because humanity exists as a community of moral life. He retained an incisive appreciation of the substance of the doctrine of original sin even if he rejected its traditional verbal form: 'There are times when I cannot think of the sins, even of the grossest sins, of other men, as though I were wholly free from the guilt of them . . . we share a common life; there is a solidarity of the race in sin; and when I condemn other men, there are times when I feel that I am condemning myself . . .'[9]

His son recalled how Dale's denunciation of sin could generate overwhelming force: 'He never stormed; but his wrath, as it grew, glowed with passion at a white heat. It swept on waves of living fire. It seemed to scorch, to shrivel, to consume' (D p. 315). Dale saw no difficulty in ascribing such personal anger to God. Sin consists in the violation of the Law of Righteousness, it is an attack on the moral fabric of the universe, and as such it incurs the wrath of God. He reasoned: 'God cannot release His creatures from the obligation to reverence and obey Him . . . A God without moral resentment against sin would be a God not worth keeping . . . Resentment against sin is an element of the very life of God. It can no more be separated from God than heat from fire.'[10]

Divine resentment is expressed in punishment, which Dale conceived as a personal and deliberate act of God. A violated moral universe and human guilt demand a punishment which is both personal and a perfect expression of God's inalienable holiness. In the self-substitution of God Dale believed he held the key to the mystery of redemption, an understanding of the cross at once penal but with immense power to heal the conscience, convince the mind, and win the surrender of the heart: 'He himself, the Lord Jesus Christ, laid aside His Eternal Glory, assumed our nature, was forsaken of God, died on the cross, that the sins of men might be remitted. It belonged to Him to assert, by His own act, that suffering is the just result of sin. He asserts it, not by inflicting suffering upon the sinner, but by enduring suffering Himself' (D p. 715). Displaying the bold originality of which Spurgeon spoke, he explained, 'The mysterious unity of the Father and the Son rendered it possible for God at once to endure and to inflict penal suffering, and to do both under conditions which constitute the infliction and the endurance the grandest moment in the moral history of God' (D p. 715).

Spiritual truth in the intellect and spiritual life in the heart. 'The highest truth . . . it most concerns Christian men to know, is in Jesus. Truth can never be rightly known when separated from Him' (E p. 309). No new knowledge could threaten the central truths of Dale's faith because he placed his trust in the living Christ as daily experienced. In doing so he did not deny the importance of theological definition but he refused to give final authority to any formula of words. Still, the lure of truth attracted the mind of Dale and the description of his own teacher's love of a good question is equally apt when applied to Dale: 'He rose to it as a hungry trout, in the dusk of evening, rises to a favourite fly' (D p. 43).

Later in life he spoke with wise humility about the failure of human language to do justice to the mysteries of the faith. Reflecting on one of his early sermons, 'Not having my own righteousness', he confided to a lifelong friend: 'Of late it has come to me with such clearness and force that I feel I never knew it before; but I cannot put it; what I say seems to miss the best part of what I have seen' (D p. 536). So the intellectual preacher who had urged the students at Yale to gain 'a despotic control over all the intellectual faculties', was driven to admit the frailty of a language unable to bear the weight of glory. Just before his death he wrote to G. G. Findlay in praise of his commentary on Ephesians. He recalled the enrichment he experienced when writing his own commentary: 'Some parts of it intoxicated me . . . but when it came to writing what [I] had seen, the colours had faded and the glory was extinguished' (D p. 637).

Dale revealed his own literary conscience when he warned the Yale students: 'The morality of a minister consists very largely in the way in which he deals with thoughts and words . . . we must do our best to form a style that shall be an accurate expression of our inner thought and life' (NL p. 177). Amongst other criticisms of the Holiness Movement, he deplored the effeminate devotional language which was 'maudlin', 'morally perilous' and 'provokes positive disgust'. He took great offence at the phrase 'sweet Calvary', a term dripping with syrupy sentiment and obscuring the moral ugliness of sin, the bitter desolation of an abandoned God and the penal anguish endured for love of sinners. He castigated the slogan value of 'the blood', a term he felt was essentially pagan unless qualified by the name of Jesus Christ. No shorthand clichés were acceptable to the 1875 Congregational lecturer whose massive exposition of the atonement had fuelled a passion for the cross that tolerated no shallow emotionalism, no slick catch-phrases and no short-circuiting the scandal of penal substitution.[11]

Early in his ministry he warned, 'There is a more intimate connection than some of us, perhaps, are inclined to believe, between spiritual truth in the intellect and spiritual life in the heart' (D p. 108). He coveted a burning ardour, 'a logic of the heart' and complained: 'There are a great many very good people who seem unwilling to do anything for the maintenance of their religious life that requires the use of their understanding; as a result, their life suffers in depth and force' (D p. 661). He contended bluntly for congregations prepared to think. Advised that Carr's Lane would not stand long doctrinal sermons he had replied stubbornly, 'They'll have to like it'. In the last year of his life he was still pleading for a faith vitalized by profound experience, undergirded by careful definition and lifted above the mundane by soaring thought. Such faith would require each preacher to be a philosopher of the heart, a theologian familiar with Scripture and unintimidated by secular thought, one who would 'put in position on the summit of his granite walls, his heaviest artillery of Scripture and logic'.[12]

Words are essential to construct thought and communicate spiritual truth. The Christian mind must articulate experience and insight so that the Word again becomes flesh. But however conscientious in study and however rich in experience, the Christian, in seeking to share the vision, will always 'seem to miss the best part of what he has seen'. Yet Dale believed the effort must be made. The obligation to think hard and reflect deeply is integral to Christian obedience and though there are horizons which fade into mystery, sometimes glorious and sometimes unnerving, the elucidation of the gospel should still command the deepest devotion of the Christian mind.

The life which He makes ours.

Some time in the 1860s Dale passed through an Easter experience so momentous that it left its mark on him for the rest of his life. While writing an Easter sermon the reality of Christ's resurrection dawned on him with such power that it forced a re-alignment of theological priorities. Interrupted in his sermon preparation, he recalled: ' "Christ is alive", I said to myself; "alive"! and then I paused; – "alive"! and then I paused again; "alive"! Can that really be true? Living as really as I myself am? I got up and walked about repeating "Christ is living!" "Christ is living!" At first it seemed strange and hardly true, but at last it came upon me as a burst of sudden glory; yes, Christ is living. It was to me a new discovery' (D pp. 642–3). The living Christ, and the possibility of personal relationship to him as risen Lord became for Dale a dominant reality, a further source of theological power in his spiritual life.

Belief in the personal lordship of Christ exerts decisive moral control over every Christian life. Christ the moral ruler is not to be confined to history or remotely enthroned in heaven. As living Lord his precepts and commands are invested with regal authority now. Moral authority inspiring holy fear is a more effective motivation to obedience than a Christian's subjective feelings of gratitude to infinite love. By insisting on the moral law Dale refused to empty infinite love of moral seriousness. Where entire devotion to Christ is absent, God suffers 'the pain of an infinite love which is thwarted and repelled in its desire to bless men with perfect righteousness and perfect joy' (J p. 136). Grace is not less gracious because God refuses to relax his moral demand. Grace is seen in 'the exactingness of an infinite love, which cannot be content with anything less than our complete restoration to the image of the Divine holiness, and our perfect fellowship with the Divine joy'. By grace, 'that which God asks for He gives . . . Every precept is but the reverse of a promise; every command is but the prophecy of a grace' (J p. 136).

Dale did not believe that by an act of consecration the believer makes Christ Lord. By virtue of creation, incarnation, redeeming death and resurrection authority, Christ already is Lord. Every human life belongs to him, comes under his sovereign ownership and owes moral obedience to him alone. Christian saints are his slaves, 'not because their spirit was crushed by a tyrannical authority which they had no power or courage to resist, but because His divine majesty, His infinite love for them, and the glory of His personal perfection, kindled their imagination, commanded the homage of their conscience, and won their hearts' (C p. 395). Personal devotion to Christ means, 'he is enthroned over all the forces of our moral and spiritual nature' (C p. 396).

But Dale goes further. The actual life of God which was the source of Christ's living, becomes, by faith, the life of the Christian: 'This does not mean that we may become all that He was . . . What He was personally we cannot become; it is not the personal dignity, but the Life which He makes ours' (C p. 539). 'In Christ our whole nature has been penetrated with the Divine life, drawn up into the divine glory' (D p. 96). The life of Christ makes the imitation of Christ possible because his life is reproduced in Christian character.

In the power of that life all righteousness is possible.

Devotion to Christ implies not only obedience to the letter but understanding of the spirit of his command, and insight into their applications to daily life. The education of the conscience becomes then a primary Christian responsibility, closely related to the devotion of the intellect. In a careful exposition of 'The Christian Method of Moral Regeneration', Dale spelt out an Evangelical asceticism of the heart: 'Self-renunciation retaining nothing of the previous moral personality'; a moral revolution 'carried through in detail by a long, laborious and sometimes painful self-discipline'; repentance leading to moral reformation; the renewal of the mind by the Spirit of Christ restoring its 'practical force and authority' as the faculty of moral reflection; the formation of habits which open the life to the continuing influence and ethical guidance of the Spirit of Christ; these are the renovative processes which facilitate Christian growth.[13]

Dale did not advocate self-help spiritual development. He looked beyond human effort to divine gift. Commenting on the apostolic injunction to 'put on Christ', he urged, 'We are to make our own every separate element of His righteousness and holiness'. Then follows a comprehensive review of the character of Jesus, setting a standard of holiness in which 'His life [is] the law of mine'; 'He is Divine. His human perfection was really human, but it was the translation into a human character and history of the life of God. He is living still. The fountains of my life are in Him' (E p. 320). The incarnate, crucified and living Christ is the source of all spiritual life, the reproduction in human experience of the life of God: 'Christ is the prophecy of our righteousness . . . he came down from heaven to give the very life of God to man, and in the power of that life all righteousness is possible' (E p. 321).

The gift of the divine life though appropriated by faith must be nurtured by a reverent obedience, sustained by dependent trust, vitalized by grateful love, and given ethical content by the development of a Christian conscience. Christ did not give a definitive and detailed list of laws. Christian conscience and skill in ethical judgement are the end-product of lifelong education. Christian obedience does not consist in childish learning of rules by rote; moral freedom implies responsibility not only to do the will of God, but also to learn it, and to learn it out of love for the Lawgiver. The Christian must discern the mind of Christ by seeking the underlying principles of his teaching, reflecting long and deeply on the meaning of life, death and resurrection, so that by exposure of mind and conscience to the living Christ as encountered in Scripture and prayer, they will come by a process of education to know what is the good and perfect will of God.

Spiritual obedience depends upon the authority of Christ being recognized by the conscience, and his laws being understood and applied by a mind renewed and informed by a whole network of spiritual influences. 'The Bible has a way of finding us', of speaking with two-edged sharpness to our condition. We must therefore 'think of it, brood over it, let it take root in our hearts'. Devotional 'use' of Scripture had little appeal to Dale. The Bible was to him a repository of divine truth and moral insight. Supremely in the Gospels it is the source-book for the divine life manifested in Jesus and as such deserved the most strenuous thought, patient reflection and loving attention of which a renewed mind was capable.

Prayer too played its part in the development of ethical intuition. He avoided the suggestion that there is power in prayer, preferring to speak of answered prayer as the deliberate personal act of God. The condition of absolute dependence on God is acknowledged each time the Christian prays. In rather sonorous words he spoke of the divine–human relationship: 'God is the Fountain of our life and of our strength; but the streams flow not under the compulsion of necessity but according to His free volitions' (E p. 436). Dale insisted that prayer makes an objective difference to the doing of God's will in the world and a subjective difference in the heart of the praying Christian. Intercession corrects the self-regarding bias of prayer. Paul's phrase 'with all the saints' appealed to the generous catholicity of Dale and reinforced his preference for a less individualistic spirituality.[14] He used the word 'commonalty' as an expression of corporate Christian commitment, believing that the common life of Christians acted as a corrective to the intense individualism of some forms of piety. The Bible, prayer, the fellowship and example of others, the 'personal history' of each soul's failures and triumphs and the enlightening of the Spirit of Christ, represent the spiritual tributaries which inform the mind and educate the Christian conscience towards maturity in Christ.

Righteousness and saintliness are Christian ideals, but Dale hesitated to speak of Christian perfection. His major criticism of the Higher Life movement was its claim to a 'condition in which the will never swerves from its loyalty to God, never consents to thought or act that is known to be sinful, never refuses to meet the obligations of any recognized duty' (J p. 199). Yet, he reasoned, 'an infallible perception of what is sinful and a complete knowledge of duty' is impossible. 'Christian perfection? It may be so; who can tell – but God?' In later years Dale reviewed his life, finding little evidence to suggest the possibility of perfection: 'There has remained in our nature a huge, stubborn, inert mass, which offered invincible resistance to every effort to break it up, to crush, and scatter it . . . The central evil has remained: it is a want of conformity to the mind of Christ, a hardness of heart which must be subdued and melted by the grace and truth of God . . .'[15] To desire holiness, to feel the 'heart tremble with a blended reverence and joy', remains the Christian goal, but its fulfilment lay in the future 'when in the clear light of God, we shall know perfectly the perfect life, and shall never, through a false judgment, mistake the will of the Eternal' (J p. 200).

Christian worldliness.

Meanwhile holiness is to be pursued by conscientious involvement in human affairs. Dale was far less suspicious of the world than many of his Evangelical contemporaries. He frequently criticized Evangelical piety for modelling itself on a world-denying lifestyle. The 'sanctity of misery', 'holy melancholy' and 'habitual gloom' were attitudes of the penitent rather than the saint.[16] The stereotype saint drew scorn from Dale. Quiet, placid, subdued, 'if he has a touch of melancholy we are better pleased. He must not be too strong, he must be a little pale' (LC p. 226). One wonders what Moody made of Dale's opinion that the American was closer to the New Testament ideal: 'A great evangelist like Mr Moody, with his restless energy, his audacity, his physical vigour, his humour and his fun, speaking night after night to crowds of people is hardly an ideal saint' (C p. 710). But Moody was precisely Dale's idea of sanctity: life-affirming, energetic, loudly humorous, rooted in human affairs and at home amongst all kinds of people. A whole argument on behalf of celebration is contained in one observation: 'No one who wanted a wedding to pass off cheerfully would have invited John the Baptist; our Lord was a welcome guest' (LC p. 221).

He dismissed as destructive scrupulousness the assumption that beauty of art, literature and creation is a snare. 'This wonderful world . . . is to pass away; but God made it.' Physical need and provision in creation are 'expressions of the Divine thought', and 'what God thought worth giving should be received gratefully and heartily enjoyed' (LC p. 219). The world of industry and commerce, politics and social development was also embraced in Dale's Christian worldliness. Athletics tracks, art galleries, libraries, drainage, slum clearance, safe gas supplies, clean water, public gardens and parks were all legitimate concerns for Christian people seeking to serve Christ in the world. The 'Municipal Gospel' of the day was simply the trial of Christ's laws in the arena of public affairs. Many of Dale's sermons were on Christian morality in the market place: 'The Sacredness of Property', 'Everyday Business a Divine Calling' and 'The Christian Rule of Justice' tackled business ethics. Anger, cheerfulness, amusements, Christmas parties, telling the truth, summer holidays and the discipline of the body were shown to be matters of Christian discipleship as well as personal morality.[17]

In his Yale lectures Dale gave what has become his classic statement on Christian worldliness: 'For men to claim the right to neglect their duties to the state on the ground of their piety, while they insist on the state protecting their persons . . . their property . . . their religious meetings in which this exquisitely delicate and valetudinarian spirituality is developed, is gross unrighteousness' (NL p. 258). Someone sent him a 'good little book' and wrote, 'There are no politics in heaven; there is where your life should be; sad, sad that it is otherwise.' Dale replied in the outraged tone of an Old Testament prophet:

> No politics in heaven! Well I suppose not; but there are no agricultural labourers there living on twelve shillings a week . . . there are no hereditary paupers there . . . there are no gaols . . . to which little children . . . are sent for an offence committed in ignorance . . . no unjust wars to be prevented . . . Politics un-Christian! . . . by going on to Boards of Works and Town Councils, and improving the drainage of great towns, and removing the causes of fever, men are but following in Christ's footsteps.
>
> (LC p. 268)

The combination of worldly wisdom, theological reconstruction and moral analysis is unusual, and gives to Dale's spirituality a quality of spaciousness. In political activity he was not confined by the scruples of an Evangelicalism defensively suspicious of 'the world'; he entered that world equipped with a profound faith in Christ's redemptive power and righteous purpose. Nor could his intellect remain within the frontiers of Calvinist orthodoxy when modern knowledge cast doubt on such an interpretation of the faith; he embarked on the task of restatement because he was convinced that the essential truths remained unchanged though their propositional form was discredited. In his view of the spiritual life he offered an analysis which encouraged freedom and responsibility under Christ, and presupposed an ongoing process of growth in moral wisdom and discernment. At the centre of political, theological and spiritual life he placed Christ, the Moral Ruler of the universe, the crucified and risen Lord. So Dale was an atypical Evangelical, largely free from the rigid adherence to the received tradition so important to a man like Spurgeon. Yet Spurgeon too broke new ground and through a distinctive spirituality gave back to Evangelical piety more than he received.

Young man, you look very miserable.

Between the ages of one and six years Charles Haddon Spurgeon lived in Stambourne with his grandparents. As one of seventeen children, nine of whom died in infancy, his stay there was probably intended to ease the burdens at home. By the time he was seven Spurgeon had read *Pilgrim's Progress*, the first of more than one hundred pilgrimages he would make through Bunyan's book. He pored over *Foxe's Book of Martyrs*, and memorized Watt's hymns for his grandmother at a penny a time, until his grandfather offered a shilling for each rat he caught and Spurgeon accepted the more lucrative contract. He attended various schools after returning home showing a proficiency in mathematics and demonstrating a remarkable memory.

In his teenage years he grew anxious about his unsaved condition. The law of God was a 'sword of fire', a 'ten-thonged whip', a divine implement with which God was ploughing his soul, ten black horses in his team – the Ten Commandments (F p. 29). Like Dale he agonized over his personal salvation, reading Bunyan's *Grace Abounding*, Baxter's *Call to the Unconverted*, and James' *Anxious Enquirer*. The long search came to a sudden conclusion one Sunday morning in Colchester Primitive Methodist Church. A snowstorm prevented him from going to his regular church and he decided to risk worshipping with a people who had 'a reputation for singing so loudly that they made people's heads ache'. The preacher, struggling to fill the time with scant material, singled out the anxious young visitor. Spurgeon's recollection is now a classic of Evangelical testimony:

> Just fixing his eyes on me, as if he knew all my heart, he said, 'Young man, you look very miserable . . . and you always will be miserable – miserable in life, and miserable in death – if you don't obey my text; but if you obey now, this moment, you will be saved.' Then lifting up his hands, he shouted, as only a Primitive Methodist could do, 'Young man, look to Jesus Christ. Look! Look! Look! You have nothin' to do but to look and live' . . . I looked until I could almost have looked my eyes away . . . the cloud was gone . . . I saw the sun . . .

> I could understand what John Bunyan meant, when he declared he wanted to tell the crows on the ploughed land all about his conversion.[18]

He was baptized by immersion and received into membership of St Andrew's Street Baptist Church in Cambridge. A surge of spiritual energy was released and channelled into tract distribution, evangelistic visiting (which peaked at seventy visits one Saturday), Sunday School teaching and lay preaching. He became sole pastor of a little church in Waterbeach at the age of seventeen and was called to the New Park Street Baptist Church before his twentieth birthday. His success as a preacher was unparalleled in the nineteenth century. In order to contain the crowds a new and much larger building would be required. From its opening in 1861, Spurgeon's work and reputation became inseparable from the Metropolitan Tabernacle.

Five years earlier, the large crowds which flocked to hear him had to be accommodated in music halls and other secular premises. Following a crowd panic at one such meeting, caused by a false fire alarm, seven people died and twenty-eight were injured. Spurgeon was prostrated and suffered such inconsolable depression he felt he was going insane. He always believed later that in his grief and guilt Jesus brought healing to his overwrought mind: 'On a sudden the name of Jesus flashed through my mind. The person of Christ seemed visible to me. I stood still. The burning lava of my soul was cooled. My agonies were hushed. I bowed myself there, and the garden that had seemed a Gethsemane became to me a Paradise.'[19]

Yea, he is altogether lovely!

That Jesus became real to his looking eyes at conversion, and Christ seemed visible to his adoring gaze in the aftermath of his sorrow, are observations of some significance in understanding the spirituality of Spurgeon. His love for Jesus and his sense of a presence almost tangible, and visible to faith, is one of the recurring themes in his writing. It was this sense of a living, intimate relationship between his soul and Christ that led one admirer to rank him and Bunyan the two greatest English Evangelical mystics.[20]

The term mystic is fully justified. The believer's union with

Christ was a theme on which Spurgeon reflected, preached and at times rhapsodized. Unlike Dale, Spurgeon had no hesitation in spiritualizing the Old Testament, given several guidelines to keep exposition within the bounds of commonsense.[21] The Book of Joshua could be construed as a type of the believer's spiritual battles; Leviticus could yield 'views of our Lord's atoning work taken from different standpoints'; Ruth 2.14, 'At mealtimes come thou hither and eat of the bread', suggested a sermon entitled 'Mealtime in the Cornfields' and leads to a meditation on the Lord's Supper.[22] But it was in the Song of Solomon that Spurgeon found language and imagery capable of conducting the powerful current of his spiritual love for Christ.

Where Dale cautioned against concentration on the allegorical use of texts potent with sensual imagery, Spurgeon sensed no danger; only the appropriateness of ecstatic, even explicit, language to convey the deepest feelings of his soul. In this debate Spurgeon had the support of a long tradition behind him, including the Puritans, though Calvin ignored the book in his preaching and writing.[23]

In a Communion address at Mentone, his favourite holiday resort in the south of France, he expounded the phrase, 'Yea, He is altogether lovely'. It is a sustained eulogy on the beauty of Jesus as experienced by a man of powerful emotional capacity: 'All loveliness meets in Him. He is the gathering up of all sorts of loveliness. He is the climax of beauty.' Admiration glows into affection and intimacy. 'His is an approachable beauty . . . He has within himself an unquenchable flame of love, which sets our soul on fire . . . Put together all loves . . . and they only make a drop compared with His great deeps of love, unexplored and unexplorable' (THC pp. 100–1). The images of flame, fire, ice and ocean depths, and the related verbs of burning, consuming, melting and flowing are the standard vocabulary of the mystic. Spurgeon gives them a typically surprising addition: 'It is a torrent which sweeps all before it when its fount breaks forth within the soul. It is a Gulf Stream in which all icebergs melt' (THC p. 102).

'Forgive me that I speak so coolly!' he apologized, 'I dare not enter fully into a theme which would pull up the sluices of my heart.' The theme which threatened to inundate his listeners was the sacrifice of Christ on Calvary: 'To see Him suffering for my sin on the tree, was as the opening of the gates of the morning to my darkened soul . . . Here our guilty conscience finds peace; here we see ourselves made comely in His comeliness' (THC pp.105, 108). The comeliness of Jesus is most apparent in the 'balance' of his loveliness; there is in Jesus nothing lacking or excessive: 'You never find His kindness lessening His holiness, nor His holiness eclipsing His wisdom, nor His wisdom abating His courage, nor His courage injuring His meekness' (THC p. 106).

The union of the believer with Christ depends on electing grace rather than human consent: 'The immovable basis of communion [was] laid of old in the eternal union which subsisted between Christ and His elect.' The Calvinistic tenor of Spurgeon's spiritual experience is made explicit in a sermon on union with Christ: 'The believer was in the loins of Jesus Christ the Mediator when in old eternity the covenant settlements of grace were decreed, ratified and made sure forever' (THC p. 183). Since the relationship with Christ is anchored in a strong theology of election, it does not change with the vicissitudes of existence. The electing love of God is the believer's guarantee, and in that security love is consummated in the union of believer and Saviour.

Indeed, Spurgeon speaks of a reciprocal indwelling, the believer in Christ and Christ in the believer. The spiritual mechanism by which such mutual belonging operates is shrouded in mystery. Spurgeon's own explanation has the ring of personal testimony, and though lacking the logical coherence of the theologically precise, his words carry the conviction of the participant rather than the spectator:

> Faith lays hold upon the Lord Jesus with a firm and determined grasp. She knows His excellence and worth, and no temptation can induce her to repose her trust elsewhere; and Christ Jesus is so delighted with this heavenly grace, that he never ceases to strengthen and sustain her by the loving embrace and all-sufficient support of His eternal arms. Here, then, is established a living, sensible, and delightful union, which casts forth streams of love, confidence, sympathy, complacency and joy . . . When the eye is clear, and the soul can evidently perceive this oneness between itself and Christ, the pulse may be felt as beating for both, and the one blood may be known as flowing through the veins of each.
>
> (THC pp. 192–3)

Remember Him till you begin to be like Him.

'The one pulse beating for both' and the 'one blood flowing through the veins' are images of entire dependence, of lives inseparably intermingled in a shared existence of mutual belonging. Spurgeon's experience of such a vivid and vital union with Christ added depth to his theology of the Lord's Supper. It grieved him deeply that the Communion service had become a primary focus of theological and ecclesiastical dispute. In response to the encroaching sacramentalism he perceived in the Church of England, he urged a return to the simplicity of the New Testament, where the Supper was a feast not a ceremony, to be received sitting at the table, not kneeling at the altar. He dreaded sacramentalism because it seemed to locate grace elsewhere than in Christ the Redeemer and to compromise the once for all sacrifice of Calvary. At the same time he was dissatisfied with the common Baptist emphasis on the Supper as a memorial because too often the primary reference of the ordinance was backwards. Neither view took seriously the present reality of the indwelling Christ and all the potential for a communion of love which his real presence conveyed.[24]

In a number of sermons Spurgeon refurbished the memorial emphasis by appealing to the personal experience of the communicant. At the Communion service memory must not degenerate into a rehearsal of historical facts, or a revision of doctrinal commonplaces. Spurgeon valued memory as a rich resource of spiritual nourishment when informed by a personal experience of Christ such as his own. Such inward reflection was controlled by referring all back to Christ as experienced by each Christian believer: 'Remember Jesus Himself . . . and think neither of pardon, nor of justification, nor of sanctification apart from Him. The streams of love, I trace up to the fountain in the heart of Christ . . .' (MTP 34 p. 448). With Christ as the focus, Spurgeon urged loving reflection on the cross and all its benefits to the individual soul, these benefits to be gratefully acknowledged in the act of receiving the bread and wine: 'The suffering body of the incarnate God is the spiritual food for our souls, but we must partake of it if it is to nourish us; and this emblematic bread must not only be broken, but eaten, – a significant type of our receiving Jesus by faith, and depending upon Him, taking Him to be the nutriment of our new spiritual life' (MTP 54 p. 317).

A strong sense of the corporate nature of the Lord's Supper adds further depth to his thought. A vision of the Christian community as a fellowship of those eternally indebted to Christ occurs in many of his Communion sermons. The mood of adoration and grateful recollection at the Lord's Supper was enriched for him by the knowledge that he celebrated 'together with all the saints'. At every feast the glorious scope of the gospel was set forth as a demonstration of the work of Christ for all his people: 'This supper is virtually the outward and visible sign of ten thousand times ten thousand broken hearts that have been bound up, tearful eyes that have been made to flash with holy joy, aching consciences that have been eased, and hearts that could sooner cease to beat than cease to love' (MTP 50 p. 103).

He finished one sermon with a litany of exhortations to remember, which took the congregation through a wide range of Evangelical experience: 'Remember that all your hope hangs upon Him who hung upon the cross . . . Remember that when He died you died in Him . . . Remember Him . . . till your love burns within you . . . Remember Him till all the church militant and all the church triumphant, too, seem gathered around your heart, and you commune with the whole church of Christ in heaven and earth . . . Remember Jesus till you feel He is with you, till His joy gets into your soul . . . Remember Him till you begin to be like Him . . .' (MTP 54 p. 320). By such imaginative spiritual direction Spurgeon endowed the Communion service with a profounder sense of the presence of Christ.

Even then, Spurgeon was clearly not satisfied. While denying any location of the Real Presence in the actual bread and wine, he did believe that Christ was really present by his Spirit and in the acts of breaking and eating bread and pouring and drinking wine. His close attachment to the Communion service is given devotional expression in the words of his hymn, 'Amidst us our Beloved stands'. The rapturous joy Spurgeon experienced in his union with Christ lent mysterious depth to the meaning of Jesus' words 'This is my Body which is for you'.[25]

'We cannot literally eat his body or drink His blood . . . but we can do it and we must do it, spiritually, by having our minds resting upon what Christ is, and what he has done, and so feeding upon our Lord Jesus Christ' (MTP 45 p. 429). The Lord's Supper provides opportunity for spiritual replenishment, though what the relation is between such replenishment and the bread and wine is not made clear. However in a sermon with the intriguing title 'The Spiced Wine of my Pomegranate' Spurgeon is more explicit and moved beyond the memorial theme:

> Amid the profusion of His gifts, never forget that the chief gift is Himself . . . He clothes thee, but it is with Himself, with His own spotless righteousness and character. He washes thee, but His innermost self, His own heart's blood, is the stream with which the fountain overflows. He feeds thee with the bread of heaven, but be not unmindful that the bread is Himself, His own body which he gives to be the food of souls. Never be satisfied with a less communication than a whole Christ.
>
> (THC p. 135)

Such thinking shows clearly the way Spurgeon's sense of intimacy with Christ by faith penetrated his eucharistic theology. These words, and the following, invest the Lord's Supper with a spiritual potential far exceeding even an enriched memorial emphasis:

> The Lord's Supper represents the giving of the whole body of Christ to us, to enter into us for food; surely, if we enter into its true meaning, we may expect to be revived and vitalized; for we have here more than a mere touch of the hand, it is the whole Christ who enters into us spiritually, and so comes into contact with our innermost being . . . No power on earth can henceforth take from me the piece of bread which I have just eaten, it has gone where it will be made up into blood, and nerve, and muscle and bone. It is within me and of me. That drop of wine has coursed through my veins and is part and parcel of my being. So he that takes Jesus by faith to be his Saviour has chosen the good part . . . he has received the Christ into his inward parts . . .
>
> (THC pp. 354, 319)

Holy Communion is, therefore, a demonstration of the whole spiritual process of assimilation, of Christian identity being absorbed into Christlikeness; but even more, to Spurgeon it was a means of grace ordained by Christ himself to strengthen and progressively deepen the love between the Christian soul and the 'Altogether Lovely One'.

Give us to live as we ought to live.

Complementing the mystical strain in Spurgeon was an energetic commitment to practical affairs and a temperament in which firmness of conviction was expressed in a somewhat unmystical dogmatism. In his own life the central truths of the Evangelical faith inspired tireless service and he believed they must be defended as non-negotiable assets entrusted to the Church.

The activism of Spurgeon's early years increased in intensity as time passed. He was minister in the largest Nonconformist congregation in Europe, in a city which was in the throes of expansion in trade, industrial development and international influence. Half a million commuters poured into it each working day creating a bustling marketplace, and a mission field which would absorb his energy and stimulate his gifts. The Pastor's Training College which trained over nine hundred ministers during his lifetime, the non-denominational Orphanage which eventually housed five hundred children and the Colportage Association which employed ninety-six colporteurs, achieved sales of £153,784 and made twelve million visits by 1891, imposed a sufficiently punishing work-load.

By 1891, 14,460 had been baptized and joined the church under his ministry. On one day he counselled thirty enquirers, he carried on a voluminous correspondence, edited the monthly *Sword and Trowel* and preached three or more times a week for the whole of his life, holidays and periods of illness excepted.[26] He wrote 135 books, edited a further 28, and from 1855 published one sermon each week until his death. The Metropolitan Tabernacle Pulpit is an unparalleled collection of one man's preaching, numbering 3,653 sermons, some published eventually in forty languages and with a normal weekly circulation of 25,000. Stories abound about the influence of these sermons on individual lives as far apart as the British garrison in India and the penal colonies of South America.[27]

What emerges from this catalogue of achievements is a man often over-worked, suffering increasing ill-health, yet constantly pouring himself out in preaching, writing and organizing. It was the age of the self-made man, when initiative, drive and enterprise were admired and encouraged. He lived up to his own adage: 'A Christian man is generally right when he is doing more than he can; and when he goes still further beyond this point, he will be even more nearly right' (ARM p. 22). Exertion in the service of Jesus was simply the outside of that inner experience of loving communion which was so real to Spurgeon. As an older man he regretted the loss of 'elasticity of spirit, the dash, the courage, the hopefulness of days gone by' (ARM p. 131). One of his prayers reveals a fear of living below potential: 'May we not live as earthworms crawling back into our holes and dragging now and then a sere leaf with us; but, Oh, give us to live as we ought to live . . . that ours may not be a fruitless wasted life; that no faculty of ours may lay by and rust' (P pp. 36, 56). But the magnitude of Spurgeon's output argues such a total commitment to Christ that it is easy to see why he reacted strongly against any threat to his understanding of the gospel. A whole edifice of spiritual activity was founded on the faith as Spurgeon held it.

Undergirding all this self-expenditure was a disciplined life of prayer. Not surprisingly Spurgeon had no patience with the more passive forms of devotion. He could reduce prayer to the simplicity of a business transaction: 'I believe in business prayers . . . I mean prayers in which you take to God one of the many precious promises which he has given us in His word, and expect it to be fulfilled as certainly as we look for the money to be given to us when we go to the bank to cash a cheque or a note' (K p. 378). The same utilitarian view is urged on student ministers: 'We bow the knee because we believe that, into the ear of the Eternal God, we speak our wants, and that His ear is linked with a heart feeling for us, and a hand working on our behalf. To us true prayer is true power.'[28]

In his public prayers other sides of Spurgeon can be glimpsed. The unemployed, the poor, orphans, 'those who have fallen by strong drink, unchastity or dishonesty', the 'working classes and the poor rich' are all included in intercession. Biblical allusions and phrases abound: 'the horrible pit and the miry clay', 'the harp hanging on the willows', 'divers trials' and 'men of Anak' would all test the memory of the most assiduous Bible student. Plain language and homely imagery are sometimes used to produce a beautiful simplicity of devotion: 'May there be no false note in all the singing of our life, but all be according to that sacred score which is written out so fully in the music of our Lord' (P p. 55): 'Lord wake up dead hearts . . . may the bulb down at the heart send forth its golden cup and drink in of the light, the life of God' (P p. 107). An agile mind was required to say Amen to the conundrum: 'If we think we love Thee more than we do, we pray that we may yet love Thee more than we think' (P p. 9). The combination of practical affairs and mystical awareness gives these prayers a disconcerting unpredictability. Paragraphs of quite elevated emotion are followed by the most basic requests; which is as it should be in a man whose spirituality contained the same mixture.

Coals of orthodoxy are necessary to fires of piety.

The self-imposed limits to Spurgeon's intellectual life played a crucial part in his spiritual development. He has been called anti-intellectual and in some ways that is true enough. He gave his students the alarming advice: 'When you hear that a learned man has made a new discovery which contradicts the Scriptures . . . do not imagine that he is really a great man, but believe that he is just an educated idiot, or a self-conceited fool' (ARM p. 26). To make sense of this attitude requires some sympathy with Spurgeon's own standpoint.

Dale had struck the nail on the head when he described Spurgeon as an old Puritan. His library was replete with Puritan early editions, he valued Puritan commentaries highly, describing them quaintly, but with a connoisseur's appreciation of their spiritual value. Dickson on the Psalms 'drops fatness', Sibbes 'scatters pearls and diamonds with both hands', Ferguson of Ayrshire is 'a grand, gracious, savoury divine'. His mind was steeped in the theology and religious psychology of Puritanism; books like *Precious Remedies for Satan's Devices* and Gurnall's *Christian in Complete Armour* were read carefully and some volumes repeatedly. One critic suggests Spurgeon's erudition in Puritan practical theology was both his chief strength and only weakness. One inescapable consequence of his Puritanism was an inability to sympathize with the movements of mind and spirit in his own age.[29] The ominous note of hostility to contemporary thought surfaced often: 'We declare that there are certain verities – essential, abiding, eternal – from which it is ruinous to swerve . . . I have been charged with being a mere echo of the Puritans, but I would rather be an echo of the truth than the voice of falsehood. Rest assured that there is nothing new in theology except that which is false' (K p. 374). Consistent with his creed, he stuck loyally to Calvinistic doctrines 'because they tally with my soul's best experience' (ARM p. 25).

The Christian mind must be loyal to the truth; that much Spurgeon shared with Dale. But Spurgeon allowed no distinction between theological definition and theological substance. Restatement of doctrinal truth in the language of the present all too easily became an act of betrayal, accommodating the gospel to the spirit of the age. The shift from penal substitution to a display of divine love, as the key to the atonement; the weakening of the doctrines of hell, judgement and wrath in favour of a benevolent divine Fatherhood; the sentimental and reductionist portrayals of Jesus the man and the inevitable lowering of christological claims, and all of these arising from a virulent anti-biblical spirit, alarmed Spurgeon and drove a barrier between his faith and the modern mind. In contrast to the 'boiling mud-showers of modern heresy' and the corrosive free-thinking he saw around him, Spurgeon urged a vigorous, biblically controlled orthodoxy. 'O for a church of believers in Jesus who know why they believe in Him; persons who believe the Bible and know what it contains; who believe the doctrines of grace, and know the bearings of those truths' (ARM p. 172).

'Our ministry demands mind', he insisted, though he was careful to distinguish the Christian mind from 'the enlightenment of the age'. Even his public prayers warned of the dangers of doctrinal error. 'Purge us of everything unscriptural . . . keep thy sheep free from the poisonous pastures of error . . . take away the itching for new doctrine . . . turn the current of thought which sets so strong in the wrong direction.' For Spurgeon spiritual health depended on right doctrine, for it is doctrine rightly understood, and that in Calvinist terms, which had enabled him to interpret his own experience.

Spurgeon was no enemy of new knowledge as such. 'A brain', he advised, 'is a very hungry thing indeed, and he who possesses it must constantly feed it by reading and thinking' (ARM p. 167). No one familiar with the sermons, or *The Treasury of David*, his extensive commentary on the Psalms, could accuse Spurgeon of being an unthinking or shallow preacher. His breadth of reading and speed of assimilation were remarkable. He spoke of 'lying a-soak in my text . . . then after I have bathed in it, I delight to lie down in it and let it soak into me' (ARM p. 124). His knowledge of the Bible, his grasp of 'the goodly land from Dan to Beersheba', the immersion of his mind in biblical commentaries and the colossal demands of his ministry created a mind which, in the end, only felt secure in biblical categories. He freely confessed, 'I have always loved safe things, I have not, that I know of, one grain of speculation in my nature' (K p. 369). What Spurgeon never did was to interrogate the text. Modern critical methods betrayed presumption, a lack of humble receptiveness destructive of spiritual insight. It was this perceived arrogance that Spurgeon deeply resented. His own ideal of Christian scholarship reflected the characteristic loyalty he felt to the truth of Christ: 'Perhaps the highest form of adoration possible, on this side of the veil, is the bowing of our entire mental and spiritual being before the revealed mind of God; the kneeling of the understanding in that sacred presence . . . We shall continue to learn even in Heaven, and shall still be looking deeper and deeper into the abyss of the Divine love' (ARM pp. 181, 167).

Given Spurgeon's adherence to the doctrines of Calvinistic Puritanism and his identification of loyalty to Christ with loyalty to the truth as he had come to know it, it is not surprising that his spirituality was conservationist. 'I have been told that it would require a surgical operation to get a new idea into my head', he admitted without apology. There is no sense of theological exploration or careful definition of truth as in Dale's doctrinal sermons. In his defence of the faith Spurgeon relied on his own rich and often dramatic experience of Christ, a Bible rock-solid against all destructive criticism, and a gift of preaching which by his very success seemed to confirm the rightness of his stance. Dale's moral sermons, for all their worthiness as lessons in Christian ethics, found no counterpart in Spurgeon's sermons; there would be too little of Christ in them for Spurgeon's liking.

To read Dale's *Ephesians* and Spurgeon's sermons is to become aware of two minds, powerful in different ways. Devotion to Christ is unmistakeable in both; but Spurgeon found Christ in the whole Bible, and to cast doubt on any part was to cast a shadow over the integrity of the One to whom the Bible bore witness. Dale never invested that amount of spiritual capital in his view of the Bible and yet his love for Christ and his sense of the living reality of his presence was just as powerful and life-enhancing. The same differences of temperament, of attitude to the world of human thought, of personal experience, become evident in comparing the way they experienced, reflected upon, preached and expounded the atoning death of Christ. Spurgeon's preaching could rise to glorious heights of vision and articulation of the great mystery of the cross, confident in proclamation, passionate in evangelism, imaginative in sympathetic insight into the eternal depths of holiness and love in relation to human guilt. For his part, Dale bequeathed one of the milestone works on the atonement, carefully argued, all the New Testament evidence marshalled and evaluated and great care taken to reconstruct a view of the cross that was morally consistent with eternal law and infinite love.

Dale's yearning to question, rethink and if possible understand the Evangelical tradition he loved, and Spurgeon's glowing love and passionate defensiveness of the faith 'once delivered to the saints' ensured that the two men were allies. The experienced reality in their hearts, of Christ crucified and risen, brought them, despite other differences, to the same place of adoring wonder. In a sermon on 'The Three Hours' Darkness' Spurgeon approached the deepest mystery of all with a hesitancy which is shot through with passionate conviction. His words that Easter morning make all theological articulation provisional; and at that point he and Dale were of one heart: 'God veiled the Cross in darkness, and in darkness much of its deep meaning lies, not because God would not reveal it, but because we have not the capacity to discern it all . . . God only knows the love of God' (MTP 32 pp. 223–4).

Sources frequently cited

Dale, A. W., *Life of R. W. Dale of Birmingham*. London 1898. (D)
Dale, R. W., *The Congregationalist*. 1876. (C)
——, *The Epistle of James*. London 1895. (J)
——, *Laws of Christ for Common Life*. London 1903. (LC)
——, *Lectures on the Ephesians*. London 1895. (E)
——, *Nine Lectures on Preaching*. London 1877. (NL)
Fullerton, W. Y., *C. H. Spurgeon*. London 1920. (F)
Kruppa, P. S., *Charles Haddon Spurgeon: Preacher's Progress*. New York 1982. (K)
Spurgeon, C. H., *An All Round Ministry*. London 1960. (ARM)
——, *C. H. Spurgeon's Prayers*. London 1905. (P)
——, *Till He Come*. Tain, Focus publications, 1989. (THC)
——, *Metropolitan Tabernacle Pulpit*. (MTP)

Additional reading

Bebbington, D. W., *The Nonconformist Conscience*. London 1982.
Dale, R. W., *The Evangelical Revival*. London 1880.
——, *Christian Doctrine*. London 1894.
——, *Fellowship with Christ*. London 1891.
Dallimore, A., *Spurgeon*. Edinburgh 1984.
Glover, W. B., *Evangelical Nonconformists and Higher Criticism in the Nineteenth Century*. London 1954.
Hopkins, M., 'Baptists, Congregationalists, and Theological Change; Some Late Nineteenth Century leaders and Controversies', D.Phil. Oxford 1988.
Hough, L. H., 'R. W. Dale', *Congregational Quarterly* (1929), pp. 417–24.
Mozely, J. K., 'R. W. Dale', in *Great Christians*, ed. R. S. Forman, London 1933.
Nicoll, W. R., *Princes of the Church*. London 1921.
Spurgeon, C. H., *Autobiography*, 2 vols. Edinburgh 1962, 1973.
Spurr, F. C., 'C. H. Spurgeon', in *Great Christians*, op. cit.
Walker, M., 'Theology of the Lord's Supper amongst Baptists in the Nineteenth Century', PH.D, New College, London, 1988.

Notes

1. *The Congregationalist* (1873), p. 191.
2. Spurgeon, *Commenting and Commentaries* (London 1893), p. 186.
3. Dale, *Life*, pp. 161–78; Kruppa, *Spurgeon*, pp. 254–81. Even the venerable Canon Ryle came into the firing line of *The Congregationalist*. See 1875, p. 306.
4. Dale, *Life*, pp. 341f.; Hopkins, pp. 96–136; *Congregationalist* (1878), pp. 326–32.
5. Hopkins, pp. 213–67; Kruppa, *Spurgeon*, pp. 408–44; Bebbington, *Evangelicalism in Modern Britain* (London 1989), pp. 143–6. Spurgeon's defence of orthodox theology, and the rearguard action he felt compelled to take is apparent in his preaching, MTP vol. 34, especially sermons 2007, 2013, and 2047; Hopkins' analysis is the most plausible so far.
6. Dale, *Life*, p. 111. The title sermon of *The Evangelical Revival* shows Dale's constructive criticisms of a too narrow Evangelicalism. The theme of an ethical Revival is also dealt with in *Congregationalist* (1878), pp. 1–2.
7. Hopkins gives a very clear portrayal of the intellectual and theological climate.
8. Dale, *Life*, p. 16. Dale wrote the biography of J. A. James.
9. Dale, *Christian Doctrine*, p. 216.
10. Dale, *Life*, p. 715. The whole sermon, 'The Forgiveness of Sins', is included in *The Evangelical Revival*, pp. 149f. Dale distinguished

between the removal of subjective pain from the conscience and the removal of the moral offence by God. Only the second is forgiveness.

11. *The Congregationalist* (1876), pp. 78f.
12. *Expository Times*, I (1889), p. 591.
13. Dale's Christian moral philosophy can be studied in *Ephesians*, ch. 17.; *Evangelical Revival*, pp. 41–148; the series of articles on 'The New Testament Theory of Sanctification', *Congregationalist* (1876).
14. Dale, *Life*, pp. 173–4, is a fine statement of Evangelical catholicity. But see p. 294 for an equally powerful criticism of Catholicism.
15. *Evangelical Revival*, p. 236; Dale, *Life*, p. 591.
16. For other examples of Dale's view of joy-making as a spiritual obligation see 'Increase Gladness: a Forgotten Ministerial Duty', *Congregationalist* (1873), p. 452; 'A Merry Heart', *Congregationalist* (1886), pp. 705f.; Cheerfulness, in *Week Day Sermons* (London 1867).
17. Dale, *Life*, ch. 16; other examples are in *Week Day Sermons*, and *Laws of Christ*.
18. Spurgeon, *Autobiography*, vol. 1, pp. 88–9.
19. Hopkins, p. 142; Fullerton, *Spurgeon*, chooses another autobiographical fragment, p. 94.
20. T. H. Darlow, *W. Robertson Nicoll: Life and Letters* (London 1925), p. 402.
21. See *Lectures to My Students*, 'On Spiritualising'. For a virtuoso performance see 'The Apple Tree', THC pp. 37–53.
22. MTP 9, p. 421; MTP 30, p. 157.
23. He spoke highly of Beza's Sermons on the Song; he prized the contribution of his favourite Puritan, Richard Sibbes; as usual he acknowledged indebtedness to Matthew Henry. His attachment to Rutherford's letters perhaps encouraged the use of the Song's more sensuous imagery and certainly provided a precedent for the 'personal union with Christ' theology which enriches Spurgeon's spirituality. Many of Spurgeon's sermons on the Song were published in one volume *The Most Holy Place*, reprinted Pasadena 1974.
24. Dale also redefined the meaning of the Lord's Supper, in language which provoked controversy. See Dale, *Life*, pp. 355f.; 'The Christian Sacraments and Christian Worship', *Congregationalist* (1885), pp. 12–20.
25. It is noteworthy that Spurgeon accepts the RV rendering of 1 Cor. 11.24 and omits the word 'broken'. MTP 45, p. 428.
26. Spurgeon was dogged by ill-health from his thirties onwards. See Fullerton, *Spurgeon*, pp. 88, 113, 180; Kruppa, *Spurgeon*, pp. 93–4, 459f.; THC pp. 57–70 is a sermon on depression with many autobiographical echoes, printed in MTP 58 only in 1912, therefore not edited by Spurgeon.
27. A good analysis of the sermons in Kruppa, pp. 233–54.
28. ARM pp. 12, 13. 'He approached the burning bush with cheerful aplomb.' This and other observations are to be found in a good cameo of Spurgeon in O. Chadwick, *The Victorian Church*, vol. i, pp. 417–21.

29. The critic in question claimed that 'Spurgeon was the one great teacher of the century whose mind was steeped in Puritan ideas, theology and literature', Fullerton, p. 195. Dr Alexander Whyte had at least an equal claim. See Chapter 9.

7
DWIGHT L. MOODY and FRANCES R. HAVERGAL

By Thy call of mercy, by Thy grace divine.
HAVERGAL

In 1873 an Anglican vicar organized a mission in the town of Bewdley. Preparations included door-to-door visitation, prayer meetings and hymn practices. Meetings were held in school-houses, halls and even factories, with after meetings for enquirers. Maria and Frances Havergal were involved in the preparations, and did some of the preaching and singing at the meetings. A subsequent mission in 1878 had speakers from the Evangelisation Society, the meetings were held in a large tent erected on the green and Frances' contribution was largely 'to preach the gospel in song'. Professionalism in organization, financial backing by sympathetic businessmen, vigorous publicity, the use of a neutral venue, the careful setting of solo and choir singing within the overall context of the meeting and the more ambitious scale of the whole enterprise were hallmarks of a new style of campaign. The change of evangelistic technique was due to the influence of the American Dwight Lyman Moody.

By the time Moody came to Britain in 1873, Frances Ridley Havergal was, at least in England, the undisputed doyenne of contemporary Evangelical hymnody and a leading writer of popular and devotional prose. She was a tireless evangelist in her own right, using her singing and writing to bring people to a 'decision for Jesus'. Though the two evangelists had much in common, particularly their commitment to saving souls, in other ways comparison virtually takes the form of contrast.

Earnest determination to be a Christian.

Moody was born in the agricultural township of Northfield, Massachussetts, in 1837. At that time the town consisted of a cluster of farms producing mainly oats and hops, but already under the influence of nearby Boston it was becoming a growing centre for industrial and cultural activity. His father, a skilled mason, died when Moody was aged four, leaving his mother, described by her grandson as 'a thrifty puritanical matriarch', to hold the large family together.

Moody's educational attainments were modest and throughout his life he felt the inadequacy of his early schooling. His spelling and grammatical idiosyncrasies are justly famous. One day he asked his grown-up family, 'How do you spell Philadelphia?' He answered it himself thus: 'F-i-l or F-e-l? Well never mind; I'll write it so that they can't tell which it is – e or i.'[1] Moody made up for educational disadvantage by native wit, practical commonsense and an ability to learn from experience which, over the years, distilled into a wise and highly developed pragmatism. Moody did not need to learn lessons twice.

In 1854 he became a shoe salesman in Boston. He joined the Y.M.C.A. mainly for the social contact it provided. Some months later his Sunday School teacher told him of Christ's love for him and the love Christ wanted in return. Moody made a simple 'decision' for Christ, and 'the following day the old sun shone a good deal brighter than it ever had before . . . I fell in love with the birds . . . It seemed to me I was in love with all creation' (F pp. 49–50). The causes of his joy were so theologically vague that the deacons of Mount Vernon Congregational Church refused his application for membership. When asked what Christ had done which entitles him to our love Moody answered: 'I don't know, I think Christ has done a great deal for us; but I don't think of anything in particular as I know of' (G p. 22). A year later Moody still struggled to articulate his experience in language recognizably evangelical, but was eventually received into membership 'in view of his evident sincerity and earnest determination to be a Christian' (F p. 51).

Moody moved to Chicago the following year. He shared the materialistic aspirations of a city whose mainspring of action was 'the desire for wealth and the growing prospect of success,' (F p. 58). He wrote home, with the usual spelling oddities, 'I can make more hear in a weak than I could in Boston in a month' (F p. 59). He became increasingly involved in evangelistic activity, starting an independent Sunday School which soon developed into a vigorous church. The revivals of the late fifties, growing success as a preacher and personal evangelist and his growing skills in organization, publicity, fund raising and motivation, were among the factors which determined Moody's career. He had the ambition, the abilities and the self confidence to succeed in business. In his first four years he had saved $7,000 and become an imaginative, persuasive and persistent shoe salesman.

But he lacked the ruthless killer instinct of the opportunist businessman. His outbursts of sentiment and apology when he had offended someone revealed a vulnerability to others' hurt which would be construed as weakness in a highly motivated man of affairs. He was good-natured, extrovert and often allowed his uproarious sense of humour to get the better of him. He clearly revelled in the frenetic pace he set himself while working, but enjoyed the slower lifestyle on the Northfield farm. Neighbours familiar with Moody hurtling along on his buggy at breakneck speed, or feeding his chickens in leisurely fashion, were able to observe the two sides of his nature. In the work of God he was energetic, outgoing, impatient of obstacles, decisive and imaginative, but in the home and on the farm he enjoyed the leisure to ponder and reflect. Undoubtedly the activist streak was dominant.

In 1861 he gave up business to work full time as an evangelist. By 1864 his mission had become the Illinois Street Independent Church catering especially for immigrant families. Public exposure as President of the Chicago Y.M.C.A. for four years ensured a growing reputation as preacher and revival leader. The Great Chicago Fire of 1871 destroyed his home, his church and the Y.M.C.A. After an exhausting campaign, raising funds to restore them, he decided to concentrate his energies on itinerant evangelism. He and his song-leader Sankey arrived in Britain in 1873. Their initial impact was disappointing but interest grew, reaching unprecedented levels in Glasgow in 1874 and in London in the summer of 1875. Moody's impact on Glasgow was felt at several levels. Day refuges for destitute children and free breakfasts for the homeless were directly inspired by his message. The Bible Training Institute was founded to train evangelistic workers and mission centres such as the Tent Hall were established to carry on the work.[2]

Evangelism remained Moody's consuming interest but as time passed he began to see the strategic value of basic education and Bible training. In 1889 he established the Institute for Home and Foreign Missions, later known as Moody Bible Institute. Other educational projects included two Northfield secondary schools. In addition he had initiated a series of international conferences for the deepening of the spiritual life at Northfield training centre which attracted such speakers as Campbell Morgan and F. B. Meyer. Northfield had close parallels with the Mildmay holiness conventions though Moody never explicitly placed himself within the Higher Life movement. In the spheres of Christian social concern, education, ecumenical co-operation in evangelism and Christian publishing Moody exerted an enduring influence.[3] Mass evangelistic services, the gospel appeal in the music of Ira D. Sankey, the effects on congregations of hymns intended to move the emotions and the encouragement of lay activity by making personal evangelism a requirement of Christian discipleship, were aspects of Moody's method and message which decisively changed the features of popular Evangelical piety.[4]

It was the love of God that broke my heart.

The centre of Moody's gospel was Christ as the expression of the love of God. Soon after his move to Chicago he felt a personal compulsion to save souls. Once he became involved in evangelism, and had begun to study the Bible seriously, he no longer had any difficulty answering the question, What has Christ done for us to deserve our love? Christ died in our place, taking our punishment because God loves us.

Moody combined the subjective and objective views of the atonement in his preaching. The death of Christ was a climactic demonstration of the love of God. Moody used all his powers of persuasion to describe that love against the background of human sinfulness. 'Grace breaks the hardest heart . . . and then the fountain of love flows out' (SG pp. 44–5). But Jesus also suffered the penalty for sin and Moody was unflinching in his account of human ruin and divine judgement. Demonstrative love for the sinner and penal satisfaction in substitution for the sinner were ideas which dwelt without conflict in the mind of Moody. He resisted the inroads made by liberal theology into the doctrine of substitutionary atonement: 'It is not Christ's sympathy – His life – we preach, it is His death . . . The moment a man breaks away from this doctrine of the blood, religion becomes a sham, because the whole teaching of this book is of one story . . . that Christ came into the world and died for our sins'. Yet 'it is sheer love which gave Christ for us . . . if you want to know how much God loves you, you must go to Calvary to find out' (G pp. 111–14).

These three words, 'blood', standing for the sacrificial death of Christ, 'love' as the motive underlying the eternal purpose of God, and 'Calvary', his favourite word for the atonement, provide the basic vocabulary of the gospel Moody preached. In uncomplicated language he spoke of God giving Christ, and Christ for love of his Father willingly offering his life for the redemption of humanity. In an autobiographical aside in his sermon on 'Love that Passeth Knowledge' he told his hearers: 'I used to think a good deal more of Christ than I did of the Father. Somehow or other I had the idea that God was a stern judge; that Christ came between me and God, and appeased the anger of God. But after I became a father, and for years had an only son, as I looked at my boy I thought of the Father giving His Son to die' (CSG p. 15).

Such anecdotal theology and down-to-earth domesticity gave Moody's preaching a popular appeal: 'Many of us think we know something of God's love . . . Columbus discovered America: but what did he know about the great lakes, rivers, forests and the Mississippi valley? So many of us have discovered something of the love of God; but there are heights, depths and lengths of it we do not know' (CSG p. 9). An even more incongruous illustration involves the potent and solemn symbol of 'the blood' being compared in its efficacy to a train ticket (SG p. 101). Miraculous deliverances in the Civil War, a pardon from Abraham Lincoln at the last minute, a condemned spy being covered with the British and American flags to prevent Cuban soldiers from carrying out an execution, these and many other homely, unusual and even far-fetched stories were told to great effect.

Human response to the gospel involves repentance and faith as prerequisites of regeneration. Repentance is not fear, remorse or even forsaking of sin; it is 'to walk in an exactly contrary direction' (CSG p. 96). Conversion is an 'instantaneous decision'.

The walking is a lifetime journey but the turning is immediate. Moody deliberately preached for that response. He used the language of immediacy: 'He will do it this minute . . . the moment we open our lips . . . today . . . now, this minute.' He built up a close rapport with his audience: 'Dear friends, let me put this question to you: Are you full of Grace? I see some of you shaking your heads . . .' Pointing to his vast audience he declared, 'That little boy there knows how to take a gift . . .', and again with a disarming impatience he pleaded: 'I wish I could get this whole audience to drop the word try and put the word trust in its place. The forgiving grace of God is wonderful. He will save you this very minute if you are willing to be saved' (SG p. 23).

This urgent, pointed preaching was set in a musical context intended to create responsiveness in the audience. One worried traditionalist enquired: 'How are we to be let down from the fever heat of these meetings to the quiet, old-fashioned manifestations of the Christian life? The life born of such excitement will have great difficulty in surviving in the cold atmosphere of our work-a-day world' (F p. 157). The combination of Moody's preaching and Ira D. Sankey's singing was novel and spectacularly effective. The evocative imagery of 'There were ninety and nine', the rumbustious joy of 'O Happy Day', the 'heart-racking' pathos of 'Almost Persuaded' and countless other 'Sacred Songs and Solos', were used to create spiritual longing and move people to give their lives to the Christ who had given himself for them. Moody and Sankey were convinced that 'people want to sing not what they think, but what they feel' (F p. 177). Consequently the hymns tended to be subjective, describing the inner experiences of Evangelical doctrine, and applying it in explicit personal terms. 'Rock of Ages cleft for ME', 'I am so glad that Jesus loves ME', 'I Need Thee Every Hour' and 'What a Friend WE Have in Jesus', are hymns which eschew objective praise and doctrinal precision in favour of gospel experience. They are not intended to inform but to move. They may, like 'Rock of Ages', contain solid Evangelical teaching, but their use was governed by evangelistic not educational purposes. The primary intention of Moody's preaching and Sankey's singing was the personal salvation of the listeners.[5]

Moody preached personal salvation as a supernatural work of regeneration through the Holy Spirit by means of which the trusting sinner is made new. Regeneration gives the believer new moral purpose and creates new resources which purify motives, govern newly perceived values and focus the affections on Christ instead of 'self' or the 'world'. By regeneration the Christian experiences the impartation of the life of God, or in Moody's bold phrase he 'receives God's nature'. It is this crisis of conversion, involving repentance, faith and regeneration, which Moody's preaching aimed to achieve. The moving force behind him was a profound apprehension of the love of God for every fallen human being, a love displayed in the crucified Christ. To reject that love was to fall under eternal judgement. Moody seldom preached on hell. He avoided the emotional excesses of hell-fire revivalists though an account of the sermon on hell he preached at Manchester in 1874, contained the solemn observation, 'We seemed to be looking across the gulf that divides time from eternity and beholding the torments of the self destroyed victims of a broken law and a rejected gospel.'[6] Predominantly however, Moody preached God's love, because 'love produces sons whereas fear produces slaves'. That said, Moody left his hearers in no doubt; 'to despise the blood is to despise God's love' (G p. 114).

Power from on high.

The demand for decision and the accompanying theology of instant conversion is at variance with Moody's own experience. Though he dated his conversion to April 1855, at that time he had little grasp of the three primary doctrines of the gospel he later preached, namely man ruined by the fall, redeemed by the blood and regenerated by the Spirit.[7] He once stated that there were three red-letter days in his early spiritual experience: 'The first was when I was converted; the next was when I got my lips opened and I began to confess Christ; the third was when I began to work for the salvation of others' (SG p. 59). In 1871, in the aftermath of the Chicago fire, an exhausted and disillusioned Moody experienced a profound renewal of inner resources. His later articulation of this experience lacks clear theological definition: 'I can only say that God revealed Himself to me, and I had such an experience of His love that I had to ask Him to stay His hand'.[8]

In his book, *Power From on High*, he expounded the work of the Holy Spirit in the life of the believer. 'I think it is clearly shown in the Scripture that every believer has the Holy Ghost dwelling in him' (CSG p. 172). The deficiency of so many Christian lives is not the absence of the Holy Spirit but the restricted flow of the Spirit's power. 'The moment our hearts are emptied of pride, selfishness, ambition and self-seeking, and everything that is contrary to God's law, the Holy Ghost will come and fill every corner of our hearts' (CSG p. 170). In Moody's thought there is a clear distinction between the Holy Spirit in us and the Holy Spirit upon us for power.

The love of God revealed to his mind and released into his heart wrought in Moody a further moral transformation, and thereafter he consistently applied the ethical test to all such experience. He exulted in Paul's words, 'The love of God is shed abroad in our hearts by the Holy Ghost . . .' (Rom. 5.5). Love is the 'crown of crowns worn by the Triune God'. Christians are to be reservoirs of divine love. Positively that means the love implanted deep in the new nature will overflow in spontaneous expression. One of Moody's favourite metaphors for this is the *Shekinah*, the glory of God filling the tabernacle, suffusing its structure with the beauty of holiness (Exod. 40). Negatively, Moody contended: 'If a man has not the love of God shed abroad in his heart he has never been regenerated' (CSG p. 157). God is love and those who are born of God love because it is their nature to do so.

The love of God shed abroad in the heart is accompanied by a new spiritual power, urgency and efficiency in the work of God. For that reason Moody was hard on all attitudes and actions which hindered or contradicted the love of God. The anointing of the Holy Spirit is for power: 'But he is not going to give that power to an impatient man; he will never give it to an ambitious man whose aim is selfish until he is first emptied of self . . . let it be God's glory and not our own that we seek' (CSG pp. 182f.). It is hard to resist the feeling that Moody was here reflecting on his own self-confidence and even conceit earlier in his career just prior to his 'baptism of power'. The Spirit purged him from self-assertive evangelism and energetic brashness, creating in him a liberating dependence on God's grace: 'I was all the time tugging and carrying water. But now I have a river that carries me.'[9]

The fruit of the Spirit and the evidence of spiritual power is a life controlled by the love of Christ. Love is the 'badge of discipleship', the 'great motive power of life', the 'fire burning on the altar'. All offences against love are hindrances to the power of the Spirit and such offences are detected by the litmus test of the fruit of the Spirit.

Similarly, he argued that lack of power in the life of the Christian community was due to behaviour which 'grieves the Spirit'. Worldly amusements like gambling, bazaars, theatres, opera music and 'unconverted choirs' drew biting criticism from Moody. In his judgement fashionable churches and complacent undemanding religiosity were the death of vital Christianity. On the growing practice of opera music in the church he chides: 'They hire ungodly men, unconverted men; and these men will sometimes get the Sunday papers, and get back in the organ loft, and the moment the minister begins his sermon, they will take out their newspapers and read them. The organist, provided he does not go out for a walk – if he happen to keep awake, will read his paper, or, perhaps, a novel, while the minister is preaching; and the minister wonders why God does not revive his work' (CSG p. 255).

Moody tended to emphasize the functional role of the Spirit. Power is given for service not for the private enjoyment of the recipient. The energy, imagination and drive of Moody involved colossal self-expenditure. He believed he survived only because of inner replenishment by the Holy Spirit. Others may judge spiritual health by a cultured prayer life, or diligent Bible study or even impressive experience, but Moody's criterion was work: 'We work from the cross, not toward it; we work because we are saved, not to be saved . . . you don't work for salvation but work day and night after you have got it' (G p. 145). Studied impatience with a moribund church underlies his comment, 'We don't read resolutions of the Apostles but the Acts. We must work and not talk' (F p. 247). Some of the titles of Moody's books betray that same preoccupation with efficient action. *Prevailing Prayer*, *To the Work*, *The Faith which Overcomes* and *Power from on High*, all contain ideas of accomplishment, success and power to achieve.

My faith bows down before the inspired word.

Moody may have lacked formal theological training but his written addresses reveal considerable indebtedness to the Protestant divines. Frequently he introduces a long quotation with 'Someone has said . . .'. A little source criticism reveals such sources as Luther, Thomas Goodwin, George Herbert, William Cowper and Charles Spurgeon. Acknowledged sources include the Thirty-Nine Articles, Matthew Henry, J. C. Ryle, and a string of Puritans. But the Bible commanded Moody's best attention. He preached and wrote widely on the value of diligent reflective Bible study, though for spiritual balance Bible study must be accompanied by prayer: 'If we read the Word and do not pray, we may become puffed up with knowledge, without the love that buildeth up. If we pray without reading the Word, we shall be ignorant of the mind and will of God, and become mystical and fanatical, and liable to be blown about by every wind of doctrine' (PP p. vi). A strong view of inspiration and a conviction that the Bible was the sole authority for all matters of Christian belief and practice created a stern resistance to any weakening of biblical authority. In his reading Moody adopted an unquestioning submissiveness to the plain meaning of the text. The words of Scripture are the Word of God, and they testify to the Eternal Word made flesh in Jesus. 'You can never separate Jesus the Word made flesh from the written Word' (G p. 204). Any questioning of the trustworthiness of the Bible was seen as an attack on the integrity of the gospel.

A defective view of biblical inspiration, Moody believed, raised serious questions about Christian status. Consequently Unitarians, German critics, geologists, sceptics and Deists all came into his firing line. Perhaps only a mind that had never felt the force of intellectual doubt could ask such beside-the-point questions as: 'What can the geologist tell you about the Rock of Ages? What can the astronomer tell you of the Bright and Morning Star?'[10] According to Moody the 'true' Christian loves the Bible, reads, studies and obeys. Criticism and obedience require opposing dispositions. Interrogation of a text by a questioning mind seeking answers is incompatible with rumination on a text by a hungry heart seeking nourishment. Against the 'so called conclusions of destructive criticism' Moody affirmed his reverence for the 'Bible as it stands'.

As an evangelist Moody was committed to defending the integrity of the Bible as the medium through which God speaks and converts. In Christian living he had felt and experienced the authority of the Bible at a level far beyond the reach of 'infidel critics'. The dependability of God's promises, the authority of

God's commands and the power of the Word proclaimed had been proven in the study, not of the critics, but of the evangelistic arena.

In his preaching Moody often retold Bible stories with imagination and power. By prolonged private meditation he entered the story with keen observation, a full range of sympathies and an eye for legitimate embellishment. His treatment of the story of Elisha and the widow's cruse of oil is a good example. Skilful use of the present tense gives it immediacy; the responses of neighbours, widow's sons, prophet and onlookers are touched in with a few deft words; the curious neighbours let him have a sly dig at those who crane their necks to see what goes on in the enquirer's room, and the sceptics of Moab are seen to be just as wrong as those of today, 'Faith asks no questions!'

Docile receptiveness to the Word of God is the ideal attitude of the Bible-loving Christian: 'The doctrines, the promises, the messages of love, are as fresh today as when first spoken. Pass on the message; be obedient to the commands; waste no time in discussion; let speculation and theorizing pass into the hands of those who like that kind of study.'[11]

The 'full-orbed Christian' studies the Bible, works at evangelism and is disciplined in prayer. Prayer meetings were an essential part of revival strategy. Sometimes they were geared to planned evangelistic campaigns, and sometimes they were part of a regular church programme. The prayer meeting is, 'the life of the church, the expression of its desire for the salvation of sinners, the united power it puts forth to bring down the blessing' (F p. 113). As in most other things, Moody judged prayer by its results. Prayer must prevail, and he gives plenty of practical advice. Long prayers are wearisome so 'let our prayers be brief and to the point'. Fussiness or an over-developed humility was no use. 'What we want is to get hold of God in prayer', an assertion which mixes hesitation before the mystery of God with unabashed forwardness expressed in the language of 'getting', a verb Moody uses often in relation to spiritual blessings. We 'get' if we have faith, which he defines as 'fervency', or earnest 'heart-sense': 'Unbelief sees something in God's hand and says "I cannot get it"; Faith sees it, and says, "I will have it" ' (PP p. 76).

The fiercest attacks are made on the strongest forts.

Such hard-edged pragmatism is tempered by less aggressive devotional attitudes. Adoration is prayer stripped of self-concern and focused on God, not for what we can 'get' but simply for who he is. To adore is to 'render divine honour, including reverence, esteem and love'; it is to sense the glorious holiness and beauty of God. Confession is a 'deep work' of inner inspection. It is not merely self-scrutiny but involves openness to God, allowing him to search and try deepest thought and secret motive.

Moral victory in daily life is only possible for the renewed soul. Unconverted people cannot 'overcome the world . . . they might as well try to cut down the American forest with their penknifes' (FWO p. 9). But if victory is possible it is hard won. Moral conflict is a sign of spiritual vitality. Moody treated Gal. 2.20 with unsophisticated directness. Paul declared: 'I am crucified with Christ: nevertheless I live; yet not I, but Christ liveth in me: and the life which I now live in the flesh I live by faith in the Son of God who loved me and gave himself for me.' Moody highlights the faith reference but gives the merest sideglance at the profound theology and complex spirituality of Paul's thought. Pragmatism displaces reflection as one of the New Testament's most penetrating insights into the believer's union with Christ, is reduced to 'We get this life by faith'. Romans chapter seven is understood as the believer's experience of conflict, though again liberty from sin is by living the overcoming life of faith. The possibility of overcoming by faith seems to be negated by his assertion: 'The old Adam never dies . . . When we are born of God, we receive his nature; but He does not immediately take away all the old nature' (FWO p. 18).

The lingering effects of the sinful nature are to be combated, and here Moody refuses to be deflected from his conviction that spirituality must pass the ethical test of character and relationships: 'An impulsive man like myself has to [apologize] often . . . Christianity is not worth a snap of your fingers if it doesn't straighten out your character' (FWO p. 22). With glorious head-on simplicity he says the cure for temper is an apology and the cure for covetousness is to strangle it by generous dissipation. A dangerous source of temptation was discerned in 'the world'. Worldliness was defined as 'forgetfulness of the eternal future by reason of love for passing things' (FWO p. 28). The Christian must guard against worldly habits, pleasure and business, and such worldliness is to be overcome by faith in Christ. At times Moody was arguing for a progressive mastery over self, a gradual draining of life from the old Adam as the indwelling Christ is trusted more and more. The unresolved tension remained and will only be resolved when Christian faith is consummated in heaven. Each Christian is committed to a life of continuous spiritual warfare, requiring to be alert to all the wiles and subterfuges of the world the flesh and the devil, and demanding ethical discipline and inward honesty.

Moody was not introspective by nature, and the well-being of his soul was affected more by the success or failure of the work than by fluctuating moods and recurring questions of the inner life. His is the spirituality of the evangelist, the Christian who is utterly captivated by the message, and whose activism on the grand scale is devotion writ large. He exemplifies the uncomplicated spirituality of the Christian extrovert, less preoccupied with the profounder notes sounded by guilt, self-doubt and spiritual restlessness. Some of these profounder notes were sounded and explored, then written, published and set to music by Frances Ridley Havergal.

Then and there I committed my soul.

Frances Ridley Havergal was born in 1836. Her father, W. H. Havergal, was an Anglican clergyman. He was an eminent church musician and composer, a keen Bible student, enthusiastic supporter of overseas missions, a fervent opponent of Roman Catholicism, a conscientious and busy pastor, and, according to one awe-struck parishioner, 'a man who could preach and put a stop to sin' (Gr p. 12).

Havergal was remarkably gifted. When her formal education was complete she had a working knowledge of Hebrew, Greek and Latin, and could speak German, French and Italian. As a toddler she sat on her father's shoulders as he played the seraphine at family hymn-singing sessions. She could play many of the major works of Handel, Beethoven and Mendelssohn from memory when she was twenty. The same prodigious memory captured word perfect the Gospels, Epistles, Revelation, Psalms and Isaiah. She was an accomplished pianist, better than average at composition and was recognized by a leading European musician as having an exceptional ability in harmonization. Grudging admiration underlay his judgement that she had 'talent, feeling, taste and brains' (M p. 89).

At first Havergal's intellect frustrated her search for salvation. When she later wrote, 'Take my intellect and use, every power as Thou shalt choose', she was speaking of a personal trait which constantly dogged her pursuit of holiness. Less than a year after her conversion she admitted, 'I cannot bear to be ignorant and behind others in learning' (M p. 41). Her critically reflective nature required a commitment to Christ which arose from conscious settled conviction. However much she tried to persuade herself God would accept her, chronic discontent with her level of moral achievement frustrated her increasingly desperate desire to become a Christian. Torn between hesitation and desire she was unable to 'decide for Christ'.

She complained in her autobiography: 'At any time I would willingly have suffered anything, might it but have brought me to the attainment of full assurance' (M p. 38). The result of such vacillation was a state of emotional suspense. At Belmont, a solidly Evangelical school for girls, Mrs Teed the headmistress regularly made powerful evangelistic appeals. She was commended in 'The Sunday Home' for her pursuit of 'seriousness'. Amongst other moral adjustments to the syllabus she removed ballroom dancing, 'that she might not be responsible for preparing pupils for scenes of worldly gaiety and dissipation' (Gr p. 31). The religious discipline of the Havergal home, the inevitable loneliness of the late child, the emotional intensity of Belmont, the example of other girls making their 'decisions' and finding joyful relief, memories of a sermon on hell convincingly preached during her childhood, the sharing of the sacrament with her dying mother and the dislocation of relationships by her removal from home combined to produce a weight of anxiety which threatened to break Frances in her teenage years.

While on holiday at her sister's home in Okehampton, and following a conversation with her sister's friend, Havergal reached a spiritual crisis. Previously she had heartily disliked being 'spoken to' by urgent soul-winners but on this occasion she was more receptive: 'Then and there I committed my soul to the Saviour, I do not mean to say without any trembling or fear, but I did, and heaven and earth seemed bright from that moment – I did trust the Lord Jesus.' As she looked back on her experience, she recorded: 'Over and over again I renewed that giving up my soul to the Saviour which had made entrance for the joy' (M p. 39). Commitment as a repetitive act of faith, involving a fully surrendered will, and resulting in joy, were to be three keynotes of her spirituality.

That she may be thine forever.

Her faith was formally and publicly confirmed when she was seventeen. She took the confirmation prayer 'that she may be Thine forever . . .' with great seriousness, and wrote a short verse to express the totality of her devotion:

Oh! 'Thine for ever', what a blessed thing,
  To be for ever His who died for me.
My Saviour, all my life thy praise I'll sing,
  Nor cease my song throughout eternity.
    In the Cathedral, 17 July 1854 (Gr p. 50)

Havergal spent the rest of her life trying to express her total love for Christ. 'The thing which beyond any other temporal gift I most value is affection. I feel as if I had a perfect greed of love' (Gr p. 82). As well as making an honest confession of her need for approval, she was providing a clue to her passionate and at times extravagantly expressed love for the Christ who alone satisfied her need to love and be loved.

Following her conversion she busily pursued an exhausting programme of varied evangelistic activity. Personal counselling started when, aged nine, she taught her first Sunday School class. Enthusiastic support for the Hibernian Bible Society and the Church Missionary Society was channelled into persistent and successful fund-raising. At different stages of her life she organized milliner's and dressmaking classes for young girls, she participated in diocesan missions, evangelistic meetings in workplaces, cottage visitation, relief work at a mining disaster, and she took a leading part in the Y.W.C.A. and the Christian Progress League. The number of singing and musical engagements she fulfilled is staggering. Personal correspondence demanded enormous discipline, for, she believed, 'letters must be answered'; in a six-month period at the height of her popularity she dealt with six hundred personal letters.

The multi-talented evangelist was in danger of self-dissipation.

She would have to comply with the natural limitations of time, energy and, later, ill-health. But the regime of Christian activism she pursued was supplementary to her real ambition. She wrote to her sister Maria in 1864: 'If I had my choice, I should like to be a "Christian poetess", but I do not feel I have the ability ever to turn this line to much account. I feel as if music were a stronger talent, tho' in neither am I doing anything serious. Most of all would I like to be your ideal – a winner of souls . . .' (Gr p. 78). The lack of self-confidence she felt eventually gave way to a productiveness and a purposefulness which resulted in a constant flow of prose articles, hymns, poems and verses on demand for baptismal cards, bereavement cards and other Christian ephemera. Her most significant publications were in the 1870s when she issued several collections of poetry and hymns and a series of devotional pocketbooks reflecting on the theme of Christ's kingship.[12]

In the preface to the collected edition of Frances' poems Maria explained that some of the poems were 'impromptu verses', the 'utterance of rapid imaginings' while others were 'sweet simplicities' and others 'higher soarings'. Whatever the end product Frances believed her poetic aptitude and musical talent were God-given and each hymn a direct gift from God. 'Writing' she said 'is praying with me' (Gr pp. 104–7).

She candidly admitted some of her attempts were sub-standard: 'I cannot write, and never yet have written beyond my own personal experience.' Any verse which was 'manufactured' was disqualified. She believed God must reveal a subject to her own soul before she could write upon it. God's giving and withholding of such revealed truth explained periodic dryness and inability to write on demand. Spiritual responsiveness, perhaps even mood, rather than acquired technique provides the key to Havergal's output. Music was both a medium through which she communicated her spiritual experience and an important formative influence upon it.[13] She exulted in a Handel chorus and enthused, 'Let the ocean of sound flow in upon your soul, till you feel that it has absorbed your individual being into itself' (Gr p. 85).

However her questioning temperament often led her to view her musical gifts with ambivalence. Although music provided endless opportunities to 'serve the Master', just as frequently it caused her to feel the temptation to pride. An educated self-distrust detected the slightest hint of impure motivation so that the joy of achievement, and the exultation of performance became for her real occasions of temptation. She complained of herself: 'A power utterly new and unexpected was given (of music and composition) and rejoicing in this I forgot the Giver' (Gr p. 73). The search for sincere motivation and freedom from pride and self-concern, began to intensify.

To be forever His who died for me.

Gospel hymns of the period made use of striking contrasts to highlight the before and after of conversion. For example black and white comparisons would be drawn between the sin of the world and the anticipated purity of heaven, the anxious turmoil of the Christless soul and the rest enjoyed by those who come to the Saviour, or the weakness of will which makes sin inevitable and the strength of the will renewed by the Holy Spirit.[14] The polarity of such hymns is given personal intensity by the subjective tone, and an urgent invitation to sinners to move from one sphere, via Christ, into the other.

Havergal used this approach in many of her hymns. 'By Thy Cross and Passion' begins with a prayer for spiritual insight into the mystery of the love revealed on the cross:

> What hast Thou done for me, O mighty Friend,
>   Who lovest to the end!
> Reveal Thyself, that I may now behold
>   Thy love unknown, untold . . .
>
> (PW p. 682)

The connection between humanity's lostness and Christ's atoning death is portrayed in a series of substitutionary exchanges in which Christ confers the opposite of what in his passion he experienced on humanity's behalf:

> O Thou wast crowned with thorns, that I might wear
>   A crown of glory fair:
> 'Exceeding sorrowful' that I might be
>   Exceeding glad in Thee;
> 'Rejected and despised' that I might stand
> Accepted and complete on Thy right hand.

Explicit echoes of the Suffering Servant, the deliberate contrast of 'me' with 'Thee' and 'mine' with 'Thine', and the black and white nature of the contrasts (curse-blessing; sorrow-joy; bruising-healing; death-life) give the hymn a powerful emotional undercurrent. The last verse seeks to make sense of the whole mystery, not by intellectual penetration, but by the offer of loving service which is the climax of worship:

> Thy cross and passion, and Thy precious death,
> While I have mortal breath,
> Shall be my spring of love, and work, and praise,
> The life of all my days;
> Till all this mystery of love supreme
> Be solved in glory – glory's endless theme.

Full surrender before full blessedness.

On Advent Sunday, 2 December 1873, Havergal made an act of full consecration. Like Moody she denied any explicit connection between this new spiritual development and the various holiness conferences of the period: 'I am so conscious of His direct teaching and guidance through His word and Spirit in the matter . . .' (M p. 131). She described her experience as an intellectual vision: 'I saw it as a flash of electric light, and what you see you can never unsee' (M p. 126). Through this distinct, dateable experience she discovered that consecration involves full surrender of self which must be consummated from God's side by an acceptance which implies his approval of the gift. Such assurance changed her whole spiritual perspective; longing was replaced by satisfaction, self-recrimination by a more positive sense of being loved, and emotional fluctuation gave way to a new spiritual stability: 'I was so delighted about it, and I was so distinctly and joyously conscious that I was not only His, but entirely His, that it came nearer to "satisfied" than anything else yet . . . He has taken away now all the fear of going back into the weary old up-and-down life' (Gr p. 142).

In one of her best poems, 'Thoughts of God', she offers, not her own faltering thoughts, but a bold description of the inner mind of the Almighty. She knew she was treading on holy ground and her imagination hesitates before being drawn inwards and upwards by the beauty of her vision. The poem ends in serenity, repose and the contemplative joy of those who know they are loved:

> They say there is a hollow, safe and still,
> A point of coolness and repose

Within the centre of a flame, where life might dwell
Unharmed and unconsumed, as in a luminous shell,
  Which the bright walls of fire enclose
In breachless splendour, barrier that no foes
  Could pass at will . . .

So in the centre of these thoughts of God,
Cyclones of power, consuming glory fire –
  As we fall o'erawed
Upon our faces, and are lifted higher
By His great gentleness, and carried nigher
Than unredeemed angels, till we stand
  Even in the hollow of His hand –
Nay, more! we lean upon His breast–
There, there we find a point of perfect rest
  And glorious safety. There we see
  His thoughts to usward, thoughts of peace
That stoop to tenderest love; that still increase
With increase of our need; that never change,
That never fail, or falter, or forget . . . [15]

Gentleness, intimacy, perfect rest, tenderest love, grace that increases with increase of need, and a thoughtful God who never fails or falters or forgets, are ideas which provide the secure emotional substructure of her consecrational theology.

With such a vision of God it was possible to look on personal sin without entirely despairing. Believing as she did in the sinfulness of even redeemed human nature, she held that consecration must always imply cleansing. She found the biblical foundation for her experience in the text, 'the blood of Jesus Christ his Son cleanseth us from all sin'. The conditions of such cleansing were simple dependence and the abandonment of the will to Christ. By a decisive emphasis on the present tense she claimed Christ cleanses and keeps the yielded life by a present and continuous work of grace. Her straightforward literal approach to biblical promises enabled her to speak with disconcerting definiteness. 'Why should we pare down the commands and promises of God to the level of what we have hitherto experienced . . . ?' She was fascinated by the word 'all' in the Bible, putting great emphasis on such phrases as 'cleansed from all sin', 'all grace abounds towards you' and 'all peace in believing'. These were open invitations to 'take God at His word'.

'Full and glad surrender' can and must be renewed, each

renewal involving a fuller surrender as God reveals areas of life as yet unyielded. Firmly in the Calvinist tradition, she spoke of sanctification in progressive terms. Even the love which she offered to Christ she felt was first given to her so that she might be 'made holy by the continual sanctifying power of God's Spirit; to be kept from grieving the Lord Jesus; to be kept from thinking or doing whatever is not accordant with His holy will'.[16] Assurance of cleansing was accompanied by an intensified view of sin: 'One does not shrink from painful discoveries of evil, because one so wants to have unknown depths of it cleansed as well as what comes to the surface' (M p. 131). She strongly rejected perfectionist language: 'It is not perfection, nor perfectionism, because if it were I should not need, and desire and claim that wonderful perpetual present tense' (Gr p. 145).

Kept for the Master's use.

Need, desire and claim remained basic spiritual attitudes throughout her life and they are key ideas in *Loyal Responses*, an important collection of her consecration poems. 'Take my life', her best known hymn, was originally written in couplets, and identified the different elements of personality or aspects of human existence requiring to be consecrated. It is comprehensive and specific in its terms, representing the spiritual equivalent of a watertight contract. It is simple, embroidered with biblical allusion, deeply personal and was often used by her at evangelistic meetings. Her own commentary on it is a searching devotional manual important in its own right, entitled *Kept for the Master's Use*. She devoted a chapter to each couplet revealing her characteristic concern to explain consecration as a two-way spiritual transaction. The original hymn used 'take' as an expression denoting human consent and divine acceptance. In the book she substituted the word 'keep' suggesting that consecration is an act which can only become a continuous reality by the keeping power of God. The whole poem then becomes a prayer for a sense of perpetual belonging.

The hymn is clearly autobiographical, the individual petitions referring to Havergal's own desire for self-abnegation. 'Take my hands and let them move, at the impulse of Thy love' recalls gospel incidents where Jesus touched lepers, the dying and the broken. For a woman who wrote letters, poems, books and music and whose manual dexterity was used in high quality needlework, carpentry (she made her own music stand) and sign language with the deaf and dumb, such a prayer involved her in a constant examination of her impulses to action.

'Take my silver and my gold, not a mite would I withhold', drew some criticism from those who felt it encouraged unrealistic and thus insincere responses. She spelt out her meaning carefully. 'We are to spend what is really needful on ourselves but not for ourselves'.[17] A gentleman's annual wine bill of £100 drew the reproving comment that it was 'more than enough to keep a scripture reader always at work in some populous district'. There is a surprisingly modern awareness of the value of recycled rubbish; old clothes could be 'done up'. She confided, 'My sister trimmed 70 or 80 hats every spring for several years with the contents of friends' rubbish drawers' so that children could go tidy to Sunday School. 'Little scraps of carpet, torn old curtains, faded blinds, and all such gear' help 'to make poor cottagers comfortable'. She herself sent off most of her jewellery to be sold and the proceeds donated to the Church Missionary Society. But in Christian discipleship there was neither reason nor excuse for shabbiness. 'The outer should be the expression of the inner . . . If the king's daughter is to be "all glorious within", she must not be outwardly a fright!' (Gr p. 163).

She frequently used the figure of 'pouring' as an expression for extravagant, uncalculating service. Her desire to give herself utterly is evident in her prayer, 'Let me pour my life's best wine for Thee, my heart's best gold . . .' (PW p. 688). Energetic and unsparing participation in multifarious projects became a process of self-oblation, pouring out into physical activity an inner love which refused to be confined to feeling. 'I never knew any idle Christian really a rejoicing one' (M p. 232). 'Take my love, my Lord I pour/At Thy feet its treasure store', was the prayer of a woman who never felt that she had quite enough being to convey her indebtedness. With playful overstatement she commented, 'I cannot write at all, how good He is, the ink would boil in my pen!' (M p. 255). The combination of contentment with unfulfilled yearning is given lyrical expression in a letter written from her Swiss holiday resort:'. . . the joy of giving myself, and my will, and my all to Him seems as if it were . . . superseded by the deeper joy of a conscious certainty that He has taken all that

He led me to give . . . so having entrusted my very trust to Him I look forward ever so happily to the future' (M p. 147).

Havergal on holiday is an entirely different personality. Away from public scrutiny she seemed to be less inclined to introspection. Her accounts of her holidays belie the suggestion she was an emotionally overwrought and physically fragile Victorian. In her Alpine travels she could outlast some of her guides, expending so much energy she mischievously reported to her sister, 'We actually went up in our petticoats'. She achieved heights of 10,000 feet in the Sparrenhorn and 11,000 feet on the Col de St Théodule. In *Swiss Letters* there are passages of descriptive prose which are a good corrective to the impression of extreme inwardness some of her more devotional books convey. Looking at the Rhine Falls at Neuhausen she exulted in what she saw and heard:

> You look up and see bright masses, mountains of white, bright water hurled everlastingly and irresistibly down, down, down, with a sort of exuberance of the joy of utter strength. You look across and see shattered diamonds by millions, leaping and glittering in the sunshine. You look down, and it is a tremendous wrestling and sinking and overcoming of flood upon flood, all the more weirdly grand that it is half hidden in the clouds of spray. Only one cannot look long, it is so dazzling, so intensely white, every drop so full of light, that the eye soon wearies and memory has to begin her work. Oh, if one were only all spirit!
>
> (Gr p. 118)

Her fascination with Alpine beauty is reflected in her poetry. The arrangement of one verse has the contour of a mountain, a technique reminiscent of George Herbert's 'Easter Wings':

And now
We only bow,
And gaze above
In raptured awe and silent love;
For mortal speech
Can never reach
A word of meetly-moulded praise,
For one glimpse of the blessed rays,
Ineffable and purely bright,
Outflowing ever from the Unapproached Light.[18]

The kingship of Christ was another of her favourite themes. The sovereign claims of his love, the majestic demands of his law, his exclusive rights as legitimate monarch and the resplendent glory of his royal personage provided her with a rich source for devotional reflection. In Bible study she totally ignored the canons of sober exegesis in her pursuit of texts which contained the vocabulary of royalty and kingship. 'The Throne, the Palace, the Royal Bounty, the Wisdom, the Favour of the King', and much more of the same imagery, she expounded chiefly from Old Testament texts. The method employed was typology, a form of Bible study favoured by many Evangelicals which has its own internal logic. Texts were searched for words and ideas applicable to Christ and used for meditation. For example, 2 Sam. 14.17 has a marginal reading 'the word of my Lord the King shall now be for rest'. Irrespective of the context, which happens to be the sordid power struggle surrounding the banished Absalom, these words are simply lifted clear of their historical reference and interpreted as words of reassurance spoken by Christ to his believing subjects.

Some of Havergal's reasoning on the subject of obedience will win her few friends amongst modern Christian women sensitive to feminist issues: 'O Master! It is perhaps my favourite title, because it implies rule and submission; and this is what love craves. Men may feel differently, but a true woman's submission is inseparable from deep love'.[19] That kind of reasoning gave the metaphors of king and master decisive control over her understanding of obedience. She used Exod. 21.5 as a paradigm for consecration. 'I love my Master; I will not go out free', becomes the affirmation of the Christian slave. 'Master, speak thy servant heareth' indicates the availability of the servant; 'Speak to me by name O master. Let me *know* it is to me', shows the anxious concern of the faithful servant to be sure of the Master's instructions. Another hymn asks, 'Lord speak to me that I may speak, in living echoes of Thy tone', a good example of a hymn intended to further evangelism by encouraging Christians to speak for Christ to God's 'erring children', the 'wandering and the wavering', the 'hungering' and the 'wrestlers with troubled seas'.

Concentration on surrender and absolute submission of the moral will can easily degenerate into a desire for self-oblivion. Like others using the vocabulary of slavery, she often came near to suggesting that a Christian was an instrument for Christ to use rather than a person being shaped by grace and consent into conformity with Christ. 'O use me Lord, use even me/Just as Thou wilt, and when, and where', conveys the impression that obedience and even value are related to usefulness. Havergal avoids such a distortion by her understanding of love and grace as revealed in Christ and expressed on the cross. There is nothing arbitrary, unwise or inconsiderate in the divine will, nor is divine love capable of calculation. The value of each soul is infinite; the freedom of each soul inviolate; and the redemption of each soul the prayer of God, articulated on Calvary. Early in her Christian experience she spoke of God as one 'whose power is love and whose love is power'. Obedience to a loving wise God is not blind submission, or moral abdication. It is the response of reasonable faith made vital by grateful love to a God whose purpose is to redeem and restore human personality.

Cultural background, temperament, natural gifts and spiritual experience are basic constituents of Christian spirituality. In all of these there were wide divergences between Moody and Havergal. Moody was unself-conscious, an energetic innovator who did not mind the limelight. Though aware of the dangers of popularity he enjoyed and sought to use his success in the propagation of the gospel. Organizational ability, rhetorical skill, a salesman's instinct for publicity, boisterous humour and the combination of a practical mind with an emotional nature are not the usual characteristics of Evangelical sanctity. But exploited in the service of Christ they contributed to educational and social reform, set in progress a wave of interdenominational co-operation in evangelism and established centres of training for thousands of Christian workers. In all this, Moody forced a change in the church's understanding and practice of mission.

The practical gospel strategist revealed a mind capable of vigorous planning and a level of pragmatism and flexibility which left little room for detailed self-scrutiny. He was well aware of personal unworthiness, but his practical and uncomplicated view of forgiveness, cleansing, faith in the indwelling Christ and the power of the Spirit upon him for service, freed him from the persistent sense of spiritual inadequacy which dogged Havergal for most of her life. Description of her spiritual experience demands compound nouns using the word 'self', as for example self-distrust, self-denial and self-surrender. The climax of her consecration hymn suggests what for her was the apex of Christian devotion. 'Take myself and I will be,/Ever, only, all for Thee.'[20] The last line has three consecutive absolutes, 'ever . . . only . . . all', and she never compromised with absolutes. They stood for ideals intended to be striven for. Introspective and intense, she was delicately sensitive to inner fluctuation. Combined with a highly intelligent intellect such a temperament was likely to be restless, enquiring and utterly devoid of complacency.

Her workload of singing engagements, writing of letters, poems and devotional books, her musical compositions and hymn book editing, personal counselling and non-stop evangelistic involvement burned up limited resources. Like Moody, her activism was the outward expression of a powerful inner dynamic drawing energy from an ineradicable sense of gratitude. Havergal, whose ambition was to be a Christian poetess given over to the service of her Redeemer, prayed that her life might become 'One rhythmic cadence in the flow of God's great poetry'. Moody spoke more plainly, but with an equally determined love: 'Because He died for me, I love Him. Because He died for me I will serve Him. I will work for Him, I will give Him my very life.'

Sources frequently cited

Findlay, J. F., *Dwight L. Moody, American Evangelist, 1837–1899*. Chicago 1969. (F)

Grierson, J., *Frances Ridley Havergal*. Worcester 1979. (Gr)

Gundry, S. N., *Love Them In: The Life and Theology of D. L. Moody*. Grand Rapids 1976. (G)

Havergal, M. V. G., *Memorials of Frances Ridley Havergal*. London 1880. (M)

Havergal, F. R., *Poetical Works*, 1 vol. edn. London n.d. (PW)

Moody, D. L., *Prevailing Prayer: What Hinders It*. London n.d. (PP)

——, *Sovereign Grace, and Other Addresses*. London n.d. (SG)

——, *Conversion, Service and Glory*. London n.d. (CSG)

——, *Faith Which Overcomes*. London n.d. (FWO)

Additional reading

Adey, L., *Class and Idol in the English Hymn*. Vancouver, University of British Columbia Press, 1988.

Chapman, J. W., *The Life and Work of D. L. Moody*. London 1900.

Daniels, W. H., *D. L. Moody and His Work*. London 1875.

Havergal, F. R., *Kept for the Master's Use*. London 1880.

——, *Swiss Letters*. London 1881.

Havergal, M. V. G., *Autobiography*. London 1887.

Kent, J., *Holding the Fort: Studies in Victorian Revivalism*. London 1978.

Moody, W. R., *The Life of D. L. Moody*. London n.d.

Pollock, J. C., *Moody Without Sankey*. London 1963.

Sizer, S. S., *Gospel Hymns and Social Religion*. Philadelphia 1978.

Notes

1. Daniels, *D. L. Moody*, p. 15.
2. Daniels is a good contemporary source for the 1873–5 British campaigns; also Findlay, *Moody*, ch. 5. Kent, *Holding the Fort*, chaps. 4–6, makes many telling criticisms. Similar criticisms were made in 1875, many of them firmly answered by R. W. Dale, 'Mr Moody and Mr Sankey', *The Congregationalist* (1875), pp. 129–47. Dale was less enthusiastic after the 1883 campaigns when he detected a 'do penance gospel' had replaced an exultant free grace gospel. Dale, *Life*, pp. 529–30.
3. 'The Unconventional D. L. Moody', *Christian History*, issue 25, no. 1 (1990), contains several good articles summarizing Moody's permanent influence on revivalism, his theology and his achievements in education.
4. ibid., D. W. Bebbington, 'How Moody Changed Revivalism', pp. 22–5.
5. See Kent, *Holding the Fort*, ch. 6, 'Sacred Songs and Sankey'; Sizer, *Gospel Hymns*, and Adey, *Class and Idol*, offer many insights into revivalist hymnology; interestingly, R. W. Dale makes some shrewd comments on hymnology in his mainly appreciative *Congregationalist* article, pp. 136–8.
6. Kent, *Holding the Fort*, p. 193: See also pp. 193–204 and Gundry, *Love Them In*, pp. 96–101, for contrasting views on Moody's use of hell in evangelism.
7. Gundry, *Love Them In*, especially chaps 3, 4, 5.
8. Pollock, *Moody without Sankey*, p. 87.
9. ibid.
10. Chapman, *Moody*, p. 386; cf. J. R. Moore, 'Evangelicals and Evolution', *Scottish Journal of Theology*, vol. 38 (1985), pp. 383f., reveals Moody's magnanimity in judgement and tolerance in doctrinal matters. He cites the case of Henry Drummond, the Scottish evangelist who was frequently Moody's associate. Drummond was a speculat-

who was frequently Moody's associate. Drummond was a speculative scientist who tried to combine the biblical account of creation and evolutionary thought. But he was first an effective evangelist, 'Moody's man with a microscope'. He offended fundamentalist opinion at the Northfield Bible conference and Moody refused to distance himself from him, showing a courageous 'disregard for the barkings of religious watchdogs'. A recent thesis instances Moody's warm catholicity as evidence that he did not share the narrow spirit of Fundamentalism. See M. J. Toone, 'Evangelism in Transition: a comparative analysis of the work and theology of D. L. Moody and his protegés, H. Drummond and R. A. Torrey', Ph.D. St Andrews (1988).

11. W. R. Moody, pp. 426.
12. *My King*, 1877; *Royal Bounty*, 1877; *Royal Commandments*, 1877; *Royal Invitation*, 1878.
13. H. O. J. Brown, 'Frances Havergal: a Clarity of Spiritual Conviction', *Christianity Today*, 23 (May 1979), pp. 34–5; M. G. De Jong, 'I want to be like Jesus: The Self-Defining Power of Evangelical Hymnody,' *Journal of American Academy of Religion*, liv (1986), pp. 461–93.
14. Sizer, *Gospel Hymns*, ch. 2. Adey, *Class and Idol*, is particularly helpful on thematic content and underlying imagery in Evangelical hymnody. See the full index in his book.
15. The poem has the distinction of being included in *The Oxford Book of Mystical Verse* (Oxford 1917), pp. 285f.
16. *Memorials*, pp. 124–32. She was reading the Puritan Thomas Goodwin as it was being issued by James Nicholl, the Edinburgh publisher.
17. Havergal, *Kept For the Master's Use* (London 1879), p. 100.
18. Grierson, *Havergal*, pp. 114–15. Ch. 12 'Alpine Travels' is a good account of Havergal's Swiss experience. See also F. Havergal, *Swiss Letters*.
19. *Memorials*, p. 138; De Jong analyses the stereotypes of male dominance and female submission pervading much hymnody of the period.
20. On the consecration hymn, Adey comments with prosaic realism: 'Such all-embracing dedication [was] quite beyond the majority who must earn a living and raise children', p. 202.

8

HANDLEY C. G. MOULE and JOHN C. RYLE

The expulsive power of grace.
RYLE

At the Brighton Holiness Convention in 1875 an invitation was issued to Christians of every section of the Church of God to come to Keswick for three days of 'union meetings for the promotion of practical holiness'. This and subsequent Keswick Conventions were part of a wider but unco-ordinated movement concerned with the attainment of a spiritual condition variously called 'the higher life', the 'victorious life' or, in the title of a best-selling book, *The Christian's Secret of a Happy Life*.

Many Christians were growing weary of repeated failure, constant struggle and limited achievement in holiness as the norm in Christian living. In contrast to the 'miserable sinner' experience, Keswick taught a second experience of grace, the gift of sanctification received by faith. The believer trusts God for justification and finds peace; by a similar act of faith God can be trusted for sanctification. The Christian soul, yielded entirely to Christ, no longer struggles against sin by 'self-energised efforts' but having found grace sufficient to neutralize the power of the sinful self, the Christian enters the rest of faith. Such a theology of sanctification needed careful qualification and clear definition.

In the early Keswick period there was a decided reluctance to pin down a vital experience for the purpose of doctrinal analysis. The evidence of changed lives and characters was recognized even by opponents, and in any case those who received the blessing claimed that it was self-vindicating. Nevertheless the control of right doctrine was felt to be a necessary safeguard to prevent Christian truth from being distorted by experience. The Bible must be seen to be normative in establishing the validity of spiritual experience. While one of Keswick's founding figures warned against 'leaving out the mystical element in our teaching and keeping to the hard lines of scientific theology', many sensed the danger of allowing experience to dictate the content of theology.

The theologically conservative Church of England paper, *The Record*, deplored a movement which 'would substitute emotional sentimentalism and visionary mysticism for solid piety, and scriptural experimentalism founded on the Word of God'.[1] In a massive critique of the Higher Life movements, B. B. Warfield commented with considered sarcasm: 'Men grow weary of serving the Lord; they do not wish to fight to win the prize; they prefer to be carried to the skies on flowery beds of ease'.[2] In fairness, while there were sections of the movement guilty of exaggerated claims and unorthodox theology, Keswick was restrained and the preaching scripturally reasoned.

It is within this context of required theological definition during the controversy surrounding Keswick that we meet two leading Evangelical bishops of the Church of England. Handley Moule was at first critical of Keswick in general and Evan Hopkins in particular. Hopkins was a mining engineer prior to his ordination into the Church of England. He became the new movement's most persuasive theological spokesman. Moule subjected Hopkin's book, *The Law of Liberty in the Spiritual Life*, to the scrutiny of a highly trained intellect, soaked in Scripture and massive in integrity. Concern for correct exegesis, theological proportion and truth made vital by experience, ensured that Moule's review was not unfairly dismissive. He agreed he 'could find fault with this or that bit of scripture exegesis and with a lack of proportion in the whole; but could he say that he knew in his own experience all that a true exegesis showed to be the Christian's privilege?'[3]

In 1877 J. C. Ryle published a collection of papers in a volume called *Holiness: Its Nature, Hindrances, Difficulties and Roots*. Within three years the author would be Bishop of Liverpool and a recognized leader of the Evangelical party in the Church of England. Even the more balanced teaching of Keswick was thought by Ryle to be doctrinally erroneous and pastorally dangerous. 'True holiness is much more than tears and sighs . . . A holy violence, a conflict, a warfare, a fight, a soldier's life, a wrestling . . . are spoken of as characteristic of the true Christian

(H pp. x, xvi). The contrast with Moule is instructive. 'It does not depend on wearisome struggle', Moule suggested, 'but on God's power to take the consecrated soul and keep him . . . Keswick stands distinctively for this; Christ our righteousness, upon Calvary, received by faith, is also Christ our holiness, in the heart that submits to Him and relies on Him . . . the open secret of inward victory for liberty in life and service through the trusted power of an indwelling Christ.'[4]

A sense of spiritual deficiency.

Moule was a son of the vicarage. His father combined Evangelical zeal with strong social concern. In his preaching he emphasized the need for personal conversion while at the same time involving himself in agitation for better drainage to prevent cholera. He also succeeded in having annual race meetings cancelled due to their anti-social effects. Handley Carr Glynn was one of eight gifted children. One would be a missionary and later a bishop in China and another would become a lecturer and examiner in classics. One would become an archdeacon in China, another would become curator of the County Museum and another chaplain in an asylum.

The stimulus of such a large able family is evident in the number of interests they each pursued. Wood carving, classical Chinese, the art of bell-ringing and fly-fishing were among the pastimes of his brothers. Handley himself became a keen player of the double harmonium, an interest he never lost. He took a degree in classics, and from such study, in an atmosphere of exact and disciplined learning, he derived a reverence and respect for the integrity of a text which was apparent in all his later writing. He was converted in 1866 when, in words written forty years later, he said: 'I was permitted to realise the presence, pardon and personal love of the Lord, not reasoned, just received' (HM p. 49).

In 1873 Moule was appointed Dean of Trinity College, Cambridge. During his time there he wrote his masterly, compact commentary on Romans. In 1880 he accepted the post of Principal of Ridley Hall, a newly formed college intended to resist ritualism and rationalism by equipping its students with solid Evangelical learning. He had a reputation for saintliness and was looked on by many as an exemplar of Christian character. His own self-estimate was more critical. In a later biographical passage he suggests that by 1885 he was aware of a sense of spiritual deficiency: 'I had begun to feel, after my years of converted life and ministerial work, guilty of discreditable failures in patience and charity and humbleness. I knew that I was not satisfied and I knew that I ought to find what would satisfy me.'[5] Around this time he reviewed Hopkins' book and though critical of details, he was becoming convinced that the overall argument reflected the experience of New Testament Christianity. In September 1885 he heard Hopkins preach at a holiness convention in Polmont, Scotland. He recalled: 'It was a long ordered piling up of the promises of God to the soul that will do two things towards him – surrender itself into His hands and trust Him for the mighty victory within' (HM pp. 127–8). He had found the answer to inner deficiency and Keswick had found an eloquent spokesman of impeccable standing amongst Evangelicals and one in whom were combined the critical eye of the scholar and the loving insight of the saint.[6]

In a series of modest pocket-sized books Moule shared with his readership his *Thoughts on Christian Sanctity, Spiritual Life, Union with Christ, Secret Prayer* and *Holy Communion*. The seminal ideas in his spirituality are visible in two particularly important books. *Thoughts on Christian Sanctity* consists of several addresses delivered at Cambridge in October 1885, barely one month after his crisis experience. In this small, and deceptively simple, book he began to fit together spiritual experience and biblical truth. The other book is his second commentary on *Romans*, published in the Expositors' Bible series and containing some of his most impressive writing. A mind trained to examine an ancient text, with a respect for its integrity, and a heart sensitive to the spiritual truths which had revitalized and redirected his own inner life, combined to produce a commentary which explores the spiritual experience of the commentator himself. What makes the book even more significant are the differences in interpretation between his 1894 commentary and the earlier Cambridge commentary of 1879.

Thoughts on Christian sanctity.

Moule welcomed the contemporary interest in the promotion of holiness. He conceded that sometimes the new teaching 'veered into error and sometimes it moved steadily on lines of eternal truth'. In an obvious attempt to reassure critics he promised: 'Never I hope, in one solitary sentence shall I forget the great lines of revealed truth and received doctrine' (CS p. 11). It is significant that he included Bible references in the margins of these books. The Keswick apologist had started his work.

The basic thrust of all Christian living must be towards a greater and more costly obedience. Moule recognized that while the Christian ideal is total loyalty of the heart to Christ, there will always be a real possibility of sin and failure. 'To the last it will be a sinner who walks with God.' Yet if the possibility of sin abounds, the possibility of victory through the indwelling Christ abounds even more: 'It is possible, by unreserved resort to divine power, under divine conditions, to become strongest . . . at our weakest point' (CS p. 18). Sin does not indicate the failure of grace but the imperfect receptivity of the believer.

The view that sin is neither necessary nor inevitable was Moule's conviction from the start. In his 1879 Romans commentary he had argued that sin was an invasion of human personality. The self is not inherently, essentially or irreversibly evil. Sin is 'an alien thing, an invasion, which (at the Fall) broke in on Man's nature created upright . . . the self is the subject on and in which the evil principle works; but it is not therefore identical with it and is capable of being worked on and in by the Divine principle'.[7] Even at the deepest levels of motive and sub-conscious predispositions, he argued, it is the consent of the self which constitutes sin.

Since it is the consenting self that yields to sin, it must be dethroned and replaced by Christ as the moral and spiritual centre of life. Moule is aware of the theological conundrum of how a selfish self can dethrone itself! 'Can self deny self? Can the centre of my acts and thoughts dislodge itself? Can I will that for which I am unwilling? Can I spring away, once and for all, from my own shadow?' (CS p. 37). He resorts to the technique Hopkins used to such effect in the sermon which won Moule. He strung seventeen texts together in a catena of promises and reminded his readers of Baxter's advice, 'Take ten looks at Christ for one at self' (CS pp. 39–40).

This is not a tactic of evasion. Moule is trying to analyse the experience of progress in holiness by indicating its twofold reference. Spiritual victory is complete only when the self is dethroned and then replaced by Christ. The controlling principle of spiritual life is the acknowledged Lordship of Christ: 'He is the Master, the master of a veritable slave, and that slave, here, now, always, everywhere, myself' (CS p. 47). If that sense of being a slave of Christ is lost, if Christ is regarded as having less than absolute authority in the soul, then the way is opened for compromise and inevitable failure. On the other hand to cultivate the mental habit of servitude to Christ leads to an almost intuitive obedience. Before the second experience of grace the self was still a slave to sin; in the act of total self-surrender the soul does obeisance to Christ and the power of sin is broken in the soul, and will remain broken so long as Christ is allowed to reign. As a result, when temptation comes, '[the Christian] says no. It is against orders. And the orders speak now in the region where to speak is to control' (CS p. 53). Moule had no qualms about using the strongest vocabulary to describe Christ's sovereign Lordship. Christ is Master, Possessor, Despot. Using oriental imagery he offered to 'put the neck of self beneath His feet', an image of servility defensible only alongside other balancing images from the New Testament such as sonship, fellowship and friendship. Moule wanted to emphasize the absoluteness of Christ's claims on the redeemed soul but in doing so he failed to allow due weight to the differences between a despot however benevolent, and one who said to his disciples, 'I no longer call you servants but friends' (John 15.15). He is surely again using hyperbole when he says Christ 'claims to own me and to use me as despotically as if I were inanimate' (CS p. 77).

In the routine circumstances, changing moods and varied demands of everyday life, Moule perceived countless occasions to renew obeisance. Each moral decision is a real choice between the Lordship of Christ and the lordship of self. In the spiritual union with Christ the will is never deprived of its moral freedom. Rather it is 'willingly yielded to it, a very different thing' (CS p. 65). Moule was guarding against a spirituality that assumes the loss of personal moral identity. The presence of Christ is such an immense reality to the believer that it will be 'as if the victory over temptation, the deliverance from sinning, the animation to love . . . were the independent and isolated action in me, of another . . . I am so to realise Him in this mighty "not myself" of His will and work, as to trust Him for immeasurable modes of purifying and preserving power in me and on me, quite beyond my analysis' (CS p. 67). Several times he admits that the working of Christ in the soul is beyond descriptive analysis.

He is struggling here to keep his exposition on 'the great lines of revealed truth and received doctrine'. However, the problem of internal evil persists. Granted the New Testament experience of 'no longer I that live but Christ who lives in me', there remains in the Christian soul the intractable problem of indwelling and besetting sin. Moule introduced what was to become a typical Keswick concept, the counteracting force of the indwelling Christ (R p. 221). In regeneration the believer is united to Christ and the effects of that union are apparent, not only in the deepest recesses of the self but also in conduct which is visible and open to public scrutiny. By the inner working of the Holy Spirit the regenerate will is made receptive, affections are kindled, and the surrender of the will, far from being an extorted submission, becomes an act of grateful love: 'In this dwelling of Christ in the heart there is involved that self-surrender which, without the Spirit's grace is unwelcome . . . It needs a divine force beneath our will to make us, without reserve and with open eyes, assent to this and welcome Him in' (CS p. 87).

The motive behind spiritual submission to Christ is to be found in the vicarious death of Christ. The believer feels a 'spiritual love to the holy Christ, love continually regenerated as faith lays hold on truth and promise' (CS p. 88). To love and trust the indwelling Christ involves more than one critical act of self-surrender. Daily, moment-by-moment repetition is required. By meditating on the beauty, holiness and love of Jesus for sinners, a Christian gathers ethical strength, spiritual love is reinforced and from the recollection of utter indebtedness there follows a desire to live a life of continuous obedience.

In this book Moule was working out a biblical theology of what had happened to him. He was not writing neutral theology but carefully interpreting his experience within revealed truth and received doctrine. Where there was apparent contradiction between his experience and Scripture he allowed the tension to stand. Here we are watching a spirituality in transition, and whatever its weaknesses, it is unmistakably Christ-centred. The fine words of Thomas Scott, 'I have found more in Christ than I ever expected to want', seem to encapsulate Moule's spirituality. In a footnote in an almost forgotten manual of English Church teaching Moule confided: 'The writer cannot express the help he has derived from one simple instance of the witness of the Scriptures to Christ. In some editions of Bagster's Bible is printed a classified collection of texts giving the names, titles, offices etc. of the Lord Jesus found in the Scriptures. An accidental opening of those pages in a friend's Bible gave him an impression never to be forgotten of the unsearchable riches of Christ in His personal glory and in His work for us'.[8] In his atoning death and risen life Christ is infinitely resourceful, all-sufficient and ever available to the open heart. The grace of Christ is not experienced as an outside reinforcement, but as an indwelling presence creating spiritual union between believer and Saviour. That this experience of realized union with Christ was seen by Moule to be a distinct and second stage in Christian experience is worked out fully in the 1894 Romans commentary.

A used Christ.

Union with Christ makes available a new power with which to live the 'grateful life', a power residing, 'not in Justification itself, but in what it opens up' (R p. 161). United with Christ in his death, the old man is crucified 'that the body of sin might be cancelled'. Precisely here, where perfectionist claims could intrude, Moule warns 'there is still a foe within' (R p. 165). Only through him who died is the body of sin 'in abeyance as to the power of temptation over the soul'. Cancelled does not mean annihilated; it is for the Christian to veto sin's suggestions, but less by confronting sin and more by surrender to Christ. Union with Christ in his death and resurrection, by a voluntary act of faith, involves an actual transfer of ownership, a complete change of control at the moral centre of the person. After such a 'definite and critical act of the thankful will' the disruptive power of sin is neutralized and life has settled, after its long friction, into gear (R p. 178). Two wills which before had ground and jumped in a damaging mis-match, have now been synchronized.

How does such a view of defeated sin fit in with the tortured wrestling of Romans chapter seven? In the earlier commentary Moule had understood the chapter to be a description of the normal Christian experience of spiritual conflict: '[The] man who here does what he hates is one who has so felt the absolute sanctity of God and of his law as to see sin in the slightest deviation of will and affection from its standard. Such penitence for such sin is not only possible in a life of Christian rectitude, but may be said to be a natural element in it.'[9]

In 1889 a new edition had a rather unconvincing qualification of his treatment of this passage. By 1894 he had arrived at what was to become the recognized 'Keswick' interpretation. The embattled soul of chapter 7 is an illustration of a believer who is not fully using the definitely sought power of the Holy Ghost. 'And when he does not, the resultant failure – though it be but a thought of vanity, a flush of unexpressed anger, a microscopic flaw in the practice of truthfulness, an unhallowed imagination darting in a moment through the soul – is to him sorrow, burthen and shame' (R p. 195). Failure, defeat and frustrating inner conflicts are the outcome of self-effort at sanctification. United to Christ by faith, with access to the immeasureable riches of grace, strength and love, the Christian need not battle, but simply trust, appeal and confide. Like many others, Moule was impressed by the frequent use of 'I' in Romans seven and the absence of any reference to the Holy Spirit, while the exact opposite is the case in chapter eight. The conflict occurs every time Paul 'acts out of character as a regenerate man' and the victory is experienced only when he 'adequately uses God' (R pp. 198f).

'A used Christ', 'using the fact of our union', and even the almost irreverent phrase, 'a used God', are typical of Moule. He is not suggesting that grace can be used in the mechanical sense, but rather that Christians should possess what they own, and use the riches of Christ instead of struggling to make ends meet. Deficiency in spiritual life is not inevitable. Certainly sin remains: 'You are a sinner still; always, actually, in defect, and in tendency . . . for whatever the presence of the Spirit in you has done, it has not so altered you that, if He should go away you would not instantly revert to the type of unholiness' (R p. 193). But the counteracting force of the indwelling Christ is available to be used if only the believer will 'act upon the fact of union with Him, and assume victory in His victory.'[10]

Moule's transitional comment on Romans chapter eight is a superb piece of devotional theology deserving lengthy quotation:

> If we are indeed in Christ, the Spirit is in us, dwelling in us, and we are in the Spirit. And so, possessed and filled by the

blessed Power, we indeed have power to walk and obey. Nothing is mechanical, automatic; we are full persons still; He who annexes and possesses our personality does not for a moment violate it. But then He DOES possess it; and the Christian, so possessing and so possessed, is not only bound but enabled, in humble but practical reality, in a liberty otherwise unknown, to fulfil the just demand of the law, to please God in a life lived, not to self but to Him.

(R p. 208)

Sacred work . . . turned Godward.

There is an undoubted strain of passivity in much of Moule's thought. But he never conceived of the spiritual life as a way of short-circuiting spiritual discipline or the means of grace. Prayer, Bible study and Holy Communion are appointed aids to Christian growth, and each must have its place in the life of faith. Prayer is a 'sacred work of thought, will and affection turned Godward'; it is 'the occasion of all others for cultivating a deep individual insight into yourself and your personal needs, and into . . . God in Christ in all His glory and grace for you'.[11] Moule was known to pace his garden from seven to seven-thirty each morning, 'with eyes closed and a shawl on his shoulders, saying his prayers' (HM pp. 311f). He found he prayed best aloud, the spoken word giving his thoughts definiteness and a force which silent discursive meditation lacked. He filled much of his prayer time reflecting on the person and work of Christ as applied to his own life. He knew how to use silence by 'quietening the articulate activities of the mind' so that consciousness can recollect the Lord in the profound quiet of 'an adoring and ruminating spirit'.

In a series of Lent meditations on the cross he urged the practice of considering the meaning of Christ's death in relation to personal need: 'The penitent spirit when it has had a real vision of itself, and of the Crucified, knows that in Him, accepted, trusted, welcomed, is the only, and the perfect, and the present and the perpetual peace of life.'[12] Prayer is a prerequisite to assurance; to reflect upon the love of the Crucified is to strengthen the sense of being loved: 'The love of the Crucified, that love which He IS, turns the words "redemption", "possession", "servitude" into the inmost voice of an infinite affection.'[13]

Intercession and petition are equally important as disciplines revealing faith in God's providence and his love for the world. When he was Bishop of Durham he prayed each morning for one of his thirteen rural deaneries mentioning each of the clergy by name. Such detailed, faithful and informed prayer is the reflection in Christian devotion of the all-inclusive love of God. He encouraged explicitness in petitionary prayer; prayers for others should be 'reverent, regular, unhurried, detailed, confiding, and expectant'. The time allotted to prayer should be regular, punctual and generous. He had a deep aversion to shoddiness in spiritual things. He warned against the 'moral impossibility of combining adoration and slovenliness'. Without being presumptuous the Christian must adopt a tone of reverent outspokenness as one who is welcome in the Divine presence. Prayer for others is an act of profound unselfishness; it is to love others in the presence of God. Intercessory prayer 'goes out, simply out, to the Lord, and asks Him in His own way to act in other directions, in other regions than our own'.[14] Prayer lists, prayer groups, a diary 'distributing names and subjects among the days of the week', though simple enough devices, were valued as modest aids to disciplined regular prayer.

Early training in textual translation, a lifelong exposure to the written Word of God, and a deep concern to ensure that his teaching was founded on Scripture, enabled Moule to handle the Bible with skill and sympathy. He believed that 'Christian life for its fullness, stability, strength and health, its adult efficiency as a life for God, requires scriptural nourishment' (HM pp. 312f). He commented ruefully that justification comes by faith but knowledge of the Bible by works. He had a high view of Scripture, believing that the Spirit was the author and interpreter, who takes of the things of Christ and reveals them to the Christian heart. His own practice was explained in a short tract. 'I keep time sacred each morning for some careful reading of the New Testament. I use a large copy and I keep a pencil in my hand to make notes in the margin or to draw lines of connection across the page.' He did the same with the Old Testament in the evening. Always in his Bible study he was looking for clues and insights into the person and work of Christ. He reckoned he had read the Gospels over attentively between fifty and sixty times.[15]

Moule revered the service of Holy Communion. He encouraged evening communion, and allowed the reservation of the sacrament provided it was for special use and not for adoration. In

1895 he was awarded the D. D. for his scholarly edition of Bishop Ridley's volume, *On the Lord's Supper*. In 'unsettled times' when the atmosphere was prickly with suspicions about ritualism and 'sacerdotalism', Moule sought to retain richness and mystery by emphasizing the spiritual reality of Christ's presence in Holy Communion. He tried to avoid stripping the sacrament of solemn efficacy as a means of grace which really set forth Christ, while at the same time resisting developments which would turn a sacrament into a sacrifice. He speaks with judicious firmness in the *Manual of English Church Teaching*: 'The Holy Supper of the Lord is an occasion for our sacrifice of praise and our sacrifice of self. But it is not a Sacrifice; it is a Sacrament. It is not to be offered; it is to be taken; it is not our gift to God; it is God's gift to us.'[16] Holy Communion is 'a single thing meant for a use full of wonder, full of blessing, full of God'.

The consistent focus of Moule's theology of the Lord's Supper is the cross. In the atoning death of Jesus lies the origin, the meaning, the efficacy, and the theological centre of Holy Communion: 'It is our self-sacrificed God's own way of setting in the very midst of our faith, and of our worship, and of our love, that supreme, amazing, soul-filling fact; His suffering for us, His bodily and spiritual suffering unfathomable, that we, through Him, believed, received, assimilated, used, might live in purity and peace.'[17] The true communicant is a consistent Christian. Communion is not merely an act of worship, it is a way of life, a quality of relationship to Christ. Such a relationship of loving trust is 'strengthened and fixed' by Holy Communion when it is received by one whose mind and heart are thoroughly prepared. In this, as in other aspects of Christian living, he displayed a 'spiritual painstaking', a seriousness about holy things that only just stopped short of being overdone.

The spirituality of Handley Moule reveals a determination to interpret his experience within the framework of biblical truth and received orthodoxy. In contrast to some other expositions of holiness, Moule made Scripture the controlling factor. He firmly anchored justification and sanctification in the finished work of Christ. He sought to expound Paul's theology of the crucified, risen and indwelling Christ in a way that made sense of Christ as he had experienced him. Yet his concentration on union with Christ, self-surrender to Christ as Master and consequent victory over sin, undoubtedly influenced his exegesis. Consequently his interpretation of Romans seven, his doctrine of union with Christ in relation to victory over sin, and his insistance on rest by faith rather than victory within conflict left important questions hanging. J. C. Ryle, by 1880 Bishop of Liverpool, was critical of the new holiness movement, perceiving in the teaching a weakened doctrine of sin, a latent perfectionism and a dangerous tendency to passivity.

Fairly launched as a Christian.

John Charles Ryle enjoyed the advantages of being a child in an affluent early Victorian home. He was educated at Eton and Oxford and there was every likelihood that he would succeed to the family banking business. His father had been a Methodist but later joined the Church of England. In the home an attitude of tolerant restraint prevailed where religious matters were concerned. Evangelicals were regarded as 'well meaning, extravagant, fanatical enthusiasts, who carried things a great deal too far in religion' (T p. 24). The impression is given, that in the Ryle home, to carry things too far in religion would be the epitome of bad manners! Ryle later recalled that the main difference between Sunday and other days was more physical than spiritual; plum pudding for dinner and occasionally oysters for supper (T p. 24).

Ryle first heard consistent Evangelical preaching at St George's, Macclesfield. He then witnessed the conversions of his cousin and sister, and became increasingly dissatisfied with the moral ambiguities of Oxford life. A period of illness confined him to bed, providing an opportunity to read the Bible, pray and reflect seriously on the shortcomings of his own inner life. In an autobiographical fragment, written almost a quarter of a century later, he only loosely dated his conversion, saying that 'from midsummer 1837 till Christmas of the same year' his life had irrevocably changed and he was, by early 1838, 'fairly launched as a Christian'.[18] Apparently the personal crisis point was reached during a singularly unmemorable afternoon service. The one exception to this severe judgement was when the second lesson from Ephesians chapter two was read slowly and emphatically by a skilled and sensitive reader. With pauses to allow time for reflection verse 8 spoke with decisive force to Ryle: 'By grace . . .

you are saved . . . through faith . . . not of works . . . the gift of God' (T p. 26).

In 1841 the family bank collapsed and the Ryles were ruined. By the end of that year J. C. Ryle had been ordained curate at Exbury in the parish of Fawley. Except for a few months in Winchester, he spent the next thirty-nine years in country parishes before being offered the new see of Liverpool, at the age of sixty-four. During a long life Ryle experienced many hardships. In addition to the emotional and physical upheaval resulting from financial ruin, he lost his first wife after only three years of marriage. His second wife died ten years later after a protracted illness which took its toll on his own health. Rather than sleep away from home when on preaching engagements, he would travel round journeys of up to thirty miles in an open carriage. With no time for holidays or recreation, and with the responsibility of three boys, he later reflected: 'The whole state of things was a heavy strain upon me, in body and mind, and I often wondered how I lived through it' (T p. 45).

He was happiest in pulpit or study, where, perhaps people could not come so threateningly close. Yet he could also be remarkably affectionate and sensitive to the needs of individuals. As a pastor he was loved by his people, serving them gladly as a servant of Christ. It is a strange paradox that someone in whom the combative instinct was so strong could also be an effective conciliator. Ryle encouraged the holding of Church Congresses because they helped Christians understand each other, and this at a time when most Evangelicals thought them High Church snares. He was a regular attender and took a full part in discussions on doctrinal differences. He urged Evangelicals to organize and learn to live and work together. In his later years he made appeals for brotherly love and tolerance. In his Farewell to the Diocese in 1900 he urged his clergy: 'Cultivate and study the habit of being at peace with all your brother ministers. Beware of divisions. One thing the world can always understand if they do not understand doctrines; that thing is angry quarrelling and controversy. Be at peace among yourselves' (T p. 100).

However, when it came to defending Evangelical principles, courtesy and tolerance did not extend to indulgence. His book, *Holiness*, is a weighty defence of the Calvinist spiritual tradition, convincingly argued, with no punches pulled, based on solid biblical exegesis and enriched by the writings of the Reformed and Puritan divines. The Canon's target was undoubtedly the new holiness movements, and by the date of the second edition, 1879, Keswick was clearly in his firing line.

It is instructive to read Moule and Ryle to compare their respective styles. In tone, Moule tends to be persuasive, gentle, sometimes using long discursive sentences to explain the spiritual experience he wishes the reader to seek. Describing the condition of submission to Christ he promised:

> Where, through His grace, that condition, in its true sense, is accepted, there an element, essentially of strength and gladness will be found to develop within the life; a cheerful assurance of a companionship most warm and tender, because divine, of a vivid sympathy meeting every true need of grief or happiness, of a wisdom which concerns itself with every detail of every day, of an affection to which the best endearments of earth can but point to their glorious archetype.

On a similar theme Ryle asserts: 'When I speak of a man growing in grace – I mean simply this, that his sense of sin is becoming deeper, his faith stronger, his hope brighter, his love more extensive, his spiritual mindedness more marked.'[19]

Where Moule is misty but warm and utterly typical of the embroidered Victorian style, Ryle in his crisp, clear and easy to follow prose sounds surprisingly modern. He worked hard at his style, aiming to write with punch, clarity and an absence of the elevated vagueness that makes Moule's writing devotionally attractive but conceptually elusive. Ryle deplored the overuse of the comma, the colon and the semi-colon. He wrote in language which was 'plain and pointed' in words picked and packed.[20] The note of warning is always in the background and he used the question mark with remorseless persistence, forcing the reader to think, to examine the argument and decide. Many of his writings were polemical, characterized by trenchant criticism of woolly theology or shaky exegesis. A mind well trained and soaked in the writings of traditional Reformed orthodoxy, neat footwork in argument and determination to stand his ground on Evangelical principle, are tactics more suggestive of the Christian pugilist than the Church of England clergyman. Ryle was both. Utterly loyal to his understanding of the historic reformed Church of England, and standing on the theological foundation of the Thirty-Nine Articles, the Prayer Book and the Bible, Ryle fought tirelessly against any perceived weakening of the old faith.

Light from old times.

Ryle distrusted novelty. In a non-pejorative sense, he was old-fashioned. Theologically he preferred the 'old and regular . . . the beaten paths of our forefathers'. He even used the dictum, 'The old is better'. The spirit of the age might dismiss 'effete systems, old world creeds, fossil theology, worn out doctrines, old fashioned divinity' in favour of a new theology, but Ryle clung to the old (UR p. 80). He conceded that, at the age of sixty, 'my mind perhaps stiffens and I cannot perhaps receive easily any new doctrines' (H p. xvii). Yet his resistance to new ideas had a more constructive explanation than the inflexibility of a mind that has settled for premature retirement.

'Let me impress the absolute necessity of resisting the current of the age' (UR p. 75). Lying behind these reactionary words was the conviction of a clergyman who had held a long tenure of a small rural living, that the intellectual ferment, the burgeoning of religious practice as a social rather than a spiritual activity, and the economic and industrial development of Victorian society were potentially perilous to the spiritual life. In Ryle's view it was an age determined to 'cross examine ancient opinions', 'impatient of restraint' characterized by 'an idolatry of the intellect'. On the other hand there was a regrettable unwillingness to investigate the great fundamental evidence of divine revelation.[21] The rise of the affluent and influential middle class is reflected in the complaint that: 'Half the lay Churchmen seem so absorbed in politics, or fine arts, or cotton, or iron, or coal, or corn, or shipping, or railways, that you cannot get them to look at religious questions' (UR p. 427).

The problem was not, however, a lack of religious activity or interest. Ryle recognized, and frequently lamented, the high profile religion was given in respectable lives. His complaint was that so much religion lacked vitality, seriousness and the kind of stability only deep roots could give. He was suspicious of religious ferment, discerning beneath the frothy, shallowness, a 'craving for novelty' and a religion-while-you-wait mentality. He had real hesitations about mass conversions though he respected Moody and approved of his doctrine. He never resolved his theological differences with Keswick though he respected the integrity of its leadership. Higher criticism of the Bible, the sacramentalism of the Oxford Movement, evolution with its attendant mood of optimism about human progress, and its consequent weakening of the doctrine of sin, were only some of the elements of the changing thought of Victorian culture with which Ryle collided.

One of his favourite words was 'solid'. In contrast to the liquidity of a free-thinking generation, whose creed Ryle labelled 'Nothingarianism', he stood for a spirituality which rested firmly on the 'old evangelical doctrines' which in turn were founded on Scripture. He spoke often of 'neglected doctrines', and engaged in theological spring-cleaning, unearthing valuable dust-covered truth and restoring it to useful life. Doctrinal error was not a mere theological peculiarity to be examined dispassionately like some suspect philosophical premise. Ryle believed that the gospel of salvation from sin by the death of Christ in the sinner's place could only become effectively real in experience. To his mind it was axiomatic that right doctrine, founded on Scripture, defined the gospel and moulded the pattern of experience. So he never saw himself as contending for peripheral issues. He laboured to defend and explore and commend the fundamental convictions which were so central to the gospel that without them it ceases to be Christian. In a passionate paper on the cross he stated that without the cross (by which he meant substitutionary atonement), 'your religion is a heaven without a sun, an arch without a keystone, a compass without a needle, a clock without spring or weights, a lamp without oil'.[22]

The Evangelical succession was traced by Ryle to the Reformers, the Puritans and the leaders of the Evangelical Revival. He produced many papers of historical appreciation and biography in an attempt to reintroduce his contemporaries to the original sources of Evangelical religion. The studies are crisply written, vivid, anecdotal but with the theological emphases woven in. They are in no sense 'modern critical' biographies. They are a restrained form of theological salesmanship and an unshamed declaration of the Church's indebtedness to such figures as Latimer, Baxter, Whitefield, Wesley and Fletcher of Madeley. The last two are deliberately mentioned here because they were leading Arminian theologians and therefore not of Ryle's school. But they were Evangelicals, and what Ryle meant by that can best be seen in his warmly appreciative words on

Wesley. He encouraged Calvinists who had lightly dismissed Wesley to think again: 'He was a bold fighter on Christ's side . . . he honoured the Bible. He cried down sin. He made much of Christ's blood. He exalted holiness. He taught the absolute need of repentence, faith and conversion.'[23]

Sin is a vast moral disease.

'The slightest outward or inward departure from absolute mathematical parallelism with God's revealed will and character constitutes a sin . . .' (H p. 2). Ryle believed that each person is by nature a sinner with a 'will to the thing that is evil'. In his treatment of sin there is a stern impatience with any attempt to lessen moral culpability by appealing to environment, social conditioning, heredity or any other mitigating factor. The warm sentimental glow which often surrounds the new-born baby is briskly dispersed by a cold draught of Ryle's realism: 'He is not a little "innocent", he is a little "sinner" . . . As it lies smiling and crowing in its cradle that little creature carries in its heart the seeds of every kind of wickedness' (H p. 3). As a drastic consequence of the fall the will to sin has become a constituent part of human nature. Further, sin has so distorted the moral vision that it is impossible for the sinner to realize the full extent of his sinfulness. Because of the incurable capacity for self-deceit and the filtering effects of self-love, any knowledge of the self man has gained is inherently untrustworthy. A permeating corruption so poisons the very sources of moral personality that its every expression is compromised. 'The best things that we do have something in them to be pardoned', he warned (H p. 9).

In an amazing piece of moral arithmetic Ryle challenged his readers to 'sit down and make a sum'. Assuming a person is awake and accountable fifteen hours a day and allowing a mere two sins per hour the mathematics of guilt work out at two hundred and ten sins a week, ten thousand and eighty sins per year and over one hundred thousand sins each decade of life.[24] In the face of that 'damning sum' Ryle expects the reader to capitulate and acknowledge the reality of sin. He is not being morbid and he is well aware that the whole process can be ridiculed. But he will not have the essential fact overlooked; every human being is inherently and intransigently set against God and can never be otherwise without God's intervention.

Ryle traced the errors of perfectionism to an inadequate doctrine of sin. Christian theology with a weak view of human corruption is not 'full measure . . . sixteen ounces to the pound'. Any claim to have enjoyed long periods of uninterrupted communion with God seemed to be both theologically wrong and pastorally dangerous. He was convinced that sin is so enmeshed in human personality that even the regenerate heart remains infected throughout life:

> The greatest proof of the extent and power of sin is the pertinacity with which it cleaves to man even after he is converted . . . It is checked, controlled, mortified and crucified by the expulsive power of a new principle of grace. But the very struggles which go on within his bosom, the fight that he finds it needful to fight daily . . . the contest between the flesh and the spirit . . . the inward groanings . . . all, all testify to the . . . enormous power and vitality of sin.
>
> (H p. 5)

Renewed after the image of God.

A complete 'transforming and altering of all the inner man' is essential for salvation. Sin has so distorted the image of God that the heart of man, the source of personality, must be re-created. 'To melt a lump of iron and forge it into a watch spring' is merely to produce the same thing in another form. A true Christian is someone who is made 'altogether new', who has experienced a 'spiritual resurrection' by which the person becomes what he was not and could not be before. This work of regeneration is accomplished by the Holy Spirit, and it results in a new spiritual awareness. Sin is seen and hated for what it is, while the cross, God's remedy for sin, takes on a personal reference. It reveals the cost of sin, the reality of divine judgement and the immensity of God's love. It is the work of the Spirit to nourish and nurture the new nature by enabling it in opposition to sin and in obedience to Christ.

Ryle worried about the spiritual consequences of neglecting the role of the Holy Spirit in sanctification. The Keswick doctrine of the indwelling Christ threatened to make the Holy Spirit redundant. Moule seemed to suggest that Christ displaces the self, and that sanctification involved the negation of the self.

There is both realism and balance in Ryle's caution. 'Christ in us' must never be forced to the point of eliminating personal identity or moral responsibility. Holiness does not consist in the loss of self but rather in the gradual transformation and maturing of a Christian character through the operation of the Holy Spirit and the diligent use of means of grace: 'We need the work of the Holy Spirit as well as the work of Christ; we need renewal of the heart as well as atoning blood' (H p. 23). That is not theological hair-splitting; it is pastoral wisdom. Regeneration sets in motion a lifelong process of spiritual growth, characterized by discipline, conflict and effort.

Ryle rejected the Keswick pattern of conversion – consecration. Deliverance from the guilt and dominion of sin is the result of union with Christ, which is the privilege of every Christian. The contention of Moule was that such deliverance was notably absent in experience. The discrepancy is explained by the argument that potential resources available in Christ remain unused until an act of absolute surrender to Christ. But such theology seemed to Ryle to weaken the doctrine of the new birth as a radical and unrepeatable new beginning. The idea that spiritual assets are frozen until a second crisis seemed to Ryle to be unscriptural and untrue to experience. 'The Spirit never lies dormant or idle'; his work is to stimulate growth, enable obedience and produce the fruits and evidences of the new birth.

Each Christian must work out their own salvation in fear and trembling. The gifts of grace, a new heart and a new nature must be improved by the 'diligent use of means'. Consistent Christian living is not simply there for the asking. Holiness is not achieved in an instant, and is not merely a matter of rest and surrender to Christ. The New Testament never suggests 'let go and let God'. It urges stand firm, put on armour, take a sword, fight, endure.

Appointed channels . . . of fresh supplies of grace.

Christian growth is the result of disciplined toil and self-exertion. To have 'an habitual respect for God's law' and a constant desire to do the will of Christ requires moral resilience developed through moral struggle. Prayer, Bible study, regular attendance at worship, corporate prayer, listening to sermons and taking Holy Communion are spiritual exercises which are obligatory for the Christian. They are means of growth in holiness and are not to be dismissed as a post-graduate course for keen Christians. One evidence of regeneration is a new spiritual-mindedness which replaces previous complacency. Amongst other changes, and with not a little optimism, Ryle suggested: 'Sermons appear a thousand times more interesting than they used to do; and he would no more be inattentive or willingly go to sleep under them, than a prisoner would upon his trial.'[25]

The Victorian age produced a superfluity of Bibles many of which, Ryle lamented, either gathered dust or had only ornamental value. His resistance to biblical criticism was unrelenting not only because he held a high view of inspiration, but because he believed the Bible provided the source-book of Evangelical truth and experience.[26] It is 'the grand instrument' by which souls are converted and the chief means by which souls are built up. 'The man who has the Bible and the Holy Spirit in his heart has everything which is absolutely needful to make him spiritually wise.'[27] Ryle encouraged and exemplified an obedient, docile receptivity to the plain meaning of Scripture, eschewing the obscurantism of the professional scholar or 'unfriendly critic'. The Bible contains 'the unchanging mind of the King of Kings'. It is to be read daily, comprehensively and with the 'thoroughness of a prospector digging for Australian gold'. Sustained exposure to the Bible moulds and shapes the mind, producing imperceptible changes in character and effecting a gradual formation of spiritual values and moral strength. True Christians live in and love the Scriptures. 'Their ears are like a dry soil, ever thirsting to drink in the water of life.'[28]

For a number of years Ryle worked at a series of *Expository Thoughts on the Gospels*, intended primarily for the use of the average Christian family. The portion would be read, and Ryle's practical and edifying comment would follow. These books had enormous popularity and drew enthusiastic if qualified praise from Spurgeon: 'We prize these volumes. They are diffuse, but not more so than family reading requires.'[29] The three volumes of John are less accessible to the 'average Christian family', and rank as a sound, scholarly if devoutly conservative commentary on John replete with references and quotations from now forgotten authors.

'The pith, marrow and backbone' of practical piety is private prayer. Ryle was so sure of this that he judged whether or not a person was converted by their attitude to prayer. 'Converted people always pray.'[30] His writings contain many reprimands of those who mutter their prayers in bed or who repeat a few sentences picked up in the nursery. Prayer is 'simply speaking to God'; 'any place can be the presence of God'. Lack of time or inclination are inadequate excuses for neglecting a discipline so formative in the shaping of Christian character. The incompatibility of sin and prayer was felt deeply by Ryle. In prayer the soul is exposed to the consuming holiness of God so that time spent in the presence of God, with the heart humbled by its sin yet gratefully receptive to grace, purifies the springs of motive, sharpens the conscience and creates a deeper love for God. Ryle understood the reflexive effect of prayer. Through prayerful discipline the spiritually stagnant are refreshed, those burdened by the monotony of personal failure discover new moral resources and those impatient with mediocrity in discipleship gain a new vision of the possibilities of grace.

'Praying out of a book is a habit I cannot praise', he observed.[31] Ryle thought of prayer as conversation with God and such intimacy does not require a script. Extempore prayer may not facilitate elegant syntax and balanced cadence but the language of friendship has no need of such devices. Ryle does not expound a theory of prayer, or examine cases or explore its psychology. His writing is a substantial plea for Christians to pray, just to get on with it!

True Christianity is a fight.

Bible reading, prayer and the other means of grace keep the soil of spirituality nutritious and fertile. But diligence is costly and excuses are easily found. Even in the pursuit of holiness Christians will feel the downward drag of indwelling sin, and the frustrating persistence of the inner tension between the new nature and the old. 'With a corrupt heart, a busy devil and an ensnaring world the Christian must either "fight" or be lost' (H p. 53). A life free of conflict is suspect and may signal an inner capitulation to the enemy. The fight for righteousness, the struggle to increase in holiness is a sign of spiritual health. Since the devil will not attack his own loyal subjects, the embattled Christian can be sure that his experience of spiritual hostility is proof of spiritual progress. Ryle believed in the immediate personal malice of the devil, seeing in the trials and testings of each individual life a reflection of the vast spiritual conflict between the loving holy purpose of God and the frustrating activity of Satan.

'There is no holiness without a warfare', he warned. 'Saved souls will always be found to have fought a fight' (H p. 55). With Keswick in his sights Ryle let loose several volleys of New Testament references describing Christian life as a warfare, a struggle and a fight. Yielding to God, the rest of faith and any other passive interpretation of holiness is 'a great mistake'. Ryle will not have the pain and frustration of indwelling sin explained away by what he sees as exegetical contortions. The tortured wrestling, the anguished penitence and the desperate pleas of Romans chapter seven 'precisely tally with the recorded experience of the most eminent saints' (H p. xi). Paul's account stands as solid scriptural evidence of the normality of an inner conflict that will not be finally resolved till the believer is glorified in heaven.

Ryle almost conceded the Keswick condition if not the Keswick method. In his treatment of assurance he admits: 'There have been . . . many believers who have appeared to walk in almost uninterrupted fellowship with the Father and the Son . . . who have seemed to enjoy an almost unceasing sense of the light of God's reconciled countenance' (H pp. 105–6). But the 'almost' is a significant qualification. Freedom from sin may by God's grace be tantalizingly within reach, but not quite. Victory depends entirely on faith in Christ's adequacy. Again the sentence, 'The more faith the more victory, the more faith the more inward peace', could have been the slogan of Keswick (H p. 57). But Ryle is not saying *only* yield, *only* believe. Faith is not the antidote to conflict but the attitude of the believer embroiled in the tensions and ambiguities of moral obedience in a fallen world. Faith is an attitude of trust which lays hold of the weapons of warfare in the confidence that God will give the victory and which focuses attention on Christ, the companion of the embattled soul. Ryle strongly advised the struggler:

> Cultivate the habit of fixing your eye more simply on Jesus Christ, and try to know more of the fulness there is laid up in Him for every one of His believing people. Do not be always poring down over the imperfections of your own heart, and

> dissecting your own besetting sins. Look up. Look more to your risen Head in heaven . . . who is ever living at God's right hand as your Priest, your Advocate, and your Almighty Friend.
>
> (UR p. 228).

That two such godly men as Moule and Ryle should differ so markedly in their understanding of holiness is due in part to differences in temperament and experience. They both sought to anchor their spirituality in the Bible, using Scripture as the primary resource for doctrine and for the interpretation of Christian experience. They shared deep convictions about the fallenness of man, the vicarious death of Christ for sinners, the need for a personal experience of Christ in repentence and conversion, and they agreed that personal holiness was the goal of Christian life. How such holiness was achieved was their major point of disagreement.

For Ryle Christian life is struggle and endurance, and sanctification required discipline and strenuous spiritual effort. Sin could only be kept at bay by a sustained battle in the soul. He vigorously denied the possibility of uninterrupted communion with God and insisted that the Christian soul is committed to a life of unremitting warfare. Moule, on the other hand, urged the need for a second crisis of grace, an absolute surrender of the will to Christ, resulting in victory over the tyranny of self through the power of a trusted Christ.[31]

In one of Ryle's warmly conciliatory passages – and there are many in the writings of this accomplished controversialist – he looked forward to the fellowship of believers in heaven. One sentence puts the whole controversy between these two devout protagonists in its proper perspective. 'Old doctrinal peculiarities, fiercely wrangled for upon earth, will be covered over by one common sense of debt to Christ' (H p. 245). The 'one common sense of debt to Christ' evident in the lives and writings of these two Evangelical bishops, was what ultimately informed and inspired their attempts to promote and expound true gospel holiness.

Sources frequently cited

Harford, J. B., and MacDonald, F. C., *Bishop Handley Moule*. London 1923. (HM)
Moule, H. C. G., *Thoughts on Christian Sanctity*. London 1886. (CS)
——, *The Epistle to the Romans*. London 1894. (R)
Ryle, J. C., *The Upper Room*. Edinburgh 1977. (UR)
——, *Holiness*. London 1952. (H)
Toon, P., *John Charles Ryle*. London 1976. (T)

Additional reading

Barabas, S., *So Great Salvation*. London 1952.
Farley, I., 'John Charles Ryle–Episcopal Evangelist: a study in Late Victorian Evangelicalism'. Durham Ph.D, 1988.
Girdlestone, R. B., Moule, H. C. G., and Drury, T. W., *English Church Teaching on Faith Life and Order* (London 1897), part II, pp. 55–152.
'Keswick at Home', *Expository Times*, vol. iv (1890), pp. 28f., 108f., 164f., 378f.
Loane, M., *John Charles Ryle*. London 1983.
——, *Makers of Our Heritage* (London 1967), chaps. 1, 2.
Macgregor, G. H. C., *So Great Salvation*. Edinburgh 1892.
Moule, H. C. G., *Christ is All*. London 1892.
——, *Outlines of Christian Doctrine*. London 1910.
——, *The Call of Lent*. London 1917.
——, *Thoughts on Union with Christ*. London 1886.
——, *Veni Creator*. London 1890.
Pollock, J., *The Keswick Story*. London 1964.
Ryle, J. C., *Practical Religion*. London 1900.
——, *Old Paths*. London 1977.
——, *Self Portrait*. P. Toon, ed., London 1975.

Notes

1. Pollock, *Keswick*, p. 33.
2. B. B. Warfield, *Perfectionism* (New York 1931), p. 244.
3. Harford, *Moule*, pp. 127–8; Barabas, *So Great Salvation*, pp. 158–60; A. Smellie, *Evan H. Hopkins* (London 1920).
4. Pollock, *Keswick*, p. 74.
5. Barabas, *Salvation*, p. 171.
6. See J. Baird, *The Spiritual Unfolding of Bishop Moule* (London 1926).
7. *Romans* (Cambridge 1879), p. 128. Moule contributed the volumes on *Ephesians, Philippians* and *Colossians* in the same series. Later he wrote three parallel volumes of devotional studies on the same

epistles. Taken together, and alongside the two Romans commentaries, they form a contribution to Pauline exegesis, which, though dated, still penetrates to depths of New Testament spirituality largely unexplored in modern exegesis.

8. Girdlestone, *Manual*, p. 146.
9. *Romans* (Cambridge), p. 131.
10. Moule, *Thoughts on the Spiritual Life* (London 1887), p. 15.
11. Moule, *Call of Lent*, p. 76; *Secret Prayer*, p. 25.
12. Moule, *The Call of Lent*, p. 96.
13. ibid., p. 99.
14. H. C. G. Moule, *Secret Prayer* (London 1898), p. 112.
15. Harford, *Moule*, pp. 311–14, gives a long extract from one of Moule's tracts, *Reading the Bible*.
16. Girdlestone, *Manual*, p. 126.
17. *Call of Lent*, p. 82; *At the Holy Communion* (London 1895), p. 2; see Girdlestone, *Manual*, pp. 112–32, for an extended treatment.
18. Loane, *Ryle*, pp. 31–3.
19. Moule, *The Secret of the Presence* (London 1900), p. 85; Ryle, *Holiness*, p. 85.
20. Ryle, *Upper Room*, pp. 35–55, 'Simplicity in Preaching', contains solid advice on clear communication; Toon, p. 49.
21. Ryle, *Upper Room*, pp. 195, 163, 427.
22. Ryle, *Old Paths*, p. 248.
23. J. C. Ryle, *Christian Leaders of the 18th Century* (Edinburgh 1978), p. 104.
24. Ryle, *Old Paths*, pp. 154–5.
25. Ryle, *The True Christian* (Welwyn 1978), p. 51.
26. G. W. Hart, 'J. C. Ryle: Evangelical Bishop', *Expository Times*, vol. 93 (1982), pp. 270–3.
27. Ryle, *Practical Religion*, p. 113.
28. Ryle, *The True Christian*, p. 120.
29. C. H. Spurgeon, *Commenting and Commentaries* (London 1893), p. 149.
30. Ryle, *Practical Religion*, p. 66.
31. ibid., p. 88.
32. The Keswick–Reformed debate continues. See J. I. Packer, ' "Keswick" and the Reformed Doctrine of Sanctification', *Evangelical Quarterly*, 27 No. 3 (July 1955), pp. 153–67; Packer, *Keep in Step with the Spirit* (Leicester 1984), pp. 145–63. The schematized programme of previous years, well expounded by Barabas, has now given way to a more flexible approach. For example John Stott has spoken several times in the past twenty-five years. His *Men Made New* (Leicester 1965), expounds Romans chapter seven along Reformed lines. See also B. L. Maddox, 'The use of the aorist tense in Holiness exegesis', *Wesley Theological Journal*, 16 (1981), pp. 106–18.

9

PETER T. FORSYTH and ALEXANDER WHYTE

In grace we live and move and have our being.

WHYTE

Born in the north east of Scotland, Forsyth and Whyte both came from poor homes where their parents struggled to provide the money for a good education. Later both trained at King's College, Aberdeen; Forsyth became Chairman of the Congregational Union of England and Wales in 1904 and Whyte became Moderator of the Free Church of Scotland in 1898; Forsyth became Principal of Hackney College and Whyte was appointed Principal of New College, Edinburgh. They both died in 1921.

In an inhospitable climate they stoutly refused to trivialize sin or understate the extent of human corruption. Forsyth's major emphasis was on the holy love of God expressed in an objective atonement, while Whyte insisted that the sinfulness of sin made spiritual conflict an inescapable reality in Christian experience. Both emphases ran counter to the prevailing atmosphere of optimistic liberalism characteristic of late-Victorian Britain.

They came by different roads to a similar theology. Forsyth in his early ministry was a lover of culture, modernist in theological sympathy and deeply involved in social and political issues. Following a crisis in Christian experience his theology was melted down, reminted and stamped with a new character in which the cross was the dominant motif. By contrast Whyte experienced a slow progressive growth into a life of faith in Christ, interpreted largely in Calvinistic terms. The piety of his mother, the phenomena surrounding the 1859 Revivals and his careful study of the Puritan divines each helped to form a faith in which intellect and heart carried equal weight. Whyte came later in life to value the mystical writers of other Christian traditions.

Though equally cultured and open to the prevailing winds of modern thought, Forsyth was more cautious, more critical but equally catholic in his tastes, being immensely well-read in German theology.[1] It is difficult to imagine Forsyth eagerly seeking an interview with Cardinal Newman, yet Whyte did, and later wrote a warm, if critical, appreciation of Newman's writings. Forsyth shared Whyte's indebtedness to the Puritans, finding in such writers as Owen and Goodwin a religion of living faith. The Puritans were men who had 'passed from death to life by Christ's cross, who lived that life upon their Bible, and interpreted it in the Holy Ghost by sanctified commonsense applied to individual experience of the evangelical kind'.[2] Forsyth and Whyte, drawing inspiration from such giants of theology, themselves represent a spirituality which is vigorously biblical, unashamedly doctrinal and consistently pastoral.

God has atoned . . . what love!

In five successive city pastorates Forsyth became increasingly aware of the impotence of mere learning and culture when faced with human brokenness. Pastoral preaching and counsel forced him to explore and puzzle over the relation of the gospel to human need, not as an intellectual exercise with theological peers, but 'in the context of life, duty and responsibility to others'. 'It pleased God by a revelation of His holiness and grace to bring me to my sin in a way that submerged all the school questions in weight, urgency and poignancy.'[3]

By temperament Forsyth was incapable of detached study. The truth of the gospel demands committed response not dispassionate analysis. The theologian's own experience of sin and atonement, of guilt and forgiveness, is the marrow that puts life and urgency into theologizing. In the cross Forsyth 'found his soul's magnetic north', a fixed point of reference by which the accuracy of all other theological statements were tested.[4] To read Forsyth is to encounter a passionate temperament feeling deeply the most vital truths; and having examined the full transforming force of that truth in his own intellect, conscience and will, he preached and wrote. Much of Forsyth's writing is hard to follow. Perhaps one reason among many was Forsyth's refusal to reduce the mystery and poignancy of the cross to manageable theological proportions. He admitted his own limitations: 'Words are hard to stretch to the measure of eternal things without breaking under us somewhere.'[5] His daughter recalled: 'He wrote with a physical and nervous intensity, which shook the desk, and which after an hour or two left him utterly spent, stretched out white and still upon his study couch, until the Spirit drove him back to pen and paper.'[6] One student of Forsyth rather playfully compares him to a village blacksmith trying to make a new precision tooled drive-shaft for an upmarket car, using only a forge, a hammer and an anvil.

In Forsyth's view, sin vitiates the whole conscience. It is a radical alienation from God, a broken communion which man is helpless to restore. There is a whole mystery of iniquity that lies at the heart of human life, a baleful influence that frustrates and mars, that insinuates itself into human structures and gives rise to life's most intractable problems of injustice, suffering and human corruption. Sin is both a pervasive and invasive force of evil that is rooted in the human psyche. It is so radically destructive that man's guilt cannot be described as mere shame. Guilt is not only the subjective pain of the violated conscience; it is objective accountability to a God who is holy love and whose law has been broken. Guilt, then, is the recoil of the soul from the moral majesty of God. Sin 'holds man suspended, not over the shallows of time, but over the abyss of eternity, the abyss of God'.[7]

The response of God to the tragedy of fallen humanity is consistent with his divine character as holy love. In 1896 Forsyth preached a sermon entitled 'The Holy Father' in which he expounded the love of God in profoundly moral terms. 'Do not say God is love. Why atone? . . . the New Testament says God has atoned! What love!' (HF p. 4). Divine love is not simply goodwill, nor is God indifferent to human sin. Neither is God to be thought of as a benevolent father wringing his hands in grief over his children's sin, but finally helpless to prevent or cure it. Love is 'the outward movement of holiness . . . you can go behind love to holiness but behind holiness you cannot go' (HF p. 5). This was a more muscular theology of God's love in which Forsyth took issue with the sentimental flabbiness of liberal theology which, in his view, emptied the cross of offence, took wrath out of judgement and trivialized sin by removing its tragic consequences. Forsyth's spirituality holds together in creative tension the tragic brokenness of human life and the tragic triumph of the cross. True religion, he believed, must 'hallow the tragic note' which is ever present in the encounter of holy love with sinful humanity.

Writing during the First World War, Forsyth pointed to the cross as the place where God decisively intervened to deal with sin. 'A holy God, self-atoned in Christ, is the moral centre of the world.'[8] Man's justification is inextricably related to the cross where God justified himself. God himself bore the penalty of sin; redemption has been accomplished by the total self-giving of God. Sundered communion is restored by the gracious, generous initiative of holy love.

'The Holy Father's first care is holiness. The first charge on a redeemer is satisfaction to that holiness. The Holy Father is one who does and must atone. As Holy Father he offers a sacrifice rent from his own heart. It is made to him by no third party, but by himself in his Son, and it is made to no foreign power but to his own holy nature and law' (HF p. 4). The only appropriate response to holy love is a trustful commitment to the God revealed in Christ crucified. Such faith is not only a single act but a continuous appropriation of forgiveness. Christian spirituality is the continual outworking in life of the experience of redemption. 'The essence of Christianity is not just to be spiritual; it is to answer God's manner of spirituality which you find in Jesus Christ and in Him crucified.'[9] Forsyth will not allow Christian faith to become a vague floating mysticism, unearthed in biblical truth. Christian faith is revelation, the content of faith given: 'Its revelation is the holiness in judgement of the spiritual and loving God. Love is only divine as it is holy; and spirituality is Christian only as it meets the conditions of holy love in the way the cross did, as the crisis of holy judgement and holy grace.'[10] Christian spirituality is rooted in the experience of redeeming grace. Christian living is simply, but demandingly, to live out the consequences of grace.

Sail by the cross and you will sail into holiness.

Forsyth carefully analysed the nature of the human response to God's holy love. God himself does not ostentatiously parade the cost of redemption. Indeed to point out the cost of love would mar the graciousness of grace. At the same time the returned prodigal, if his penitence is real, will begin to reflect on the suffering and sacrifice that distinguishes costly forgiveness from easy indulgence. The redeemed heart will increasingly feel the offensiveness of sin and tremble in awe at the self-expenditure of God. 'We must gain some reasonable sense of the mystery we cannot fathom. We must weigh the gravity of sin in the face of holiness, for the sake of worshipping the Saviour's grace and love's earnestness about its holy law' (HF p. 23). To grow in grace and knowledge of Christ involves an ever deepening and an ever more personal grasp of the inner meaning of the cross. 'He must be personal to us. He must be our Saviour in our situations, our needs, loves, shames, sins. He must not only live but mingle with our lives' (HF p. 96). It is with the quickened heart of the penitent and with the awakened wonder of the forgiven that the Christian gazes on the cross with a hushed and grateful joy. 'It is all beyond thought, beyond poetry . . . God himself in that mighty joy, refrains from words' (HF p. 37).

Forsyth honestly faced the problem of ongoing sin in the life of the redeemed Christian. In *Christian Perfection* he argued that Christian holiness is always tinged with penitence. Sin keeps the Christian humbly aware of dependence on God's mercy. God can have no communion with a heart that is uncritical of itself. 'Every defect of ours is a motive for faith. To cease to feel defect is to cease to trust' (HF p. 102). Sin and grace will coexist as opposing principles so long as life lasts. Sin is a daily occurrence and forgiveness is a daily need:

> There is the great forgiveness once for all, when the man passes from death to life, to a new relationship with God; and there is the daily forgiveness which renews in detail and keeps the channel of grace clean, once it has been cut, and prevents it silting up . . . There is the bathing of the whole man into the regeneration in which he is born of God, and there is the washing, which is the cleansing of the feet daily exposed and daily soiled.
>
> (HF p. 114)

The vital question for Forsyth concerns the soul's final allegiance: 'Perfection is not sinlessness but the loyalty of the soul by faith to Christ' (HF p. 110). Undeniably sin is an act of will involving the consent of the whole person. Though he never understated the gravity of sin he believed the occasional sin, the lapse from obedience to disobedience is quite different from the life lived in service to sin. Sin is never the Christian's native element nor is it the overriding principle which governs conduct. Love to God is the controlling principle of Christian living, the set of the will is toward holiness and the basic underlying drive of life is the obedience of faith. Christians love much because they have been forgiven much, and that grateful love acts as an invasive force that occupies the heart and overflows in praise-filled worship and costly service.

The redeemed life is life turned into a new way, vowed to a new Lord and lived in a new power. To the Christian, sin is both a reality and a cause of godly sorrow. Though life is a constant conflict, the underlying continuity is a sense of sorrow for sin, gratitude for forgiveness and a resolve, daily renewed, to love God. It follows that Christian perfection can never be understood as freedom from temptation and sin. To be perfect is to be 'in a right relation to God in Christ, not the complete achievement of Christian character' (HF p. 119). In a sense sanctification is justification repeatedly experienced, the relation with God repaired as soon as ruined: 'The great justification does not dispense with the daily forgiveness' (HF p. 114). Forsyth's logic is: if the relation is right the behaviour will follow. To be perfect is not to be fully sanctified but to be duly justified. Entire sinlessness, or an abstract ideal of perfection, is alien to a gospel of redemption and grace. Christian progress is dynamic. The very nature of personality makes nonsense of a static perfection or a plateau of achievement. Forsyth reduces such abstractions to absurdity: 'Perfect Christians would be complete . . . and empty; dead and done with; finished futilities' (HF p. 135). Continuous growth is a condition of living personality; it is the operation of grace enabling each Christian to become what they are, to come to all they can be in Christ, to be in tune with their redeemed destiny. That is the true fulfilment of Christian personality.

Sanctification is the process by which what is implicit in a soul justified in Christ is made explicit in Christian character and conduct. God who sees the end from the beginning, the saint in the penitent, declares the believer righteous. Perfection, in these terms, has to do with realizing potential. It is the perfection of the seed which contains the promise and the power of becoming the perfect tree (HF pp. 125f).

Sanctification no less than justification is the outcome of a faith which is essentially trust in 'God's love, redemption and providence amidst the duties, pleasures, enterprises, perils, fears, guilts, gains, losses of active life' (HF p. 142). Clearly Forsyth had little use for a faith that made the occasional extravagant gesture but disdained the discipline of daily duty. Nor did he encourage a type of pious faith that might act as a spiritual double-glazing to keep out the worst of the world's disturbing noise. Faith is the fundamental attitude to God which produces a life and character confident in Christ, patient of God's purpose and growing out of a will really and inly broken with Christ on the cross: 'Seek first for the Kingdom and sanctification will be added; care for Christ and he will take care of your soul; sail by the cross and you will sail into holiness.'[11]

Our soul is fulfilled.

In approaching the holy Father Christians must acquire that delicate balance of penitence and boldness in the presence of a God who is holy love, both gracious and demanding. As redeemed, reconciled and forgiven sinners, prayer must always take place beneath the cross, and is only possible at all because of the cross. The soul's civil war, the inner tension between sin and holiness, the pull of temptation and the pull of faith seeking to be obedient, drives the Christian to prayer. Inevitably such prayer is experienced as conflict, as an inner turmoil of argument for moral victory. Further, truly Christian prayer will seek to bring human life in all its brokenness and emptiness, with all its failures and futilities, its chaos and catastrophe, beneath the shadow of the cross so that the world's despair can be seen in the light of God's great redemptive act. The realities of sin and atonement preserve Christian prayer from degenerating into a spiritual self-culture on the one hand and a mere tinkering with human structures on the other. Through prayer a Christian enters the cosmic struggle between sin in all its destructiveness and holy love in all its redemptive power: 'As there are thoughts that seem to think themselves in us, so there are prayers that pray themselves in us. And, as those are the best thoughts, these are the best prayers.

For it is Christ at prayer who lives in us, and we are conduits of the Eternal Intercession.'[12]

In Forsyth's thought, conflict and struggle are almost a means of grace. Prayerful wrestling is a process which involves concentration of energy and a determination of purpose inevitably producing resilience of character. In Forsyth's thought, life is so constructed that each soul is confronted with its own obstacles. Frustrations and problems which refuse to disappear and which God declines to remove are essential to Christian growth. To grapple with difficulty and come to terms with failure develops the resourcefulness of the will and educates the soul into a faith which will not demand that God take all the trouble out of life. Exploring the connection between God's will, life's hardships and Christian prayer, Forsyth suggests the purpose of prayer is to resist the problems that confront and confound. Each problem is there by the initial will of God, to be overcome by prayer and effort, which is his higher will. The valuable by-product of moral and spiritual resistance is a more vigorous and assertive faith and the development of a sacred forwardness with God.

'Resisting His will may be doing His will' (SP p. 82). That is precisely the kind of thought which makes Forsyth's arguments hard to understand and his words difficult to forget. 'We obey God . . . as much when we try to change his will as when we bow to it' (SP p. 90). Forsyth was suspicious of Quietism, an attitude of passivity in the apparent will of God: 'Let us beware,' he warned, 'of a pietist fatalism which thins the spiritual life, saps the vigour of character, makes humility mere aquiescence' (SP p. 91). Any view of prayer which deprives the Christian of the right to argue, to petition and to plead with God is theologically suspect to Forsyth, because it robs prayer of vigour and moral energy, and suppresses freedom of thought and will, two essential aspects of human personality. With scornful impatience Forsyth dismisses the claim that the highest prayer is the prayer of utter submission. Quietist prayer 'may consecrate manners, but it impoverishes the mind . . . It may feed certain pensive emotions but it may emasculate will, secularise energy and empty character. And so we decline to a state of things in which we have no shocking sins – yes and no splendid souls; when all souls are dully correct, as like as shillings, but as thin and as cheap' (SP pp. 91–2).

Prevailing prayer assumes an understanding of God which

allows of change both in circumstances and in the divine purpose. God is neither inflexible omnipotence nor is he the divine chess player who dictates every move man makes until the final checkmate. A view of God in which prayer has no decisive effect on the divine will would create 'a Hell of ceaseless, passionate, fruitless, hopeless, gnawing prayer. It is the heart churning, churning, grinding itself out in misery' (SP p. 61). Will-lessness before God is not, and cannot be, the highest form of devotion. Indeed Forsyth rejects it as an unworthy ideal. The aim and purpose of prayer, the reason for praying at all, is rooted in the belief that prayer prevails with God, that God's will is not fixed and frozen but is open to the influence of pleading and argument. Prayer is power with God, it is a power 'momentous in the affairs of life and history', it is the 'assimilating of a holy God's moral strength' (SP pp. 54, 12).

Forsyth carefully avoids the suggestion that prayer changes things, as if it were possible to manipulate God. God changes things and prayer is wrestling with God. The holy Father hears the prayers of his children and is to be trusted with the consequences. 'He says no in the spirit of yes' (SP p. 67). Prayer is never unanswered. Goodwin has a passage in which he likens God's faithfulness in answering prayer to the conscientious correspondent who keep his friends' letters in a conspicuous place till they are answered. The present writer possesses a letter from Forsyth to one of his friends, to whom he apologizes for neglecting to send an answer. His explanation was that he had met the postman on the way out, had read the letter, put it in his overcoat pocket and promptly forgot all about it. By contrast, God can be trusted to respond to every prayer: 'God has old prayers of yours long maturing by him' (SP p. 67). 'We shall come one day to a heaven where we shall gratefully know that God's great refusals were sometimes the truest answers to our truest prayer. Our soul is fulfilled if our petition is not' (SP p. 14).

'Our soul is fulfilled.' Though Forsyth does not limit the efficacy of prayer to its effects on the praying person, it is his contention that prayer makes a decisive contribution to Christian health and growth. 'The greatest, deepest, truest thought of God is generated in prayer . . . theology cannot be denuded of prayer' and neither can prayer be emptied of theology. Prayer is the proper context for theology and theology suggests the proper practice of prayer. In Forsyth's judgement, thinking about God reduced to passive reflection or discursive meditation reveals a lack of moral and spiritual discipline, and the absence of a biblically controlled devotion: 'The Bible is the most copious spring of prayer', which provides prayer with 'the large humane note of a universal gospel' (SP p. 78). Prayer arising from the Bible is inevitably theological and will be characterized by a level of thinking, a breadth of expression, a range of emotion and a respect for doctrinal truth, worthy of the God in whose presence prayer is made. God is not honoured by thoughtless hurried devotion, nor by habits of piety meticulously observed, but by 'considered prayer', 'prayer on the scale of the whole gospel and at the depth of searching faith' (SP p. 79). Prayer is the Christian thinking theologically. Forsyth recognizes the validity of more passive forms of prayer but he firmly resists the view that they are the higher or more spiritual forms. Nevertheless he values the prayer of quiet in which 'we are regathered in soul from the fancies that bewilder us and the distractions that dissolve us into the dust of the world. We are collected into peace, power and sound judgement' (SP p. 47).

Prayer has a formative influence on character and conduct. For example, prayer helps in the repulsion and defeat of selfishness. In prayer 'our egoism retires and into the clearance there comes with our Father our brother' (SP p. 11). The soul is never more obedient to God than when at prayer. However mixed up and ambiguous a person's motives might be in other areas of life, the simple desire to pray is beyond censure: 'What puts us right morally, right with a Holy God (as prayer does), must have a great shaping power on every part and juncture of life' (SP p. 26). Part of that shaping power resides in the commitment each prayer implies: 'A prayer is also a promise. Every true prayer carries with it a vow' (SP p. 27). This is especially true in intercession. Intercessory prayer is an act of self-giving, a volunteering for active duty so that the Christian's actions, attitudes and lifestyle must be consistent with a life of prayer. Intercession is not only inner desire expressed in words; it is a declaration of intent and a making of the self available to God as part of the answer to the prayers we pray. 'Prayer establishes the soul of a man or of a people, creates the moral personality day by day, spreads outward the new heart through society and goes to make a new ethos in mankind' (SP p. 48).

In the spirituality of P. T. Forsyth the key element is not

prayer, church, sacrament, ethics or even love. Each of these is essential in a balanced spirituality. To Forsyth's mind the cross makes Christian spirituality vital. The cross gives prayer its guarantees and its moral power; the cross lies at the heart of the Church's message and mission and gives the sacraments meaning and content. It is only in the cross that the true nature of divine love is revealed as holy love, an ethical principle commanding the soul's submission. Only a clear perception of the cross preserves the truth that grace is the intervention of God on man's behalf:

> Our greatest hope is our greatest humiliation. And where grace abounds there does sin abound. The Christian life is repentant praise; if much praise, much grief; if much good labour, also much deep sorrow; if much confidence also much amazement. And sin is always the more deeply confessed for ourselves and our world because we confess much more than sin – a Saviour to our own worst depths and to the wide ends of the earth.[13]

The hospitable-hearted Evangelical.

When it came to sounding and exploring 'our own worst depths' Alexander Whyte was both specialist and consultant. Through his reading, preaching and prayers he devoted his life to the study of human character in relation to divine holiness. The recurring themes in his sermons, prayers and books are conscience, the soul's conflict with indwelling sin, the toil and struggle of the road to holiness and the impelling hunger that drives each person to search for God. During a long life he engaged in a detailed study of the internal workings of conscience and motivation as they govern moral behaviour. He reflected on the development of human character as it co-operated with grace or connived with sin. His findings were then tested by ruthlessly comparing them with his own experience of sin, failure and puzzlingly slow progress on the road to holiness. Whatever Whyte learned in all his research he sought to apply to his own experience. He was an experiential theologian whose spirituality was the inimitable result of one soul's conflicts and triumphs.[14]

Whyte exerted enormous influence during his ministry at Free St George's, Edinburgh, from 1873 to 1921. He was part of a galaxy of scholarship and spirituality that enriched Scottish church life at the end of the nineteenth century. In such men as James Denney, R. S. Candlish, A. B. Bruce, Marcus Dods, T. M. Lindsay and George Adam Smith the Free Church of Scotland produced an influential array of men in whom intellectual gift and spiritual vitality coincided. Unlike many of his contemporaries, Whyte did not pursue a career in pure scholarship, though in intellectual power and breadth of knowledge he was their equal. Whyte's best energies were poured into his lifelong research project, the problems of the spiritual life, and especially the soul's conflict.

Whyte lived with the ambiguity of his parentage from boyhood to old age. His father never married his mother and emigrated to America soon after Whyte's birth. The influence of his mother, a woman of strong character, sound commonsense and a disciplined and devout faith, shaped his early religious experience. His sense of a call to the ministry was encouraged by his minister, fuelled further by his discussions with a rather free-thinking uncle, and sustained through the years of his apprenticeship as a shoemaker, then for several more years as a low paid teacher in a country school. When he eventually entered King's College, Aberdeen, he positively revelled in the intellectual give and take of class work, and he spent hours trawling in the sea of literature and theology. In a rather patronizing letter to his friend John Dickson he exhorts him, 'I hope your spiritual and intellectual life is growing. Read, Pray, Think' (B p. 70). These three words sum up Whyte's spirituality.

The time he spent in Aberdeen coincided with the Revivals of 1859. The awakenings gave him his first opportunity to preach the gospel. The style of preaching throughout the Revival period was passionate, searching and to the point, so that one witness recalled, 'Every hearer present was asked whether he had come under personal allegiance to Christ.' The sense of personal sin, the heightened religious awareness in the community, the evidence of many converted, of lives changed and of answered prayer, and through it all the repeated testimony to a thrilling sense of joy and forgiveness, permanently coloured Whyte's understanding of Christian experience (B pp. 92–3).

Under the influence of Alexander Bain, Professor of Logic and Psychology, Whyte's naturally wide-ranging mind was trained to think with clarity, precision and disciplined concentration. The permanent influence of Bain can be seen firstly in Whyte's lifelong refusal to dissipate his mental energies in pursuit of a broad but shallow culture and secondly in his fascination with motive, the inner springs of moral action.

By 1873, when he took up the charge of Free St George's, the main features of his mature spirituality were visible. His own religious experience, the spiritual quickening of the Revivals, the honing of intellect under Bain, and the formation of a scholarly discipline, he owed to Aberdeen. The creation of a theological framework that was Calvinist and experimental, he owed to his own church tradition and his careful and constant study of the Puritans. In the crucial stage of translating his reading, thinking and praying into the language of daily life and experience, he was helped by the pastoral demands of a first pastorate in the heart of industrial Glasgow.

In Free St George's, Edinburgh, there was ample scope for reading, praying and thinking. The daily discipline of faithful, tireless reading constantly replenished the deep well from which he drew during fifty years of mind-stretching and soul-searching preaching. In Whyte's spiritual formation the influence of the Puritans was decisive. In 1907 on a hill walk in the Scottish Highlands, Whyte received what he was convinced was a direct message from God: 'Go back and boldly finish the work that has been given you to do. Speak out and fear not. Make them at any cost to see themselves in God's holy law as in a glass. Do you that, for no one else will do it . . . Go home and spend what is left of your life in your appointed task of showing My people their sin and their need of My salvation' (B p. 532). This profoundly personal experience rekindled the ardour and authority of Whyte's preaching, and sent him back to the Puritans for spiritual fuel. The Puritans were 'an inestimable treasure, used aright'. For Whyte those heavy, often ponderous volumes of practical divinity were definitive textbooks on the psychology of temptation, the anatomy of sin and the pathology of guilt. Nevertheless, used aright, they were doctors to his soul, offering the healing of divine mercy, the consolation of grace and the cordials of hope and faith. All of this strengthened the framework of his Calvinist theology, characterized by spiritual conflict, perseverance and the quest for assurance.

Whyte's knowledge of the Puritans was legendary, and his love of doctrine provoked a friend into complaining that 'he would talk doctrine for a year on end' (B p. 118). The Puritan preacher

Thomas Brooks advised, 'Christ, the Scripture, your own heart and Satan's devices are the four things that should be first and most studied and searched!'[15] These four hallmarks of Puritan theology were firmly stamped on all Whyte's preaching and writing.

A special place in Whyte's affection was reserved for Thomas Goodwin. After procuring the new edition of Goodwin's works Whyte admits he read no other so much or so often. The index volume of the collected works was prepared by Whyte. Such detailed and devoted work produced a subject index which is virtually a condensation of Goodwin's theology. Goodwin was a moderate Calvinist whose works combined mystical devotion and doctrinal clarity. The preparation of the index 'wrought both the style and the matter of the great Puritan's thinking into the very fibre of his apt and devoted pupil's mind' (B p. 118). In Goodwin, Whyte found a doctrinally disciplined account of Christian experience which was intellectually satisfying, spiritually nourishing and, most importantly, was confirmed by his own experience.

In the search for spiritual truth he was a man with few boundaries. He read widely and sympathetically. When he disagreed with an author, he did so with firmness and courtesy. It is a tribute to his criticism that his appreciation of Saint Teresa was used in a monastery and had been warmly commended in the *Tablet* and the *Catholic Times*. The combination of evangelical conviction and an enquiring teachable spirit enabled Whyte to appreciate and assimilate truth from all points of the spiritual compass. He once defined the true catholic as 'the well read, the open minded, the hospitable hearted, the spiritually exercised evangelical' (B p. 389n). In his reading Whyte was alert for certain common features; the conscience as the basis of moral personality and the arbiter of moral behaviour; the need for reality in penitence and perseverance in prayer, sanctification and the practice of the presence of God (B p. 390).

When Whyte took up the study of an author, the operative word was appreciation. Amongst the authors he commended in his book *Thirteen Appreciations* were Boehme, the Lutheran speculative philosopher; Lancelot Andrewes, the high Anglican bishop whose prayer book teaches 'the grace of tears'; John Henry Newman, the Roman Catholic Cardinal, and Father John, a Russian Orthodox spiritual director, both of them contemporaries from whom Whyte received personal correspondence. Then there was Rutherford the Presbyterian Covenanter, Teresa the Carmelite nun, Law the Non-juror and mystic, and Butler, the cool analytic moral philosopher.[16]

This awful inward cross.

With characteristic honesty, and taking his congregation into his confidence, Whyte once admitted his puzzlement as to the cause of personal declension in spiritual life. 'I have tried hard to find out some of the reasons for that declension, both in myself and in other men, but I am not satisfied with what I have found as yet. If I succeed in my study of that painful matter, I shall tell you more about it another time.'[17] Though Whyte would spend his life exploring the 'labyrinthine intricacies' of his own heart he never felt he had solved the riddle of his inner self. Longing for holiness seemed to coexist with an ineradicable sense of sin.

Whyte had little patience with any weakening of the doctrine of sin. The question of a genuinely sincere young Anglican clergyman, concerning the possibility of freedom from sin here and now, was answered with adamantine certainty: 'No sir, no man who knows what God is would say a thing like that – no man who has seen the exquisite holiness of God would say a thing like that' (B p. 532). A broken and a contrite heart is, and must always be, the lifelong experience of the forgiven sinner, God's grace not only conferring forgiveness but working on to form in his people a penitential mind. 'Great sins forgiven must never for a single day be forgotten.'[18]

From such brokenness of heart is born a deeper aversion from sin, a profounder sense of gratitude and a more resolute walk with God. Sin breaks the heart, but in penitence the sinner gathers the debris and offers it to God who in grace and mercy restores the joy of salvation so 'that broken bones may joy'. The rhythm of sin, penitence, forgiveness, reminds the Christian of utter dependence on grace and lends depth and pathos to Christian joy which is at its most grace-ful as the joy of the forgiven. Nevertheless in the daily walk with God sin remains as a continuing reality, and the Christian believer lives with a contradiction.

Whyte tackled this tension between sin and holiness in his various sermons which allude to Romans seven, a chapter in which he recognizes 'the sighs sobs and agonizing cries of the divided soul'. This inner contradiction arises from the fact that the believer who is 'in Christ' is also still 'in the flesh', thus creating a dualism in present experience, an unresolved tension between the 'now' and 'not yet'. In Whyte's view Romans seven does not say that holiness is impossible for Paul, but that the reality never matches Paul's aspirations. Alongside the exquisite holiness of God Paul is aware of his impurity in thought and action so that chapter seven is to be understood as the anguished prayer of a soul redeemed from sin yet living on in an unredeemed world. This conflict between sin and holiness is felt most acutely at the centre of personality. 'Here heaven and hell meet, as nowhere else in heaven or hell; and that too, for their last grapple together for the everlasting possession of that immortal soul.'[19]

The 'gnashing agony of Paul's heart' is that he is a 'self sold slave'; in the final analysis he has consented to his bondage, but he has consented against his will. Whyte explains the notion of consenting unwillingly in terms of the relation between mind, will and heart. According to Whyte, in effectual calling, the believer's mind is savingly enlightened and the will is savingly renewed, 'but not yet his heart . . . not yet his whole spirit, and disposition and inclination and affection' (SL p. 111). As a believer: 'Paul's whole will was now wholly set upon always thinking and feeling and wishing what was good . . . But with all that there were still the remains of his original sin lurking deep down in his imperfectly sanctified heart. And thus it was that his better mind and better will were so often forerun and forestalled; overrun and overborne by the uprush of the inward sinfulness that still dwelt deep down within him' (SL pp. 111f).

Only this interpretation of Romans seven did justice to Whyte's own experience of inner conflict in which, like Paul, Whyte's sanctified mind and will were 'everlastingly warring within him against his still unrenewed heart'. Romans 7.25 expresses pungently the frustration of every sinner striving after sanctity: 'So then, with the mind I myself serve the law of God: but with the flesh the law of sin' (AV). This chapter was central to Whyte's spirituality, so much so that he would not give shelf room to any commentary that suggested the second half referred to Paul's pre-Christian experience. With a sublimely simple logic, Whyte argued, if this was Paul's experience as a Christian, it must be normal, and if it is normal, it must be part of the mystery of sanctification. Relying on the strength of a sufficient grace, the cleansing of a sufficient sacrifice and the counteraction of the indwelling Spirit of God, he resolved to 'take up this awful inward cross of mine' (SL p. 113).

Whyte contended that indwelling sin is ultimately a means of sanctification. 'Anything and everything that breaks your heart every day is good.' As indwelling sin breaks the heart it produces humility and patience with God. Patience produces prayerfulness, trust and an increasing love for Jesus Christ who through the whole experience 'is longing to get his right place with you and within you' (SL p. 119).

Relying heavily on the Puritans, Whyte pursued the origins of sin in the human heart. By 'some aboriginal catastrophe' the 'every protoplasm, so to call it, out of which Paul's whole inward man had been made, was already tainted and vitiated in every original atom of it' (SL p. 122). From this grim view of the human psyche Whyte argues that long after new birth from above 'the old and aboriginal sinfulness' continues to 'taint, to infect, to corrupt and to pollute' the whole of life. Original sin is so deep, so secret in its movements and so sudden in its eruption that the Christian is 'ensnared and enslaved', taken completely by surprise; every sin is a 'coup d'état' within the Christian soul.

In the words of John Owen, Whyte offers pastoral comfort to struggling believers. 'The heaviest cross a Christian can carry is a heart full of involuntary sin.' The notion of involuntary sin is further explained as 'the total inability even of the regenerate will to rule and restrain the first sinful motions of the soul' (SL p. 124). To the charge that the idea of involuntary sin leads to a slackening of moral demand, Whyte would reply that the essence of regeneration is the renewed will and it is the opposition of the renewed will that creates the conflict in the first place. Further, just as the will is renewed, so the affections are redirected positively in love for Christ and negatively in hatred of sin. 'O wretched man that I am. For what I hate like hell I am every day swept away into doing' (SL p. 123). Through the renewed will and the redirected affections, a positive desire for holiness and freedom from sin is set up in opposition to the subversive forces of sin. The inner anguish of the embattled and often defeated Christian is, in reality, a positive resistance to the power of sin.

God at his God-like work.

One of Whyte's former deacons suggested that Dr Whyte's approach was like some weather forecasts, 'occasional sunny spells'. When Whyte turned his attention from sin to Christ he could startle with originality. In one sermon he tried to imagine the first thoughts of Christ awakening in the tomb; disorientation, surprise at the finality of the stone and the grave-clothes, evidence of his disciples' pessimistic conclusions; then 'a great sob of relief' as the Saviour of sinners cried again, this time with joy, 'It is finished'. The same deacon recalled words of passionate gratitude in a sermon on 'I if I be lifted up . . .'; 'Blessed be His name he draws me – draws me as no other does; not God unless he be God in Christ; not man unless it be the man Christ Jesus; not Christ Himself, unless it be Christ crucified.'[20] Passionate gratitude draws the heart towards obedience and pulls it away from the sin that seduces the heart and subverts the most devout aspiration. The spiritual conflict waged at the centre of redeemed personality is ultimately a conflict between love and hatred and between holiness and sin. The Christian heart enters that conflict with a bias towards the loveliness and purity of Christ but with no guaranteed outcome.

The painful sense of being always a sinner and always needing forgiveness did not lead Whyte to spiritual despair. His experience of indwelling sin and spiritual conflict made him realistic in his expectations. The believer is righteous by faith in Christ, but the downward drag of the natural man remains. The Christian must come to terms with slow, organic growth into holiness. Sanctification is gradual, an arduous progressive work of God in the heart: 'The new heart of a saint of God was never attained at a bound. A new life of motive . . . disposition . . . intention . . . aim and end is not the growth of a day or of a year. All this present life is allotted by God to His saints to make them a new heart' (WM p. 52). Whyte describes God as a master craftsman, shaping, moulding and bringing into being the finished work of art, his own original creation in each unique redeemed soul. 'What a laboratory, what a forge, what a crucible is the soul of man, and my soul. What living materials to be worked upon . . .' (WM p. 63).

Like Paul, Whyte saw that 'God at work within you' has its necessary corollary in 'Work out your own salvation with fear and trembling'. Grace does not preclude moral effort; it enables it. God's work does not make the believer redundant, it stimulates a life of disciplined love and spiritual culture. Grace is simply 'God at His God-like work of making me to will and to do'. Whyte urged: 'Work on at your souls while a spot or a speck, a taint or a tarnish of sin is left . . . Do not throw down the slow work, in disgust and despair. Work on at it.' One of Whyte's favourite expressions sums up the dogged hopefulness which underlay his pessimistic view of human nature. 'The perseverance of the saints is made up of ever new beginnings' (B p. 331). If the predominant mood of Whyte is governed by unrelenting moral seriousness, there is nevertheless a cautious optimism, an edge of light relieving his inner gloom: 'That is not to be despaired of surely – that which God has on His hands and on His heart' (WM p. 67).

The motions of prayer . . . love . . . hopefulness.

At the more immediate level of the Christian's present experience, Whyte believed there were 'good original motions in the heart' towards love, joy, peace: 'When these good motions come up out of the depths of our souls and find a renewed will waiting to receive and assist them in the upper regions of our souls . . . they soon cover the whole life with works of righteousness and true holiness.' Nevertheless, Romans seven remains for Whyte the only adequate explanation for indwelling sin. He does however suggest that the hold of sin over the heart can be weakened. 'Saturate your soul continually with every part of scripture . . . pour down into your evil heart gospel doctrines and gospel promises . . . till the first motions of your deepest heart shall be motions no longer of the poison of sin, but instead of that the motions of prayer, praise, faith, hope, love and holiness' (SL p. 129).

Saturate the soul with Scripture was the advice of a lifelong Bible student. Whyte was a staunch defender of William Robertson Smith who was arraigned before the Free Church of Scotland General Assembly for views which threatened the received doctrine of inspiration. Whyte insisted that criticism was the devotion of the mind to the truth of God. He pleaded for 'Free, learned and evangelical churches', three adjectives defining the kind of church within which Christians could grow into the stature of the fulness of Christ. He warned the General Assembly of the Free Church of Scotland: 'The world of mind does not stand still and the theological mind will stand still at its peril' (B p. 219). The Bible must be approached with a conscience devoted to truth, a mind nourished by unfettered scholarship and a heart ignited by the glory of the gospel.

His own approach was an intuitive and psychological study of character. He seemed less concerned to exegete the text than to penetrate the mysterious connections between human personality and divine grace. As a commentary on the biblical text his character studies are diffuse, selective and even sketchy; but as searching studies of religious psychology applied to the experience of every Christian they can be peculiarly persuasive. The process of establishing accurate critical conclusions was of less immediate importance to Whyte than arriving at an authentic interpretation of human life viewed through the life circumstances of the biblical characters. He advised his hearers: 'The Bible deserves all our labour and all our fidelity; and we are repaid with usury for all the student-like industry we lay upon it.'[21]

Whyte's teaching on prayer is, like all else in his spirituality, a reflection of his experience. First and foremost prayer is disciplined practice. He highlights the constant unremitting practice of Daniel, and he bluntly warns that without such disciplined continuity 'you will be a bungler at it all your days'.[22] There is a gentle chiding and practical common sense in his sermon on 'Time in our Devotions'. He gives advice on how to 'get that dreary and guilty hour filled up'; he reminds his hearers that Christ is not a taskmaster with a stop-watch; and gives the liberating advice: 'Do anything you like. Prayer is the most elastic exercise possible' (WM p. 75). The regularity of prayer helps to redeem time. Each Christian must take seriously the relation between judgement and the way time is used. Every past hour should be commended to God's mercy and each new hour sanctified and consecrated by prayer.

Secondly, prayer is a sanctifying influence. Whyte often returned to the matter of broken relationships when he spoke of holiness. He saw prayer as an ethical corrective and suggested resentments should be prayed through. By prayer the Christian should put himself in the place of the person who has been hurt and move from the place of complacent self-forgiveness to the place where 'we take to heart all [our] sin against [our] neighbour as he takes it to his heart' (LT p. 47). In another sermon he commends the practice of ejaculatory prayer, short immediate prayers in response to immediate situations; these prayers he defines as 'upward arrows with all their points sharpened by love' (LT pp. 63–4). It is noteworthy that Whyte, for all his highly developed theology of sin and sanctification, rooted holiness at the level of daily moral behaviour, and particularly the level of ordinary obligations to other people. The most telling tests of a holy life often concern the practice of prayer and the quality maintained in personal relationships.

Another feature of Whyte's practice of prayer is best described as intensity. He preached on the text, 'Elijah prayed his prayers' (Jas. 5.17 RV marg.). Prayer is not conversation but passionate intreaty. Such emotional engagement invests reasoning with God with energy, drive and personal force so that prayer becomes an expression of the whole being, the communication of the total person. Such communion is self-consuming. Prayer must be intense, passionate: 'We have passions enough to make us saints in heaven or a devil in hell . . . we have plenty of passion, but it is all missing the mark' (LT p. 71). Whyte is arguing that the sacred gift of feeling, the drives and energies of human personality should be channelled and released God-ward. This is especially significant in petitionary prayer. Requests should be made to God with the whole heart involved in the outcome. Whyte describes some prayer as pleading and arguing; pleading prayer is a sharp exchange of marshalled evidence and persuasive argument, and often the basis of the argument is the nature of God himself. In pleading prayer the Christian 'reminds' God of his faithfulness, mercy, love and promises. This is no casual conversation; it is a meeting of wills, and an expression of the heart's deepest longings to God.

Sometimes God is absent despite the yearning of the soul. After his Christmas holiday in Bonskeid, in central Perthshire, he confided in his congregation, sharing with them an experience which began in desolation and ended in glory:

> Last week I became very miserable as I saw my [holiday] slipping away and my vow not performed. I therefore one afternoon stole into my coat and hat, and took my staff, and slipped out of the house in secret. For two hours, for an hour and three-quarters, I walked alone and prayed: but pray as I

would, I got not one step nearer God all these seven or eight cold miles. My guilty conscience mocked me to my face, and said to me: Is it any wonder that God has cast off a minister and father like thee? For two hours I struggled on, forsaken by God, and met neither God nor man all that chill afternoon. When at last, standing still, and looking at Schiehallion clothed in white from top to bottom, this from David shot up into my heart: 'Wash me and I shall be whiter than snow!' In a moment I was with God. Or, rather, God, as I believe, was with me.
(LT pp. 233–4)

In a winter sun at the foot of one of Scotland's finest mountains Whyte glimpsed the glistening purity of holiness, and in Schiehallion's dominant beauty he sensed the power, the presence and the purifying love of God.

Whyte complained that too many prayers were theologically undernourished: 'There is little Scripture substance, strength, depth and height in your prayers . . . The reason why so many of our prayers are so dry . . . cold . . . and full of repetition is just because there is so little Christology in them.'[23] Whyte wanted prayer to be the interweaving of experience and doctrine; sin, guilt, atonement, forgiveness, the risen Christ, the work of the Holy Spirit, the person of Jesus were not simply theological ideas. They were explanations of experience, and the raw material from which a wholesome Christian spirituality can be formed. Christological devotion is the spiritual expression of a theology that majors on sin and atonement through the death of Christ. To pray in the name of Jesus is to make a condensed theological statement that has become deeply personal to each Christian: ' "The Name of Christ" in a true believer's prayer is not a written word or an uttered sound; it is rather our richest conception and utterance of all that Scripture teaches us of the divinity, incarnation, sacrifice and intercession of Him we call Christ.'[24]

The influence of the Puritans with their emphasis on the nature and origins of moral behaviour left an indelible mark on both Whyte and Forsyth. By temperament Whyte was introspective; he was fascinated by motivation in human conduct, and a writer like Goodwin strongly reinforced his natural self-distrust. Consequently Whyte was remorseless in exposing sin, stern in his denunciations of it and extremely adept at detecting it. Yet his pastoral ministry was widely appreciated by those who found in him a fellow traveller on the road of Christian holiness.[25] Forsyth called the Puritan achievement 'divine cartography'; they provided a guide to the landscape of Christian experience. Much of his own knowledge of the spiritual terrain is derived from Goodwin and Owen, his Congregational forebears. In Puritanism both men found an account of their experience which was intellectually nourishing and psychologically satisfying, especially in the treatment of sin, atonement and the struggle for holiness in redeemed personality.

They shared a strong aversion to perfectionist teaching, even in the milder more qualified teaching of Keswick. Whyte's eagle-eyed survey of human character enabled him to pierce the murky gloom of subconscious motivation and pervasive self-love which frustrated the desire for holiness. Such pessimism about human nature, and distrust of even the redeemed heart, give Whyte's writing an air of heavy solemnity, amounting almost to joylessness. His own experience is recounted in terms of grim demanding moral struggle which gave him little patience with a sunnier theology of 'resting in faith', or of 'victory' conceived as a normal constant in Christian spirituality. One wonders if H. C. G. Moule's second commentary on Romans was one of those sent back to Whyte's bookseller, rejected because it took the comfort out of Romans seven? Forsyth too could be searingly critical of any claim to solve the problem of moral conflict in the Christian soul. Conflict, he argued, is not a problem; it is the fire within which Christian character is forged.

Whyte read widely with a taste critically appreciative. He represented open-hearted Evangelicalism gratefully absorbing truth from an astonishing range of sources in the Christian tradition. Forsyth was more distrustful of mystical theology, sensing a dangerous vagueness and an emphasis on will-lessness that was morally subversive. In their understanding of prayer and Christian progress both men issued a call to costly struggle. No ultimate deliverance is promised in this life; the soul in conflict is the soul being formed.

The pursuit of holiness is incompatible with spiritual contentment. The struggle after God tests devotion to the limit; frustration, darkness and remorse which is both the aftermath of sin and love expressing regret over its own failure, are all part of the process by which the moral personality is brought into an obedient devotion. Both Forsyth and Whyte sensed the abysmal depth of sin and grace, and recoiled from any suggestion of a facile solution to the mystery of iniquity. If at times Whyte was overwhelmed by his own unworthiness, there were times too, perhaps all too rare, when his faith soared and he anticipated the glory of life in God. 'If we seek God, and seek Him out to the end of our life – feeble as our faith is, and smoking flax as our love is – yet by His grace, after all our partial discoveries of God, and all our occasional experiences of Him, we also in our measure shall receive, and shall forever possess, enjoy, very God Almighty Himself for our Reward, forever' (LT p. 292).

Exultation in Christ and all that he is for humanity is woven through much of Forsyth's writing. His last book ends with a powerful description of eternal life as it impinges on life now: 'We begin living the eternal life here, with its endless selfless energy, vaster than we feel, and surer than we know. That life is not a mere spirituality but a sanctity; for we are not mystic beings in our destiny, but moral and holy . . . The Christian idea is not happiness and it is not power, but it is perfection – which is the growth of God's image and glory as our destiny.'[26]

Sources frequently cited

Barbour, G. F., *Alexander Whyte*. London 1923. (B)
Forsyth, P. T., *God the Holy Father*. London 1957. (HF)
——, *The Soul of Prayer*. London 1949. (SP)
Whyte, A., *Lord Teach Us to Pray*. London n.d. (LT)
——, *The Spiritual Life*. Edinburgh 1917. (SL)
——, *With Mercy and With Judgment*. London n.d. (WM)

Additional reading

Binfield, C., 'Principal when Pastor: P. T. Forsyth, 1876–1901', From *Studies in Church History*, ed. Diana Ward, vol. 26. Oxford 1989.
Bradley, W. L., *P. T. Forsyth: The Man and His Work*. London 1952.
Escott, H., *P. T. Forsyth: Director of Souls*. London 1948.
Forsyth, P. T., *The Church and the Sacraments*. London 1947.
——, *The Cruciality of the Cross*. London 1948.
——, *The Work of Christ* (London 1938); this volume has an important memoir by Forsyth's daughter.
Hunter, A. M., *P. T. Forsyth: Per crucem ad Lucem*. London 1974.
Nicoll, W. R., *Princes of the Church* (London 1921), pp. 312–24.

Rodgers, J. H., *The Theology of P. T. Forsyth*. London 1965.
Turnbull, R. G., *A History of Preaching*, vol. 3 (Grand Rapids 1974), pp. 474–7; pp. 509–14.
Whyte, A., *Bible Characters*, 6 vols, Edinburgh 1892 onwards.
——, *Thirteen Appreciations*. Edinburgh 1913.
Wood, R. C., 'P. T. Forsyth among the liberals; Christ on Parnassus', *Literature and Theology* (2 March 1988), pp. 83–95.

Notes

1. See Binfield, 'Principal when Pastor', for examples of Forsyth's considerable cultural awareness; also Wood, 'P. T. Forsyth among the Liberals', for comment on Forsyth's ambiguous theological status amongst Evangelicals.
2. Forsyth, *Faith, Freedom and the Future* (London 1955), p. 105. Most of Forsyth's work was reprinted by the Independent Press in a uniform edition in the middle of this century. All references are to this edition.
3. Escott, *Forsyth* (London 1948), p. 8; Forsyth, *Work of Christ*, p. xvi.
4. Escott, p. 18.
5. Forsyth, *Work of Christ*, p. 210.
6. ibid., p. xxvi.
7. See H. H. Farmer, *The Word of Reconciliation* (Welwyn 1966); Forsyth would approve of Farmer's view of sin as moral catastrophe.
8. Forsyth, *The Justification of God* (London 1948), p. 94.
9. Quoted in Turnbull, *History of Preaching*, p. 476.
10. *Work of Christ*, p. xxxi. From many articles on Forsyth's theology, see B. G. Worrall, 'The Authority of Grace in P. T. Forsyth', in *Scottish Journal of Theology*, vol. 25 (1972), pp. 58–74; M. W. Anderson, 'P. T. Forsyth: 'Prophet of the Cross', in *The Evangelical Quarterly*, vol. 47, pp. 146–61.
11. Hunter, *Forsyth* (London 1974), p. 67.
12. Escott, *Forsyth*, p. 77.
13. Forsyth, *Revelation Old and New* (London 1962), p. 84.
14. R. Mackintosh, 'Dr Whyte As I Remember Him', *Congregational Quarterly*, vol. 2 (1924), pp. 196–205.
15. *Works of Thomas Goodwin*, ed. Nicholl (1861), vol. 1 p. xvi.
16. Whyte, *Thirteen Appreciations*, p. 169.
17. Whyte, *Thomas Shepard, Pilgrim Father and Founder of Harvard*, (Edinburgh 1909), p. 59.
18. ibid., p. 75.
19. Whyte, *Bible Characters*, vol. vi, pp. 212–20.
20. Mackintosh, 'Dr Whyte', *Congregational Quarterly*, p. 199.
21. Whyte, *Bible Characters*, vol. iii, p. 290.
22. ibid., p. 169.
23. Whyte, *Bible Characters*, vol. vi, p. 170.

24. Whyte, *The Shorter Catechism* (Edinburgh, reprinted 1954), p. 191.
25. J. M. Barrie, the Scottish playwright, a native of Kirriemuir and Whyte's friend, considered him the most uplifting preacher in the land. See *Letters of J. M. Barrie* (London 1942), pp. 31–2; see also Peter Davidson, 'The Main Themes of Alexander Whyte', *Evangelical Quarterly*, vol. 27, pp. 93–107.
26. Forsyth, *This Life and the Next* (London 1953), p. 87.

10

SAMUEL CHADWICK and GEORGE CAMPBELL MORGAN

Love in action – that is grace.
CAMPBELL MORGAN

Samuel Chadwick was born in 1860 in Burnley, which he remembered as a drab industrial town where factories dominated the scenery and pavements were the only playgrounds. His father, a cotton weaver at Hopwoods' Oak Mount Mill, was compliant, gentle, deeply religious and a lifelong Methodist. His mother, the more dominant personality, was a sensible and straightforwardly honest woman reputed to speak with 'the terseness of a telegram and the force of a catapult'. Chadwick later described her with undisguised admiration: 'She was intellectual without learning, regal without vanity, saintly without ritual, capable without fussiness, witty without venom, humorous without malice and merry without being frivolous' (D pp. 21–2).

At the age of eight Samuel was at work in the mill from six a.m. His family were poor but respectable and throughout his life he retained a defensive affection for 'saints in clogs'. When he was ten years old he was converted in circumstances which were entirely unremarkable. With the uncomplicated logic of a child he looked critically at the boots he had just cleaned for his father and decided they would not be clean enough for Jesus to wear: 'I took up the boots again . . . it was the adoption of a fixed principle . . . I got into the habit of doing the simplest duties as unto Jesus Christ . . . I was only a lad but I knew Jesus. Taking up the boot a second time to do it for Jesus was the confession of my choice. It registered my decision' (D. pp.

24–5). Later, at the age of fifteen, the earlier experience was more sharply defined and he began to feel an inner compulsion to preach. His early hopes of becoming a preacher were discouraged by an unsympathetic circuit superintendent on the grounds of his lack of culture and formal education. A year before he died he recalled his earliest aspirations: 'Everything was against it. My people were poor, my health was indifferent, my education neglected and such gifts as I had were of the microscopic order, and nobody troubled to look for them.'[1]

In 1881 he was appointed Methodist lay-agent at Stacksteads. His zeal and conscientious application to duty is carefully recorded in the small journal he kept of his first year.[2] In one week he paid 104 visits and complained he only managed to call on fourteen people on a 'bad day'. His pugnacious humour is apparent in the entry: 'Sung in the streets at 6.45 a.m. much to the annoyance of folks who had headache as the relic of Saturday night's debauch'. He quickly sensed his own ineffectiveness as a preacher and after a brief period of spiritual search he emerged from a spiritual crisis which he afterwards referred to as his Pentecost. From this time, in 1881, he turned into a gospel activist working in Edinburgh, Clydebank, London and Leeds; editing *Joyful News* ('that breezy organ of Evangelical Wesleyanism') from 1905 to 1932; preaching and teaching at holiness conventions in Britain and overseas, particularly at Southport; becoming Principal of Cliff College in 1913, serving as President of the Methodist Conference in 1918 and holding office as President of the Free Church Council in 1921.

A compromised religion.

During his time as editor of *Joyful News* the paper developed as an organ devoted to encouraging on the one hand an intensive and experiential personal piety, and on the other a stringent social criticism which was sometimes enlightened but not infrequently simplistic. Over a period of several years, for example, the paper commented on housing conditions, the plight of starving Russian refugees, the basis of a just peace following the armistice, the Irish question, miners' strikes, educational policy, sabbath observance, temperance, debt and gambling. On some occasions Chadwick spoke with weight and experience, forging powerful arguments from a Christian moral perspective. At other times he seemed to underestimate the complexity of the issues which were taxing the minds of those he criticized. Nevertheless the moral vigilance, spiritual warmth and straightforward language of *Joyful News* made it an effective medium for Chadwick's distinctive emphases. Almost all of his published work is contained in or derived from *Joyful News* articles.[3]

Chadwick's style was tailor-made for a popular paper. He was a lifetime student of words. He told his students he had read slowly through Chambers' dictionary four times. Short sentences, strong verbs of action, contrasting clauses, a feel for the right word and a preacher's preference for the imperative mood make his writing lively and vigorous.

As President of the Conference he received many letters soliciting his help. This important collection of correspondence gives many insights into the personality of Chadwick. Nurses needing work references, a case of embezzlement, marital breakdown, advice on the suitability of ministerial candidates, a request that a flirtatious student be disciplined, the alleged use of denominational property for Labour Party meetings and even the question of proper remuneration for a lay missioner who had become a Roman Catholic and joined Buckfast Abbey, were referred to him for advice.

The spirituality represented by Chadwick grew out of an older style of Evangelical Methodism which was being put under pressure by social changes. Urban growth in industrialized towns presented to the churches the evangelistic challenge of an increasing population accessible in large numbers, but largely unreached. The decline in religious interest and church attendance seemed to point accusingly to the churches' failed mission. Intellectually Evangelicals tended to be on the defensive against advances in science, philosophy and biblical criticism. In addition, Free Church Evangelicals shared the ecclesiastical concerns of their allies within the established Church over the revival of Anglo-Catholicism. But however gallant the rearguard action, a church in retreat was to a man like Chadwick a contradiction in terms. His diagnosis was uncompromising and the treatment he prescribed was a wholehearted return to the spiritual first principles of Methodism. These he understood as conversion, leading to a life of personal discipleship, sanctification which is the perfection of love and holiness expressed through Christian character, and mission which demanded the recovery of evangelistic zeal and a church committed to 'saving souls'.

In his critique of the church he complained about preaching which was vaguely apologetic and over-anxious to accommodate the gospel to the spirit of the age: 'The modern pulpit is strong in philosophy but weak in witnessing, emphatic on ethics and silent in testimony . . . Every truth proclaimed should be backed by a proved experience.'[4] Not only ministers, but also the members of the churches, were reluctant witnesses, and Chadwick suspected the cause was a deficient experience. He argued for a more overt and aggressive discipleship: 'The demand is for an open avowal of Christ as Lord; a personal confession of a choice and an allegiance; a personal witness of what Christ is to the soul. He will not consent to clandestine relationship.'[5] Underlying Chadwick's zeal was the conviction that the church was diminishing the gospel by minimizing its personal demand: 'Religion loses its grip when it substitutes concession for conviction, when it urges what it dare not expect . . . a compromised religion has no power of attraction.'[6]

Chadwick was a radical; he returned to the spiritual roots of Methodism to find a spirituality vital enough to revive the churches. His radical Methodism was amply demonstrated by the effects of his own evangelistic efforts; it was disseminated through the 2000 lay evangelists who came to Cliff College during Chadwick's principalship for biblical education and training in evangelism; and it was popularized by over thirty years of hard-hitting religious journalism. Such zealous activism was the external expression of spiritual energy generated inwardly by personal and immediate experience of God.

Theology vitalized by experience

Chadwick came to Stacksteads with fifteen carefully prepared sermons. Several weeks into his work he was discouraged by the lack of conversions. He had begun to think through the doctrine of scriptural holiness, and especially the demand for absolute surrender of the whole person. At 3 a.m., after a protracted spiritual struggle, he kindled a fire and burnt his sermons as an act of self-renunciation. At the early morning prayer meeting he spoke of an experience of sanctification and thereafter he repeatedly attributed his zeal and success in evangelism to the ongoing reality of that crisis experience of the Holy Spirit (D p. 32). Chadwick believed that Calvary and Pentecost must be recapitulated in the private experience of each believer. The historical sequence of crucifixion – resurrection and Ascension – Pentecost is not accidental but provides the normative pattern for Christian spirituality. Such a sequence answered to Chadwick's own experience of two crises.

Conversion he defined as 'the crisis of the soul in which it turns to God'. His theology of conversion held true to the classic tension between the initiative of God and the response of man. While 'omnipotence waits for man's consent' and 'grace can only save when man yields', it remains true that 'God's grace is needed for the turning'.[7] Such a critical turning to God unifies the heart in love to God, sets it in opposition to sin and simultaneously cleanses, corrects and redirects the will. Chadwick's definition of conversion was generous and accommodating: 'The types [of conversion] are as varied as human temperament. With some it is sudden, convulsive and exciting; with others it is gradual, gentle, and almost imperceptible.' The wise experience of an evangelist lies behind his comment that 'Convulsion is no necessary part of conversion, but consent to the will of God is as its very soul'.[8]

Conversion is response to the grace of God which was decisively revealed in the cross. For Chadwick, 'Love is the big word of the Cross'. The cross originates in the love of God for a sinful world and that love is fulfilled only when it has turned the heart of the sinner to God and overcome the destructive corrupting power of sin: 'Sin abounds. It begins in lawlessness, fails to attain its destined order, passes into transgression, issues in spiritual alienation, moral dislocation and social disorder.'[9] Nevertheless there is a tenacious optimism in Chadwick's view of grace: 'Let sin run as it will . . . it never passes beyond the boundary of the infinite and eternal grace. Sin is always confronted and enveloped in grace.'[10]

The source of Chadwick's optimism is to be found in his view of God's love: 'Love is not amiable complacency. Love is fire.' Chadwick finds no conflict between love and holiness, grace and judgement: 'The death of Christ for sin is the supreme demonstration of the love of God. God was in Christ, not against Him. The love of God is not conceded to the Cross, but commended in it. The Cross manifests the love of God, but it did not procure it' (GC p. 17). The eternal nature of God is displayed in awesome sacrifice, in a moral recreation through submission to sin's penalty, in a forgiveness which reaches beyond remission of sins to the recreation of moral personality: 'The cross begets Godlikeness in those who receive its gospel' (GC p. 18). God's eternal love yearns for fellowship with created humanity and his eternal righteousness flashes judgement on the sin of fallen humanity. The cross is the historic meeting place of love and righteousness where judgement is transformed into redemption through sacrificial love: 'The Cross is an incident, the sacrifice is eternal. The Lamb slain from the foundation of the world is in the midst of the Throne. The Throne is the Throne of Grace' (GC p. 18). The death of Christ completely accepted and proclaimed is 'the basis of faith, the substance of the gospel, the centre of fellowship, the standard of life and the badge of discipleship' (GC p. 19).

Chadwick's Lenten practice was dominated by the passion of Christ: 'Usually the days are with "set face" toward the Cross'. Catholic devotional manuals, books on the atonement and carefully chosen Bible passages were vehicles for meditation on the Passion.[11] Appropriate verses from Psalms and Prophets were prayed through, the mind ruminating on the mysteries of the Suffering Servant of Isaiah, the abandoned soul of Psalm 22 and the promises of redemption, cleansing, pardon and the joy of restored fellowship. The critical reverence of the Bible student gave way to the humble research of a soul seeking illumination, 'turning leisurely and prayerfully from one great passage to another, to track out words and trace their unfolding in the book of God'. Chadwick's proclamation of the cross has much of Forsyth's moral penetration of the mystery of sacrifice, aided by a vocabulary honed to a fine cutting edge. The demands of popular journalism produced skills which enabled Chadwick to communicate his vision of the cross in a masterly display of language subordinated to devotion. A Passion Sunday meditation on Christ in Gethsemane is a good example:

> The Cross symbolized His life. The crude material expression repulsed him. His mind shrank, his soul shivered, but His face never flinched. It was wet with blood and tears, but His eyes kept their steady resolute gaze. He prayed in unutterable anguish. The Cross is still in the will of the Father. 'If it be

> possible let this cup pass from Me. Nevertheless not as I wilt but as Thou wilt.' So it had always been . . . His Cross was where it had always been: in the Will of the Father . . . He shrank from it; but he never shirked it.[12]

Christ is not imitated but reproduced.

The consent of the will lay at the heart of Chadwick's own second experience. He called it 'a crisis of obedience' and claimed it gave him the key to all his thinking, all his service and all his life. 'There came into my soul a deep peace, a thrilling joy and a new sense of power' (WPen p. 32). Just as the original Pentecost had brought 'illumination of mind, assurance of heart, intensity of love, fullness of power and exuberance of joy' so the believer's personal Pentecost carries an equally potent spiritual payload.

Chadwick made bold claims for this second experience of grace. In matters concerning the life of the soul 'The Spirit-filled are not left in uncertainty as to the mind of God'. The experience of prayer is decisively changed because, 'before Pentecost we pray in the Spirit, after Pentecost the Spirit prays through us' (PP p. 41). In describing the overall benefits of what he calls the 'Baptism of the Holy Spirit' he uses absolute terms with total confidence: 'All fullness of life, all resources of vitality, all certainty of assurance, all victory over sin and the flesh, all prevailing power in prayer, all certitude of glory – all and everything is in the Indwelling Presence and Power of the Holy Spirit of God in Christ Jesus our Lord' (WPen p. 36). That last complex clause contains the key elements of Chadwick's spiritual thought.

In John's Gospel Jesus had promised, '[The Spirit] abideth with you and will be in you'. Chadwick pushed the prepositions to their theological limits, arguing that 'inwardness is the distinctive feature of the Spirit'. Indwelling is not simply the felt presence of God; it is the actual, personal, spiritual presence of God, objectively real and subjectively realized within human personality: 'It is a personality within a personality by which the Spirit becomes the life of my life, the soul of my soul . . . an indwelling that secures identity without confusion and possession without absorption.'[13] Chadwick seemed to be claiming that the incarnation is perpetuated in the Body of Christ through the indwelling presence of the Holy Spirit in the consecrated body of each believer.

One of his favourite texts is Judges 6.34: 'The Spirit clothed himself with Gideon'. He suggested that the Spirit clothing himself with humanity is another miracle of incarnation. He did not intend to diminish or compromise the unique once-for-allness of the historic incarnation of Christ. He was concerned to establish the 'real presence' of Christ, by his Spirit, in the life of each Spirit-filled believer. Nor did he intend to suggest that such indwelling destroyed the integrity and identity of human personality. Rather, the Spirit-filled personality is enabled to find its fullest and highest expression only through the vitalizing and cleansing influence of the divine presence. In his teaching on divine indwelling, Chadwick comes as close as his Evangelical theology will allow to the notion of a conscious union with God. But such union with God is not the end result of a process of mystical devotion; it is by faith, in an instant, and is the spiritual consequence in the life of the believer of the historic acts of God in the crucifixion – resurrection and Ascension – Pentecost. Conversion involves the birth of a new life in which the soul is regenerated by the Holy Spirit; baptism with the Holy Spirit is the filling of that life with the presence of the risen Christ. Through these two acts of faith the Christian becomes the dwelling-place of God.

Consequently when Chadwick spoke of Christlikeness he meant much more than the imitation of a model: 'Christ lives in men through the Spirit. He is no longer a model but a living Presence. Christian faith does not copy Him; it lives Him. Christ is not imitated; He is reproduced' (WPen p. 76). It is part of the creative work of the Holy Spirit to bring all the soul's qualities, potential and actual, to their intended completion. The Spirit awakens the dormant and develops the latent faculties of each indwelt personality. In this way each Christian becomes an embodiment of the Spirit, the expression in human existence of the life of the triune God: 'The love of the Father is the origin of Grace; the grace of the Lord Jesus Christ is the medium of redeeming love; and through the Spirit is communicated both the grace of the Son and the love of the Father' (WPen p. 46). The same trinitarian perspective informs his comment on Eph. 3.14–19: 'The Spirit strengthens the inner man, the Son reveals the Divine love to the heart, and the Infinite God fills the whole being with Divine fullness of love, blessedness and power' (WPen p. 51).

In his exposition of the theological basis of the second blessing Chadwick can be hard to follow, raising as many questions as he answers. By contrast, when dealing with the practical question of how this experience is to be obtained, he reduces a whole spiritual theology to four simple steps. The first step is simply to ask, not for the gift, or for the power, but simply for the constant presence of Christ through his Spirit. It is an important spiritual principle that Christ is to be sought for himself and not for the benefits he brings. Secondly, sins of the spirit which hinder the blessing must be forsaken in repentance; 'There is generally a bonfire when the Fire of God falls'. Thirdly the gift requested must be received, through a confident faith which trusts God's promises and claims the promised gift. The fourth step is a life of continual obedience. When obedience fails the blessing is lost.[14]

ASK, REPENT, RECEIVE, OBEY. It all seems too easy and the simple scheme reads like a slick piece of theological salesmanship. But Chadwick was writing pastorally for a readership of widely differing ability. Alongside such step-by-step simplicity there are impressive passages of serious theological reflection, illuminated by his own experience and intended to encourage similar experience in his readers. He was trying to map out a practical procedure for 'obtaining the blessing'. In doing so he had to describe a complex process of interaction between the human soul and the triune God in all the mystery of his being, and to do so in such a way that the incalculable resources of divine grace could become immediately and effectively available.

The moral energy of holiness.

Chadwick shared Wesley's conviction that holiness is an experience to be sought, and once received must be expressed in a life of perfect love. The issues surrounding Christian perfection are of such importance for Christian spirituality that Chadwick believed it demanded 'clearness of thought, intelligence of faith and instruction on the implications of experience'. In practical terms Christian perfection was defined as fitness for a specific function, the 'perfection of grace for efficiency in all the will of God' (CCP p. 94). Perfection is defined, then, as fitness to receive and express the indwelling presence through sanctified personality. Such fitness is by the expulsion of sin from the heart by a definite act of faith, with the specific aim of claiming the promised cleansing. The Christian thus cleansed is not only able to resist sin, but the desire to sin is 'rooted up and cast out of the heart'. Chadwick had preached through W. B. Pope's three-volume *Compendium of Christian Theology*. Pope was the leading Methodist theologian of Chadwick's generation who taught entire sanctification by faith, providing substantial theological confirmation of Chadwick's experience.[15]

In Chadwick's view, love is the essential element and the infallible test of perfection. At the 1912 Southport Holiness Convention, Chadwick examined the basis of Christian ethics using 1 John.[16] He suggested four ethical principles; First, 'Christian experience is verified in a new ethic'. Second, 'by ethics we mean for practical purposes, a system of moral rules and precepts for the regulation of life'. Third, the Christian ethic is more than that; 'its precepts and principles of conduct may be accepted without its vital experience'. So, fourthly, 'Christ is inseparable from the Christian; there must be an abiding relationship'.

This 'vital experience' and 'abiding relationship' are developed in his address on 'God is Love'. Love is 'the impulse to give – the mysterious power by which we live in the life of another.' By implication the love of God is that same mysterious power by which he lives in the life of the believer. That mutual fellowship of personalities, the communion of love between God and the Christian, was what Chadwick meant by abiding. The love of God poured into the heart is nothing less than the divine gift of the real presence and power of God. Love is the basis of the Christian's relationship with God; abiding in love the aim of all Christian obedience and the essential condition of divine indwelling.

Obedience is more than adherence to received rules. It consists in an attitude of moral fidelity sustained and guided by the renewed mind. It is the work of the Holy Spirit to lead the mind into truth, to take the things of Christ and reveal them: 'The mind furnishes the raw material of character . . . and the character is transformed, not by spiritual ecstasies but by the renewing of the mind; and the mind is renewed by truth.'[17] Consistent holiness involves constant obedience. For such obedience to be possible the Christian requires the spiritual resources of an infinite grace, the moral discernment of an awakened and informed conscience and the intellectual discipline of a renewed mind devoted to discovering 'the good and perfect and acceptable will of God'. The model of obedience is Christ, who became 'obedient unto death': '[It is] to His death we are to have the likeness of living correspondence. Christian obedience is inherently sacrificial. He loved . . . He gave. That is the whole story when Faith has filled in the gaps . . . To be conformed to His death is to love as He loved, and give as He gave.'[18]

There is a close relationship between obedience, the Christian mind and the practice of prayer. Chadwick interpreted the biblical injunction 'Watch and pray' as a call to creative reflection on the data of human experience. By waiting in the divine presence, seeking divine wisdom and instruction, the Christian mind is being attuned to the needs of the world. When daily life is subjected to compassionate scrutiny in the search for meaning and appropriate Christian response, prayer becomes intercession. Such spiritual thinking can have the same creative outcome as when the Spirit brooded over the primeval chaos: 'If prayer is a lost art it is because meditation is a lost habit. Great supplicants have always been great brooders.'[19]

In the prayer of solitude a deep cleansing of the heart takes place. The soul is alone, naked and vulnerable, for once silent and humbled in 'the presence of God Who is shadowless light'. By such prayer 'life and motive are examined in the light of his countenance'. Divine majesty mediated through grace is experienced as fatherly love. Intimacy and trusting faith are characteristic of Christian prayer. By the help of the indwelling Holy Spirit the heart cries out, sometimes with inarticulate joy, sometimes with wordless longing and sometimes with the Christian cry of recognition, 'Abba, Father.' Chadwick laid great weight on the ministry of the Holy Spirit as the one who prays through the praying heart, making intercession with 'groanings which cannot be uttered'.

Christian activism in mission and evangelism provided much 'fuel' for petitionary prayer. Chadwick urged that petitions should be specific, bold and persistent. *Joyful News* carried a regular column, 'Requests for prayer', which included in one issue requests that, 'a young widow with ten children should prosper in business', a local preacher would be cured of sciatica, and that 'a young man be kept from debt'.[20] Beneath the list, Chadwick wrote encouragingly: 'It is particularly requested that notification should be sent when answers have been received.' Prayer was to be regarded as an appointed means of obtaining blessings from the Father.

On one occasion Chadwick wrote, 'I live in the grip of a quest; and preach with the joy of a find.'[21] His spirituality confirms both claims. Chadwick was gripped by the overwhelming reality of God. The degree of immediacy and even intimacy which underlay his experience of God fired his heart with a fervour which gave his evangelistic preaching power and his words to a languishing church a sharp prophetic edge. A member of his Leeds church described him with obvious affection: 'Slight of stature, with a striking head, an aggressive nose, eyes that seemed to be looking both inwardly at some vision, and through to the heart and mind of the object in front . . . ; a manner somewhat assertive and pugnacious; without any trace of indecision or fear; consequently dominating most men and circumstances, yet, withal, as gentle as a child, as humble as the poorest, as forgetful as a saint'.[22] Stern self-discipline, a staggering workload and increasing leadership responsibilities did not seem to drain the joy from his pursuit of God. Chadwick was undoubtedly a potent preacher and a formidable controversialist but of at least equal significance was a personality passionately determined and ruthlessly honest, yet humbly open to the full range of New Testament experience as interpreted within his own tradition. While Chadwick was resisting what he saw as the erosion of vital and experiential Christianity, by controversy, by evangelistic urgency and indirectly by the influence of his personal testimony, his close friend George Campbell Morgan was conducting his own assault on spiritual mediocrity.

Chadwick summed up the most influential expository ministry of his generation when he wrote a review of a controversial sermon preached by Morgan at Westminster Chapel: 'He is pre-eminently a teacher of the Word . . . he was set for the defence of the Word, not by Apologetics but by Interpretation . . . to make known again the authority, completeness and finality of the divinely inspired Word of God' (M p. 210).

That bible found me!

George Campbell Morgan's father was a Baptist minister who later joined the Plymouth Brethren. He lived a life of devout austerity and claimed he had 'never read a novel in all the 80 years of his life'. Morgan's upbringing was characterized by 'plain living and an absence of almost all counter attractions and few friends of his own age' (M p. 31). He described the late Victorian period as a time when 'youth was held within restrictions unnatural to itself'. His own upbringing imposed just such restrictions (M p. 37).

Though his first sermon, preached when he was only 13, was delivered in Monmouth Methodist Chapel, Morgan shares with Chadwick the dubious distinction of being turned down for the Methodist ministry. His pastoral work was done mainly in Congregational churches, first in Stone, Rugeley and Birmingham, then in New Court, Tollington Park, a church with a long distinguished Nonconformist tradition, numbering amongst its previous ministers the Puritan Thomas Manton. He worked as an evangelist in the slums of Hull, the villages of Staffordshire and the commercial centres of the great cities in Britain and the U.S.A. Two periods at Westminster Chapel in London were the cornerstone of a remarkably wide ministry in which he crossed the Atlantic fifty-four times (by sea!), and spoke at every major annual Bible convention, of which eleven 'regulars' are listed in the biography. He spent thirteen years in itinerant preaching in the United States, wrote over seventy books, was President of Cheshunt, the Congregational College, and created then disseminated the 'Westminster Method' of Bible teaching until there were nineteen such Bible schools in London and fifty-three nationally. 'Restlessness was said to be his besetting sin'; on the selective evidence adduced that seems to be an understatement.

The cloistered Evangelicalism in which he was raised left Morgan largely unprepared for the much more severe intellectual climate of an increasingly secular society. He had no crisis experience of conversion, his spiritual development being nurtured and shaped by home influences, parental expectations and an uncritical receptiveness to religious training. Until he was sixteen 'it never occurred to him to doubt the authority of the Bible'. Teacher training exposed him to a new world of knowledge which was often critical of the Bible. His faith, 'while not undermined was eclipsed . . . when the sun is eclipsed it is not killed it is hidden' (M p. 38). Confused, hurt and deprived of religious certainty, he locked away all his books and bought a new Bible: 'I am no longer sure that this is what my father claims it to be

– the Word of God. But of this I am sure. If it be the Word of God, and if I come to it with an unprejudiced and open mind, it will bring assurance to my soul itself . . . That Bible *found* me' (M pp. 39–40). That is the testimony of a young Christian divesting himself of a faith received second-hand and searching for a faith authentically and inalienably his own. It is significant that it is his father's faith which is being tested.

Not by apologetics but by persuasion.

When Morgan came to Westminster Chapel he started a Friday evening Bible Lecture which gave full scope to his teaching gifts and his conviction that the Bible is the primary text-book of Christian spirituality. The 'Westminster Method' involved teaching the Bible 'patiently, persistently and consecutively', analyzing whole books or major themes. A selective, piecemeal, text-hunting ministry he considered neither fair to the Bible nor adequate as a spiritual diet. His lectures and books reveal a careful verse by verse exposition, comprehensive analysis of the whole book and textual comparisons showing the interconnectedness of the whole counsel of God. By teaching and example he encouraged daily, personal, detailed study of the Bible. He once told a gathering of Bible students to go and buy concordances and he would teach them individually how to use them. When travelling by rail he often had his Bible open with pencil and notebook on his knee. It was his practice to read a biblical book through fifty times aloud before beginning to preach on it. He was appreciative but discerning in his use of critical scholarship, on one occasion using a break in a conference to consult the latest German scholarship on the Gospel of John in the new edition of the *Encyclopaedia Brittanica*. His early career in teaching included time at the Jewish Collegiate School in Birmingham. From his friendship with E. Levy the headmaster he developed an imaginative sympathy for Old Testament Judaism.

Morgan understood Bible study as a means to an end. It must issue in evangelism and service. Bible knowledge which fails to make the connection between the gospel and human life is at best a form of spiritual self-culture, and at worst a muffling of the demands made by the Word of God. Bible study must always provoke action; hearing and doing are constituent elements of a Bible-centred obedience. The authority of the Bible is primarily moral and spiritual. It is the business of the Bible teacher to interpret and apply to life 'the eternal principles revealed in the Bible, which being obeyed, all other things fall into their proper place and proportion'.[23]

The man who preached in 1919 on the need to regulate drainage and smoke pollution was clearly prepared to apply 'eternal principles' to the most earthy issues.[24] He confessed his indebtedness to writers like Kingsley, Dickens and Ruskin, and he could speak with prophetic force about the failure of Christian people to allow Christian principles to permeate daily social life: 'The most terrible blasphemy of the age is not the blasphemy of the slums, but the blasphemy of the place of worship where men pray such prayers (as Thy Kingdom come) and then go out to deny every principle of divine government in their lives.'[25] That is almost a paraphrase of Amos' complaint. Yet Morgan also held firmly to the importance of individual conversion. 'You say, Can't we improve the dwellings of the poor? Yes, God help us to do it. But one of the best ways is to improve the man that lives in the dwelling.'[26]

The Bible, then, is God's chosen medium through which the divine imperative is conveyed to mind and heart. For that reason Morgan spared no labour to establish the meaning of Scripture; and he had little patience with those whose preaching revealed a lack of such careful thought. His diary records a visit to a local church: 'Heard a capital sermon with which I did not at all agree, on a text which bore no relation to the subject. Text Proverbs 9. 5: subject Holy Communion' (M p. 188). Responsible exegesis requires a firm refusal to violate a text and use it to demonstrate homiletic virtuosity. Morgan's opposition to such liberties arose from his belief that the teacher of the Word of God is not only teaching what the Word says, but how such truth is to be discovered. The preacher/teacher's own methods influence the hearer, and Morgan desired a Christian public schooled in the creative and controlling disciplines of Bible study. One newspaper reviewer was unable to make up his mind whether Morgan represented a spiritual intellectuality or an intellectual spirituality (M p. 216). Certainly he laid primary emphasis on the need for mental work and regular discipline as qualities of the Bible student; and he assumed that each Christian was obliged to be such a lifelong Bible student.

Morgan valued the Bible as an indispensable means of discerning the mind of Christ, as essential food without which the Christian soul suffers spiritual starvation and as God's appointed means of spiritual nurture, education and encounter with himself. The verse sung at the beginning of each Friday night Bible school expresses well his reverence for the Bible as a means of grace:

> Break Thou the Bread of Life, dear Lord to me,
> As Thou dids't break the loaves beside the sea;
> Beyond the sacred page, I seek Thee Lord,
> My spirit pants for Thee, O Living Word.

The Bible is bread to be broken, shared and assimilated. Christians who search into the Bible are seeking not knowledge about God but God himself. The hunger that drives them is not hunger for facts but for a presence, the presence of the risen living Word of God who still looks with compassion on harassed helpless people and breaks bread to feed them. That was the vision which lay behind the biblical framework of Morgan's spirituality.

Before a biblical text Morgan's demeanour was docile, receptive and utterly honest, enabling him to teach what he had learned with a rare combination of humility and authority. When an honest interpretation of Scripture conflicted with a system of dogmatics the system and not the text should be examined, and if need be adjusted. He was often content to leave tensions unresolved, not because a solution could not be suggested with a little ingenuity but because an imposed solution would violate the richly dynamic meaning of the biblical text. Such principles were upheld by Morgan when he resigned an influential teaching position in defence of a colleague whose book had antagonized Fundamentalist opinion. His own temperament, his understanding of the gospel as a gracious invitation, and his profound humility in the face of the mystery of grace, made him suspicious of slogan theology, or creeds used as a doctrinal means test. He regarded the phrase 'hold the truth' as a 'hateful expression', for the truth of the gospel can never be adequately held by any one group.

The Passion of God.

Morgan understood sin as rebellion, as inordinate self-will. Those who deny the radical nature of human sinfulness, or who rationalize personal failure, or become complacent about moral inadequacy are merely exhibiting the subterfuge of the self skilfully but unsuccessfully trying to evade an encounter with God in his holiness.[27] Such wilfulness is not to be quelled but converted, and that not by coercion but by the persuasion of love. By love Morgan does not mean an over-indulgent goodwill which ignores the moral tragedy of sin: 'It is because of love that God never turned His back upon man; but that love is the sternest foe of sin' (BC p. 48). Unfailing love for sinners and unyielding opposition to sin create a divine dilemma which can be resolved only by God's total involvement in all the consequences of sin. And since gracious unfailing love is of the very nature of God, that love leaves him no option; he must bear the suffering of those he loves. The mystery of the cross is the mystery of the passion of God.

In his commentary, *Hosea: the Heart and Holiness of God*, Morgan expounded the compassion of God with daring emphasis on the divine vulnerability. When there is every justification for God abandoning sinful Israel, giving up his people, letting his love for them die and allowing them to perish, God is overheard in an anguished cry, 'How can I give you up?' There is an inner argument in the heart of God. Sin and repeated failure persist, but love will not give up in defeat. The anguish of God is awesome to contemplate and impossible to comprehend: 'Here we are in the presence of Love . . . love that becomes an agony; love that becomes a tragedy' (H p. 131). From this truth of the divine suffering it is a natural step to the cross. The event of the crucifixion was 'the working out into visibility [of] all the underlying eternal truth of the passion of His love'.

Basic to Morgan's spirituality was the reality and destructiveness of sin, but of sin enveloped in grace, deprived of its executive power in the heart of the forgiven. In the cross the perversity of the human will is confronted by the passion of God and instead of expected annihilation the sinner is met by suffering love: 'In the moment in which man sinned against God, God gathered into his own heart of love, the issue of that sin, and it is not by the death of a Man, but by the mystery of the passion of God, that He is able to keep His face turned in love toward wandering men . . . and had there been no passion in His heart, no love, no suffering of Deity, no man could ever have returned to Him' (BC p. 50).

By the mystery of the passion of God, 'the great healing love that wins through suffering' was released with reconciling power into a fallen universe: 'In the actual outpouring of the blood of the Man of Nazareth there was symbolised that infinite mystery of essential love bending to suffering, and pain and death, gathering into itself that which is against itself in inherent principle, and suffering, in order that through that suffering there might be accomplished something which cannot be accomplished without it' (BC p. 67). What cannot be accomplished without the cross is forgiveness, by which the heart is freed from the guilt, pollution and power of sin.

The objections of the fastidious to blood vocabulary carried little weight with Morgan. It is not by Jesus' life, but by Jesus' life laid down, that redemption is won; it is not by the attractiveness and beauty of a perfect life that hostile wills are forgiven and recruited to obedience, but by the mystery of that life willingly given to be broken for the sins of all people. Rather than empty the atonement of objective significance by rephrasing such terms as 'through His blood', Morgan conceded the 'vulgarity' of the image. The offensiveness of the cross merely emphasizes the extent and expense of the passion of God: 'Vulgar Cross; but that in it which is vulgar is my sin. Shining through it is the light that comes from the throne; and flowing through it is the great river of His grace' (BC p. 74).

Christ the centre and circumference.

The cross as the evidence of the suffering love of God applied personally to our own sins is the main motivational spring of Christian devotion. Christian spirituality is a living out of the experience of grace, and in that sense is essentially responsive. Underlying the cross are principles which inform, direct and inspire Christian spirituality. Jesus' death on the cross was the culmination of a life lived in absolute conformity to the will of God, and that conformity was no exacted compliance, but a trusting filial obedience. Conformity to Christ's death must therefore mean that doing the will of God becomes the overriding directive of Christian living. The cross, experienced as God's suffering love reaching out to sinners, is pure gift; but when in conformity to Christ, each Christian takes up a personal cross, it becomes a shaping principle, an act of responsive love. The total self-surrender of God is only answerable by an equivalent act of self-surrender. Grace demands the response of obedience, not as its condition, but as its consequence.

The spiritual life originates in the grace of God and that grace is most fully revealed and mediated through Jesus. 'The Incarnation is God's final Self-interpretation, the Speech of Himself to man in the terms of humanity, that man may grasp the truth concerning Deity' (H p. 131). And as we have seen, the truth concerning Deity is that in Christ righteousness and love coincide so that moral requirement and gracious gift do not cancel each other out. Christ is the fulfilling of both, for 'His redemption of the human soul is not a pity that agrees to ignore sin; but a power that cancels it and sets free from its dominion' (H p. 133).

The crucified and risen Christ not only breaks the dominion of sin, but establishes his own rule by becoming 'the centre and circumference of Christian life'. Morgan declared early in his Westminster ministry: 'No man will ever be welcome in this pulpit who is likely to degrade His person, or limit His purpose or question His power' (M p. 144). The person of Jesus, his life and inner experience, were areas of constant interest to Morgan. Some of his finest writing is devoted to the exploration of Jesus' teaching. He wrote commentaries on all four Gospels, and on the parables, miracles and teaching of Jesus. Each of these, with his own favourite, a series of reflections on the *Crises of the Christ*, show how he used imagination and sympathy to penetrate the mystery and genius of Jesus' ministry. He summed up the centrality of Christ in his own spirituality thus: 'In Christ I find God. In Christ my heart learns to love God, and can do no other than love God. In Christ therefore I find the secret of the change in the output of energy that transforms my energy from hurtfulness to beneficence. You and I live with God, walk with God, talk with God, and have fellowship with God, through Jesus Christ.'[28]

One baptism, many fillings.

Christ is the self-expression of God, and the Holy Spirit is the effective presence of the risen Christ in the life of the believer. Morgan took issue with 'the popular and prevalent idea that the Holy Spirit is to be asked for and waited for'. The Holy Spirit is not a gift to be requested but is Christ's gift made available through his finished work. A perceived absence of the Holy

Spirit in the life of the Christian is due to human disobedience obstructing the Spirit's power. It is not due to divine tardiness. In Morgan's view, a generous self-giving God does not wait to be asked to bestow himself. On the invitation of obedient minds and hearts, 'He takes possession and dwells within'. Here he is differing from those who taught a second experience of grace, whether called the second blessing or the baptism of the Spirit.

Against such teaching as Chadwick's, he argued that the baptism of the Holy Spirit is equivalent to and simultaneous with conversion and regeneration. Every person who is born again is baptized in the Spirit, and such baptism marks the initiation of spiritual life, not its advanced development. The spiritual deficiency detected by many Christians was not caused by the absence of the Spirit but by failure to surrender the whole self to the indwelling God. The delay in full spiritual effectiveness is 'not the waiting of man for the Spirit, but the waiting of the Spirit for man' (SG p. 173). There is no need of a second gift; there is no two-stage process of Christian discipleship modelled on Calvary and Pentecost. There is only the 'appalling miracle' of regeneration by repentance and faith by which the human life becomes the temple of God. In that experience all the potential riches of Christ are available from the start. The Spirit-filled life is the normal condition of the believer.

Morgan explained the low level of spiritual life which many Christians experienced in terms other than a second-blessing theology. Ignorance of the possibilities of grace, moral disobedience, and lack of faith hinder the free expression of the Holy Spirit in the life of the believer. Only when the will is fully surrendered, and the self is wholly available, can the Spirit endue life with power and holiness. 'Be filled with the Spirit' is an imperative, placing the responsibility for spiritual adequacy on the individual believer. The availability of grace is not in question; the willingness and the adventurousness of the heart is.

Thus the New Testament pattern is baptism and filling as the one experience simultaneous with conversion. But in reality many Christians experience one baptism but many fillings. The filling of the Spirit is not a privilege of the few but an imperative for all; it is not a counsel of perfection but an act of obedience. Christians conscious of spiritual mediocrity must fulfil two conditions, abandonment and abiding: 'Wherever whole-hearted, absolute, unquestioning, positive, final abandonment of the life to God obtains, the life becomes filled with the Spirit' (SG p. 227). Spirit filling requires an unconditional surrender, negotiated at the power centre of the self. Negatively, surrender results in moral purification from 'everything that is unlike His own perfection of beauty'. Positively it is availability for service.

To keep the commands of God is to obey, and to live a life of continual obedience is to abide. Faith and love sum up the commands; faith is 'the absolute dependence of the soul upon Christ and the consequent life of obedience to Him' (SG p. 231). Love is outgoing service to others for Christ's sake. So faith working by love provides for Morgan an adequate ethic of discipleship. In the whole discussion of the work of the Spirit Morgan picks his way carefully through the biblical evidence, refusing to construct a set pattern of experience to be reproduced in every life, but trying to establish biblical principles which must be operative in every life however varied the experience.

The fruit of the spirit is love.

Chadwick and Morgan had few significant theological differences. They shared a total commitment to biblical authority, and a profound reverence for the Bible as the Word of God. For both preachers the cross as the manifestation of divine love and divine justice was utterly central. They were equally insistent on the need for conversion, that is, a new birth through the Holy Spirit by faith in Christ's atoning work, and in their preaching there was a definite call for such explicit commitment. On the relationship between the ministry of the Holy Spirit and the life of the believer they differed, firstly because their own experience differed and secondly because their exegetical conclusions differed. Undoubtedly the latter was influenced by the former! But even where they disagreed on precisely how a Christian is filled with the Spirit they agreed as to what constitutes the valid evidence for such filling; power for effective service, Christlikeness of character and in particular, the growth and development of love as the controlling impulse of Christian behaviour.

Morgan defined holiness as 'approximation to the character of God, indeed it is the character of God reproduced at the centre of personality' (WP iii p. 279). This is achieved by the indwelling Spirit who contradicts, negatives and counteracts the downward gravitational pull of sin. The idea of the counteracting Spirit is typical Keswick teaching, as is Morgan's treatment of Romans seven.[29] His contention that all necessary resources for Christian growth are already available in 'the riches of His grace', was consistent with his own experience. His view that 'all Christ is, He is for me and in me' is a claim echoed in countless Holiness conferences. But Morgan was more sympathetic to failure, giving an emphasis to motive and intention which reveals a gentle pastoral realism: 'I know the call is to a life, high, noble, pure, but I know the God who calls. He is a God of patience; he judges the motive, the aspiration. If I am his child, though I tremble and fail, He in infinite love counts my life blameless when the master passion of the whole endeavour is the pleasing of His heart' (WP iii p. 301).

'The fruit of the Spirit is love' (Gal. 5. 22). Morgan's grammatical vigilance, perhaps even his pedantry, influence his treatment of this verse. The 'ungrammatical "is" ' followed by nine singular nouns, demands some explanation. He argues that love is an all-inclusive virtue, providing the basic vocabulary of Christian ethics. Love is the final quality control on Christian behaviour. All other aspects of Christian character are Christian only insofar as they are expressions of love. Joy is love's consciousness; peace is love's confidence; long-temperedness is love's habit; kindness is love's activity; goodness is love's quality; faithfulness is love's quantity; meekness is love's tone; temperance is love's victory. The fruit of the Spirit is not ninefold but one. It is Love. Not a vapid romanticized emotion, nor a 'fragrance which cannot be analysed'. It is the categorical imperative of Christian living. Love is most perfectly expressed in terms of law: 'If you love me keep my commandments' (John 14.15). Obedience proves love and love is the inspiration of obedience. By continuing obedience the Christian remains within the sphere of a loving communion and harmony of wills, allowing the love of God to flow through life unchecked. Though he does not use the metaphor, Morgan likens the outworking of love to an efficient irrigation system, reclaiming barren areas, exploiting potential fertility and bringing life to moral fruition.

But Campbell Morgan did not believe the benefits of spiritual life were one-sided. In a daring passage, again reflecting on the dilemma of God in Hosea ('How shall I give you up, O Ephraim'), Morgan writes, 'That is the cry of a Being hungry for love' (WP i p. 171). God is love, and his being hungers for love and can be satisfied with nothing less. 'The fruit of the Spirit which is for the sustenance of God's own heart in its hunger, is love,' (WP i p. 170). Here he is reflecting on love from the viewpoint of God in his need. It is not that he reduces God to dependence on human affection; it is that he takes seriously the nature of love as a quality of relationship, requiring reciprocation for fulfilment. If love is only fulfilled in a process of exchange in which there is neither calculation nor limitation, and if God is indeed love, then God, in the deepest reality of his being, needs to love and to receive love. 'Love is sustenance for God's hunger.' It is the work of the Holy Spirit to produce that love; such love is the gift of God himself to the human heart; it is the fruit of the cross, the reproduction in the redeemed heart of a love capable of self-giving. God gives what we need so that in grateful joy and costly love heart is united to heart in a mutuality of self gift.[30]

Such exalted spiritual thought arises from intense experience and serious biblical reflection. Chadwick, guided by his own two-stage experience, understood obedience as a crisis and the baptism of the Holy Spirit as a once-for-all second blessing. Morgan, also reflecting his experience, but with more exegetical precision, argued that obedience was not a once-for-all surrender in order to *receive* the Holy Spirit. Rather, obedience is a continuing imperative urging the Christian to a life of unbroken loyalty to Christ so that the Holy Spirit *already possessed* might have freedom of expression through consecrated personality. While differing in their interpretation of how the Spirit works, they both discerned the absolute necessity of obedience expressed in love. They shared a vision of God's love as unlimited grace and as a prior, initiating and reconciling power released into the world through the death of Christ. From such a high view of the divine love they developed a spiritual theology in which the love of God is seen to be a creative force capable of transforming human personality. The love of God, poured into the heart by the Holy Spirit, evokes response from the whole person. The mind is convinced by the evidence of crucified love; the will is moved to surrender to a self-surrendered God; the energy of the emotional life is gathered and focused on 'The Son of God who loved me and gave Himself for me'.

Christian love is understood not only as response to God's love. It is the expression through redeemed personality of the nature of God himself. God is love, and by the 'awesome miracle' of new birth he is the indwelling God. The obedient Christian, responsive to the Lord Jesus Christ, and filled with the Spirit of God, becomes a medium through which the very nature of God is glimpsed. 'The fruit of the Spirit is love . . . God's love has been poured into our hearts by the Holy Spirit . . . He who loves is born of God and God's love is perfected in him . . .' Chadwick and Morgan reflected deeply on such phrases, and sensing their vitalizing importance they trusted to the vision of divine love revealed in Christ and sought to be open to its recreative power.

Sources frequently cited

Chadwick, S., *The Call to Christian Perfection*. London 1936. (CCP)
——, *The Gospel of the Cross*. London 1934. (GC)
——, *The Path of Prayer*. London 1968. (PP)
——, *The Way to Pentecost*. London 1951. (WPen)
Dunning, N., *Samuel Chadwick*. London 1935. (D)
Morgan, G. C., *The Bible and the Cross*. London 1909. (BC)
——, *Hosea: The Heart and the Holiness of God*. London 1934. (H)
——, *The Spirit of God*. London n.d. (SG)
——, *The Westminster Pulpit*, 10 vols. London 1951–. (WP)
Morgan, J., *A Man of the Word*. London 1951. (M)

Additional reading

Davies, R., and Rupp, G., *A History of the Methodist Church in Great Britain*, vol. 2, London 1978; vol. 4, London 1989.
Harries, J., *G. Campbell Morgan: The Man and His Ministry*. Chicago 1930.
Howarth, D. H., 'Samuel Chadwick and Some Aspects of Wesleyan Methodist Evangelism, 1860–1932'. Lancaster, M. Litt. 1977.
——, *How Great a Flame*. Cliff College 1983.
——, 'Joyful News', *Proceedings of the Wesley Historical Society*, vol. 44, pp. 2f.
Lambert, D. W., *The Testament of Samuel Chadwick*. London 1957.
Morgan, G. C., *The Crises of the Christ*. London 1903.
——, *The Practice of Prayer*. London 1906.
——, *The Acts of the Apostles*. London 1924.
——, *The Prophecy of Jeremiah*. New York 1931.
Murray, H., *Campbell Morgan, Bible Teacher*. London 1938.
Turnbull, R. G., *The History of Preaching*, vol. 3 (Grand Rapids 1974), pp. 434–41.

Notes

1. *Sheffield Daily Telegraph*, 17 Oct. 1932.
2. This journal is still extant and is kept along with many other Chadwick MSS at Cliff College, Calver, Sheffield.
3. S. Chadwick, *Joyful News* 1905–1932. Cliff College holds the most complete run of *Joyful News* known to me.
4. *Joyful News* (12 June 1913), p. 5.
5. ibid.
6. *Joyful News* (12 June 1913), p. 5.
7. *What is Meant by Conversion?*, S. Chadwick (London n.d.), p. 8. One of a series of 'Popular Lectures by Eminent Men in the World of Religious Thought'. The Superintendent of the Wesleyan Mission, Oxford Place, Leeds, with his love for 'saints in clogs' and pride in his working class roots must have enjoyed such an effusive publisher's blurb!
8. ibid., pp. 14–15.
9. *Joyful News* (7 Dec. 1916), p. 5.
10. This quotation is from his friend Campbell Morgan.
11. Chadwick's search for a spirituality deeper than what was on offer in contemporary Evangelicalism is noted by J. M. Turner, *Conflict and Reconciliation* (London 1985), p. 166.
12. D. W. Lambert, *Through the Year with Samuel Chadwick* (London 1960), p. 30.
13. Chadwick, *Pentecost*, pp. 43, 51, 102.
14. While the sequence in the original *Joyful News* article (28 May 1914, p. 5), is ASK, REPENT, RECEIVE, OBEY, in the volume of Chadwick's articles, issued as *The Way to Pentecost*, the sequence has been changed by the editor to REPENT, ASK, RECEIVE, OBEY. It is not a simple misprint for the paragraphs have been transposed and sentences altered to make the sequence fit. It looks suspiciously like an attempt to make Chadwick's teaching fit with the typical holiness emphasis on cleansing from sin before there can be legitimate asking. Chadwick's point is too important to be quietly corrected. 'There must be desire that is focused into petition . . . God waits to give, but He is a God of discretion and waits to be asked . . .' To ask is to want, and the importance of desire for God, and for the realization of all God has to give as a prerequisite for God's response lies at the very heart of Chadwick's spirituality. Want it, want it enough to forsake sin, want it enough to believe God will give it, then go on wanting it so much that implicit obedience to Christ is gladly offered. 'The blessing of Pentecost may be lost, and it is always lost when obedience fails.' The suspicion of a little theological tidying up is strengthened by the omission of a sentence which, by the canons of textual criticism, is the 'hard reading'. In the section on repentance Chadwick stated in the original article, 'Regeneration saves from sinning. A soul born of God can no more sin than a teetotaller can get drunk.' That first short sentence is too unguarded

to be included; the second is *vintage* Chadwick! He gave his own classic account of his second experience in the *Methodist Recorder*, Winter 1897.

15. See A. Sell, 'An Englishman, an Irishman and a Scotsman . . .', in *Scottish Journal of Theology*, vol. 38, pp.41–83; and G. Slater, 'Ministerial Training: William Burt Pope (1822–1903)', in *Epworth Review*, vol. 15, no. 2 (May 1988), pp. 59–66.
16. The whole set of fairly full outlines is available in neat, legible handwriting. See n. 2 above.
17. *Joyful News*, 4 March 1920, p. 1.
18. *Joyful News*, 1 April 1926, p. 1.
19. Disbound pamphlet amongst Chadwick's papers at Cliff College.
20. *Joyful News*, 24 Oct. 1912, p. 5.
21. ibid.
22. D. Howarth, *How Great a Flame*, p. 18.
23. Harries, *G. Campbell Morgan*, p. 197.
24. Bebbington, *Evangelicalism*, p. 211.
25. Murray, *Campbell Morgan*, p. 114.
26. ibid., p. 108; *Westminster Pulpit*, vol. x, pp. 115f.
27. G. C. Morgan, *Preaching*, London n.d.
28. Murray, *Campbell Morgan*, p. 109.
29. Morgan, *Westminster Pulpit*, vol. iii, p. 285.
30. In *The Prophecy of Jeremiah* (New York 1931), Campbell Morgan shows the same ability to look at a text with bold originality. This from the foremost Evangelical Bible teacher of his generation, over sixty years ago: 'The first responsibility of womanhood is that women should discover their personal rights in God, should realize that they bear to God a relationship which man does not affect, nor can; that they have a right of access to God, for the realization of that which they are in themselves, without the interference of man in any way' (pp. 273–4). This passage was brought to my attention by Kate Durie from whose well-stored mind my own thinking has often benefited.

11
DAVID MARTYN LLOYD-JONES and JOHN R. W. STOTT

The call of God is a call of grace.
STOTT

On 18 October 1966, Dr Martyn Lloyd-Jones, minister of Westminster Chapel, was scheduled to speak at the opening meeting of the National Assembly of Evangelicals on the issue of Christian unity. His address was a clear call for Evangelicals to leave doctrinally compromised denominations and form an Evangelical fellowship of churches. Consistent with his known position, Lloyd-Jones asserted that Evangelical loyalty to a biblical gospel must transcend denominational allegiance. The chairman of the meeting was the Reverend John Stott, rector of All Soul's church, Langham Place, in central London. As a convinced churchman, he felt it impossible to remain silently neutral. He stood at the end of the address to argue for a different biblical view of unity. The incident was to 'dramatise a fracture in the Evangelical world'.[1]

Evangelical Christianity is theological in its character . . .

Lloyd-Jones was Welsh, of powerfully independent mind and nurtured within Calvinistic Methodism. His theology was quarried and hewn into shape through a careful study of Reformed and Puritan thought. He believed Evangelical convictions carried with them an obligation to resist the ecumenical manoeuverings of churches which, in his view, had become moribund through uncertainty about the essentials of the gospel.

Immensely well read in church history and biography, Lloyd-

Jones habitually appealed to the past to find truth which would provide a corrective to the unbalanced and unhealthy emphases in contemporary Evangelical Christianity. He refused to be identified with the 'decision' style of evangelism associated with Billy Graham campaigns, arguing that such a practice oversimplified doctrine and turned the scriptural example of Christ receiving sinners into the more man-centred theology of sinners receiving Christ. As a Reformed theologian he remained cautious in his attitude to Keswick holiness teaching and never preached at the convention. While not unsympathetic to the emerging charismatic emphasis on the ministry and gifts of the Holy Spirit, he discerned a serious lack of doctrinal control over experience. As various Evangelical agencies came into closer contact with ecumenical and other liberalizing developments, Lloyd-Jones withdrew, so that over the years his ties faded significantly with such groups as Inter-Varsity Fellowship, London Bible College and the journal, *The Evangelical Quarterly*.[2]

John Stott had co-operated closely with Lloyd-Jones during the fifties when both were involved in university missions.[3] Despite differences in emphasis they held each other in deep respect before and after 1966. But the differences were significant. Stott had no hesitation in giving public support to the Billy Graham campaigns and ensured that 150 people referred to his church were given adequate spiritual guidance.[4] Unlike Lloyd-Jones, Stott has given the Bible readings at Keswick. Indeed in 1965 he expounded that crux of Keswick spirituality, Romans chapter seven.[5] As a Church of England clergyman Stott expresses deep, though not unquestioning, loyalty to his own tradition. He does not feel so strongly Lloyd-Jones' fears that co-operation with non-Evangelicals would seriously compromise the gospel. It is his contention that Evangelicalism can offer a vision for the Church that is biblical, intellectually coherent, socially and ethically aware, and humbly open to the insights of other Christians.

In the 1950s co-operative evangelism had provided an informal testing ground for ecumenism. Lloyd-Jones sensed in the post-war ecumenical euphoria a blurring of doctrinal distinctives. From 1956 to 1961, at the invitation of the British Council of Churches, he participated in discussions to find common ground between Evangelicals and other Christians. Lloyd-Jones sought to present the essence of Evangelical theology as he understood it. Original sin imputed through Adam, penal substitution, and the new birth, were just three issues on which the discussions eventually foundered. The reports of the meetings reveal a mind soaked in Pauline theology of a Reformed flavour, arguing with firm courtesy for sound doctrine.[6] It is not without significance that his monumental exposition of Romans began in 1955. Precisely the issues being discussed were being preached on with passionate power in Westminster Chapel week by week for more than a decade.

His keen mind, together with his unswerving loyalty to the Bible and Reformed theology made him inexorable in pursuit of error, and tenacious in his hold of truth. Temperamentally ill-at-ease with the notion of dialogue, he was immensely secure in his fundamental convictions. One of his earliest books was entitled *Truth Unchanged Unchanging*. The phrase encapsulates the spirituality of one for whom precise doctrinal definition, careful biblical statement and radical spiritual change must coalesce in any adequate account of Christian experience.

In 1967 the National Evangelical Anglican Congress met at Keele. For the first time Evangelical Anglicans stated their willingness to become fully involved in ecumenical dialogue. The Congress further affirmed that 'Evangelism and compassionate service belong together in the mission of God'.[7] *Keele 67*, as it came to be known, was organized by a committee whose chairman was John Stott. He claimed that, for Evangelical Anglicans, Keele represented 'our conversion from the negative and defensive . . . a formal public, penitent renunciation of pietism', which he defined as '. . . an exaggerated religious individualism . . . retirement into self-made security with God . . . contracting out of our responsibility to the visible church and to the world'.[8]

In the last twenty-five years Stott has emerged as a leading Evangelical statesman whose spheres of influence have included the World Council of Churches, the Lausanne Congress on World Evangelization in 1974 and the second National Evangelical Anglican Congress at Nottingham in 1977, which he chaired. More recently he represented Evangelicals in dialogue with the Roman Catholic Church, and gave several Bible readings at Lausanne II, held at Manila in 1989.[9] In addition to such wide-ranging ecumenical activity, Stott has written profusely, contributing to the realignment of Evangelical thought on social and moral issues, ranging from specific issues of ethical concern such as unemployment, nuclear arms control and abortion, to broader issues of justice and poverty, and extending into questions of the relationship between gospel and culture.

The influence these two leading figures have exerted within their respective spheres has been enormous; Lloyd-Jones amongst Evangelicals who endorse principled separatism and Stott amongst Evangelicals across the denominations seeking dialogue with the wider Christian world. Theological consistency, biblical thinking and personal integrity have been the common and constant features of two ministries characterized above all by Christ-centred devotion.

It was entirely God's doing.

David Martyn Lloyd-Jones was born in Cardiff on 20 December 1899. His father, who kept a general store, was something of a pioneer as a salesman of mechanized farm implements. The family moved to Cardiganshire (now part of Dyfed) in 1906. Lloyd-Jones' passionate love for rural Welsh-speaking Wales dates from that time. At school Martyn's application had been mediocre until he became aware of his father's financial difficulties. In 1910 a fire had put an intolerable strain on the family business and eventually in 1914 his father moved the family to London and acquired a milk delivery business. Though there were times when he had to rise at 5.30 a.m. to fill in for absentee workers, Martyn now excelled at school, a teacher commenting, 'What Martyn knows he knows' (M1 p. 28).

In 1916, at the age of sixteen, he was enrolled at St Bartholomew's Hospital in London, taking his MRCS and LRCP degrees in July 1921 and his MB and BS in October, with distinction in medicine. His abilities were recognized by Sir Thomas Horder, one of the most eminent physicians of the age. After graduation Dr Lloyd-Jones became his assistant. In teaching, Horder relied on the Socratic method of instruction, eliciting truth by question and answer, a technique intended to train the mind in quick, clear thinking. Lloyd-Jones was to use that method in Bible discussion groups, in pastoral counsel and above all as an approach to biblical exposition in which he first dealt with the negative, exposing the logical weakness of a position by following where it led, and then argued the position he believed correct.

In his early twenties he passed through a period of spiritual change: 'For many years I thought I was a Christian when in fact I was not. It was only later that I came to see that I had never been a Christian and became one. But I was a member of a church and attended my church and its services regularly' (PP p. 146). In 1923 he heard Dr John A. Hutton, the new minister of Westminster Chapel, and later explained, 'He impressed me with the power of God to change men's lives' (M1 p. 61). He began to reflect deeply on the human condition, and the connection between sin and much of the suffering he encountered. Later he confessed: 'I am a Christian solely and entirely by the grace of God . . . He brought me to see that the real cause of my troubles and ills and that of all men, was an evil and fallen nature which hated God and loved sin. My trouble was not only that I did things that were wrong, but that I myself was wrong at the very centre of my being' (M1 p. 64). Lloyd-Jones never dated his conversion, preferring to interpret his experience as a process. Through the sovereign grace of God, his life was turned round by the revelation of his own sinfulness and God's love.

Increasing unease about the values that should govern his career, the discovery of Puritans like Richard Baxter who were urgent in the work of saving souls, a persistent inward compulsion to the ministry of preaching and a passionate regret over the decline of Evangelical Christianity in Wales, culminated in resignation from his medical position. In 1927 he was appointed missioner at Sandfields, in Aberavon, South Wales. A local correspondent wrote: 'The Sandfields district of Aberavon is a dead end. Even when the sun shines, sandy wastes and dreary, crowded houses convey a sense of desolation, almost of hopelessness. Into this desperate little world came the young physician–minister, preaching, living the gospel of old-new hope' (M1 p. 224).

This glorious message of the cross.

The twelve years spent ministering in Wales left indelible marks on Lloyd-Jones. Ever since his schoolmaster had given him a booklet on Howell Harris, the Calvinistic Methodist preacher of the eighteenth century, he had come to value the contribution such men had made to Welsh Christianity. Prior to his leaving medicine he provoked a storm of protest by a talk he gave on the tragedy of modern Wales. Now he had deliberately come to a struggling congregation intent on offering the same uncompromising gospel ministry which had been so effective nearly two hundred years before. Much of his thinking was influenced by his reading of the Calvinistic Methodist revival: 'When I saw something which was so different from the high spirituality and the deep godliness of the Methodist Fathers, I did not have a struggle over whether to follow it or not' (M1 p. 195). He loved all things Welsh, the historical accounts of the Welsh Methodist fathers, the hymns of William Williams, the Welsh tradition of radical politics, and the genius of the Welsh Christian character which he believed was a combination of doctrinal thinking and passionate experience.[10]

The new missioner of Sandfields was soon in enormous demand as an itinerant gospel preacher. The minister of one church made the disconcerting comment that he could not decide whether Lloyd-Jones was a hyper-Calvinist or a Quaker. In explanation he told Lloyd-Jones: 'You talk of God's action like a hyper-Calvinist and of spiritual experience like a Quaker, but the cross and the work of Christ have little place in your preaching' (M1 p. 191). Later in life the American theologian and journalist, Carl Henry, asked the searching question, 'Was there some ambiguity about evangelical doctrine in your own earliest preaching?' With disarming frankness Lloyd-Jones replied: 'In the early part of my ministry I preached regeneration as the great message not justification . . . I preached what I was sure of. I neglected the Atonement, but within about two years I came to see that was an incomplete message.' Three classics of Evangelical theology recommended by a local Congregational minister permanently changed the emphasis of his preaching.[11] Over thirty years later he told his Westminster Chapel congregation: 'There is no end to this glorious message of the cross . . . there is always something new and fresh and entrancing and moving and uplifting that one has never seen before' (C p. 13).

Lloyd-Jones believed the offensiveness of the cross was part of its power. The doctrine of substitutionary atonement challenged the best moral wisdom and the most coherent human philosophy, pointing to realities subversive of all human self-sufficiency. 'The cross proclaims at once that we are not saved by ideas. We are not saved by thought or by understanding' (C p. 47). The unregenerate mind, he argued, is incapable of submitting to gospel truth. The offensiveness of such doctrines as original sin, imputed guilt and penal substitution does not arise from moral insight but from moral blindness caused by intellectual pride.

The mind must therefore be brought to see the true nature of human iniquity. Sin is not mere weakness requiring understanding, or brokenness requiring healing, or even guilt requiring forgiveness. Sin is enmity with God and hatred of God's law, a state of moral rebellion requiring punishment. In a startling juxtaposition of biblical ideas, he argued that God had brought all into being by the mere word of his power but this same God 'cannot forgive sin just by saying "I forgive". A word is enough to create [a world] but a word is not enough to forgive' (C p. 159). The cross proclaims the moral consistency of God. The demands of a righteous God cannot be circumvented even by his own love: 'If there is one place in all history and in the whole of the universe where you see the immutability and the unchangeableness of God more clearly than anywhere else, it is on the cross' (C p. 79). The love of God for fallen humanity is such that 'he himself smites the Son . . . pours out his eternal wrath on Him' (C p. 81). That, said Lloyd-Jones, is the gospel offence, and that is what must be preached in any evangelism claiming biblical warrant.

I stressed engaging the intellect to its maximum.

To Lloyd-Jones, theological reflection by a reverent mind was a spiritually formative discipline, an exercise in passionate wisdom, a fusion of logic and prayer. From P. T. Forsyth he had discovered the cruciality of the cross in preaching the gospel. In Jonathan Edwards he found a writer so convincing that his influence pervaded his spiritual psychology. Edwards' vision of the sovereign majesty of God and the total ruin of humanity provided much of the theological substructure of his arguments against man-centred evangelism. The Princeton theologian B. B. Warfield's powerfully apologetic writings gripped his mind and became foundational resources in his defence of biblical infallability.

Reading the Puritans provided spiritual nourishment, the more satisfying because they dealt with the problems of sin and redemption in a way that answered his own experience. His debt to Richard Sibbes, acknowledged in his lectures on preaching, shows clearly how reading could become for him a means of grace. The practical Sibbes 'quietened, soothed, comforted, encouraged and healed me'.[12] In the Puritans he found 'that outlook and teaching which put its emphasis upon a life of spiritual, personal religion, an intense realisation of the presence of God, a devotion of the entire being to him' (M2 p. 460).

Though aware of contemporary trends, he apparently gained little help from such thinkers as Karl Barth, William Temple and C. H. Dodd.[13] Still, no man who regularly took the Bampton or Gifford lectures as holiday reading can be accused of intellectual parochialism. W. H. C. Frend's heavy tome, *The Donatist Church*, Kenneth Kirk's masterly survey of ascetic theology, *The Vision of God*, and the detailed, meandering biographies of Whitefield and Wesley by the Victorian Luke Tyerman, all books he enjoyed reading, demonstrate how seriously Lloyd-Jones took the New Testament injunction, 'gird up the loins of your mind' (1 Pet. 1.13). His daughter's delightful account of a typical morning on holiday has deservedly become part of the received tradition of Evangelical folklore. When everyone else was on the beach bathing and playing in glorious sunshine, she recalled: 'In front of a rock, over at one corner of the beach, was my father, fully clothed, in a grey suit, with a hat upon his head, his usual hat, shoes, socks, waistcoat, the whole thing, sitting bolt upright, leaning against the rock and reading *The Divine Imperative* by Brunner' (CG p. 140).

In a sermon on spiritual thinking Lloyd-Jones asserted: 'The first thing that happens to us when we become Christians is that we find that we are thinking in a different way . . . we have a new understanding, we are thinking spiritually.' Indeed, 'one of the hallmarks of the Christian should be the capacity to think logically, clearly and spiritually.'[14] Even the Christian intellect, he held, does not discover truth by power of reason: 'You can never find [truth] by looking for it. Truth is revealed to us, all we do is reason about it after having seen it' (M1 p. 92). Truth is God-given. That conviction should galvanize the Christian mind not only to explore but to assimilate truth as an enlivening gift of God.

The process whereby truth and spiritual experience are integrated was explained in a sermon on a key text, Romans 6.17. Truth, he claimed, is addressed primarily to the mind: 'As the mind grasps it, and understands it, the affections are kindled and moved, and so in turn the will is persuaded and obedience is the outcome' (CG p. 84). The relation of mind, heart and will was central to Lloyd-Jones' understanding of Christian experience. God's greatest gift to humanity is 'the mind with its capacity for apprehending truth' (SD p. 61). Given genuine faith in Christ and frank acknowledgement of sin, the gospel of truth 'can satisfy man's mind completely, it can move his heart entirely and it can lead to wholehearted obedience in the realm of the will' (SD p. 60).

When he came to London in 1938, Lloyd-Jones sensed in Evangelical circles an unhealthy reliance on feelings, a superficial spirituality dependent on meetings and above all an anti-intellectual bias which he believed was detrimental to the gospel. As a remedy for 'non-theological, pietistic and sentimental' spirituality, he told Carl Henry, 'I stressed engaging the intellect to its maximum' (CG p. 102). It is one of Lloyd-Jones' major achievements that he was a powerful originating force behind the post-war renaissance of Reformed theology.

Lloyd-Jones consistently encouraged various agencies committed to the recovery of doctrinally secure Christianity. He was instrumental in forming the Evangelical Library and was for a time closely associated with the London Bible College and *The Evangelical Quarterly*. Under his initial guidance the Inter-Varsity Fellowship changed from being an intellectually unadventurous Christian club into a vigorous evangelistic agency fostering Evangelical scholarship. He was a founding member of the Banner of Truth Trust, the publishing house primarily responsible for the republication in recent years of many Puritan and Reformed works. He encouraged and hosted the annual Westminster Puritan Conferences, further stimulating interest in Puritanism.[15] His major series of sermons on Romans and Ephesians, spanning the years 1954–68, present a carefully balanced spirituality of doctrine, experience and ethics, corresponding in Christian experience to mind, heart and will.

The reader of the sermons is unlikely to be swept away by their rhetorical power and even less likely to be cosily comforted by devotional cotton wool.[16] The appeal is primarily to the intellect. 'The truth is something which can be defined and analysed and stated in propositions', he stated boldly. Hearers and readers alike are cornered by argument: 'What I am asserting and arguing is based on elementary logic and thinking and upon honest dealing with the Word of God.'[17] This sense of being hemmed in by logic could convince the hearer with remarkable results. During his last American tour, as he 'ascended the ladder of Paul's logic in Romans', a mathematician was so deeply moved that he vandalized the hymn-book by tearing out the page containing the words of the final hymn. He confessed, 'As he was preaching I said, "Ah yes, but – then he answered the but, until I had no buts left'.[18]

Christ in the heart.

Much of Lloyd-Jones' spirituality was mediated through intellectual engagement. Equally certain, his spiritual experience transcended the categories of logic. With great reticence, he spoke occasionally of experiences in which the love of God flooded his being. As a young doctor, and later as an exhausted preacher, he had experiences of which he said: 'It was entirely God's doing. I have known what it is to be really filled with a joy unspeakable and full of glory' (M1 p. 101). Overwhelming joy, conscious intimacy with God and the sense of the heart being enfolded in love and filled with Christ himself, suggest a rare quality of spiritual experience. Through his expository preaching he compared his own relationship with Christ to the New Testament norms. At such times intellectual confidence gave way to the more affective, mystical strain in his nature which acted as a powerful lens through which, with reverent hesitation, he interpreted the subtleties of Pauline spirituality and his own experience.[19]

It is possible for the personal relationship between Christ and the believer to reach a degree of intimacy so complete that Paul described it as Christ dwelling in the heart through faith. 'It means that He Himself in some mystical sense that we cannot begin to understand really does dwell in us' (E p. 150). To know Christ, in all the glory and fulness of his being, is the height of spiritual aspiration. Language becomes inadequate; even Paul spoke of 'knowing the love of Christ which surpasses knowledge' (Eph. 3.19). Lloyd-Jones acknowledged defeat: 'You cannot dissect an aroma, you cannot analyse love' (E p. 155). But inability to articulate spiritual blessing does not remove the obligation to 'delve into mystery' and seek the deepest communion with Christ of which the redeemed personality is capable.

Lloyd-Jones made much of the 'sealing of the Spirit', an experience he interpreted as immediate assurance of salvation.[20] The experience of Christ dwelling in the heart is of a different order. There is 'a greater element of permanence', a 'deeper fellowship'. From the objective truth of Christ *for* us, the Christian moves to the subjective experience of Christ *in* us. 'We have advanced to the position in which we are mainly concerned about Christ, not as the one who died for us, but as the Christ who is our life, Christ as the One . . . who takes up his abode within our lives and within our consciousness' (E p. 159). More explicitly: 'It is Christ dwelling within the believer – not as an influence, not as a memory, not merely through His teaching, not merely through the Holy Spirit. It is Christ *Himself* dwelling within him in a mystical relationship . . . The Lord Jesus Christ is in heaven, but he is also in me' (E p. 160). Such indwelling is a direct communication of Christ in all the plenitude of his grace. The One 'in whom all the fulness of God was pleased to dwell' seeks accommodation in the human heart.

In his exposition of Ephesians 3.14–21, he exults in the all-sufficient and all-comprehending love of God which fills the believer with 'all the fulness of God'. 'This statement must not be reduced to the level of general blessing. [Paul] means what he says . . . He is standing on one of the great peaks of God's plan of redemption, than which there is no higher' (E p. 280). He warned, 'The love of God is so great and powerful that a man feels his physical frame beginning to crack beneath it' (E p. 213). Even the Christian mind, renewed and enabled by the Holy Spirit, is incapable of bearing the weight of such glory unless 'strengthened with might by his Spirit in the inner man'. But given such reinforcement, believers bring mind, heart and will in an attitude of humble but active longing, praying that Christ may dwell within, and that they may know the love of God and be filled with his fulness.

Rooted and grounded in love.

True Christian knowledge 'is knowledge of a Person. God is love. Christ is love incarnate. So to know God and to know Christ of necessity leads to love' (E p. 186). 'Love . . . can build us up and make us strong, and make us look like representatives and reproductions of the life of the Lord Jesus Christ Himself' (E p. 187). 'Love is God's own motive', and so the child of God is one in whom love constrains, energizes and compels. Every Christian is called to be perfect as God is perfect, holy as God is holy, as loving to the unlovely as God has been to them. Countless unremembered acts of compassion as well as the costly acts of reconciling love which leave their mark on the soul, will one day be 'seen to be of great value with the arc-light of God's love shed upon them' (E p. 191).

Unknown to many of the Westminster Chapel congregation who heard these words, Lloyd-Jones was still remembered in Aberavon as one whose generous compassion made many lives easier. Other people's rent arrears, mortgage difficulties and financial shortages cost him 'a small fortune'; on one of his holidays the person forwarding his mail sent ninety letters, mostly from people seeking advice and help. Lloyd-Jones did not minimize the absolute negatives of Paul in 1 Corinthians 13. Without love all other expression of Christian devotion are useless: 'That is a shattering and alarming statement, but it is obviously the simple truth. It must be so because the Christian life is a Christ-like life, and everything in Him had its source in love' (E p. 190).

'The greatest characteristic of the greatest saints in all ages has always been their realisation of God's love to them' (M2 p. 767). During a university mission he expressed regret that he had not been sufficiently animated by love. Adding urgency to that sense of failure, and silencing any disclaimer from those who knew him and judged him more generously, was his deepest experience of God's patient, forgiving and demanding love. His friend and biographer recalled the fervour with which he sung words from Wesley's hymn, 'O love divine, how sweet Thou art':

> God only knows the love of God;
> O that it now were shed abroad
> In this poor stony heart!
>
> (M2 p. 767)

The standard by which he measured love is set impossibly high: 'God's perfect love is self-generated; it does not depend on anything outside Himself; it is love that starts within and goes out to others' (E p. 203). He goes on, 'Your love and mine must be the same. It will be so when our life is grounded in love.' Asked how life is to be rooted and grounded in love, Lloyd-Jones would urge his hearers to 'put themselves in the way of blessing', to pray, to read the Scriptures, to seek the Lord himself. His was not a spirituality based on creating certain conditions as a way to 'get' or 'claim' blessing. But to seek God with a mind open to his truth, a heart longing for his presence and a will responsive to his commands, is a process of personal preparation and an expression of desire for God, that God in his grace will not leave unrewarded.

Devotion must have its discipline, and for Lloyd-Jones that meant before all else time with the Bible. He read it through each year using McCheyne's calendar. It was the primary means of grace in his life. He reminded his hearers of the saints who 'had their greatest personal experiences of the love of Christ as they were reading the Scriptures. Suddenly He seems to meet them through a particular word; He comes out of the book, as it were, and they know that He personally is speaking to them' (E p. 266). He was again betraying his own practice when he said: 'True reading of the Bible involves thought, meditation, preparation of ourselves, and above all expectancy . . . a looking for Him, and a readiness to find Him everywhere' (E p. 268). In the Bible Lloyd-Jones was entirely at home, mentally at ease, aware that this book demanded his best thinking and would deepen his communion with God. The slightest intimation of God's presence, the subtle pressure of truth on the mind, the first discernible tremor of conscience should be given immediate and total attention; and then Bible study and prayer become the one act of communion.

The communion of love is prayer at its most formative. 'Love is something which can be contemplated . . . love itself always has a contemplative element in it' (E p. 232). Intellectual apprehension, theological reflection, even spiritual thinking must give way to 'the study of love. We are no longer looking at the love of Christ externally with a sense of wonder and amazement; we are now experiencing it, being bathed in it, enveloped by it, being ravished by and filled with it' (E p. 234). Here the expositor of Paul reveals his own soul and speaks in the language of an Evangelical mystic. In prayer the Christian may come with heartfelt confession, bold petitions, love-inspired intercession, but the highest prayer is the longing for an increased capacity for God. 'Contemplation of God, adoration and worship are the highest expression of our love to God' (E p. 198).

John Stott ended a historical sketch of the glory of preaching with warm reference to the stature of Martyn Lloyd-Jones. He explained the impact of Lloyd-Jones' preaching by mentioning: 'His medical training and early practice as a physician, his unshakeable commitment to the authority of Scripture and to the Christ of Scripture, his keen analytical mind, his penetrating insight into the human heart, and his passionate Welsh fire . . .'[21] The same qualities explain the main features of his spirituality, for in Martyn Lloyd-Jones, spirituality and preaching were inextricably linked.

Yesterday really was an eventful day.

Sir Arnold Stott trained at St Bartholomew's Hospital, later becoming an eminent Harley Street physician and consultant at Westminster Hospital. His wife was a devout Lutheran, he a scientific secularist. Their only son, John Robert Walmsley Stott, was born on 27 April 1921. The name of John Stott is inextricably entwined with the name of the church of which he is Rector Emeritus, All Souls', Langham Place. As a boy he had discovered the mischievous joy of flicking paper pellets over the balcony on the heads of the worshippers below. In 1945 he was ordained curate, appointed Rector in 1950 and Rector Emeritus in 1975.

He referred to himself as a 'high-idealed adolescent'. Educated at Rugby, then Trinity College, Cambridge, he followed the educational route of his father. Religious interest was never far away, and he later recalled: 'I used on half holiday afternoons to creep into the Memorial Chapel by myself, in order to read religious books, absorb the atmosphere of mystery, and seek for God. But he continued to elude me' (EL p. 14). Then he encountered the Reverend E. J. H. Nash, a former school chaplain who had become a full-time evangelist. Nash organized Varsity and Public Schools Camps (nicknamed 'Bash Camps'), where he followed a deliberate policy of aiming his evangelistic efforts at 'key boys from key schools'. Whether this was strategy or snobbery, the fact remains that Canon Michael Green, The Reverend Dick Lucas, the Bishop of Liverpool, David Sheppard and John Stott were 'Bash campers' and each is a leading Church of England Evangelical.[22]

Nash was 'nothing much to look at, and certainly no ambassador for muscular Christianity', but as he preached on Pilate's question: 'What shall I do with Jesus who is called the Christ?' Stott was struck by 'the entirely novel idea' that he had to *do* anything with Jesus. As the preacher went on Stott recalled: 'To my astonishment, his presentation of Christ crucified and risen exactly corresponded with the needs of which I was aware' (EL p. 15). Using the third person, he told the story of his conversion in his bestselling book, *Basic Christianity*, published twenty years later in 1958. 'A boy in his later teens knelt at his bedside one Sunday night in the dormitory of his public school. It was about 10 p.m. on 13 February 1938. In a simple, matter-of-fact but definite way he told Christ that he had made rather a mess of his life so far; he confessed his sins, he thanked Christ for dying for him; and he asked Him to come into his life. The following day he wrote in his diary: "Yesterday really was an eventful day".'[23]

Using the words of Rev. 3.20, and Holman Hunt's picture 'The Light of the World', where Christ is depicted knocking on the door of the soul, he explained in simple language the consequences of receiving Christ into the heart: 'He will be able to apply the benefits of His death to us personally. Once inside the house His first task will be to springclean it. He will renovate, redecorate and refurnish it.' The 'unutterable joy of His friendship' is that 'He not only gives Himself to us but desires that we should give ourselves to Him.'[24] It is hard to dismiss the suspicion that the images of restoration, renovation and redecoration came easily to the mind of one who had recently acquired a run-down Welsh smallholding in Pembrokeshire and was in the process of making it a place of retreat and study.

From Nash, who for five years wrote regularly to his new convert, Stott learned to love the Bible. University training convinced him of the strategic importance of the mind in the quest for Christian maturity, as he 'wrestled painfully with the challenges of liberalism'.[25] At Ridley Hall, Cambridge, Stott challenged the opinion expressed by the principal that there was no New Testament evidence for an important doctrine. The principal's reply: 'You probably know more about the New Testament than I do', was probably true enough. More significantly, it was an incident entirely consistent with Stott's later development.

'We evangelicals are Bible people', he claimed in 1977. His writing in recent years demonstrates the leverage that claim exerts on his own mind. A book of his sermons slipped quietly onto the market in 1979. Entitled *Focus on Christ*, it displays the rich spirituality of one who is habitually Christ-centred in his thinking. A substantial book on homiletics, *I Believe in Preaching*, appeared in 1982. It contains many variations on the theme of biblical thinking related to the modern world, and explores the idea of the preacher as bridge-builder between Bible and culture. Ten years after the Lausanne Congress he produced *Issues Facing Christians Today*, a major work on Christian personal and social ethics in which he tried to deal honestly and compassionately with some of the major dilemmas of the late twentieth century. By 1986, in *The Cross of Christ* he was wrestling with what he considers the central doctrine of the New Testament, persuasively arguing for a view of the atonement which does justice to the powerful motivational pull of the cross on the Christian heart. These and many other books became the basis of *Essentials*, a volume in which David L. Edwards and John Stott engaged in a Liberal-Evangelical dialogue.

Biblical thinking, the relationship between the gospel and the modern world, the centrality of Christ and life under the cross – amongst many other features of Stott's thinking and spiritual vision, such themes have proved extraordinarily fruitful when developed in the fertile environment of a Christian mind, informed by Scripture and open to the world.

Your mind matters.

The development of a Christian mind is a basic prerequisite of Christian obedience. The loyalty of the mind to Christ, the engagement of the mind in disciplined biblical reflection, the humility of the mind committed to dialogue with others, the openness of the mind to the questions of a critical world and the fusion of mind and heart in Christian worship, are not so much themes of Stott's ministry as underlying characteristics. Still, the intellect is not everything. Stott confesses his own struggle to break out of the emotional confinement of public school training, and tells of what, for him, was the liberating discovery that Jesus cried. In a moving fragment of autobiography he told of his response to a performance of Handel's *Messiah*. As the audience dispersed he wondered: 'Is it priggish of me to say that I could not move? I had been transported into heaven, into eternity . . . It was somehow not enough for me to clap the *musicians*. I wanted to fall on my face and worship God.'[26] Emotion and intellect together give balance to Christian devotion.

The atmosphere in which the Christian mind is most at home is that of worship. 'The only worship pleasing to God is heart-worship, and heart-worship is rational worship. It is the worship of a rational God, who has made us rational beings and given us a rational revelation so that we may worship him rationally' (CC p. 165). Neither intellect nor emotion should displace that 'mixture of awe, wonder, and joy called worship'. Stott can describe with blunt precision the cause of the absence of transcendence in some forms of Christian worship. He deplores the tendency to be 'cocky, flippant, superficial and proud' in leading services which can be 'slovenly, mechanical, perfunctory, and dull'. Such a spiritual travesty will only be overcome by certain recovered emphases: Bible-centred worship in which God's voice is heard, a rediscovery of the reality of Christ in the Lord's Supper and a sincere offering of praise and prayer. In other words there must be a recovered 'sense of the greatness and glory of Almighty God'.[27]

In a book originally written as a response to the emergent charismatic movement Stott described deeper experiences of God in which truth apprehended by the mind ignites the heart:

> Sometimes [the Holy Spirit] floods our hearts with such a tidal wave of his love that we almost ask him to stay his hand lest we be drowned by it . . . Sometimes we experience a quickening of our spiritual pulse, a leaping of our heart, a kindling of our love for God and man, a pervading sense of well-being. Sometimes in the dignified reverence of public worship, or in the spontaneous fellowship of a home meeting, or at the Lord's Table, or in private prayer, invisible reality overwhelms us. Time stands still. We step into a new dimension of eternity. We become still and *know* that God is God. We fall down before him and worship.[28]

'We become still and *know* . . .' Worship and knowledge of God belong together and issue in obedience. The Christian mind does not think exclusively about 'Christian' topics but thinks about every topic 'Christianly'. For Stott the modifying adverb is seminal. The Christian mind operates with presuppositions and principles derived from Christ as revealed in the Scriptures, so that the outcome of all worship and reflection on Christ and

Scripture must be practical, moral obedience. The Christian mind is therefore a primary organ of Christian devotion for it is by disciplined Christian thinking in the context of prayer, that the will of Christ may best be discerned: 'No-one is intellectually converted if he has not submitted his mind to the mind of the Lord Christ, nor morally converted if he has not submitted his will to the will of the Lord Christ' (CC pp. 212–13).

The search for Christian insight into the human condition and the moral dilemmas of the contemporary world have left their marks on the spirituality of Stott. His involvement in dialogue with other Christian traditions and indeed with the wider world arises directly from his theology of God. In the aftermath of *Keele 67* and *Lausanne 74*, he wrote, 'The living God of the biblical revelation enters into dialogue with man. He not only speaks but listens. He asks questions and waits for answers' (CMMW p. 60). Stott readily acknowledges that his mind has 'not stood still' over the past thirty years.[29] He confesses that, faced with the complex moral and cultural questions posed by modern society, Christians, especially Evangelicals, 'have [had] a tendency to pontificate from a position of ignorance' (CMMW p. 33). In reaction to the ghetto mentality of mid-twentieth-century Evangelicalism Stott has sought to engender a mood of humility and openness to dialogue, which has become integral to his own spiritual thinking. He is convinced that the Christian mind is recognized not only by its presuppositions and principles, but by the tenor of its response to those from whom it differs. Hidden away in the preface to *Christian Mission in the Modern World* are words which give a new meaning to the phrase 'Evangelical humility': 'Life is a pilgrimage of learning, a voyage of discovery, in which our mistaken views are corrected, our distorted notions adjusted, our shallow opinions deepened and some of our vast ignorance diminished' (CMMW p. 10).

Since *Lausanne 74*, Stott's major works have shown clear signs of a mind which, in growing more catholic in sympathy, has struggled to hold together integrity of personal conviction with sensitivity where disagreement is inevitable. His contributions to ecumenical debate have been marked by courage and principle. His father's hope that John Stott would enter the diplomatic service has been entirely, if unexpectedly, fulfilled. In one year Stott was overseas for twenty weeks when he visited five countries, led fourteen conferences and gave one hundred Bible Readings and addresses.[30]

The Father's testimony to the Son through the Spirit.

In the discovery and application of truth in order to discern the will of Christ, the Christian mind must be open to the reality of the God who speaks. 'The biblical text is an inspired text', he wrote in 1988, '. . . unlike any other text, unique in its origin, nature and authority.' These apparently uncompromising words are qualified by a further statement: 'The inspired text is also to some degree closed' and requires to be opened up (BS 3 p. 364). Almost twenty years earlier Stott had argued for the same two interpretative principles: the authority of the inspired text and the need for the text to be interpreted. But he carefully spelt out what such opening up means: 'What is needed is a *translation* of the gospel into the language, idiom and thought forms of the modern world. But a genuine translation is never a fresh composition; it is a faithful rendering into another language of something which has already been written or said' (CC p. 41). These two convictions, that something has 'already been written or said', and needs now to be 'translated', have their roots fixed deep in the spirituality of the Scripture expositor. Stott has consistently traced the authority of the Bible to its function as a witness to Christ. As such, no one is entitled to take liberties with it. 'Scripture is a means to the end of finding life in Christ.' Though a means, the Bible is an indispensable means, mediating the self-disclosure of the triune God: 'The Three persons of the Trinity are all involved in Scripture, for Scripture is the Father's testimony to the Son through the Spirit' (CC p. 98).

On Lloyd-Jones' advice Stott has used McCheyne's lectionary for almost thirty years, reading three chapters each morning, studying one and reserving the fourth for the evening. He is editor of, and a major contributor to, a series significantly called 'The Bible Speaks Today'.[31] These expositions illustrate his easy familiarity with the broad terrain of Scripture. Comparison of the secondary sources used in his 1968 commentary on Galatians with those used in his recent contribution on Acts, is a revealing indicator of how Stott, and many other Evangelicals, are willing to do their Bible study in the company of the critics. Stott's own stance remains conservative, but many of his expository clues are gratefully attributed to scholars of a different theological persuasion.

In Stott's view, Bible study must be undertaken from a mental and spiritual standpoint sympathetic to the thought-forms of both the Bible and the contemporary world. Indifference to the consequences of human sin and failure, or any other sign of retreat from involvement, is intolerable to the student of a Bible whose primary purpose is to witness to Christ, the Saviour of the world. 'As true servants of Jesus Christ believers should keep their eyes open . . . to human need, and their ears cocked to the world's cries of pain.' In the same article, entitled 'The World's Challenge to the Church', his analysis of modern western culture concludes: 'Looking for transcendence, [many people] are trying to find God; looking for significance they are trying to find themselves; looking for community they are trying to find their neighbour' (BS 1 p. 132).

The evidence for these felt needs of society is gathered from an astonishing range of sources: Theodore Roszak, Alvin Toffler, Arnold Toynbee, Desmond Morris, Victor Frankl and Woody Allen are cited and their testimonies noted. As Stott reflects on Bible and world, gospel and culture, he feels deeply the need for Christians to build bridges so that a broken world might encounter the living Christ through the lived and spoken witness of the Christian Church: 'Jesus Christ we believe is the fulfilment of every truly human aspiration. To find him is to find ourselves.'[32] Stott is arguing for an approach to evangelism which retains the lifegiving note of proclamation while repenting of all kinds of insensitivity, from ignorance through indifference to full-blooded cultural imperialism: 'Humility in evangelism is a beautiful grace . . . Human beings are godlike beings! True, they are fallen from their sublime origin, and their godlikeness has been severely distorted. But it has not been destroyed' (CMMW p. 72; BS 1 p. 129).

This positive but qualified view of the created world, drawn directly from the biblical witness, gives the spirituality of John Stott a this-worldly urgency. Whether he is watching the 'disgusting habits of predatory seagulls', or tramping through an Australian swamp in pursuit of the rare, 'almost pure green' ground parrot, or admiring the thirteen species of Darwin's finch on the Galapagos Islands, Stott the ornithologist enjoys the world God made. Enjoyment is inevitably tempered by the tragic fracturing of the creation through sin: 'Original sin means that our inherited human nature is now twisted with a disastrous self-centredness. Evil is an ingrained, pervasive reality' (IFCT p. 34). Stott lists the social consequences of institutionalized self-centredness; stripped forests, man-made deserts and dust-bowls, polluted rivers, a fouled and poisoned atmosphere, are but global symptoms of man's moral incapacity. Despite human sin, the world, created and fallen, remains central to the redemptive purposes of God: 'Through the death, resurrection, and Spirit-gift of Jesus, God is fulfilling his promise of redemption and remaking marred mankind, not only as individuals but incorporating them into his new, reconciled community.' Christians are a redeemed people in an as yet unredeemed world. They look forward to the consummation of all things, when 'Jesus Christ will appear in great magnificence. He will raise the dead, judge the world, regenerate the universe and bring God's kingdom to perfection' (IFCT p. 35). The witness to that redemption is the Bible; its definitive expression is the cross.

Living under the cross.

In Stott's magnum opus, *The Cross of Christ*, cumulative biblical argument, fruitful trawling amongst historical and contemporary theologians and astute psychological observation, undergird an exposition of the cross which constitutes a personal credo. On its completion Stott looked back on the several years it had taken to write as a time of spiritual enirchment and clarified conviction: 'I have emerged . . . with a firm resolve to spend the rest of my days on earth (as I know the whole redeemed company will spend eternity in heaven), in the liberating service of Christ crucified' (CoC p. 7). His interpretation of the cross is unashamedly 'substitutionary', though he expounds 'propitiation' with considerable care: 'it is God himself who in holy wrath needs to be propitiated, God himself who in holy love undertook to do the propitiating, and God himself who in the person of his Son died for the propitiation of our sins . . . There is no crudity here to evoke our ridicule, only the profundity of holy love to evoke our worship' (CoC pp. 173–5).

Divine self-substitution on the cross is a profound mystery, an act of unqualified grace: 'The essence of sin is man substituting himself for God, while the essence of salvation is God substituting himself for man' (CoC p. 160). Sin, whether expressed in self-centred egoism, acquisitive materialism, alienated relationships, or a despoiled creation, is confronted by a God who reaches out in justice, love, wisdom and power in a once-for-all act of reconciling grace. At the cross, the gospel and world meet in a confrontation of values. Today's follower of Christ is called to live at the meeting-place of cross and contemporary culture, and, by a life of self-giving love and service, to witness to the renewing power of a self-sacrificed Saviour: 'The community of the cross is essentially a community of self-giving love, expressed in the worship of God and the service of others' (CoC p. 285). Mission and spirituality overlap in life under the cross: 'Mission sooner or later leads us into passion . . . every form of mission leads to some form of cross. The very shape of mission is cruciform.'[33]

Profound theology and courageous thinking have led Stott to a view of the cross which makes room in the heart of God for the pain of the world. The feelings and sufferings of Jesus 'are an authentic reflection of the feelings and sufferings of God himself' (CoC p. 331). The pain of God is felt 'whenever his wrath and love, justice and mercy, are in tension today'. The implications of a theology of the pain of God penetrate deeply into the Christian consciousness. Motivation for mission in costly love and Christlike service is rooted in the mysterious truth of the suffering of God: 'Christians cannot regard with equanimity the injustice which spoil God's world and demean his creatures. Injustice must bring pain to the God whose justice flared brightly at the cross; it should bring pain to God's people too' (CoC p. 293). The same logic applies to the cry of the unloved, the broken, the alienated: 'The community of the cross, which has truly absorbed the message of the cross, will always be motivated to action by the demands of justice and love' (CoC p. 293). In Stott's case the steady stream of articles and addresses on social justice, the aching emptiness of late twentieth-century Western culture, and the Church's obligation to translate the gospel into the language of contemporary need, flow from the inner imperative of love for a God who makes the pain of the world his own.

The powerful impact of the cross on Stott's spirituality is unmistakeable in a rare piece of personal comment. The comparison he draws between the Buddha and Christ is disturbingly explicit, and one senses the mixture of sadness and wonder in a passage too pain-filled to be devotional, but which probes deeply into the mysteries of sin, suffering and redemption:

> I have entered many Buddhist temples . . . and stood respectfully before the statue of the Buddha, his legs crossed, arms folded, eyes closed, the ghost of a smile playing round his mouth, a remote look on his face, detached from the agonies of the world. But each time after a while I have had to turn away. And in imagination I have turned instead to that lonely, twisted, tortured figure on the cross, nails through hands and feet, back lacerated, limbs wrenched, brow bleeding from thorn pricks, mouth dry and intolerably thirsty, plunged in God-forsaken darkness. That is the God for me! He laid aside his immunity to pain . . . our sufferings become more manageable in the light of his . . .
>
> (CoC pp. 336–7)

The community of the cross.

Through the cross God is creating a community which lives in obedience to the crucified Christ. Christian worship, growth and service take place within, and not in isolation from, the Christian community. Under the cross each Christian lives a life of new and reconciled relationships. Acceptance with God, understanding of self, love for enemies and service to the world, are all areas where the radical changes worked by the Spirit of God in the renewed community are to be most evident.

Forgiveness experienced as peace with God inspires celebration and worship which combines rejoicing with reverence: 'Humbly (as sinners) yet boldly (as forgiven sinners) we press into God's presence responding to his loving initiative with an answering love of our own' (CoC p. 257). In the Lord's Supper, '[Christ's] sacrifice on the cross is remembered, partaken of, proclaimed, acknowledged as the ground of our unity and responded to in grateful worship' (CoC p. 261). Where there is a reverent and expectant administration of the Eucharist, 'there is a real presence of Jesus Christ, not in the elements but among His people and at His table. Jesus Christ Himself objectively, really present, coming to meet the believer, ready to make Himself known in the breaking of bread . . . that he may feed on Him in his heart by faith' (BS 1 p. 127). The community of the cross is a community of celebration, 'a eucharistic community'.

The community of the cross is made up of individuals who have experienced the redeeming power of self-giving love. Whereas sin is 'being curved in on oneself', the love of God revealed on the cross is love turned outwards in grace and mercy. The cross stands as a paradigm pointing to a paradox: Christian obedience is ultimately a life in which self-denial is the way to self-affirmation.

'If we are following Christ with a cross on our shoulder, there is only one place to which we are going; the place of crucifixion' (CoC p. 279). Stott insists 'our self is a complex entity of good and evil, of glory and shame'.[34] Each human being is constituted partly as a result of creation (the image of God), and partly as a result of the fall (image defaced). The goal of Christian spirituality involves both continuous denial of the fallen self and constant strengthening and affirming of the created self. Rationality, the sense of moral obligation, sexuality, creativity, aesthetic judgement, responsible stewardship of the created world, the legitimate needs for love and community, and the sense of transcendence urging the human heart to worship, are all qualities of created humanity. Through the fall the image of God in created humanity is defaced by irrationality, moral perversity, distorted sexuality, fascination with the ugly, waste, greed and exploitation of the earth, alienated relationships and the fragmentation of community. Each member of the community of the cross must therefore 'take the hammer and nails to fasten [this] slippery fallen nature to the cross and thus do it to death' (CoC p. 279). Basic to Christian self-affirmation, and balancing the call to self-denial, is the value God has put on the true self in order to restore the image of God in each human personality.

The community of the cross was formed by love and lives by embodying that love. Stott asks the intriguing question, 'How has God solved the problem of His own invisibility?' He answers: ' "If we love one another God dwells in us and His love is perfected in us." In other words the invisible God, who once made himself visible in Christ, now makes Himself visible in Christians, if they love one another' (BS 2 p. 253). The same theme recurs in Stott's expository writing: 'It is obviously easier to love and serve a visible man than an invisible God, and if we fail in the easier task, it is absurd to claim success in the harder.'[35] 'Love for God', he warns, 'is not an emotional experience but a moral obedience.' Love is self-conscious, a decision of the renewed will, an affirmation of the whole person recreated in the image of a God, who is self-giving love.

Worship and personal spiritual development, rooted as they are in the cross, must impel the Christian community outwards in a mission of costly, even suffering service to the world: 'Every Christian should be involved. I sometimes ask people who call themselves "committed Christians" what they are committed to. Christ was committed to people. We should be also' (CMMW p. 121). The cost of living under the cross is the pain of involvement, a deliberate going into the world motivated by simple uncomplicated compassion. Love has no need to justify itself. Like God who is redeeming love, 'it merely expresses itself wherever it sees need' (CMMW p. 30).

'Mission is our human response to the divine commission . . . It is a *whole* Christian lifestyle' (IFCT p. 14.) A contemporary historian has remarked that John Stott has 'a considerable sense for the wholeness of things'.[36] This is apparent in Stott the Evangelical statesman who eschews both polarization and unprincipled compromise on divisive issues, preferring dialogue, and the open channels of persuasion. Here as in much else in Stott the influence of Charles Simeon can be discerned.

Stott's spirituality tends towards a similar pattern of balance and wholeness. The Christian mind is to be formed by the whole Bible but also informed about the beauty and the brokenness of the world. Deep and enduring gratitude to God finds authentic expression in personal devotion but also in world-affirming commitment. Therefore authentic Christian mission gives due weight to both evangelism and social action. Living under the cross the Christian community is enabled in celebration, developed in love and impelled to service. These are definite features of a spirituality 'with a sense for the wholeness of things'.

But Stott's own confession of faith, written at the age of sixty-five, suggested that the real cohesive force in his spiritual life is 'the service of Christ crucified'. To Christ, crucified and risen, the Bible bears witness, and therein lies both the authority and the attraction of Scripture; in Christ, living and dying, the love of God for his world was given definitive expression, and in his suffering the pain of the world becomes the pain of God; through Christ, the world was reconciled to God, enabling each individual to find acceptance and new life by faith in him; from Christ the community of the cross learns the meaning of fellowship in love and costly self-giving service to the world; under Christ they learn to live in obedience and joy, creating and sustaining a Christian counter-culture characterized by Christian thinking, fellowship, worship and mission; and to Christ, the focus of faith, hope and love, all things tend towards the final consummation in the redemptive purposes of God.

The confrontation between Lloyd-Jones and Stott over the issue of ecumenism has tended to obscure the many areas in which they found agreement and to eclipse other real differences between them. The emphasis on the primacy of the mind in spirituality was originally given powerful support by Lloyd-Jones. His influence was already being felt in the circles in which the young John Stott moved. In the 1950s and 1960s they were the two most influential Evangelical preachers in London and often followed the same university mission trail. Central to their spirituality is the conviction that the ability to think and study is a God-given gift, making them persuasive exponents of 'scholarly evangelism'. The foundation of all Christian thinking is the Bible. The Christian mind is to be submissive but active in study, seeking truth with heart, intellect and will geared for obedience. The focal point of their spirituality, drawing all else together, is Christ and his cross. Their interpretations of the cross differ significantly, but not their passionate belief in the substitutionary nature of Christ's death and their total conviction that faith in Christ crucified is the only way sinners can be justified in the sight of God.

On the relationship between Church and world the difference is marked. Asked if Christians are 'to work for good laws and a just society, even though they cannot hope to Christianise society', Lloyd-Jones replied: 'Certainly. Such effort prevents the world from putrefying. But I regard it as entirely negative' (CG p. 106). Stott has no such ambivalence; much of his writing and ministry has been a plea for an effective Christian presence in the world as a *Christian Counter Culture* or as *God's New Society*. The same fundamental differences in approach underlay their disagreement on inter-church relations. In the case of Lloyd-Jones, Christian thinking, theological and personal integrity involved a firm declaration of truth and strong resistance to what his biographer called 'the mentality of accommodation'; loyalty to truth has required that. For Stott, Christian thinking, theological and personal integrity have resulted in changed and developing thought, as he has continued to reflect on the biblical witness in relation to the modern world; loyalty to truth has required that.

Differences in temperament, spiritual experience, theological emphasis and in church allegiance are forced into secondary status by the one activity which has commanded all that is best in both men, preaching the word of God. 'What is preaching?', demands Lloyd-Jones. 'Logic on fire! Eloquent reason! It is theology on fire . . . theology coming through a man who is on fire. A true understanding and experience of the Truth must lead to this' (PP p. 97). Near the end of his life he made the self-revealing comment: 'The ultimate test of a preacher is what he feels like when he cannot preach' (M2 p. 738). More than anything else, Lloyd-Jones was shaped by his vocation, his deepest joys were discovered in study and realized in preaching. Like his hero Whitefield, Lloyd-Jones laboured to preach a 'felt Christ', to communicate not only truth, but truth soaked in fellowship with Christ, truth on which life's ultimate issues depended.

The same passion glows in Stott, tempered by a similar sense of privilege. His most recently published words on the spiritual experience of the preacher illustrate the intimate connection between the Word of God and the personal spirituality of the preacher:

> To enter the pulpit with the confidence that God has spoken, that He has caused what He has spoken to be written, and that this inspired text is in [my] hands, this can cause a preacher's head to swim, his heart to beat, his blood to flow, and his eyes to sparkle with the sheer glory of having God's Word in his hands and on his lips.
>
> (BS 3 p. 365)

Sources frequently cited

Catherwood, C., *Chosen of God*. Highland Books. (CG)
——, *Five Evangelical Leaders*. London 1984. (EL)
Lloyd-Jones, D. M., *The Cross*. Kingsway 1986. (C)
——, *Preaching and Preachers*. London 1971. (PP)
——, *Spiritual Depression*. London 1964. (SD)

——, *The Unsearchable Riches of Christ: Ephesians 3.1–21*. Edinburgh 1979. (E)
Murray, I. H., *D. Martyn-Lloyd-Jones: The First Forty Years 1899–1939*. Edinburgh 1982. (M1)
——, *D. Martyn Lloyd-Jones: The Fight of Faith 1939–1981*. Edinburgh 1990. (M2)
Stott, J. R. W., *Christ the Controversialist*. Leicester 1970. (CC)
——, 'Christian Ministry in the Modern World', *Bibliotheca Sacra*, vol. 145 (Apr.-Jn. 1988), pp. 123–32; (Jly-Sep. 1988), pp. 243–53; (Oct.-Dec. 1988) pp. 363–70; (Jan.-Mar. 1989), pp. 3–11. (BS)
——, *Christian Mission in the Modern World*. Falcon 1975. (CMMW)
——, *The Cross of Christ*. Leicester 1986. (CoC)
——, *Issues Facing Christians Today*. Basingstoke 1984. (IFCT)

Additional reading

Edwards, D. L., *Essentials.*, London 1988.
Lloyd-Jones, D. M., *Romans–Chapter 1–9. 39*, 8 vols. Edinburgh 1970–88.
——, *Ephesians*, 8 vols. Edinburgh 1972–82.
——, *Sanctified Through the Truth*. Kingsway 1989.
——, *Growing in the Spirit*. Kingsway 1989.
——, *Revival*. Marshall Pickering 1986.
Manwaring, R., *From Controversy to Co-Existence*. Cambridge 1985.
Peters, J., *Martyn Lloyd-Jones: Preacher*. Exeter 1986.
Stott, J. R. W., *Baptism and Fullness*. 2nd edn Leicester 1975.
——, *God's New Society*. Leicester 1979.
——, *Focus on Christ*. Fount 1979.
——, *I Believe in Preaching*. London 1982.
——, *The Message of Acts*. Leicester 1990.
——, *The Epistles of John*. Leicester 1964.

Notes

1. Bebbington, *Evangelicalism in Modern Britain* (London 1989), p. 267; Murray, *Lloyd-Jones*, vol. 2, ch. 25.
2. Lloyd-Jones' relationship with these and other agencies can be traced in the indices of Murray's two-volume biography.
3. See D. Johnson, *Contending for the Faith* (Leicester 1979).
4. Manwaring, *Controversy to Co-existence*, p. 98.
5. For Lloyd-Jones' unusual view of Rom. 7 see *Romans: The Law* (Edinburgh 1973), especially pp. 238–57. Stott's exposition was published as *Men Made New* (Leicester 1966).
6. Murray, *Lloyd-Jones*, vol. 2, pp. 314–20.

7. Bebbington, *Evangelicalism*, p. 249.
8. Murray, *Lloyd-Jones*, vol. 2, pp. 538–40; see also M. Saward, *Evangelicals on the Move* (London 1987).
9. See *The Evangelical-Roman Catholic Dialogue on Mission 1977–1984*, Exeter, 1986. Stott was a continuing member of ERCDOM, taking part in all three phases of the dialogue. In a personal note to the author John Stott makes his present position clear: 'When I was first invited to attend, as an Adviser, one of the Assemblies of the WCC (Uppsala 1968), I wrote to the General Secretary in order to clarify the basis on which I would feel able to accept the invitation. Of course, I said, I wanted to come in order to listen and to learn. But (I added), I did not share the kind of ecumenical perspective which regarded every point of view as equally valid, since I desired to be submissive to the supreme authority of Scripture. I hoped I would have the liberty, therefore, to bear witness to what I believed Scripture taught and to disagree with those who disagreed with Scripture. The General Secretary replied that this was exactly why I had been invited. So I went, in spite of some exhortation from evangelical friends not to go.'
10. Some of Lloyd-Jones' own comment on 'Welshness' can be found in Murray vol. 1, p. 315, and vol. 2, p. 757.
11. Catherwood, *Chosen of God*, p. 107; Murray, *Lloyd-Jones*, vol. 1, p. 191. The three books were R. W. Dale, *The Atonement* (London 1875); J. Denney, *The Death of Christ* (London 1902); P. T. Forsyth, *The Cruciality of the Cross* (London 1909). Stott supplements this account in *Cross of Christ*, pp. 9–10.
12. Lloyd-Jones, *Preaching*, p. 175. See also Lloyd-Jones, *The Puritans* (Edinburgh 1987).
13. Murray, *Lloyd-Jones*, vol. 2, pp. 137, 571, 318.
14. D. M. Lloyd-Jones, *Faith on Trial* (London 1965), pp. 35, 80.
15. See the important address Lloyd-Jones gave at the Puritan Conference on 'Knowledge–False and True', in *The Puritans*, pp. 24–45, which shows that Lloyd-Jones was well aware of the dangers of spiritual pride and doctrinal rectitude devoid of living experience. Testimony to Lloyd-Jones' example came from one of the last literary contributions of Professor F. F. Bruce. Reviewing Murray's second volume, he commented: 'He was a thoroughly humble man. Those who charged him with arrogance were wildly mistaken.' See *The Evangelical Quarterly*, vol. 63, no. 1 (1991), pp. 68–71.
16. Lloyd-Jones, *Preaching*, p. 174: 'I abominate devotional commentaries.'
17. V. Verbrugge, reviewed *Christian Unity*, (Eph. 4.1–16), in *Calvin Theological Journal*, 18 (1983), pp. 94–8. The writer was critical of lack of interaction with contemporary biblical scholarship but Lloyd-Jones had maintained from the beginning that he was publishing sermons not commentaries.
18. A five-dollar note was inserted to purchase a replacement! Murray, *Lloyd-Jones*, vol. 2, p. 612.
19. See Murray, *Lloyd-Jones*, vol. 2, p. 219; Lloyd-Jones, *Saved in*

Eternity (Kingsway 1988), p. 151, where Lloyd-Jones is cautious about the wrong kind of mystical quest.

20. See Michael Eaton, *Baptism With the Spirit* (Leicester 1989); Murray, *Lloyd-Jones*, vol. 2, pp. 483–91.
21. Stott, *Preaching*, p. 46.
22. Manwaring, *Controversy to Co-existence*, p. 57.
23. Stott, *Basic Christianity* (Leicester 1958), p. 131.
24. ibid., p. 127.
25. Edwards, *Essentials*, p. 35.
26. Stott, *Balanced Christianity* (London 1975).
27. BS 1 p. 127. The series of four articles published in *Bibliotheca Sacra* are hereafter referred to as BS followed by the number and page ref. Full details above.
28. Stott, *Baptism and Fullness*, p. 69.
29. Edwards, *Essentials*, p. 33.
30. *All-Souls Magazine*, Mar.-Apr., 1980.
31. Stott has contributed volumes on The Sermon on the Mount, Acts, Galatians, Ephesians and 2 Timothy.
32. Stott, *Preaching*, p. 151.
33. Quoting Douglas Webster, *Cross of Christ*, p. 291.
34. 'Love or Hatred of Self', *Christianity Today*, 28, No. 7 (20 Apr. 1984), pp. 26–8.
35. Stott, *Epistles of John* (Leicester 1964), p. 171.
36. A. Hastings, *A History of English Christianity 1920–1985* (Collins 1986), p. 456.

CONCLUSION

The end of all is the grace unspeakable.
FORSYTH

Worthy the Lamb of endless praise,
  Whose double life we here shall prove,
The pardoning and the hallowing grace,
  The dawning and the perfect love.

To make our right and title sure,
  Our dying Lord himself hath given,
His sacrifice did all procure,
  Pardon, and holiness, and heaven.

Our life of grace we here shall feel
  Shed in our loving hearts abroad,
Till Christ our glorious life reveal,
  Long hidden with himself in God.[1]

Originally written as part of a hymn on the Lord's Supper, these verses touch the heart of Evangelical spirituality. In them Charles Wesley sounds the note of exultant celebration in the presence of the Lamb of God who takes away the sins of the world. He draws a distinction between justification and sanctification, between pardon as the dawning of the life of grace, and that same grace continuing to be operative in the hallowing of life. Assurance is based on the atonement made by the dying Lord. The primary benefits of his death, conferred as gracious gifts on the believing Christian, are 'pardon, and holiness, and heaven'. Christ as the source of the life of grace, love as its expression, and re-creation in the life of God as its goal, complete Wesley's affirmation of Evangelical experience.

Through exploring such experience in the lives and writings of twenty-two Evangelical Christians, certain broad conclusions emerge which merit some reflection. First, while Evangelicals have held certain doctrinal emphases in common, those included in this study display considerable diversity within that basic unity. Second, part of this diversity is due to several influencing factors including historical and cultural context, individual temperament and the literary forms in which these Christians expressed themselves. Third, some critical reflections will help to identify weaknesses and strengths within the Evangelical spiritual tradition. Finally it is important to note the contributions which Evangelical spirituality continues to offer to the wider Christian tradition, not as exclusive insights, but as emphases which, taken together, constitute the bases of the Evangelical understanding of the spiritual life.

The grace in the heart of God.

'Conversion is the crisis of the soul in which it turns to God.'[2] With that succinct definition few Evangelicals would quarrel. However to insist on the necessity of conversion is one thing; to impose a specific pattern of experience is quite another. Conversion can be a sudden life-transforming crisis or a gradual growth into faith. Consciousness of having been made a child of God is more important than secondary matters of timing or sequence of events. Indeed such figures as Edwards, More, and Whyte placed no date on the moment of their conversion. Theirs was a spirituality entirely lacking in presumption, with a strong sense of the sinfulness of sin and profound knowledge of what is at issue in moral struggle.

While recognizing the necessity of regeneration, Whyte also urged the need for daily, continuous conversion. The only proof of his own rebirth was the manifestation of the new nature: 'The new birth that we must all every day undergo, the one all-embracing change of heart that God demands of us in His Son every day, is a complete change of end and intention, a completely new motive. The fall of man took place when God ceased to be man's motive, and when each man became his own motive and his own end.'[3] Whitefield would not have disagreed with Whyte's view, but he considered his own experience of radical, dateable change paradigmatic and so important that all his life he lived with the picture of that revelatory moment: 'I know the place! . . . whenever I go to Oxford I cannot help running to that place where Jesus Christ first revealed himself to me and gave me the new birth.'[4]

In Whitefield's case conversion was the culmination of an anguished search. But for some it seemed a natural, unforced step of faith. Chadwick registered his decision to follow Christ by cleaning a pair of boots properly; Stott knelt in his bedroom, confessed his need and made space in his life for Christ. Dale considered that the secret of Moody's success on his British tour of 1875 was the unconditional offer of forgiveness, while on his later visit in 1883 the results were disappointingly different because Moody preached forgiveness on the basis of repentance. The first message produced radiating joy in the converts, the second a burden of unassuaged anxiety.[5] Differences in personal experience and theological emphasis, however, do not alter the basic Evangelical conviction that the fundamental need of the human heart is to be made new. The process of renewal is neither predictable nor uniform. The sovereignty of grace is such that God calls each by his Spirit, working within the circumstances, temperament and experience of each individual.

The position of the cross at the centre of Evangelical thought and devotion has inevitably given rise to different interpretations of the nature of atonement. Some, like Edwards, Bonar and Lloyd-Jones, argued that the truth lies predominantly in the righteousness of God. The cross not only reveals but carries out the judgement of God on sin. The death of Christ is understood as a propitiation of God's wrath. Christ offered himself as the sinner's substitute to bear the full punishment for sin. Others, like Charles Wesley in some of his hymns or Moody in his preaching, viewed the cross as the definitive demonstration of divine love, an historical act of mercy which exposes the eternal heart of God. These two emphases are often combined, for example in Forsyth's phrase 'holy love' and in Stott's careful exposition of substitutionary atonement. The death of Christ is perhaps best presented as a mystery which defies theoretical control. It is an overpowering truth which smashes human complacency by the announcement of judgement and grace; all are sinners but all are loved with an eternal love; all are sinners under just condemnation and deserving nothing, but by grace offered pardon and infinite blessing.

Whatever theory of the atonement is preferred, Evangelicals proclaim that 'God's grace did compel this Passion of the Cross' which reveals the 'Grace in the heart of God'. Consequently 'every living experience of Christianity begins at the cross.'[6] Morgan ends his book, *The Bible and the Cross*, by presenting an argument in which logic gives way to a vision, long and reverently pondered during countless readings of the passion story: 'If there be no sin, law and love are never out of harmony with each other; truth and grace go ever hand in hand; justice and mercy sing a common anthem. If the law be broken what is love to do? If truth be violated, how can grace operate? In the presence of crime, how can justice and mercy meet? This is the problem of problems.' It is in God's solution to this dilemma that Evangelicals like Morgan have found the fulcrum of the spiritual life, in a vision of God's grace that has consequences at once immediate and eternal, personal and cosmic:

> By suffering wrought out into human history, and in the sight of all the ages through the Cross, He demonstrated that love meets law as it suffers, and fulfils it; grace satisfies the demand of truth by meeting all the issues of its violating; and mercy can operate on the basis of justice, not because God has smitten and afflicted other than Himself; but because in a mystery which baffles and bruises the intellect as it attempts to encompass it, God has gathered the whole into His own heart, and suffered to reconcile all things unto Himself.[7]

We cannot work for God without love.

In matters of faith, Evangelicals have consistently looked to the Bible as the primary authority. But in controversy between Arminian and Calvinist positions, in response to new movements with differing theological emphases, and in their attitude to the advances of critical scholarship, opinions have differed markedly regarding interpretation of Scripture. For example, the introductory chapter of J. C. Ryle's book, *Holiness*, is directed against what he saw as the novel teaching of the day about sanctification, and in defence of *scriptural holiness*. The pages are peppered with biblical references. H. C. G. Moule's finest exposition of Keswick theology is in his largest *biblical* commentary, while in his other writings there are repeated claims that his teaching is fully in accord with Scripture. He prefaced his little pocket-book, *Union with Christ*, with the claim: 'Every page is submitted reverently and entirely to the authority of the Holy Scriptures.'[8] His pages too are tapestries of scriptural phrases. Where doctrinal differences emerged, there may be claim and counter-claim about biblical interpretation; but that the matter was to be settled by appeal to the Bible was undisputed.

Spurgeon could fulminate against the critics and thinkers whose beliefs and unbeliefs reminded him of the clothes of Italian peasants, 'an agglomeration of philosophic rags, metaphysical tatters, theological remnants and heretical cast-offs.' 'We believe', he continued, 'that though the Bible has been twisted and turned about by sacrilegious hands, it is still the infallible revelation of God.'[9] Of the same generation, and with an equal desire to be true to the Bible, R. W. Dale struggled to retain the substance of biblical truth without becoming enmeshed in defending that which he felt to be intellectually untenable. Late in life he wrote an article in which he conceded Jonah could be interpreted as fiction. Around the same time he often went to his Welsh retreat: 'He would take his Bible, and read book after book with minute care, noting the truths on which, as it seemed to him, he had dwelt too lightly.'[10]

The attitude of reverent submission before the biblical text, exemplified so differently by Spurgeon and Dale, has been characteristic of Evangelical spirituality. Differences of interpretation abound, but there has been virtual unanimity in the conviction that the Bible is God's word, revealed truth, sharp, two-edged, piercing to the deepest recesses of mind and heart. The application of biblical truth to the personal life is not simply one way of obedience to God which happens to be preferred by Evangelicals. Since the Bible is God's word written its study is a required discipline, a formative and habitual submission of mind and heart to the Spirit of God. Cowper's wistful prayer, entitled 'The Waiting Soul' begins:

> Breathe from the gentle south, O Lord,
> And cheer me from the north;
> Blow on the treasures of thy word,
> And call the spices forth![11]

and reflects something of the anticipation of promised blessing which animates those who meditate upon the Bible and await God's word.

Conversion, whether sudden or gradual, creates a heightened

awareness of moral accountability to Christ. Regeneration of the self results in a replenished emotional life, a renewed and redirected will and a powerful urge to service. Joy, fear of the Lord, gratitude and many other notes are sounded in the song of the redeemed, but adding depth to the whole experience is the sense of indebtedness to the crucified Lord. Joy is the joy of being loved; the heartfelt sense of obligation, which is the legacy of forgiveness, is understood as a debt to love; the fear of the Lord is the carefulness of the Christian not to offend against the holy love of God; and gratitude is the cry of each Christian who experiences the reality behind Paul's cry, 'the Son of God who loved me and gave himself for me'. These are the inner dynamics of the missionary activism and zeal for doing which have characterized so much of Evangelical spiritual life. Horatius Bonar urged his congregation:

> Go, labour on, spend and be spent,
> Thy joy to do the Father's will,
> It is the way the Master went,
> Should not the servant tread it still?[12]

With less poetry but more punch Moody recalled the days when he started his Sunday School class with eighteen pupils. He said, 'If I am worth anything to the Christian church today, it is as much due to that work as to anything else . . . I used the little talent I had, and God kept giving me more talents.' He warned his hearers: 'Laziness belongs to the old creation, not the new. There is not a lazy hair in the head of a true Christian . . . We cannot work for God without love . . . but the moment the love of God is shed abroad in our hearts, my friends, we cannot help loving Him and working for Him.'[13]

Like a river glorious, is God's perfect peace

Sanctification is variously described as growth in holiness, the renewal of the divine image, conformity to Christ, consecration, or in the Wesleyan tradition, the perfection of love. Analysis of the nature and process of Christian growth has been a fertile ground for Evangelical disagreement. Whether sanctification should be instantaneous or gradual, by faith, discipline, or both, and whether the ideal of the Christian spiritual life should be peace which is the rest of faith or strength in the midst of conflict, are several key questions over which many prayers for understanding and blessing have been offered, and much time, paper and ink expended.

Standing between the reformed Calvinist view and the new holiness movement, Havergal spoke of a crisis experience of consecration. She wrote to her sister following her experience of consecration in 1873: 'As to "perfectionism" or "sinlessness" I have all along, and over and over again, said I never did, and do not, hold either.' That seems unequivocal enough, and she goes on, 'I believe [sinlessness] to be not only an impossibility on earth but an actual contradiction of our very being, which cannot be "sinless" till the resurrection change has passed upon us.' Two years later she wrote a passage which comes puzzlingly close to contradicting that: 'He has taken my will as I gave it to Him, and now I am really not conscious of even a wish crossing His will concerning me . . . I mean for many months He seems not to have allowed the enemy to come near me.'[14] Havergal's ambiguity highlights the tension between scriptural models and human experience.

A key text in many of these discussions has been Romans chapter seven. The orthodox view has favoured the 'miserable sinner' interpretation; conflict caused by inner contradiction is integral to Christian experience. The Keswick view, espoused by Moule amongst many others, suggests that the conflict Paul describes occurs in the heart of the regenerate soul every time Christ is not fully trusted; it is the despairing cry of the needlessly defeated, the consciously mediocre, and is caused by an unsurrendered will.[15] Havergal's hymn, despite her claimed independence of 'movements', became the classic expression of the Keswick experience. John Newton wrote from the other viewpoint with his customary unadorned honesty. Read consecutively they provide an instructive contrast:

Every joy or trial,
  Falleth from above,
Traced upon our dial
  By the Sun of Love.
We may trust Him solely
  All for us to do
They who trust Him wholly,
  Find Him wholly true.
Stayed upon Jehovah,

Hearts are fully blest,
Finding as he promised,
Perfect peace and rest.[16]

'I am aiming at things inconsistent with each other at the same instant, so that I can accomplish neither . . . I appear to rejoice and mourn, to choose and refuse, to be a conqueror and a captive. In a word I am a double person; a riddle. It is no wonder you do not know what to make of me, for I cannot tell you what to make of myself. I would and I would not, I do and I do not, I can and I cannot, I find the hardest things easy and the easiest things impossible . . .'[17]

Differences such as these make for enrichment. Often disagreement in formulating experience into theological terms is part of the process by which a tradition develops. An imposed uniformity would simply disqualify those whose experience did not fit the theological template. Sometimes Evangelicals have failed to recognize, trust and nurture the diversity of experience and emphasis which are the legitimate fruits of their own doctrinal distinctives.

Grace which like the Lord the giver
Never fails from age to age.

Contributing to the diversity of Evangelical spirituality has been the interaction between historical context and spiritual tradition. The impact of Enlightenment assumptions on Evangelical thought was considerable. Jonathan Edwards' own experience of 'a new sense' of God, his study of revival phenomenology and his treatises such as *The Freedom of the Will*, betray the Enlightenment preoccupation with knowledge. Experience and knowledge of God he considers self-evident, provided the canons of proof are clearly established. *The Religious Affections* stands as a monumental example of the desire to provide that proof and establish the validity of spiritual experience.

In the nineteenth century, Romanticism also influenced Evangelical thought. Hannah More's distaste for the Romantic poets did not prevent her from enjoying her garden with all the enthusiasm for nature of the true Romantic. More significantly a growing emphasis on feelings began to influence Evangelical piety. R. W. Dale observed, not without criticism, 'People want to sing, not what they think, but what they feel.'[18] The Keswick emphasis on immediacy of blessing to the seeking heart, the setting in the beautiful scenery of the Lake District with all its associations with Wordsworth, and the use of sentimental vocabulary, again castigated by Dale, are features which betray Romantic influence.

Not only historical context but the individuality of each personality gives colour and tone to spirituality. Alexander Whyte was an illegitimate child, born into a poor home, in a small town community in mid-Victorian Presbyterian Scotland. His deep pessimism about his own heart and his chronic sense of unworthiness cannot be unrelated to the scandal of his birth. There are times when Whyte so overstates the case that he comes close to self-hatred. Talking of the infamous Judge Jeffreys, he told the respectable Free St George's congregation: 'If you lay your ear close enough to your own heart, you will sometimes hear something of that same hiss with which that human serpent sentenced to torture and death . . . O yes, the very same hell broth that ran for blood in Judge Jeffreys' heart is in all our hearts also.'[19]

By contrast, John Newton, whose early career was about as sinful as Whyte's worst nightmares, faced his sin without minimizing it, but still revelled in grace and thoroughly enjoyed being a Christian. 'When the treble is praise, and heart humiliation the bass, the melody is pleasant and the harmony good.' Newton's best hymns reflect this confident gratitude, and his spiritual exuberance:

> Blest inhabitants of Zion,
> Washed in the Redeemer's blood,
> Jesus whom their souls rely on,
> Makes them kings and priests to God,
> 'Tis His love His people raises,
> Over self to reign as kings,
> And as priests, His solemn praises,
> Each for a thank-offering brings.[20]

Individuality and social milieu have to a large extent governed the literary forms in which Evangelical spirituality has been expressed. Evangelicalism has little that is new to offer and has been content to use treatises, hymns, letters, prayers, sermons and private journals. It is curious that of the twenty-two people studied only Spurgeon left material for an intended full-scale autobiography, issued posthumously by his widow. Wesley and

Whitefield produced journals, and others have left fragments, but Evangelicalism owns few classics of spiritual autobiography.

Hymns have been enormously influential. Charles Wesley's collection provides 'a little body of practical divinity', a modest disclaimer belied by the enormity of his achievement; the Olney Hymns aimed at communicating truth with simplicity, the plain Augustan language serving the purpose well; Bonar's versified doctrine, Havergal's hymns of consecration with their insistent call for subjective response, and Moody's use of Sankey in evangelistic appeal, each reflect the temperament of the authors and the requirements of the age.

Evangelicals made heavy use of the post. The letters of Wesley, Whitefield, Cowper, Newton and More are replete with instruction on the spiritual life, theological opinions, social comment, devotional reflection, and gossip, that essential source of historical detail. Whitefield comes alive in his letters; Newton's *Cardiphonia* is a classic of Evangelical devotion; Cowper is one of the masters of English letter writing. It seems Hannah More was unfortunate in her first biographer. Perhaps the less serious, more playful and life-affirming Hannah would have been visible if the letters had not been altered, cut and indeed 'improved' by her editor.[21]

The printed sermon was for long an immensely popular form of religious literature. Evangelical spirituality has its own corpus, of enormous volume though of admittedly mixed quality. Wesley's sermons provide part of the doctrinal standards of Methodism; Edwards' sermons make few concessions to a paperback age; Spurgeon's sermons are still valued by some critical commentators.

A spiritual tradition both nourishes and is nourished by its adherents. Individual gifts of personality, temperament and experience, interact with a whole world of influences, circumstances and people, to produce each person's history. Within Evangelical spirituality there has been a changing continuity as each generation has reinterpreted the Evangelical distinctives, responded to changing movements of thought and sought new ways of expressing the life of grace.

How can a Christian girl personate Jezebel?

The call to conversion is a call for individual response. The personal relationship with Christ, by grace, through faith in the atonement, is typical of Evangelical spirituality. The experience of conversion releases powerful resources of moral and spiritual renewal. Through forgiveness, conviction of sin and feelings of guilt are replaced by a new sense of joy and freedom. It is precisely these feelings of well-being which can degenerate into an experience-based spirituality in which feelings are more important than objective truth, and God is loved as a source of blessing rather than for himself. Lloyd-Jones sounded many warnings about the dangers of dependence on feelings: 'We are all ready to try to obtain and to thirst after special experiences – assurance of forgiveness and salvation, being freed from special sins, experiencing joy and peace, being able to live the full life and so on. All these things are part of the heritage of the Christian, but he must not live on them and be satisfied by them. To know *Him* properly is a life full of peace.'[22]

Undoubtedly there are many instances of Evangelicals indulging in spiritual self-culture. Indeed there is almost an in-built call to self-preservation in many forms of evangelism. To base a relationship with God on personal benefit is to cultivate a spirituality of prudence, a piety of self-interest. Evangelicals have not always successfully resisted that temptation. The distinction between desire for peace with God and desire for God is not always maintained.

R. W. Dale preached a remarkable sermon on forgiveness in which he took serious issue with the prevalent assumption that the important factor in forgiveness is the feeling of having been forgiven. Forgiveness, he argued, is not just about making people better in the future; it is about dealing with the wrongness of the past. Forgiveness is not primarily about removing feelings of guilt; it is about the moral resentment of God directed at the sinner but turned away by mercy. The curse of sin is not human guilt but violated law; the offence is not against our own peace, but against God's holiness. 'We like to sing hymns', he scorned, 'but hymns about ourselves not about God; hymns which tranquillise us by their peacefulness, charm us with their beauty, melt us with their sadness, or animate us with their joy.'[23] Dale is the scourge of contrived religious sentiment. He continues:

> In our very religion God has a secondary place. We have made ourselves the centre of our religious thought. We are conscious that we ourselves are alive, but He has ceased to be a living

> God, with an infinite fervour of joy in righteousness – which is obedience to His will; and an infinite fervour of hatred for sin – which is the transgression of His commandments. In morals we think of our own conscience – not of God's law; of our self-respect not of God's approval; and we are distressed by self-reproach – not by God's displeasure and anger.[24]

It is important to note such rebukes; they come from within the tradition and show something of the corrective influences at work in the Christian community.

Related to individualism and subjectivism is preoccupation with guilt. Scrupulosity is not confined to Evangelicalism; the Oxford Movement gave equal encouragement to severe self-censorship. But there is a certain quaintness in Hannah More writing a whole essay on the misuse of the word 'ascension' because she thought it was being used irreverently when applied to ballooning.[25] There are surprises too. Robert Murray McCheyne wrote to his father: 'The bottles of good things are by no means unacceptable . . . all but the whisky, to which I am a sworn enemy, though I have to drink a dram while visiting.' In a later letter to his mother he expressed a connoisseur's appreciation for fine French wines.[26]

Some Evangelicals had extremely sensitive antennae where sin was concerned. Havergal gave up singing all but sacred music because the morally meticulous Mr Snepp, who collaborated in her published work, had expressed surprise that she was willing to sing the part of Jezebel in Mendelssohn's *Elijah*: 'How can a Christian girl personate Jezebel?', he asked. No one seemed to notice that *Elijah* is sacred music.[27] Shakespeare also suffered at the hands of moral zealots. Wesley's annotated copy of the plays was burned as 'worthless lumber' by John Pawson, President of the Methodist Conference.[28] Havergal had her own reservations, expressed in moral rather than literary criticism. Looking for 'an intellect to rub against', she read Shakespeare for half an hour each day over some weeks; 'I think my motive was really that I might polish my own instruments for the Master's use. But there is so much that is entirely of the earth earthy, amid all the marvellous genius and even the sparkles of the highest truth which flash here and there, so much that jars upon one's spirit, so much that is downward instead of upward.'[29] However, since

Shakespeare was 'useful' in cultivating the intellect, he remained on her list.

Resistance to culture was part of a wider suspicion of the world as the source of dangerous temptation. The frivolity of 'card-playing', moral subversion in the theatre and the inherent dishonesty of fiction are prime examples of such 'dangers'. Early Keswick speakers isolated tobacco and bad temper as particular faults indicating an unsurrendered will.[30] The Reverend Andrew Bonar, brother of Horatius, was genuinely worried when he saw his family on holiday, 'so full of spirits in the country that they may have for the time bidden farewell to God in their heart'.[31] Much more sensible was the attitude of Charles Simeon: 'If we give ourselves up to creature comforts, we shall be disappointed . . . But if we enjoy them in subserviency to God, and in subordination to higher pursuits, we shall not find them so empty as may be imagined. For "God has given to his people all things richly to enjoy": and provided only we enjoy God in them, they are both a legitimate and an abundant spring of pure delight.'[32]

Tension inevitably developed between involvement in the world and separation from it. The strain was felt most acutely in the relationship between evangelism and social action. Hannah More's retreat from the social world of London, together with her withdrawal from the wider world of affairs, was almost monastic in its thoroughness. Though she was committed to the abolition of slavery and other programmes of philanthropy, there is always a hankering to be back in the moral safety of Christian company. The 'Christian Worldliness' of Dale represents a full-blooded affirmative response to the world. Christian involvement is not an option for the adventurous, but an obligation inherent in the gospel. Social amelioration is not a compromise but a legitimate implicate of the gospel. John Stott has frequently referred to the 'rediscovery of the Evangelical social conscience'. He has contributed significantly not only to changes of mood and attitude, but to a changed theological perspective: 'As a human being our neighbour may be defined as "a body-soul-in-community". If we love our neighbour as God created him (which is His command to us) then we shall inevitably be concerned for his total welfare, the welfare of his body, his soul and his society.'[33] Evangelical spirituality has had to accommodate a view of mission and compassionate obligation which disturbs the quietness and dissipates the cosiness of private devotions and personal witnessing.

Individualism, emphasis on feelings, guilt-making and scrupulosity, world-denying attitudes, suspicion of cultural life, withdrawal from social involvement, to which might be added, an anti-intellectual strain, a tendency to be judgemental of non-Evangelical Christians, a dismissive attitude to other spiritual traditions and sometimes an unlovely spiritual pride, are amongst the weaknesses, failings and distortions sometimes present in Evangelical piety. Some of them are qualities corrupted; the line between a sensitive conscience seeking to be loyal to Christ and over-scrupulous introspection is not easily drawn. Others are defensive attitudes which hardened into a permanent fortress mentality; loyalty to the authority of the Bible need not require that other and different traditions be ignored, only that they be subordinate to biblical truth. Many Evangelicals are increasingly recognizing the need for humility in conviction and openness to the corrective balance provided by the wider Christian community. In that exchange of fresh insight, living experience, cherished conviction and mutual listening, Evangelicals come with their gifts and insights.

O that God may fill us with His love.

Many of the criticisms suggested above are by no means universal. Of the people studied in this book, many have displayed a generous catholicity in relation to other Christians. John Newton's letters abound with expressions of goodwill to fellow-Christians, with many of whom he might disagree. He regretted 'the vanity and sinfulness of unchristian disputes' and confessed: 'I cannot see it my duty, nay, I believe it would be my sin, to attempt to beat my notions into other people's heads. Too often I have attempted it in the past; but now I judge that both my zeal and my weapons were carnal. When our dear Lord questioned Peter . . . he said not, "Art thou wise, learned, eloquent?" nay, he said not, "Art thou clear and sound and orthodox?" But this only, "Lovest thou me?" '[34]

Moody deplored the 'miserable sectarian spirit that once held despotic hold on men'. In London he declared: 'Talk not . . . of this party and that party, but solely and exclusively of the great comprehensive cause of Jesus Christ . . . in this city let us starve it out for a season, to actualize this glorious truth . . . O that God may fill us with His love, and the love of souls.'[35] Much of Moody's success in managing people was due to his intuitive tact and generously open nature. His ecumenical spirit never eclipsed his Evangelical convictions. Describing the purpose of his Northfield Conference in America, he said: 'The central idea is Christian unity . . . but it is understood that along with the idea of Christian unity goes the Bible as it stands.'[36]

Love and gratitude to Christ, crucified and risen, provide the originating source of much that is passionate and celebratory in Evangelical devotion. The ardour and joy of fellowship with Christ the Saviour released floods of lyrical affirmations of love, desire, worship and surrender. The infinite volume of the oceans, the endlessly repeated surging of the waves, and the capacity of water to fill and overflow was one of McCheyne's favourite images, used to convey something of the 'unsearchable riches of Christ'. 'Unfathomable oceans of grace are in Christ for you. Dive and dive again, you will never come to the bottom of these depths. How many millions of dazzling pearls and gems are at this moment hid in the deep recesses of the ocean caves . . . it is truest wisdom to adorn the soul with Christ and his graces.'[37] During a spell of illness McCheyne travelled to Palestine as part of a deputation investigating the possibilities for missionary work amongst Jews. While his boat was anchored off the Bay of Carmel on the Mediterranean, he wrote:

> O Lord, this swelling tideless sea
> Is like Thy love in Christ to me:
> The ceaseless waves that fill the bay
> Through flinty rocks have worn their way,
> And Thy unceasing love alone
> Hath broken through this heart of stone.[38]

A similar note of unrestrained exultation burst from Whyte as he concluded his sermon 'Under Grace':

> No mortal man has ever lived, to be called life, under the law. But grace brings true and everlasting life. Live, then, in grace, and in nothing else. Rise up every morning in grace. Congratulate yourself every morning as you wake, and say, O my soul, we are not under the law, but under grace. Go out to your day's work under grace. And return home, lie down on your bed again, ever more and more under grace. Live, and die,

and rise again, and go to judgment, and go to heaven itself, and all under grace . . . Grace reigns.[39]

The passion of Christ excites strong emotion in those who live in daily fellowship with Christ, crucified and risen. P. T. Forsyth refused to allow the evidence of his own experience of Christ to be ruled out of the courts of theological enquiry. 'Should it make no difference to the evidence for Christ's Resurrection that I have had personal dealings with the risen Christ as my Saviour? . . . Is his personal gift of forgiveness to me, in the central experience of my life, of no value in settling the objective value of his Cross and Person?'[40] The doctrinal intransigence often attributed to Evangelicals is in fact something more; inextricably linked with all theologizing, and lifting even the most reverent examinations of Christian truth to a higher plane than that of disciplined, honest scholarship, is the personal experience of a love the reality of which is beyond contradiction or rational qualification. Spurgeon well illustrates this theology of the heart's experience in words of characteristic intensity: 'Oh that I could have the cross painted on my eyeballs, that I could not see anything except through the medium of my Saviour's passion! Oh, Jesus . . . let me wear the pledge forever where it is conspicuous before my soul's eyes.'[41]

Christ-conscious not self-conscious.

Amongst Evangelicals the Bible has held an unchallenged position as the source-book of theology and the handbook of spiritual experience. John Wesley's advice to his niece Sarah assumed the Christ-centred nature of the biblical revelation: 'All you want to know of Him is contained in one book, the Bible. And all you learn is to be referred to this, either directly or remotely . . . spend at least an hour a day in reading and meditating on the Bible.'[42] Handley Moule exemplified the spirituality of a mind so immersed in the Bible that his whole thinking was dyed in scriptural colours. The Christian who practises habitual study will find that 'a something great and gracious, large and deep, loving and strong, comes out of it into his inner life, and grows there, a something such as no other reading can bring. Make that Book your friend, and you shall surely catch the contagion of its character, its way of thinking about God, about man, about sin, judgment, mercy, holiness, about virtue here and its glorification hereafter.'[43]

John Stott avoids the danger of making the Bible a substitute for Christ by maintaining a proper balance between Christ, Scripture and sacrament. 'God has given us both [Scripture and sacrament] in order to display Christ before the eyes of our heart, to attract our attention to Him and to draw out our faith in him. Scripture and sacrament alike are Christ-conscious, not self-conscious . . . They are binoculars for the magnification of Jesus Christ. We are to look through them, not at them. Our gaze is to be on Christ.'[44]

To love Christ is to live for him. Love implies intimacy of relationship and moral obedience. Though some Evangelicals have been guilty of being preoccupied with what seems morally trivial while ignoring ethical concerns of far vaster import, there can be no denying the moral seriousness felt by those whose spiritual life focuses on Calvary. R. W. Dale's words, overlaid with the solemnity of the hard thinker who has grappled with the mystery of atonement, can speak for the whole Evangelical tradition of moral seriousness in the walk with God. When there is perfect love for God:

> His statutes become songs instead of unwelcome restraints; all the currents of life flow freely in the channels defined by His will. But His statutes are His statutes still . . . they are laws which love has no desire to break. When I call Him my God, I mean that His will – not my own – is the rule of life and conduct. When I say that He is God over all, I mean that the final harmony and glory of the universe are to come from the acceptance of His will as the supreme law by all created beings; and for myself, I also mean that whoever resists and refuses to submit – be he man or angel – must perish.[45]

The maintenance of the life of grace depends upon openness to the God whose grace is life. Bible-reading, prayer, Holy Communion and the Christian community are each appointed channels of grace. The deeply mystical note in Whyte was sometimes replaced by a quite refreshing down-to-earthness when he was praying for others. Visiting a distressed elderly woman somewhere in Edinburgh, he prayed, 'O Lord, here's two poor old folk needing you sorely. You won't be too hard on us!' On a Sunday morning the noise of driving rain on the church windows took his prayer in a northerly direction! 'Lord we would remember our Highland ministers. We think of many of them on this wet day, going along a wet road, to a wet church, to preach to a few wet people.'[46]

According to Bishop Moule intercession for others is an expression of love, an imitation of Christ in his priestly, ascended role. Intercession 'witnesses to the Christian believer's living spiritual union with his brethren in Christ . . . and to his wonderful and blessed spiritual union with his Lord in new birth and new life . . . Oh for more full, more vivid, more continuous recollection of this holy spiritual solidarity with Him, and with them in Him!'[47] Bishop Ryle recognized intercession as a safety-valve which prevents prayer becoming self-absorbed. 'We should try to bear in our hearts the whole world . . . This is the highest charity. He loves me best who loves me in his prayers.'[48]

The Lord's Supper is the place at which the primary truths of the gospel converge. Incarnation, atonement, resurrection and second advent all point to the Christ-centredness of Christian faith; the one loaf and the one cup, the gathered people of God and the context of worship witness to the corporate nature of Christian worship and spirituality. Few within the Evangelical tradition have undervalued the Lord's Supper as a place of deep and holy communion with Christ. Spurgeon pin-pointed the reason for reverent and faithful attendance at Holy Communion, whatever an individual's church allegiance: 'Happy is the Christian who can say, "I scarcely need that memorial". But I am not such an one; and I fear, my brethren, that the most of us need to be reminded by that bread and wine, that Jesus died; and need to be reminded by the eating and the drinking of the same, that he died for us.'[49]

'He died for us.' That is the central affirmation of Evangelical faith, and the primary truth from which all else begins to flow. The life of grace has its source in the life of God, the God who in Christ died to save sinners. Spirituality is lived doctrine. For Evangelicals that means the cross is to be lived. The self-giving love of God in Christ, the 'grace unspeakable' of a crucified Lord, ignites within the heart of the forgiven sinner such fires of love, gratitude and wonder, that the only sufficient response is a life of self-expenditure, the total surrender of mind, heart and will.

The twenty-two people whose spiritual lives have formed the basis of this study are examples of a spirituality in which the cardinal verities of Evangelicalism have exerted decisive control. The experience of conversion in response to the divine grace, the centrality of the cross, the primary authority of the Bible and the imperative to service for Christ's sake are hallmarks of the Evangelical spiritual tradition stamped clearly on their lives. There is richness in their diversity, encouragement in their failures, inspiration in their triumphs and humour in their occasional quirkiness. There is much to be learned from the faith they expressed in word, prayer, sermon, hymn, letter and even treatise, as in their individuality, in the context of their time, they have struggled to live the life of grace.

The Evangelical tradition is a living, diverse and increasingly influential presence in the Christian Church. Not without its weaknesses, it nevertheless brings insights, indeed convictions, underwritten by the authority of personal experience. If these convictions need to be shared without arrogance, they also need to be heard without prejudice. 'Religious fellowship between Christians belonging to different churches is not merely a pleasant luxury, it is an important aid to religious knowledge and spiritual growth. It satisfies the hunger of the heart. It is a means of grace. It supplies the corrective influences to that narrowness of thought and sympathy which every man is likely to contract who is enclosed within limits of his own sect or party.'[50]

'The end of all is the grace unspeakable.' Forsyth never solved the problem of theological language. 'It is not easy to find a word that has no defect, since all words, even the greatest, are made from the dust and spring from our sandy passions, earthly needs and fleeting thoughts; and they are hard to stretch to the measure of eternal things without breaking under us somewhere.'[51] Few theologians have written theology with such passionate investment as Forsyth wrestling to speak about 'the grace unspeakable'. His own words glow with hope and wonder, and hint at the final unveiling of ineffable mystery:

> We deserved death, and death He gave us – the death of the Cross. The end of all is the grace unspeakable, the fulness of glory – all the old splendour fixed, with never one lost good; all the spent toil garnered, all the fragments gathered up, all the lost love found forever, all the lost purity transfigured in holiness, all the promises of the travailing soul now yea and amen, all sin turned to salvation. Eternal thanks be unto God,

who hath given us the victory through Jesus Christ our Lord, and by his grace, the taste of life for every man.[52]

Notes

1. F. Whaling, *John and Charles Wesley* (London 1981), pp. 255–6.
2. S. Chadwick, *What is Conversion* (London n.d.), p. 5.
3. A. Whyte, *With Mercy and With Judgment* (London 1925), p. 50.
4. A. Dallimore, *George Whitefield*, vol. 1 (Edinburgh 1970), p. 77.
5. R. W. Dale, 'Mr Moody and Mr Sankey', *Congregationalist* (1875), pp. 11–12.
6. G. C. Morgan, *The Bible and the Cross* (London 1909), pp. 81, 70.
7. ibid., p. 117.
8. H. Moule, *Union with Christ* (London 1886), p. vii.
9. C. H. Spurgeon, *An All-Round Ministry* (Edinburgh 1960), pp. 180–1.
10. A. Dale, *Life of R. W. Dale* (London 1898), pp. 590–1.
11. W. Cowper, *Poems*, vol. 1 (Oxford 1980), p. 173.
12. H. Bonar, *Hymns* (London 1904), p. 60.
13. S. Gundry, *Love Them In* (Grand Rapids 1976), pp. 146, 153.
14. M. Havergal, *Memorials* (London 1880), pp. 128, 165.
15. The Romans seven debate is updated in C. L. Mitton, 'Romans VII Reconsidered: III', *Expository Times* 65 (1954), pp. 133f.; B. L. Martin, 'Some Reflections on the Identity of ἐγώ in Romans 7.14–25', *Scottish Journal of Theology* (1981), pp. 39–47; J. Packer, *Keep in Step with the Spirit* (Leicester 1984), pp. 263–70.
16. F. Havergal, *Poetical Works* (London n.d.), p. 717.
17. J. Bull, *Letters of John Newton* (London n.d.), pp. 136–7.
18. R. W. Dale, 'Mr Moody and Mr Sankey', *Congregationalist* (1875).
19. A. Whyte, *Bunyan Characters*. First Series (Edinburgh n.d.), p. 195.
20. J. Newton, *Works*, vol. 3, p. 373.
21. *Quarterly Review*, vol. 52 (1834), pp. 416, 441.
22. I. Murray, *Lloyd-Jones*, vol. 2 (Edinburgh 1990), p. 220.
23. R. W. Dale, *The Evangelical Revival* (London 1880), p. 162.
24. ibid., p. 169.
25. *Quarterly Review*, vol. 52 (1834), p. 435.
26. Letter, 23 Nov. 1835, New College Library.
27. Havergal, *Memorials*, p. 163.
28. J. M. Turner, *Conflict and Reconciliation* (London 1985), p. 105.
29. Havergal, *Memorials*, p. 194.
30. N. C. Macfarlane, *Scotland's Keswick* (London n.d.), p. 99.
31. D. Blakey, *The Man in the Manse* (Edinburgh 1978), p. 106.
32. C. Simeon, *Horae Homileticae*, vol. 7, p. 324.
33. J. Stott, *Balanced Christianity* (London 1975), pp. 45–6.
34. J. Bull, *Letters of John Newton*, pp. 42–3.

35. S. Gundry, *Love Them In*, p. 169.
36. J. Pollock, *Moody without Sankey* (London 1963), p. 256.
37. A. Bonar, *McCheyne* (Edinburgh 1966), pp. 274–5.
38. ibid., p. 643.
39. A. Whyte, *The Apostle Paul* (Edinburgh 1903), pp. 213–14.
40. A. M. Hunter, *P. T. Forsyth* (London 1974), p. 73.
41. M. Walker, 'The Theology of the Lord's Supper amongst Baptists in the Nineteenth Century', PhD thesis (New College, London 1988), p. 231.
42. J. Telford, *Letters of John Wesley* (London 1931), vol. vii, pp. 82f.
43. H. Moule, *Call of Lent* (London 1917), p. 74.
44. J. Stott, *Christ the Controversialist* (London 1970), p. 103.
45. R. W. Dale, 'The Old Antinomianism and the New', *The Congregational Review* (1887), pp. 17–18.
46. G. Barbour, *Whyte* (London 1923), pp. 365, 429.
47. H. Moule, *Secret Prayer* (London 1898), p. 115.
48. J. C. Ryle, *Practical Religion* (London 1900), p. 94.
49. Walker, Thesis, p. 234.
50. A. Dale, *Life of R. W. Dale*, p. 173.
51. P. T. Forsyth, *Work of Christ* (London 1948), p. 210.
52. P. T. Forsyth, *Holy Father* (London 1957), p. 79.

Index of Scripture References

Index